MW00989994

LEHI IN THE DESERT

THE WORLD OF THE JAREDITES

THERE WERE JAREDITES

The Collected Works of Hugh Nibley

The Collected Works of Hugh Nibley will include volumes on the following subjects:

The Old Testament and Related Studies
Ancient History
The Pearl of Great Price
Early Christianity
The Book of Mormon
The Doctrine and Covenants and Mormonism
Education, Politics, and Society

Other volumes in this series:

Old Testament and Related Studies
Enoch the Prophet
The World and the Prophets
Mormonism and Early Christianity

The Collected Works of Hugh Nibley: Volume 5
The Book of Mormon

LEHI IN THE DESERT

THE WORLD OF THE JAREDITES

THERE WERE JAREDITES

Hugh Nibley

Edited by
John W. Welch
with
Darrell L. Matthews
and
Stephen R. Callister

Deseret Book Company
Salt Lake City, Utah
and
Foundation for Ancient Research and Mormon Studies
Provo, Utah

Printed in the United States of America

First printing January 1988

Library of Congress Cataloging-in-Publication Data

Nibley, Hugh, 1910–
Lehi in the desert, and, The world of the Jaredites / by Hugh Nibley.

p. cm. – (The Collected works of Hugh Nibley ; v. 5)
Bibliography: p.
Includes index.
ISBN 0-87579-132-8: $15.95
1. Book of Mormon. 2. Middle East—Civilization—To 622.
3. Jaredites (Mormon Church) I. Title. II. Title: Lehi in the desert. III. Title: World of the Jaredites. IV. Series: Nibley, Hugh, 1910– Works ; v. 5.
BX8627.N48 1988 87-32941
289.3'22—dc19 CIP

Contents

Key to Abbreviations

AASOR	Annual of the American Schools of Oriental Research
AJA	American Journal of Archaeology
ARAHA	Annual Report of the American Historical Association
ARW	Archiv für Religionswissenschaft
BA	Biblical Archeologist
BASOR	Bulletin of the American Schools of Oriental Research
CJ	Classical Journal
CQ	Classical Quarterly
HUCA	Hebrew Union College Annual
IE	Improvement Era
IEJ	Israel Exploration Journal
ILN	Illustrated London News
JAOS	Journal of the American Oriental Society
JBL	Journal of Biblical Literature
JE	Jewish Encyclopedia
JE	A Journal of Egyptian Archaeology
JNES	Journal of Near Eastern Studies
JPOS	Journal of the Palestine Oriental Society
JQR	Jewish Quarterly Review
JRAS	Journal of the Royal Asiatic Society
JRSAI	Journal of the Royal Society of Antiquaries of Ireland
MGWJ	Monatsschrift für Geschichte und Wissenschaft des Judentums
PEFQ	Palestine Exploration Fund Quarterly

PG	J.-P. Migne, Patrologiae Cursus Completus . . . Series Graeca (Paris: Migne, 1857-66), 161 vols.
PL	J.-P. Migne, Patrologiae Cursus Completus . . . Series Latina (Paris: Migne, 1844-64), 221 vols.
PO	Patrologia Orientalis
RB	Revue Biblique
RE	Pauly-Wissowa, Paulys Realencyclopädie der classischen Altertumswissenschaft
TAPS	Transactions of the American Philosophical Society
TSBA	Transactions of the Society of Biblical Archaeology
WPQ	Western Political Quarterly
ZASA	Zeitschrift für Ägyptische Sprache und Altertumskunde
ZDMG	Zeitschrift der deutschen morgenländischen Gesellschaft
ZDPV	Zeitschrift des Deutsch-Palästina Vereins

Foreword to the 1952 Edition

The Book of Mormon, the most interesting piece of literature in the Church, is essentially an account of three migrations from Asiatic lands to America.

The Jaredites reached here about the time of the confusion of tongues; another group arrived under the leadership of the Prophet Lehi at the time of Zedekiah, king of Israel; the third, under Mulek, arrived about the same time.

While the story of these peoples in their adopted homeland is told sufficiently well in the Book of Mormon to give the reader a good understanding of the achievements and their general philosophies, very little is said about the lives of the peoples before they began their westward journey. That makes Dr. Nibley's book doubly interesting.

The author has tried, after long and careful research, to tell the story of the people of Jared, their manner of life, and their reasons for leaving their Asiatic home to settle in the new land, now known as America. From countless sources Dr. Nibley has drawn material which, woven together, describes an early people, who, in search for God's truth, left their homes for the then unknown world. This study has been done in such a manner as to make real and understandable these early peoples, and to make them living persons to those of this day, thousands of years removed.

Dr. Nibley has done the same thing for the people who left their homes under the leadership of the Prophet Lehi and of Mulek many years later. The cultural life of Lehi's home is described in almost minute detail. Dr. Nibley answers questions which are only lightly touched upon in the Book of Mormon: Who was Lehi? What was his standing in Jerusalem? Where was his home? What caused him to move away and seek a home across the great ocean? The answers to these questions give life to these persons, who without this help would remain in the shadows. This work by Dr. Nibley also confirms the Book of Mormon story, answers the causes of migration, and explains on the basis of historical evidence why certain things mentioned in the Book of Mormon did occur.

The study of the Jaredites, of Lehi in the Desert, and of Mulek covers a territory of historical research not formerly invaded by modern scholars.

The book could not have been written except with vast acquaintance with sources of historical learning. It has been written also under the inspiration of the Spirit of God. Almost the best thing about the book is that it becomes a testimony to the truth of the claims of Joseph Smith that he was divinely inspired in the translation of the Book of Mormon as well as in his work of restoring the gospel of the Lord Jesus Christ.

Evidences for the Book of Mormon are increasing every day. For this reason this book, which becomes a powerful witness of the Book of Mormon, becomes also doubly precious to the leaders of the latter-day faith.

Dr. Nibley and the publishers should be congratulated upon bringing the articles which ran originally in *The Improvement Era* into book form.

JOHN A. WIDTSOE

Introduction to the 1988 Edition

At first light on June 6, 1944, the earliest of many allied landing craft began hitting the beaches of Normandy.[1] At Utah Beach, twelve men dangling from one of those landing jeeps cheered their rollicking driver on as they surged up from beneath the surface of the chilly English Channel waters. That driver, an army intelligence noncom holding a Ph.D. in ancient history from the University of California at Berkeley, was none other than Hugh W. Nibley, age thirty-four.

While preparing for the invasion, he had just visited several antiquarian bookstores in London—walking out with armloads of Arabic and Greek literary treasures. He had also, on the sly, slipped a copy of the Book of Mormon into one of the fifty-five pockets in his regimental intelligence corps fatigues.

The jeep ahead of Nibley's went over a sand knoll and disappeared from the face of the earth, never to be heard of or even seen again. "It was right there at Utah Beach," Hugh still vividly recalls, "as we were all a couple feet under water, that it really hit me—how astonishing the Book of Mormon truly is. It had never occurred to me before, as far as that goes, but all I could think of all that day was how wonderful this Book of Mormon was."[2]

Judged by any standard, the Book of Mormon is nothing ordinary. So it seems only right that the most illustrious scholar yet to have investigated the Book of Mormon should have become fascinated with it in no ordinary way. Since Utah Beach, Hugh Nibley was never the same again. Nor was Book of Mormon scholarship.

Hugh Nibley is probably still best known for his groundbreaking investigations into the ancient Near Eastern backgrounds of Lehi and of the Jaredites. Those classic studies are contained in this volume—the first of several books to appear in the volumes of the *Collected Works of Hugh Nibley* that deal with the Book of Mormon. To this day, Nibley remembers how excited he was while making these discoveries and writing them up.

Nevertheless, to Nibley, these and many other similar historical details only set the stage for understanding the actual messages of the Book of Mormon. Ultimately, the importance of the Book of Mormon in his opinion is that it conveys a remarkably clear and compelling picture of the plan of salvation. It exposes in unequivocal terms the foibles of the human condition and the choices all people face for temporal and spiritual survival. These messages—urgently relevant for our present day—are at the heart of the Book of Mormon for Hugh Nibley. His excursions into the history, language, culture, and backgrounds of the Book of Mormon are only one method of understanding and appreciating certain aspects of that message.

Developing this understanding has been a lifelong endeavor for Hugh Nibley. It began in 1948 with his article "The Book of Mormon as a Mirror of the East,"[3] which soon grew into three lengthy serials, "Lehi in the Desert" in 1950,[4] "The World of the Jaredites" in 1951-52,[5] and "There Were Jaredites" in 1956-57,[6] all of which were published in the *Improvement Era*. In 1952, the collected articles under the names of "Lehi in the Desert," and "The World of the Jaredites" were published as a book entitled *Lehi in the Desert and the World of the Jaredites*. That volume has enjoyed wide circulation for thirty-five years.

In the present volume, the work of the editors has been confined largely to technical tasks. The earlier texts remain substantially unchanged, but they have been edited lightly. All the information found in "The Book of Mormon as a Mirror of the East" (much of which was inserted into "Lehi in the Desert" in 1950) has been worked back into the text and notes of "Lehi in the Desert," as have most of the original illustrations. The series "There Were Jaredites" is included here for the first time, and all footnotes in this enlarged edition have been verified and made more readable, thanks especially to the labors of Stephen Callister, Darrell Matthews, and Rebecca Bishop.

Close work with these articles and their sources makes it even more apparent now than before that "The Book of Mormon as a Mirror of the East" and "Lehi in the Desert" broke completely new ground. Since that time, this novel research has spawned many other fruitful studies, corroborating the soundness of this innovative approach. Dr. Nibley's broad knowledge of the ancient Near East, and especially his fluent Arabic, allowed him to reconstruct the probable cultural backgrounds of men like Lehi and Nephi and to read between the lines in the Book of Mormon to identify evidences of their cultural world. Much of that evidence is quite direct and strong; other times it is subtle and more remote. In either case, no one else had even thought of seeing such things; yet without such insights, the lives of Lehi and the Jaredites would "remain in the shadows," as Elder John A. Widtsoe said in his foreword to the 1952 publication of *Lehi in the Desert and the World of the Jaredites*.[7]

The method of "Lehi in the Desert," as Dr. Nibley once explained, is "simply to give the Book of Mormon the benefit of the doubt." If one assumes that Lehi lived in Jerusalem around 600 B.C., a remarkably consistent picture emerges between what is now known about that historical period from a secular standpoint and what we find in the Book of Mormon itself. Likewise, if one assumes that Jared left from Mesopotamia around 2000 B.C., then the nature of society and history reflected in early accounts of his people should be consonant with those times. The kinds of ancient Near Eastern facts and observations Nibley then correlates with details in the Book of Mormon are drawn from areas of language and literature, archaeology and history, culture and politics. Taken alone, few single factors are overwhelmingly impressive, but all together they fit very convincingly into what Dr. Nibley calls "The Big Picture."

To Hugh Nibley in these early years, a significant payoff for his research came in the ammunition it provided against Book of Mormon critics. His parting shots in *Lehi in the Desert and the World of the Jaredites* drive this point home:

> There is no point at all to the question: Who wrote the Book of Mormon? It would have been quite as impossible for the most learned man alive in 1830 as it was for Joseph Smith. And whoever would account for the Book of Mormon by any theory suggested so far—save one—must completely rule out the first forty pages.[8]

> To write a history of what could have happened at the very beginning of recorded history would have been as far beyond the scope of any scholar living in 1830 as the construction of an atom bomb would have been.[9]

While the potency of his insights is hard to ignore, one should not be sated at this point. The first course is only the appetizer. Over the years, Hugh Nibley has not rested until he has understood the messages of the Book of Mormon in light of these historical backgrounds. Thus, a reader should not plan to stop at the end of this particular volume, but should look ahead to the broadening perspectives yet to come in *An Approach to the Book of Mormon,*[10] *Since Cumorah,*[11] and many subsequent articles about the prophetic meanings of the Book of Mormon. Likewise, Nibley's legacy and influence will surely continue to stimulate much more thinking about the Book of Mormon for many years to come.

This volume, however, is the essential starting place for understanding the things that Hugh Nibley has contributed over the past four decades to Book of Mormon scholarship. In these works, Dr. Nibley teaches us in many ways, as the reader will readily observe:

He makes us look more carefully at the Book of Mormon. "We need to make the Book of Mormon an object of serious study," he says. "Superficiality is quite offensive to the Lord. We have not paid enough attention to the Book of Mormon."

He challenges us to understand the Book of Mormon. "The Book of Mormon," he says, "is a debatable subject. . . . If we do not accept the challenge we will lose by default."

By rigorous examination, he shows that the Book of Mormon stands up well under close scrutiny. By looking carefully at the Book of Mormon, by ferreting out innuendos, by examining each significant word or phrase in the book, the reader repeatedly finds more than originally meets the eye.

Time and again Nibley teaches us to be surprised at what the Book of Mormon contains. He often remarks how perfectly obvious something should have been to him long before it was: "Some subjects I studied for years without it occurring to me for a moment that they had any bearing whatsoever on the Book of Mormon."

But most of all, he never loses sight of the Book of Mormon's spiritual significance. "Above all it is a witness to God's concern for all his children, and to the intimate proximity of Jesus Christ to all who will receive him."[12]

Despite his great knowledge and wisdom—or, more accurately, because of it—Hugh Nibley knows that any scientific method is by nature limited. He knows that no ultimate, empirical proof of the Book of Mormon can be had: "The evidence that will prove or disprove the Book of Mormon does not exist."[13] In his mind, all this scholarship simply sets the stage for the ultimate questions of life. Once a person explicitly realizes that he or she cannot explain everything in the Book of Mormon, that person is at last where Moroni wants him or her to be, at the point where the person must turn to God to find out if the book's contents are true. "All that Mormon and Moroni ask the reader is, don't fight it, don't block it, give it a chance!"[14]

Accordingly, Hugh Nibley speaks candidly about the book's relevance to our day. "I intend to take Moroni as my guide to the present world situation."[15] "In my youth I thought the Book of Mormon was much too preoccupied with extreme situations, situations that had little bearing on the real world of everyday life and ordinary human affairs. What on earth could the total extermination of nations have to do with life in the enlightened modern world? Today no comment on that is necessary."[16] "In the Book of Mormon, the very questions which now oppress the liberal and the fundamentalist alike, to the imminent overthrow of their fondest beliefs, are fully and clearly treated. No other book gives such a perfect and exhaustive explanation of the eschatological problem. . . . Here you will find anticipated and answered every logical objection that the intelligence and vanity of men even in this sophisticated age have been able to devise against the preaching of the word. And here one may find a description of our own age so vivid and so accurate that none can fail to recognize it."[17]

In so speaking, Nibley puts the Book of Mormon into an urgent eternal perspective. "The Book of Mormon should take priority. We have not paid enough attention to the Book of Mormon. This is very urgent!"[18] A sense of this pressing need—no less emphatic today than it was that day on Utah Beach—is the indelible stamp left by the legacy and influence of Hugh Nibley.

Since Hugh Nibley, we as a people are not the same.[19] We are warned, but reassured. In effect, we too are Lehis in the desert.

JOHN W. WELCH
EDITOR

Notes

1. This introduction has been adapted from my essay "Hugh Nibley and the Book of Mormon," *Ensign* (April 1985): 51-56.

2. Statements quoted in this introduction were gathered in interviews with Hugh Nibley conducted by Susan Roylance and me.

3. *Improvement Era* 51 (April 1948): 202-4, 249-51; reprinted *Improvement Era* 73 (1970): 115-20, 122-25.

4. *Improvement Era* 53 (January 1950) 14-16, 66-72, running serially each month until *Improvement Era* 53 (October 1950): 804-6, 824, 826, 828, 830; reprinted without illustrations and with slight modifications in *Lehi in the Desert and the World of the Jaredites* (Salt Lake City: Bookcraft, 1952), 1-139.

5. *Improvement Era* 54 (September 1951): 628-30, 673-75, running serially each month, except for April and May, until *Improvement Era* 55 (July 1952): 510, 550; reprinted without illustrations and with slight modifications in *Lehi in the Desert and the World of the Jaredites* (Salt Lake City: Bookcraft, 1952), 143-266.

6. *Improvement Era* 59 (January 1956): 30-32, 58-61, running serially each month until *Improvement Era* 60 (February 1957): 94-95, 122-24.

7. (Salt Lake City: Bookcraft, 1952), vi; page x above.

8. Ibid., 139; page 123 below.

9. Ibid., 258; page 256 below.

10. The 1957 course of study for the Melchizedek priesthood quorums of the Church of Jesus Christ of Latter-day Saints (Salt Lake City: The Council of the Twelve Apostles of the Church of Jesus Christ of Latter-day Saints, 1957); reprinted (Salt Lake City: Deseret, 1964).

11. Much of this book first appeared as a series of articles in *Improvement Era* from October 1964 to December 1966; it was then republished (Salt Lake City: Deseret, 1967).

12. Hugh W. Nibley, "The Book of Mormon: A Minimal Statement," *Concilium: Theology in the Age of Renewal* 25 (New York: Paulist Press, 1968); reprinted in Hugh W. Nibley, *Nibley on the Timely and the Timeless,* Truman G. Madsen, ed. (Provo: BYU Religious Studies Center, 1978), 151.

13. Nibley, *Since Cumorah,* viii.

14. Gary P. Gillum, *Of All Things! A Nibley Quote Book* (Salt Lake City: Signature Books, 1981), 93.

15. Ibid., 86, from "Gifts," 3.

16. Ibid., 87, from "The Prophetic Book of Mormon," 17

17. Ibid., 87, from "Historicity of the Bible," 11; reprinted in *The Collected Works of Hugh Nibley,* 1:18.

18. See also Nibley, "The Book of Mormon: A Minimal Statement," 149: "Until recently, most Mormons have not been zealous in the study of the book."

19. "Few students can talk coherently about their first class from Brother Nibley," Robert K. Thomas has observed. "For some it was simply a rite of passage, the academic equivalent of a social unit initiation. For many it was, at best, a brisk blur edged with random flashes of insight. For a few it was an intellectual implosion, from which they will never recover. For after one has stood in the presence of his first true scholar, the world loses a bit of its apparent symmetry, reveals the forces which determined its form, and invites an infinite recasting." Robert K. Thomas, "The Influence of Hugh Nibley: His Presence in the University," in John W. Welch, ed., *Tinkling Cymbals: Essays in Honor of Hugh Nibley on his 65th Birthday* (Provo: F.A.R.M.S., unpublished collection of essays, 1975), 13.

Part 1
Lehi in the Desert

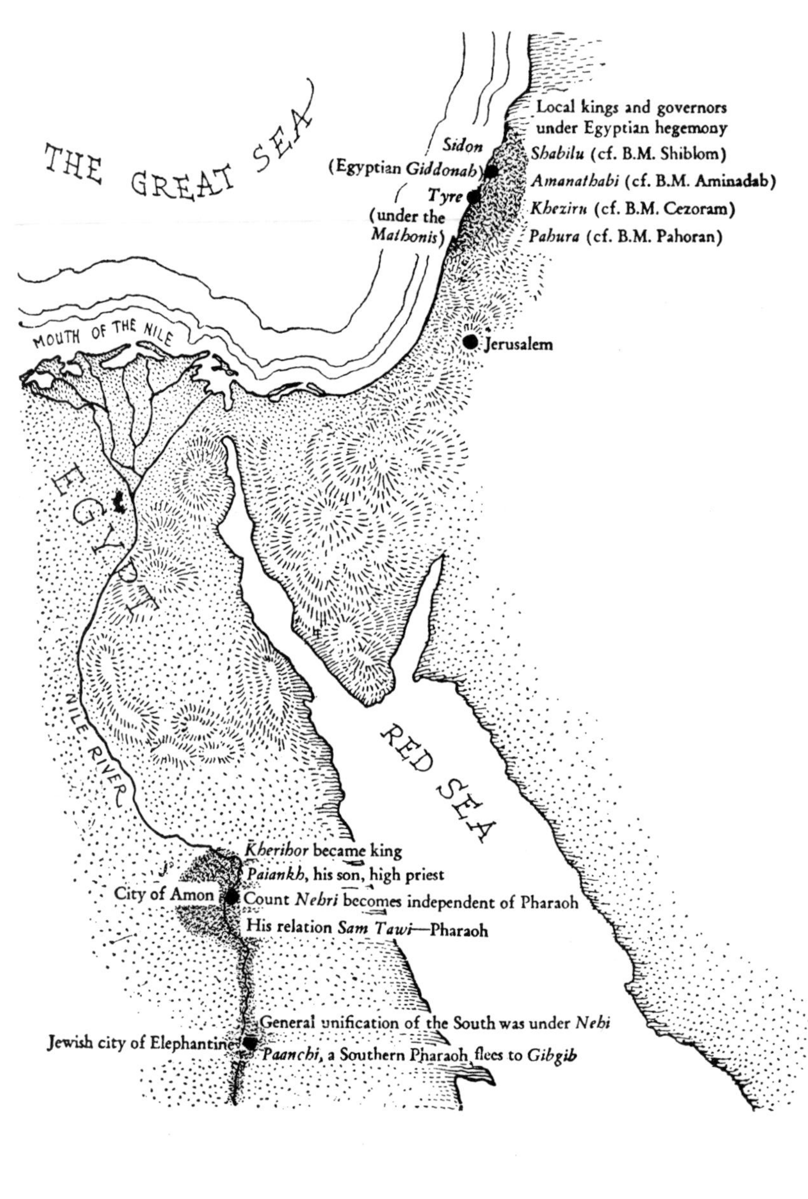
THE GREAT SEA
Sidon
(Egyptian Giddonab)
Tyre
(under the
Mathonis)
Local kings and governors
under Egyptian hegemony
Shabilu (cf. B.M. Shiblom)
Amanathabi (cf. B.M. Aminadab)
Khezirn (cf. B.M. Cezoram)
Pahura (cf. B.M. Pahoran)
MOUTH OF THE NILE
Jerusalem
EGYPT
NILE RIVER
RED SEA
Kheribor became king
Paiankh, his son, high priest
City of Amon
Count Nebri becomes independent of Pharaoh
His relation Sam Tawi—Pharaoh
General unification of the South was under Nebi
Jewish city of Elephantine
Paanchi, a Southern Pharaoh flees to Gibgib

1

The Troubled Orient

The Problem

The first eighteen chapters (approximately forty pages) of the Book of Mormon tell the story of how one Lehi led a company of Israelites from Jerusalem across Arabia to the sea at the beginning of the sixth century B.C. Since the publication of this account, other ancient travel stories have been unearthed in the Near East and been accepted as genuine or pronounced fictitious as they fulfilled or failed to fulfill certain conditions. Thus Professor Albright declares the story of the Egyptian Sinuhe to be "a substantially true account of life in its *milieu*" on the grounds (1) that its "local color [is] extremely plausible," (2) it describes a "state of social organization" which "agrees exactly with our present archaeological and documentary evidence," (3) "the Amorite personal names contained in the story are satisfactory for that period and region," and (4) "finally, there is nothing unreasonable in the story itself."[1]

The story of Wenamon the same authority accepts as true in its political history and geography, noting that "it correctly reflects the cultural horizon and the religious ideas and practices of its time."[2] Certain Egyptian episodes in the *Odyssey* Lieblein considered authentic because they posit "a rather good knowledge of Egyptian conditions and institutions" in whoever composed them.[3] On the other hand, such tales as the Shipwrecked Sailor may be regarded as fanciful because they have a "total lack of specific historical or geographic background, as well as by their *mise-en-scène,* which is either mythical or extravagantly improbable."[4]

With such examples before us, we may proceed to test the story of Lehi: does it correctly reflect "the cultural horizon and religious and social ideas and practices of the time"? Does it have authentic historical and geographical background? Is the *mise-en-scène* mythical, highly imaginative, or extravagantly improbable? Is its local color correct, and are its proper names convincing? Until recent years men were asking the same questions of the book of Exodus, and scholars were stolidly turning thumbs down until evidence accumulating in its favor began to turn the scales. As one student described it, the problem "is rather to prove, by innumerable small coincidences, that which Ebers has so well called the 'Egypticity' of the Pentateuch, than to establish any particular historical point by external and monumental evidence."[5] Just so the problem of 1 Nephi is to establish both its "Egypticity" and its "Arabicity" by like innumerable coincidences. The fact that the Book of Mormon is a modern text, and yet not modern enough to have exploited the fruits of archaeology, gives it a double handicap at the outset, and yet in view of the claims made by Joseph Smith, it can plead no immunity from the same exacting tests that have revealed the true nature of documents of known antiquity. If the book can pass those tests, there is no point to arguing about its age and authorship.

Virtually all that is known of the world in which Lehi is purported to have lived has been discovered within the last hundred years—mostly within the last thirty.[6] How does this information check with that in the book of 1 Nephi? Before we can place the two side by side for comparison, we must describe briefly the nature of the modern evidence. It falls, for us, into four classes:

1. First and most to be prized are documents found in the country of Lehi and dating from his very time. A number of these have come to light in recent years—seals, jar handles, inscriptions, and, most notably, the Lachish let-

ters discovered in 1935. These are the remains of the correspondence of a military officer stationed in the city of Lachish, about thirty-five miles southwest of Jerusalem, at the time of the destruction of both cities, and so give us an eyewitness account of the actual world of Lehi—a tiny peephole, indeed, but an unobstructed one. In these letters "we find ourselves brought into close contact with the inner religious, political, and military life of Judah at this period."[7] Since 1 Nephi pretends to bring us even closer contact with the same society, we have here an important "control."

2. The new finds have called for extensive review and reevaluation by the ablest scholars of the situation in Jerusalem at the time of its fall; these learned summaries will save us the trouble and risk of making our own.

3. Book of Mormon descriptions of life in the desert must be checked against eyewitness accounts of life in the same deserts, for the same period of time, if possible. Since the country and people concerned are among the most unchanging on earth, there are many things that are as true today as they were in 600 B.C., providing data of a well-nigh timeless, but highly specialized, nature which has been made available in:

(a) Numerous scientific journals and surveys of the country, with the *Palestine Exploration Fund Quarterly* taking the lead.

(b) A growing treasury of great classics on life among the Arabs, beginning with Burckhardt in 1829 but mostly confined to our own age: Doughty, Philby, Lawrence, Hogarth, Thomas, etc.

(c) Few Americans realize the language and cultural opportunities available to the serious student in any part of the land. No large city in the United States is without its communities of Syrians, Greeks, Armenians, etc., often fresh from the old country and full of Near Eastern lore. Who would dream that a former driver of camels, a pure-blooded Arab and devout Mohammedan, would settle in the vicinity of such a town as Provo, Utah, or that the deserts of southern California should support colonies of Arabs raising sheep, chickens, and dates, exactly as they and their ancestors have done in the deserts of the East? Such people are often marvelous informants, for they have astonishing memories and love nothing better than to reminisce over an all-night game of backgammon.[8]

4. As a check on such word-of-mouth reports we have the words of the ancient poets of the Arabs. The prose story of the *Banī Hilāl* is also very useful both as a "standard work" on desert migration and as telling a story that parallels that of Nephi very closely on some points.

Taken together these sources allow a far closer scrutiny of the book of 1 Nephi than would have been possible a generation ago. Though what follows is little more than a general survey, we believe it pursues the lines that a correct examination of the story of Lehi should take, and that enough evidence is offered to justify the remarks with which we shall conclude this study.

The Situation in Jerusalem

When we speak of Jerusalem, it is important to notice Nephi's preference for a non-Biblical expression, "the land of Jerusalem" (1 Nephi 3:10), in designating his homeland. While he and his brothers always regard "the land of Jerusalem" as their home, it is perfectly clear from a number of passages that "the land of our father's inheritance" (1 Nephi 3:16) cannot possibly be within, or even very near, the city, even though Lehi had "dwelt at Jerusalem in all his days" (1 Nephi 1:4). The terms seem confused, but they correctly reflect actual conditions, for in the Amarna letters we read of "the land of Jerusalem" as an area larger than the city itself, and even learn in one instance that "a city of the land of Jerusalem, Bet-Ninib, has been captured." It was the rule in Palestine and Syria, as the same letters show, for a large area around a city and all the inhabitants of that area to bear the name of the city.[9] This was a holdover from the times when the city and the land were a single political unit, comprising a city-state; when this was absorbed into a larger empire, the original identity was preserved, though it had lost its original political significance.[10] The same conservatism made it possible for Socrates to be an Athenian, and nothing else, even though he came from the village of Alopeke, at some distance from the city.[11] This arrangement deserves mention because many have pointed to the statement of Alma 7:10 that the Savior would be born "at Jerusalem which is the *land* of our forefathers," as sure proof of fraud. It is rather the opposite, faithfully preserving the ancient terminology to describe a system which has only been recently rediscovered.

Though he "dwelt at Jerusalem," Lehi did not live in the city, for it was after they had failed to get the plates in Jerusalem that his sons decided to "go down to the land of our father's inheritance" (1 Nephi 3:16), and there gather enough wealth to buy the plates from Laban. Loaded with the stuff, they "went up again unto the house of Laban" in Jerusalem (1 Nephi 3:23). The Book of Mormon employs the expressions "to go down" and "to go up" exactly as the Hebrews and Egyptians did with reference to the location of Jerusalem, and thus clearly establishes that Lehi's property lay somewhere in the country and not within the walls of Jerusalem.[12]

We know very little about the city government of the Jews, save that the "elders" played the principal role. By "elders" has been understood "the heads of the most influential families of a city."[13] This would make them identical with those princes, notables, and officials who are designated as *sarim* in the Lachish letters; the word *sarim* applies, according to J. W. Jack, to "members of the official class, i.e. 'officers' acting under the king as his counsellors and rulers." In the Lachish letters we find the *sarim* denouncing Jeremiah to the king and demanding that he be executed because of his bad influence on the morale of the people (Jeremiah 38:4-5).[14] In accusing the prophet of defeatism, the influential men of Jerusalem were supported both by the majority of the people and by a host of prophets by whose false oracles "Judahite chauvinism" was "whipped to a frenzy," making it, to say the least, a risky business to hold an opposite opinion.[15] For the government, with the weak and ineffectual Zedekiah at the head, had set its heart on a suicidal policy of military alliance with Egypt and "business as usual."[16]

The country had just come through a great economic boom, thanks mostly to commercial dealings with Egypt, which had produced an unparalleled efflorescence of great private fortunes. "Phoenician galleys filled the Nile mouths, and Semitic merchants . . . thronged the Delta,"[17] the bulk of sea trade passing through Sidon, which from first to last dominated the commercial scene.[18] Lists of goods imported into Egypt from Palestine show that the great men of the East took the gold of Egypt in return for their wine, oil, grain, and honey, the first three far outclassing all other commodities in importance.[19] Among inland cities like Jerusalem the caravans of the merchant princes passed as in the days of the Amarna letters, for there were no real roads until the time of the Romans.

At the turn of the century the international situation was casting a dark shadow over the picture. Babylon, suddenly freed from other concerns, moved quickly towards a showdown with Egypt, the "broken reed" with which the leaders of Judah had unwisely cast their lot. Yet the clouds of impending war were not so dark as the shadow of religious laxness and moral decay which, according to Jeremiah, followed upon excessive prosperity and an overfondness for things Egyptian (Jeremiah 43:10-13; 44:1-30; 46:11-26). It is no wonder that the *sarim,* facing problems enough in maintaining a program of "business as usual," denounced the melancholy prophet as a traitor, defeatist, and collaborator with Babylon. The country was divided into two factions, "the two parties, pro-Egyptian and pro-Babylonian, existed side by side in the land. King Zedekiah, his rulers and princes, and probably most of the people, favored Egypt . . . while the prophet Jeremiah and his followers advised submission to Babylonia."[20] It was a time of "dissension and heart burning, when divided counsels rent the unhappy city of Jerusalem,"[21] and as things became worse in an atmosphere "charged with unmixed gloom, . . . Zedekiah . . . stubbornly followed the path to ruin by conspiring with Pharaoh."[22] The alarm was justified, for when the blow finally fell it was far more catastrophic than scholars have hitherto been willing to believe, with "all, or virtually all, of the fortified towns in Judah . . . razed to the ground."[23] It was not until 1925 that we learned that "Tyre actually fell" at this time.[24]

The fatal infatuation with Egypt, which was largely responsible for the calamity, is a striking feature of the story. Why did the government of Judah stick so loyally to an Egypt that had long since lost the power to compel obedience? For one thing, we now know that cultural and economic ties were far stronger between the two nations than anyone had hitherto supposed. J. W. Jack noted in 1938 that "excavations have shown a closer connection with the land of the Pharaohs than was suspected; . . . the authorities at Lachish were probably using, or at least were accustomed to the Egyptian calendar and the Egyptian system of numeration in their local records." Though this goes for an earlier time, "all indications point to this connection with Egypt continuing unbroken right down to the end of the Jewish monarchy."[25] One anthropologist went so far as to claim that Lachish was actually an Egyptian colony, but investigation shows that the same "Egyptian" physical type and the same predominance of Egyptian culture prevails elsewhere in Palestine.[26] Recently found ivories, seals, inscriptions, and the preliminary study of mounds throughout the land all tell the same story: overwhelming and unexpected preponderance of Egyptian influence,[27] to the equally surprising exclusion of influences from Babylonia and Assyria.[28] At Jerusalem itself, where excavation is necessarily limited, sealings on jar handles attest the same long reign of Egyptian culture.[29] At the same time, the Elephantine papyri tell us another thing that scholars never dreamed of and which they were at first most reluctant to believe, namely, that colonies of Jewish soldiers and merchants were entirely at home in upper Egypt, where they enjoyed free practice of their religion.[30] The ties between Palestine and Egypt were, moreover, of a very long standing, centuries of "a common Hebrew-Egyptian environment" being necessary to produce the permeation of Egyptian modes of thought and expression into Hebrew, and to load the Egyptian vocabulary with words out of Palestine and Syria.[31] The newly identified *Aechtungstexte* show that as early as 2000 B.C. "Palestine was tributary in large part, at least, to Egypt," while the excavation of Byblos, a veritable "little Egypt," proved the presence of the Egyptian empire in later centuries.[32]

To say that Egyptian culture is predominant in an area is not necessarily to argue the presence of Egyptian dominion. According to Hogarth, Egypt exercised three degrees of empire: the first degree was rule by direct force, the second by "fear of reconquest which a few garrisons and agents and the prestige of the conqueror could keep alive in the minds of indirect administrators and native subjects," and the third degree "meant little more than a sphere of exclusive influence, from which tribute was expected but, not being secured by garrisons or representatives . . . tended to be intermittent."[33] Thus we see that the position of Egypt as "most favored nation" in Judah may represent any degree of decayed dominion—even to an "empire" of fourth degree.[34] It was the Egyptian cultural heritage rather than her government that was all-powerful, Egyptian influence being strongest in Palestine *after* Egypt had passed her peak as a world power.[35]

In the great days of Egypt the renowned Ipuwer had said, "the foreigners have become Egyptians everywhere," and a near contemporary of Lehi can boast, "behold, are not the Ethiopian, the Syrian, and all foreigners alike instructed in the language of Egypt?"[36] For centuries it was the custom of the princes of Syria to send their sons to Egypt to be educated.[37] No matter how sorry the plight of Egypt, the boastful inscriptions of her rulers—sometimes very feeble ones—proclaim the absolute and unquestioned superiority of Egyptian civilization to all others: with Egyptians that is an article of faith. Like the English in our own day, the Egyptians demonstrated time and again the ability to maintain a power and influence in the world out of all proportion to their physical resources. With no other means than a perfect and tenacious confidence in the divine superiority of Egypt and Ammon, Wenamon almost succeeded in overawing the great prince of Byblos. Is it any wonder then, that in a time when Egypt was enjoying the short but almost miraculous revival of splendor that marked the XXVI Dynasty, with its astonishing climax of world trade, the credit of that country should stand high in the land of Jerusalem?

But it is now time to turn to the book of 1 Nephi. How perfectly the author depicts the very situation we have just described! He explains that he does not intend to write a political history, and we must often look between the lines; yet the amount of information he imparts in the most casual and unlabored manner imaginable is simply astonishing. Consider first the picture of Lehi.

Lehi was a very rich Jew; he was proud of his Egyptian education, spoke and wrote Egyptian, and insisted on his sons learning the language. He possessed exceeding great wealth in the form of "gold, silver, and all manner of riches" (1 Nephi 3:16), not manufactured at Jerusalem; he had close ties with Sidon (one of the most popular names in the Book of Mormon, where it appears both in its Semitic and its Egyptian form of Giddonah); yet he lived on an estate in the country, "the land of his inheritance" (1 Nephi 2:4), and was something of an expert in vine, olive, fig, and honey culture; so there can be little doubt of the nature of his business with Egypt.

Now this man, coming from one of the oldest families and having a most unobjectionable background and education, suddenly found himself in bad with the "people that count." First, there was mockery, then, anger, and finally, plots against his life (1 Nephi 1:19-20) which, since they were serious, must have been supported in high places, for in openly siding with Jeremiah (cf. 1 Nephi 7:14) he had made himself a traitor to his class and his tradition: members of his own family turned against him, and taking the side of "the Jews who were at Jerusalem" (1 Nephi 2:13), as Nephi explains, accused their father of criminal defeatism in thinking and preaching that "the great city Jerusalem must be destroyed" (1 Nephi 1:4), exactly as the *sarim* accused Jeremiah of treasonable talk. So vehement was their support of the government party's point of view, that Lehi's two eldest sons shared with the Jews the great crime of plotting against their father's life (1 Nephi 17:44). Nowhere is the "dissension and heartburning that rent the unhappy city of Jerusalem"[38] more clearly shown forth than in those impassioned scenes within Lehi's own household. The elder sons, reared to a life of Egyptian elegance and heirs to a fortune that owed much to Egypt, were staunch defenders of the *status quo,* while the younger sons, less spoiled by all accounts, had been made aware of the real nature of the crisis in Jerusalem, which was not really an economic or a political but basically a moral one (1 Nephi

1:19). The older men could not see this at all: "the people who were in the land of Jerusalem," they protested, "were a righteous people; for they kept the statutes . . . according to the law of Moses; wherefore, we know that they are a righteous people" (1 Nephi 17:22). Such was the holy chauvinism of the false prophets with their gospel of business as usual. The atmosphere of hysteria and gloom that prevails in Nephi's story of Jerusalem is, as we have seen, strictly authentic, and the danger of utter annihilation of Jerusalem that runs like an ominous fate motif through the whole book was, as the event proved, perfectly justified.

Language and the Book of Mormon

The world has always cast a superior and mocking eye on the inordinate concern of the Book of Mormon for things Egyptian. With surprise and incredulity it is now learning that Egyptian culture counted for far more in Palestine in 600 B.C. than anyone had ever supposed. It is significant that the Book of Mormon concern with Egypt is strictly cultural—it never mentions Pharaoh or speaks of Egyptian government, but only of Egyptian culture and especially language. It makes it perfectly clear, however, that Egyptian was for Lehi a *second* language, "for he having *been taught* in the language of the Egyptians therefore he could read these engravings, and teach them to his children" (Mosiah 1:4). We have seen that Egyptian was taught to "Ethiopians, Syrians, and all other foreigners" in Lehi's day. Moroni tells us (Mormon 9:32-33) that the language of Lehi's descendants was not Hebrew or Egyptian but a mixture of both, both being corrupted in the process, so that "none other people knoweth our language," which would certainly not have been the case had they spoken only Hebrew. Ancient Hittite was just such a dual language. The reason "none other people knoweth *our* language" today is that English is the result of imposing cultivated French on native Saxon, just as cultivated Egyptian was imposed on native Hebrew in Lehi's Palestine. On a ceremonial dagger which with its handle of white gold reminds us of Laban's sword, we read the name Ja'qob-her, "Jahveh is satisfied," a name which neatly combines Egyptian and Hebrew in a process of fusion for which a great deal of evidence now exists, and which had been in progress long before Lehi's day.[39]

It was common in ancient as in modern languages to use one and the same word (e. g. English, "speech," Egyptian "ra") both for "utterance" and "language,"[40] though this common Book of Mormon usage is *not* found in Hebrew. When Nephi says, "after this manner was the language of my father in the praising of his God" (1 Nephi 1:15), he is not telling us what language his father spoke, but giving notice that he is quoting or paraphrasing an actual speech of his father. Likewise when he says, "I make a record in the language of my father" (1 Nephi 1:2), he says that he is going to quote or paraphrase a record actually written by his father (1 Nephi 1:16). He explains that his father wrote the record in Egyptian though it dealt with Jewish matters, but he never affirms that Egyptian was his father's native tongue. The clause in 1 Nephi 1:2 which begins, "which consists of . . ." does not refer back to "language" or "father," of course, but to "record." The other two are syntactically possible but don't make sense: a language does not consist of a language, but a record does. The sentence is awkward English, but like many others in the Book of Mormon closely resembles the familiar Semitic *hal* construction, and could be read, "I make a record, in the language of my father, consisting of the learning of the Jews," etc. Joseph Smith did not dictate the punctuation of the Book of Mormon.

Some have maintained that the Book of Mormon was written in Hebrew but with Egyptian characters. But Mororoni (Mormon 9:32-34) observes that the Nephites have altered their writing of Egyptian to conform to their way of speaking it, and that "the Hebrew hath been altered by us *also*," with the result that "none other people knoweth our language." Their language was neither Egyptian nor Hebrew. Moroni appreciates the accuracy and clarity of old Hebrew, which is no longer spoken by his people (Mormon 9:33), and writes reluctantly "in the characters, which are called among us the reformed Egyptian," simply because that takes up less space. Now Egyptian could be written in less space than Hebrew because in Lehi's day demotic was actually a shorthand, extremely cramped and abbreviated;[41] and it was a shorthand for the very reason that it was thoroughly idiomatic, that is, peculiarly adapted to the sounds and thought processes of one language and one language only. It could be used very economically for writing Egyptian, but not for any other language. In fact, not long after Lehi's time the Persian conquerors of Egypt learned Aramaic instead of Egyptian because the Egyptian script was too clumsy and hard to learn.[42] Now we are asked to believe that the Jews reversed this process and adopted Egyptian characters for their *own* language.

This amounts to a declaration that the Nephites denied themselves the use of their holy and superbly practical script, of which Torczyner writes: "The script of Lachish makes us realize for the first time that the Phoenician-Hebrew alphabet . . . is . . . a script invented, and used particularly, for writing in ink upon papyrus, hide (parchment) and potsherds. We now realize that the ancient Jews could write quickly and boldly, in an artistic flowing hand, with the loving penmanship of those who enjoy writing."[43] And the Nephites got rid of this to learn in its place the most awkward, difficult, and impractical system of writing ever devised by man! Why all the trouble? Simply to save space. What space? Space on valuable plates. When did the custom begin? With Lehi. Where and when did he learn "the language of the Egyptians"? In Palestine, of course, before he ever thought of himself as a record-keeper. Did the wealthy Lehi learn Egyptian characters so that he could sit in his house in the land of Jerusalem and by writing Hebrew with demotic symbols save a few cents a month on writing materials? And did he command his sons to learn Egyptian so they could save space when they kept records? Of course not: when they learned the language, neither Lehi nor his sons had any idea that some day it would be useful to keepers of records on metal plates. They had no other reason for learning Egyptian characters than to read and write Egyptian. It was only later when historians became cramped for space that they saw the advantage of continuing to write in Egyptian. And the Egyptian characters can only have been preserved for their use because the language was also preserved; for people who were *not* crowded for space would not have continued to write Hebrew in the difficult Egyptian characters for hundreds of years, when all the time they might just as well have been writing in the twenty-two simple and practical characters of the Hebrew alphabet.

Many reasons might be added for rejecting this interesting theory, but the simple statement of Moroni should be enough to banish the darling illusion that anyone who has had elementary Hebrew knows the original language of the Book of Mormon. If that were so, its translation by the gift and power of God would have been no great miracle, and instead of a Urim and Thummim a short list of Egyptian characters with their Hebrew equivalents would have been the only tool necessary to Joseph Smith's generation or our own. The fact remains that the abridging and editing of the Book of Mormon was in a language known to no other people on earth but the Nephites.

There is much in Nephi's writing to show that, as he claims, he is writing in Egyptian—not merely in Egyptian characters. When Nephi tells us that his record and that of his father are in the language of the Egyptians (*not* that the language of his father was the language of the Egyptians), we can be sure he means just that. And what could be more natural than that he should choose to record his message, addressed not only to the Jews, but also "unto all the house of Israel" (1 Nephi 19:19) and all the Gentiles (1 Nephi 13:39-40) in a world language rather than in his own tribal Hebrew? Did not later Jews adopt Greek, an international world language, in preference to Hebrew, even as a vehicle of holy writ, for the purpose of commanding the widest possible hearing not only among the Gentiles but also among the Jews themselves?

The first three verses of 1 Nephi, sharply set off from the rest of the text, are a typical *colophon,* a literary device that is highly characteristic of Egyptian compositions. Typical is the famous Bremer-Rhind Papyrus, which opens with a colophon containing (1) the date, (2) the titles of Nasim, the author, (3) the names of his parents and a word in praise of their virtues, with special mention of his father's prophetic calling, (4) a curse against anyone who might "take the book away," probably "due to fear lest a sacred book should get into impure hands."[44] Compare this with Nephi's colophon: (1) his name, (2) the merits of his parents, with special attention to the learning of his father, (3) a solemn avowal (corresponding to Nasim's curse) that the record is true, and the assertion, "I make it with mine own hand" (1 Nephi 1:3)—an indispensable condition of every true colophon, since the purpose of a colophon is to establish the identity of the actual writer-down (not merely the ultimate author) of the text. Egyptian literary writings regularly close with the formula *iw-f-pw* "thus it is," "and so it is."[45] Nephi ends the main sections of his book with the phrase, "And thus it is, Amen" (1 Nephi 9:6; 14:30; 22:31).

The great preoccupation and concern displayed in the Book of Mormon for matters of writing, Lehi's passion for writing everything down (1 Nephi 1:16), and the obvious pride of writers in their skill, are peculiarly Egyptian.

Nephi's "I Make It With Mine Own Hand," is simply the Egyptian "written with my own fingers," and we can almost hear Nephi speaking in the words of an Egyptian sage: "Copy thy fathers who have gone before thee. . . . Behold, their words are recorded in writing. Open and read and copy." Certainly Nephi himself was diligent in keeping this *seboyet.*[46] It was the Egyptian, not the Hebrew gentleman, who advertised his proficiency in the arts of the scribe.[47] Thoroughly Egyptian also is Lehi's didactic spirit and his habit of giving long formal addresses on moral and religious subjects "in the manner of the fathers" to his sons. Like a good Egyptian he wrote all this down, of course.[48] The *form* of these discourses, with their set introductions and formal imagery might have come right out of an Egyptian schoolroom, though their *content* smacks more of the "learning of the Jews," as Nephi himself observes (1 Nephi 1:2). Both in form and content, however, the writings of the prophets and the wisdom of Israel are found to resemble the prophetic and "wisdom" literature of Egypt very closely,[49] so that we need not be surprised if Lehi's prophecies do the same. At the end of the last century scholars were mystified to find that a demotic prophecy datable to the time of Bocchoris (718-712 B.C.), in which coming destructions were predicted with the promise of a Messiah to follow, was put into the mouth of "the Lamb" (*pa-hib*). Greek sources inform us that this prophecy enjoyed very great circulation in ancient times.[50] The strange wording of Lehi's great prophecy, uttered by "the Lamb" (1 Nephi 13:34, 41), is thus seen to be no anachronism, taken from Hellenistic or Christian times, as was once maintained.

Typical of the Egyptian prophets is one Neferrohu, whose prophecies, though of uncertain date, were credited with great antiquity. This man describes himself as a commoner, but withal a valiant man and "a wealthy man of great possessions," and he is proud of his skill as scribe.

Like Lehi in other things, he recalls also that he brooded much "over what should come to pass in the land," and having done so was moved to prophesy: "Up my heart, and bewail this land whence thou art sprung . . . the land is utterly perished, and nought remains . . . the earth is fallen into misery for the sake of yon food of the Bedouins who pervade the land." Yet he looks forward to a savior-king who is to come.[51] The situation is not unique but is a characteristic one both in Egypt and Judah, and no one could deny that if Lehi was not a fact, he was at least a very authentic type. Nephi says his father was but one among many prophets in his own day.

Egyptian Politics in the New World

The best possible indication of the influence of Egyptian civilization on Lehi's people may be found in an episode taken from the later history of the Nephites.[52]

Book of Mormon:

Acting on the recommendation of King Mosiah, who was anxious to avoid a throne controversy, the Nephites in the early first century B.C. substituted for the kingship a system of rule by priestly judges, "wise men to be judges, that will judge this people according to the commandments of God" (Mosiah 29:11). We are not told where Mosiah got the idea, but the eagerness and ease with which the people adopted the system imply that they were familiar with it (Mosiah 29:37-41). This is definitely indicated by the account of one Korihor, who was able to gain a great following in the land by charging "the high priest, and also the chief judge over the land" with reviving "ordinances and performances which are laid down by ancient priests, to usurp power and authority" over the country (Alma 30:21-24). That there was a real danger of reviving an ancient priest-rule is apparent from the fact that the new system had no sooner been established than a certain Nehor, in the first case to be tried by the new chief judge, is charged with being first to introduce priestcraft "among this people." The chief judge on this occasion observes that such priestcraft if allowed by the people "would prove their entire destruction" (Alma 1:12). So we are told that priestcraft had not been practiced in the New World, but that a tradition of priestcraft was vividly remembered; its origin must therefore be sought in the Old World, if we would believe the Book of Mormon.

The Old World:

From the eleventh dynasty on, the history of Egypt is largely concerned with the efforts of the priests of Amon, with the chief priest of Amon at their head, to gain control of the country. About 1085 B.C. the chief priest of Amon actually seized the throne of the south, and from that time on "the High priest of Amon . . . could and constantly did reduce the king to a position of subservience."[53] The name of the great priest who crowned himself in Thebes was Herihor or Kherihor.[54] The cornerstone of the priestly rule was a new system of popular law courts, in which the priests of Amon were the judges, and which at first competed with and then supplanted the regular courts everywhere.[55] The separatist tendency, which remains characteristic of the priestly history, may have been foreshadowed in the uniting of all the south countries as a single administrative unit under Nehi, the great governor of the Eighteenth Dynasty, as well as in the appearance, beginning with Count Nehri, of a separate ruling family at Thebes, under the patronage of Amon.[56] Nehri's successor by taking the name *Sam Tawi*, "uniter of the two lands," serves notice of a new dynasty.[57]

Whether or not *Nehi* and *Nehri* are in any way related to the name *Nephi* (there are other Egyptian names that come nearer) remains to be investigated. But no philologist will refuse to acknowledge the possible identity of the Book of Mormon *Korihor* with the Egyptian *Kherihor*, and none may deny, philologist or not, a close resemblance between *Sam* and *Sam* (the brother of Nephi).

Book of Mormon:

The so-called "people of Ammon" (Alma 30:1), a community noted for its piety, took Korihor before their leader, Ammon, "who was a high priest over that people." Thence he was "carried before the high priest, and also the chief judge over the land." This higher court in turn "sent him to the land of Zarahemla . . . before Alma, and the chief judge who was governor over all the land" (Alma 30:19-21, 29-31).

The Old World:

The chief governor of Egypt was "the high priest of Amon" (or Ammon), his title being in Egyptian *neter hem tep*—"chief servant (*Hem*) of the God."[58] *Hem* is an element in Egyptian proper names and means the same as the extremely common *'Abdi* element in western Asiatic names of the time (cf. the modern Arabic *Abdullah*, "servant of God"). It is most interesting that the brother of the earlier Ammon in the Book of Mormon actually bears the name of *Hem* (Mosiah 7:6). As for *Amon* (or *Ammon*), it is the commonest proper name in the Book of Mormon, and also the commonest and most revered name in the Egyptian Empire,[59] which at all times during the later period (after 930 B.C.) pretends to embrace Palestine and regard Jerusalem as a dependent. The reverence shown the name of *Amon* in no way indicates the slightest concession to paganism on the part of the Jews, since *Amon* is no less than the Egyptian version of their own universal, one, creator-God, the Great Spirit, who is never conceived to be in animal form nor represented by any image.[60] He first appears about 2140 B.C., in southern Egypt, at Thebes, where he seems to have been an importation from western Asia.[61]

Can he be the God of Abraham? It is significant that the name first rises to prominence in the years following the time of Abraham's sojourn in Egypt, and near a place where the most famous Jewish colony in Egypt was later located.[62]

A reflection of the Egyptian picture may be detected in the coast cities of Palestine, regularly under Egyptian influence, where government was also by priests and judges, who occasionally usurped the office of king. This happened both at Sidon and Tyre; in the latter city two priestly usurpers bore the name of *Maitena* or *Mattena*—a name which has a number of variants and strongly suggests the Book of Mormon Mathoni.

Book of Mormon:

The experiment with government by priestly judges collapsed, largely due to a rivalry for the chief judgeship among three candidates, all sons of the great chief judge, *Pahoran*. Their names are *Pahoran, Paanchi,* and *Pacumeni* (Helaman 1:1-3).

The Old World:

Such family rivalry for the office of high priest is characteristic of the Egyptian system, in which the office seems to have been hereditary not by law but by usage.[63]

The name of *Pahoran* reflects the Palestinian *Pahura,* (for the Egyptian Pa-her-an; cf. Pa-her-y, "the Syrian") which is "reformed" Egyptian, i.e., a true Egyptian title, but altered in such a way as to adapt it to the Canaanite speech. *Pahura* (also written *Puhuru*) was in Amarna times an Egyptian governor (*rabu*) of Syria. The same man, or another man with the same name, was placed by Pharaoh as governor of the Ube district, with his headquarters at *Kumedi*[64] (cf. the element *-kumen* in the Book of Mormon place names).

Paanchi is simply the well-known Egyptian *Paiankh* (also

rendered *Pianchi, Paankh,* etc.). The first important man to bear the name was none other than the son of the above-mentioned *Kherihor*. He did not succeed his father on the throne, being content with the all-powerful office of chief high priest of Amon, but his son, *Panezem* did become king.[65] In the middle of the eighth century another *Pianhki,* a king of Nubia, conquered virtually all of Egypt, and claimed for himself the office of high priest of Amon at Thebes as well as the title of Pharaoh.[66] His successor, when the Assyrians invaded Egypt, in the days of Lehi, fled to a fortified city, as yet unlocated, which bore the name of *Kipkip* or *Kibkib,* a name-form that strongly suggests the Book of Mormon city-name Gidgiddoni (cf. also *Gimgimno,* 3 Nephi 8:9).

Pacumeni, the name of the third son, resembles that borne by some of the last priest governors of Egypt, whose names are rendered *Pa-menech, Pa-mnkh, Pamenches,* etc. The Greeks (who often furnish the key to the correct reading of Egyptian names) put the guttural before the nasal *Pachomios*. The most famous man of the name commanded all the forces of the south, and was also high priest of Horus. At least one other governor-general of Egypt bore the name.[67]

A striking coincidence is the predominance among both Egyptian and Nephite judge names of the prefix *Pa-*. In late Egyptian this is extremely common, and has simply the force of the definite article.[68] Another Book of Mormon judge, *Cezoram,* has a name that suggests that of an Egyptian governor of a Syrian city: *Chi-zi-ri*.[69] It should be noted that the above *Panezem* upon becoming king took the name of *Meriamon,* which has a Book of Mormon ring, even if we don't read it *Moriamon*—a perfectly possible variant.

Sidon was the official port through which the Jews traded with Egypt. Since Lehi and his people were in the mercantile business, it is not surprising that Sidon is the only Palestinian city besides Jerusalem whose name figures prominently in Book of Mormon geography. Moreover, since Sidon was the common meeting ground between Hebrew and Egyptian, and since names in both languages occur in the Book of Mormon, one would expect the name of this most popular place to appear in its Egyptian as well as in its Hebrew form. The Egyptian form is *Dji-dw-na*, which is remarkably close to the Book of Mormon personal name *Giddonah*.[70]

We cannot conclude this brief survey of the "Egyptian question" without reference to one significant indication that Lehi's forefathers were *not* natives of Jerusalem. We learn in Mosiah 1:4 that certain plates were written "in the language of the Egyptians." Nephi informs us (1 Nephi 3:19) that these same plates were in "the language of our fathers," and that the possession of them was necessary if a knowledge of that language was to be preserved among his people. To preserve mere *characters* but a single page of Hebrew and Egyptian signs would have been necessary, and Lehi or his sons could have produced such from memory, since they had already been taught them. And if the language in question were Hebrew, Lehi's children could have produced from their own resources any number of books in their own language, so that when Nephi expresses his belief that without that one volume of plates a language will be lost—the ancient language of his fathers—he cannot possibly be speaking of Hebrew. The preservation of Hebrew would naturally require possession of the scriptures, the canon of the pure language, but these could be had anywhere in Judah and would not require the dangerous mission to Laban. The language of Lehi's forefathers was a foreign language; and when Nephi tells us it was the language of the Egyptians he means what he says. Since time immemorial Israelites had been sojourning in Egypt individually and in groups, and there is nothing the least surprising in the possibility that Lehi's ancestors were among such settlers.

2

Men of the East

Strange Names

The stamp of Egypt on Lehi's people may be clearly discerned in the names of those people and their descendants. Hebrew and Egyptian names together make up the overwhelming majority and occur in about equal strength, which is exactly what one would expect from Mormon's claim that both languages were used among them (and which would certainly *not* be the case were Hebrew the only spoken language), but Hittite, Arabic, and Ionian elements are not missing. First, consider a few Egyptian names, setting off the Book of Mormon names (BM) against their Old World equivalents (OW).[1]

Aha (BM), son of the Nephite commander in chief.
Aha (OW), a name of the first Pharaoh; it means "warrior" and is a common word.

Aminadab (BM), Nephite missionary in the time of the judges.
Amanathabi (OW), chief of a Canaanite city under Egyptian domination. The name is "reformed" Egyptian.

Ammon (BM), the commonest name in the Book of Mormon.
Ammon (Amon, Amun) (OW), the commonest name in the Egyptian Empire: the great universal God of the Empire.

Ammoni-hah (BM), name of a country and city.
Ammuni-ra (OW), prince of Beyrut under Egyptian rule. The above might stand the same relationship to this name as

Cameni-hah (BM), a Nephite general, does to

Khamuni-ra (OW), Amarna personal name, perhaps equivalent of Ammuni-ra.[2]

Cezoram (BM), Nephite chief judge.

Chiziri (OW), Egyptian governor of a Syrian city.

Giddonah (BM), a) high priest who judged Korihor, b) father of Amulek.

Dji-dw-na (OW), the Egyptian name for Sidon.

Gidgiddoni and **Gidgiddonah** (BM), Nephite generals.

Djed-djhwt-iw-f and **Djed-djhwti-iw-s** plus **ankh** (OW), Egyptian proper names meaning "Thoth hath said: he shall live," and "Thoth hath said: she shall live," respectively.[3] On this pattern the two Nephite names mean "Thoth hath said I shall live," and "Thoth hath said: we shall live," respectively.

Giddianhi (BM), robber chief and general.

Djhwti-ankhi (OW), "Thoth is my life"; see above.

Gimgim-no (BM), city of Gimgim, compare Biblical No-Amon, "City of Amon."

Kenkeme (OW), Egyptian city, cf. Kipkip, seat of the Egyptian dynasty in Nubia.

Hem (BM), brother of the earlier Ammon.

Hem (OW), means "servant," specifically of Ammon, as in the title *Hem tp n 'Imn,* "chief servant of Ammon" held by the high priest of Thebes.

Helaman (BM), great Nephite prophet.

Her-amon (OW), "in the presence of Amon," as in the Egyptian proper name Heri-i-her-imn.[4] Semitic "l" is always written "r" in Egyptian, which has no "l." Conversely, the Egyptian "r" is often written "l" in Semitic languages.

Himni (BM), a son of King Mosiah.

Hmn (OW), a name of the Egyptian hawk-god, symbol of the emperor.

Korihor (BM), a political agitator who was seized by the people of Ammon.

Kherihor (also written Khurhor, etc.) (OW), great high priest of Ammon who seized the throne of Egypt at Thebes, cir. 1085 B.C.

Manti (BM), the name of a Nephite soldier, a land, a city, and a hill.

Manti (OW), Semitic form of an Egyptian proper name, e.g., Manti-mankhi, a prince in Upper Egypt cir. 650 B.C. It is a late form of Month, god of Hermonthis.

Mathoni (BM), a Nephite disciple.

Maitena, Mattenos, etc. (OW), two judges of Tyre, who at different times made themselves king, possibly under the Egyptian auspices.

Morianton (BM), the name of a Nephite city and its founder, cf. the Nephite province Moriantum.

Meriaton and **Meriamon** (OW), names of Egyptian princes, "Beloved of Aton" and "Beloved of Amon" respectively.

Nephi (BM), founder of the Nephite nation.

Nehi, Nehri (OW), famous Egyptian noblemen. **Nfy** was the name of an Egyptian captain. Since BM insists on "ph," **Nephi** is closer to **Nihpi,** original name of the god Pa-nepi, which may even have been Nephi.[5]

Paanchi (BM), son of Pahoran, Sr., and pretender to the chief-judgeship.

Paanchi (OW), son of Kherihor, a) chief high priest of Amon, b) ruler of the south who conquered all of Egypt and was high priest of Amon at Thebes.

Pahoran (BM), a) great chief judge, b) son of the same.

Pa-her-an (OW), ambassador of Egypt in Palestine, where his name has the "reformed" reading Pahura; in Egyptian as Pa-her-y it means "the Syrian" or Asiatic.

Pacumeni (BM), son of Pahoran.

Pakamen (OW), Egyptian proper name meaning "blind man"; also *Pamenches* (Gk. *Pachomios*), commander of the south and high priest of Horus.

Pachus (BM), revolutionary leader and usurper of the throne.

Pa-ks and Pach-qs (OW), Egyptian proper name. Compare *Pa-ches-i,* "he is praised."

Sam (BM), brother of Nephi.

Sam Tawi (OW), Egyptian "uniter of the lands," title taken by the brother of Nehri upon mounting the throne.

Seezor-am and **Zeezr-om** (BM), a depraved judge, and a lawyer, resp., the latter also the name of a city.

Zoser, Zeser, etc. (OW), Third Dynasty ruler, one of the greatest Pharaohs.

Zemna-ri-hah (BM), robber chief.

Zmn-ha-re (OW), Egyptian proper name: the same elements as the above in different order—a common Egyptian practice.

Zeniff (BM), ruler of Nephite colony.

Znb, Snb (OW), very common elements in Egyptian proper names, cf. Senep-ta.

Zenoch (BM), according to various Nephite writers, an ancient Hebrew prophet.

Zenekh (OW), Egyptian proper name; once a serpent-god.

It will be noted that the names compared are rarely *exactly* alike, except in the case of the monosyllables *Sam* and *Hem*. This, strangely enough, is strong confirmation

Paiankh, son of Kherihor and Chief High Priest of Ammon. The name, in the form Paankhi, is borne by two rulers of the South, in the first and fourth kings of Dynasty XXV. It is absolutely identical with the Paanchi of Helaman 1:3.

The Egyptian form of the name Sidon reads approximately Djidonah (the "d" very strong), suggesting the Book of Mormon proper name Giddonah. The Hebrew form is very common in the Book of Mormon. (From Max Burchardt, "Altkanaanaischen Fremdworte" after W. F. Albright, "Vocalization of the Egyptian Syllabic Orthography," 67.)

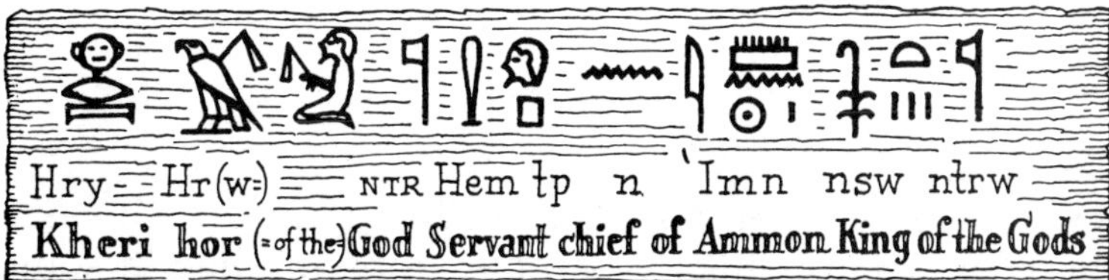

The full title of Kherihor before he became king in Thebes. In the Book of Mormon (Alma 30), Korihor is sent by Ammon, whose office of High Priest over the people of Ammon has important judicial and political functions, to be tried before "the high priest and chief judge of the land." Just such a combined and general authority was enjoyed by Kherihor in Egypt as Chief Servant (Hem) of Amon. The Ammon in the Book of Mormon has a brother by the name of Hem.

of their common origin, since names are bound to undergo some change with time and distance, whereas if the resemblance were perfect, we should be forced to attribute it, however fantastic it might seem, to mere coincidence. There *must* be differences; and what is more, those differences should not be haphazard but display definite tendencies. This brings us to a most impressive aspect of Book of Mormon names.

Let us take for example the case of *Ammon*. Being so very popular a name, one would expect it to occur in compounds as well as alone, and sure enough, it is the commonest element in compound names, in the West as in Egypt. But in compound names *Amon* or *Amun* changes form following a general rule. Gardiner in his *Egyptian Grammar* states:

> A very important class of personal names is that containing the names known as theophorous, i.e. compound names in which one element is the name of a deity. Now in Graeco-Roman transcriptions it is the rule that when such a divine name stands at the *beginning* of a compound [the italics are Gardiner's], it is less heavily vocalized than when it stands independently or at the end of a compound.[6]

The author then goes on to show that in such cases *Amon* or *Amun* regularly becomes Amen, while in some cases the vowel may disappear entirely. One need only consider the Book of Mormon *Aminidab, Aminadi, Amminihu, Amnor,* etc., to see how neatly the rule applies in the West. In the name *Helaman,* on the other hand, the strong vocalization remains, since the "divine name" is not "stated at the *beginning*" of the compound. Since the Semitic *"l"* must always be rendered as "r" in Egyptian (which has no *"l"*) *Helaman* would in "*un*reformed" Egyptian necessarily appear as the typically Egyptian *Heramon*.

The great frequency of the element *Mor-* in Book of Mormon proper names is in striking agreement with the fact that in the lists of Egyptian names compiled by Lieblein and Ranke the element *Mr* is, next to *Nfr* alone, by far the commonest.

In an article in *The Improvement Era* for April 1948, the author drew attention to the peculiar tendency of Book of Mormon names to concentrate in Upper Egypt, in and south of Thebes. At the time he was at a loss to explain such a strange phenomenon, but the answer is now clear.[7] When Jerusalem fell, most of Lehi's contemporaries who escaped went to Egypt, where their principal settlement seems to have been at Elephantine or Yeb, south of Thebes. It would seem, in fact, that the main colonization of Elephantine was at that time, and from Jerusalem.[8] What then could be more natural than that the refugees who fled to Egypt from Lehi's Jerusalem should have Book of Mormon names, since Lehi's people took their names from the same source?

One serious objection to using Book of Mormon names as philological evidence must not be passed by without an answer. Upon seeing these strange words before him, how could the illiterate Joseph Smith have known how to pronounce them? And upon hearing them, how could his half-educated scribe have known how to write them down phonetically? Remember, these names are not translations into English like the rest of the book but remain bits of the authentic Nephite language. Between them, the guesses of the prophet as to pronunciation and the guesses of Oliver Cowdery as to transcription would be bound to make complete havoc of the original titles. Only there was no guessing. According to David Whitmer and Emma Smith in interviews appearing in *The Saints Herald* and pointed out to the author by Preston Nibley, Joseph never pronounced the proper names he came upon in the plates during the translation but always *spelled them out*.[9] Hence there can be no doubt that they are meant as they stand to be as accurate and authentic as it is possible to render them in our alphabet.

But Egypt was not everything. Palestine was always a melting pot and more so than ever in Lehi's day, when the whole Near East was being thoroughly mixed by the operations of commerce and war. Lists of skilled workmen living at Babylon immediately after the fall of Jerusalem show an almost unbelievable mixture of types.[10]

Since the Old Testament was available to Joseph Smith, there is no point in listing Hebrew names, but their Book of Mormon *forms* are significant. The strong tendency to end in *-iah* is very striking, since the vast majority of Hebrew names found at Lachish end the same way, indicating that *iah* names were very fashionable in Lehi's time.[11] Hebrew names turned up on ancient jar handles from other places also have a familiar Book of Mormon ring: Hezron, Memshath, Ziph (BM Ziff), Jether, Epher, Jalon, Ezer, Menahem, Lecah, Amnon (BM Amnor), Zoheth, etc.,[12] would never be suspected if inserted into a list of Book of Mormon names. The Book of Mormon does give the right *type* of Hebrew name.

What comes as a surprise is that a number of Book of Mormon names are possibly Hittite, and some of them are undoubtedly so. Thus while Manti suggests Egyptian Mont, Manti, Menedi, etc., it also recalls the Egyptian name of a Hittite city, Manda, and a characteristic element of Hurrian names (much of Hittite is really Hurrian, as Professor Goetze has shown) -anti, -andi, likewise fairly common in the Book of Mormon.[13] So likewise *Cumeni, Kumen-onhi, Kisk-kumen* (Eg.-Hitt. Kumani, an important city), *Seantum* (Eg.-Hitt. Sandon, Sandas), *Akish* (Eg.-Hitt. Achish, a name of Cyprus), *Gadiandi* (Eg. for a Hittite city, Cadyanda).[14] Their Egyptian form implies that these names reached the people of Lehi not directly but through normal routes, though it has recently been shown that some of Lehi's important contemporaries were Hittites, and that Hittite settlements and names still survived in the hill country of Judah in his time.[15]

The occurrence of the names *Timothy* and *Lachoneus* in the Book of Mormon is strictly in order, however odd it may seem at first glance. Since the fourteenth century B.C. at latest, Syria and Palestine had been in constant contact with the Aegean world, and since the middle of the seventh century Greek mercenaries and merchants, closely bound to Egyptian interests (the best Egyptian mercenaries were Greeks), swarmed throughout the Near East.[16] Lehi's people, even apart from their mercantile activities, could not have avoided considerable contact with these people in Egypt and especially in Sidon, which Greek poets even in that day were celebrating as the great world center of trade. It is interesting to note in passing that Timothy is an Ionian name, since the Greeks in Palestine were Ionians (hence the Hebrew name for Greeks: "Sons of Javanim"), and—since "Lachoneus" means "a Laconian"—that the oldest Greek traders were Laconians, who had colonies in Cyprus (BM Akish) and of course traded with Palestine.[17]

The compiler of these studies was once greatly puzzled over the complete absence of *Baal* names from the Book of Mormon. By what unfortunate oversight had the authors of that work failed to include a single name containing the element *Baal*, which thrives among the personal names of the Old Testament? Having discovered, as we thought, that the book was in error, we spared no criticism at the time, and indeed had its neglect of *Baal* names not been strikingly vindicated in recent years it would be a black mark against it. Now we learn, however, that the stubborn prejudice of our text against *Baal* names is really the only correct attitude it could have taken, and this discovery, flying in the face of all our calculation and preconceptions, should in all fairness weigh at least as heavily in the book's favor as the supposed error did against it.

It happens that for some reason or other the Jews at the beginning of the sixth century B.C. would have nothing to do with *Baal* names. An examination of Elephantine name lists shows that "the change of Baal names, by substitution, is in agreement with Hosea's foretelling that they should be no more used by the Israelites, and consequently it is most interesting to find how the latest archaeological discoveries confirm the Prophet, for out of some four hundred personal names among the Elephantine papyri not one is compounded of *Baal*."[18]

Since Elephantine was settled largely by Israelites who fled from Jerusalem after its destruction, their personal names should show the same tendencies as those in the Book of Mormon. Though the translator of that book might by the exercise of superhuman cunning have been warned by Hosea 2:17 to eschew *Baal* names, yet the meaning of that passage is so far from obvious that Albright as late as 1942 finds it "very significant that seals and inscriptions from Judah, which . . . are very numerous in the seventh and early sixth [centuries], seem never to contain any *Baal* names."[19] It is very significant indeed, but hardly more so than the uncanny acumen which the Book of Mormon displays on this point.

Speaking of the occurrence of a few Arabic names in the Old Testament, Margoliouth observes, "Considering . . . that the recorded names are those of an infinitesimal fraction of the population, the coincidence is extraordinary."[20] This consideration applies with multiple force to the Book of Mormon, where the many names coinciding with Old World forms represent "but an infinitesimal fraction" of the Nephite population.

Lehi and the Arabs

Lehi was very rich, and he was a trader, for his wealth was in the form of "all manner of riches" (1 Nephi 3:16) such as had to be brought from many places. His world was a world of travelers and merchants. The princes of the Delta were merchants,[21] the princes of the Syrian and Palestinian cities were also, as the Amarna tablets show, merchants; the story of Wenamon tells us that the princes of Phoenicia and Philistia were merchants; the Arab princes of the desert were merchants; and the merchants of Egypt and Babylonia would meet in their tents to transact business;[22] the two wisest of the Greeks, Lehi's great contemporaries Solon and Thales, both traveled extensively in the East—on business.

Very significant is the casual notice that Lehi once had a vision in a desert place "as he went forth" (1 Nephi 1:5), *as* he went he prayed, we are told, and *as* he prayed a vision came to him. The effect of the vision was to make him hasten back "to his own house at Jerusalem" (1 Nephi 1:17), where he had yet greater visions, showing that it was not necessary for him to "go forth" either to pray or to have visions; he did not go forth expecting a vision—for when a vision came he immediately returned home—but one came to him in the course of a regular journey *as* he went about his business and forced him to change his plans.

Lehi's precious things and gold came to him in exchange for his wine, oil, figs, and honey (of which he seems to know a good deal), not only by sea (hence the great importance of Sidon), but necessarily and especially by caravan as well. "Israel," says Montgomery, "looked to the desert. There alone commercially were its possible profits, by way of the great trade routes . . . to Syria, . . . to the Mediterranean and Egypt, or . . . to the Euphrates and the Persian Gulf. To the west it was blocked off by the Egyptians, Philistines, Phoenicians, Syrians, cleverer traders than the Hebrews." Since Egypt controlled this western trade, it is easy to see how Lehi could profit by making the most of his Egyptian training and background. Though these western outlets were open in Lehi's day due to a policy of close cooperation with western powers against Babylonia, the rule always was that the desert trade, specifically that of the South Desert, was the one reliable source of wealth for the men of Jerusalem.[23]

There is ample evidence in the Book of Mormon that Lehi was an expert on caravan travel, as one might expect. Consider a few general points. Upon receiving a warning dream, he is ready apparently at a moment's notice to take his whole "family, and provisions, and tents" out into the wilderness (1 Nephi 2:4). While he took absolutely nothing but the most necessary provisions with him (1 Nephi 2:4), he knew exactly what those provisions should be, and when he had to send back to the city to supply unanticipated wants, it was for records that he sent and not for any necessaries for the journey. This argues a high degree of preparation and knowledge in the man, as does the masterly way in which he established a base camp in order to gather his forces for the great trek, in the best manner of modern explorers in Arabia.[24] Up until Lehi leaves that base camp, that is, until the day when he receives the Liahona, he seems to know just where he is going and exactly what he is doing: there is here no talk of being "led by the Spirit, not knowing beforehand" as with Nephi in the dark streets of Jerusalem (1 Nephi 4:6).

His family accuse Lehi of folly in leaving Jerusalem and do not spare his personal feelings in making fun of his dreams and visions, yet they never question his ability to lead them. They complain, like all Arabs, against the terrible and dangerous deserts through which they pass, but they do not include ignorance of the desert among their hazards, though that would be their first and last objection to his wild project were the old man nothing but a city Jew unacquainted with the wild and dangerous world of the waste places.

Lehi himself never mentions inexperience among his handicaps. Members of the family laugh contemptuously when Nephi proposes to build a ship (1 Nephi 17:17-20), and might well have quoted the ancient proverb, "Do not show an Arab the sea or to a Sidonian the desert, for their work is different."[25] But while they tell him he is "lacking in judgment" (1 Nephi 17:19) to build a ship, they never mock their brother's skill as a hunter or treat him as dude in the desert. The fact that he brought a fine steel bow with him *from home* and that he knew well how to use that difficult weapon shows that Nephi had hunted much in his short life.

Lehi has strong ties with the desert in his family background. Twenty-six hundred years ago the Jews felt themselves much closer to the people of the desert than they have in subsequent times. "We come to realize," says Montgomery, "that Israel had its face turned towards those quarters we call the Desert, and that this was its nearest neighbor." The Jews themselves were desert people originally, and they never forgot it:[26] "This constant seeping-in of desert wanderers still continues. . . . There is no barrier of race or language or caste or religion" between them and their desert cousins.[27] We have often been told that the patriarchs of old were wandering Bedouins, though far from barbaric;[28] their language was that of the desert people, many of whose words are to this day closer to Hebrew than to modern Arabic.[29] As recently as 2000 B.C. Hebrew and Arabic had not yet emerged from "what was substantially a common language, understood from the Indian Ocean to the Taurus and from the Zagros to the frontier of Egypt. This common language (excluding Accadian . . .) was probably almost as homogeneous as was Arabic a thousand years ago."[30] A curious and persistent homogeneity of culture and language has characterized the people of the Near East in every age, so that Margoliouth can affirm that "a Sabaean (south Arabian) would in fact have found little to puzzle him in the first verse of Genesis."[31] "The Hebrews remained Arabs," is the verdict of a modern authority; "their literature . . . in its recorded forms, is of Arab scheme and type."[32] It is not surprising that Professor Margoliouth holds that Arabic seems to hold "the key to every lock" in the study of the Old Testament.

Of recent years the tendency has been more and more to equate Hebrew and Arab, and Guillaume concludes the latest study on the subject with the dictum that the two names are really forms of a common original, both alike referring to "the sons of Eber."[33] The name Arab is not meant to designate any particular race, tribe, or nation and "no sharp distinction is made between Hebrews, Aramaeans, and Arabs in the days of the Patriarchs," according to Albright,[34] but the word simply designates a way of life, and was applied by the Jews to their own relatives who remained behind in the wilderness after they themselves had settled down in the city and country.[35]

One interesting tie between Israel and the Arabs should not be overlooked since it has direct application to the Book of Mormon. We refer to those Hebrew genealogies in which "the nomenclature is largely un-Hebraic, with peculiar antique formations in *-an, -on,* and in some cases of particular Arabian origin."[36] "The loss of the ending *on* is quite common in Palestinian place-names," according to Albright, referring to places mentioned in Egyptian records.[37] One can recall any number of Book of Mormon place names—Emron, Heshlon, Jashon, Moron, etc., that have preserved this archaic *-on,* indicative of a quaint conservatism among Lehi's people, and especially of ties with the desert people.

Now of all the tribes of Israel, Manasseh was the one which lived farthest out in the desert, came into most frequent contact with the Arabs, intermarried with them most frequently, and at the same time had the closest traditional bonds with Egypt.[38] And Lehi belonged to the tribe of Manasseh (Alma 10:3). The prominence of the name of Ammon in the Book of Mormon may have something to do with the fact that Ammon was Manasseh's nearest neighbor and often fought her in the deserts east of Jordan; at the same time a prehistoric connection with the Ammon of Egypt is not at all out of the question.[39] The seminomadic nature of Manasseh might explain why Lehi seems out of touch with things in Jerusalem. For the first time he "did discover" (1 Nephi 5:16), from records kept in Laban's house, that he was a direct descendant of Joseph. Why hadn't he known that all along? Nephi always speaks of "the Jews who were at Jerusalem" (1 Nephi 2:13) with a curious detachment, and no one in First Nephi ever refers to them as "the people" or "our people" but always quite impersonally as "the Jews." It is interesting in this connection that the Elephantine letters speak only of Jews and Aramaeans, never of Israelites.[40]

Not only do both Nephi and Lehi show marked coolness on the subject of tribal loyalty, but both also protest that the tribe is not a decisive factor in salvation, that the same blessings are available to all men at all times and in all parts of the world (1 Nephi 10:17-22), that "the Lord esteemeth all flesh in one" (1 Nephi 17:35), there being no such thing as an arbitrarily "chosen" people (1 Nephi 17:37-40). This is in marked contrast to the fierce chauvinism of the Jews at Jerusalem and is of a piece with Lehi's pronounced cosmopolitanism in other things. Lehi, like Moses and his own ancestor, Joseph, was a man of *three* cultures, being educated not only in "the learning of the Jews and the language of the Egyptians" (1 Nephi 1:2), but in the ways of the desert as well.[41] "There is a peculiar color and atmosphere to the biblical life," says Professor Montgomery, "which gives it its special tone. . . . And that touch comes from the expanses and the free-moving life of what we call Arabia."[42] The dual culture of Egypt and Israel would have been impossible without the all-important Arab to be the link between, just as trade between the two nations was unthinkable without the Bedouin to guide their caravans through his deserts. Without the sympathetic cooperation of the Arabs any passage through their deserts was a terrible risk when not out of the question, and the good businessman was ever the one who knew how to deal with the Arabs—which meant to be one of them.[43]

Lachish letter No. 6, in denouncing the prophet Jeremiah for spreading defeatism both in the country and in the city, shows that Lehi, a supporter of the prophet, could have been active in either area of "the land of Jerusalem" (1 Nephi 3:10). Even the remark that Lehi "dwelt at Jerusalem in all his days" (1 Nephi 1:4) would never have been made by or for people who would not think of living anywhere else, and a dwelling "at Jerusalem" would be an aid rather than a hindrance to much travel,[44] for "the wilderness of Judah is a long projection north from the Arabian deserts to the gates of Jerusalem."[45]

The proverbial ancestor of the Arabs is Ishmael. His is one of the few Old Testament names which is also at home in ancient Arabia.[46] His traditional homeland was the Tih, the desert between Palestine and Egypt, and his people were haunters of the "borders" between the desert and the town;[47] he was regarded as the legitimate offspring of Abraham by an Egyptian mother. His was not a name of good omen, for the angel had promised his mother, "he will be a wild man; his hand will be against everyone, and every man's hand against him,"[48] so the chances are that one who bore his name had good family reasons for doing it, and in Lehi's friend Ishmael we surely have a man of the desert. Lehi, faced with the prospect of a long journey in the wilderness, sent back for Ishmael, who promptly followed into the desert with a large party; this means that he must have been hardly less adept at moving than Lehi himself. The interesting thing is that Nephi takes Ishmael (unlike Zoram) completely for granted, never explaining who he is or how he fits into the picture—the act of sending for him seems to be the most natural thing in the world, as does the marriage of his daughters with Lehi's sons. Since it has ever been the custom among the desert people for a man to marry the daughter of his paternal uncle (*bint 'ammi*), it is hard to avoid the impression that Lehi and Ishmael were related.[49]

There is a remarkable association between the names of Lehi and Ishmael which ties them both to the southern desert, where the legendary birthplace and central shrine of Ishmael was at a place called Be'er Lehai-ro'i.[50] Wellhausen rendered the name "spring of the wild-ox jawbone,"[51] but Paul Haupt showed that Lehi (for so he reads the name) does not mean "jaw" but "cheek,"[52] which leaves the meaning of the strange compound still unclear. One thing is certain, however: that Lehi is a personal name. Until recently this name was entirely unknown save as a place name, but now it has turned up at Elath and elsewhere in the south in a form that has been identified by Nelson Glueck with the name *Lahai*, which "occurs quite frequently either as a part of a compound, or as a separate name of a deity or a person, particularly in Minaean, Thamudic, and Arabic texts."[53] There is a Beit Lahi, "House of Lahi," among the ancient place names of the Arab country around Gaza, but the meaning of the name has here been lost.[54] If the least be said of it, the name *Lehi* is thoroughly at home among the people of the desert and, so far as we know, nowhere else.

The name of Lemuel is not a conventional Hebrew one, for it occurs only in one chapter of the Old Testament (Proverbs 31:1, 4), where it is commonly supposed to be a rather mysterious poetic substitute for Solomon. It is, however, like Lehi, at home in the south desert, where an Edomite text from "a place occupied by tribes descended from Ishmael" bears the title, "The Words of Lemuel, King of Massa." These people, though speaking a language that was almost Arabic, were yet well within the sphere of Jewish religion, for "we have nowhere else any evidence for saying that the Edomites used any other peculiar name for their deity" than "Yahweh, the God of Hebrews."[55]

The only example of the name of Laman to be found anywhere to the writer's knowledge is its attribution to an ancient *Mukam*, or sacred place, in Palestine. Most of these

Mukams are of unknown, and many of them of prehistoric, date. In Israel only the tribe of Manasseh built them.[56] It is a striking coincidence that Conder saw in the name *Leimun*, as he renders it (the vowels must be supplied by guesswork), a possible corruption of the name Lemuel, thus bringing these two names, so closely associated in the Book of Mormon, into the most intimate relationship, and that in the one instance in which the name of Laman appears.[57] Far more popular among the Arabs as among the Nephites was the name Alma, which can mean a young man, a coat of mail, a mountain, or a sign.[58] While Sam is a perfectly good Egyptian name, it is also the normal Arabic form of Shem, the son of Noah.

It should be noted here that archaeology has fully demonstrated that the Israelites, then as now, had not the slightest aversion to giving their children non-Jewish names, even when those names smacked of a pagan background.[59] One might, in a speculative mood, even detect something of Lehi's personal history in the names he gave to his sons. The first two have Arabic names—do they recall his early days in the caravan trade? The second two have Egyptian names, and indeed they were born in the days of his prosperity. The last two, born amid tribulations in the desert, were called, with fitting humility, Jacob and Joseph. Whether the names of the first four were meant, as those of the last two sons certainly were (2 Nephi 2:1; 3:1), to call to mind the circumstances under which they were born, the names are certainly a striking indication of their triple heritage.

3

Into the Desert

Lehi the Dreamer

Lehi possesses in a high degree the traits and characteristics of the model *sheikh* of the desert. He is generous, noble, impulsive, fervent, devout, and visionary, and he possesses a wonderful capacity for eloquence and dreams. As to the dreams, when the Arabs wander, they feel they must be guided by dreams, and their *sheikhs* are often gifted dreamers.[1] The substance of Lehi's dreams is highly significant, since men's dreams necessarily represent, even when inspired, the things they see by day, albeit in strange and wonderful combinations. It is common for men in every age, for example, to dream of ships, but a man in Lehi's day must dream of particular kinds of ships, and no others will do.

In his dreams Lehi finds himself wandering "in a dark and dreary waste," a "dark and dreary wilderness," where he must travel "for the space of many hours in darkness," lost and helpless (1 Nephi 8:4-8). Of all the images that haunt the early Arab poets this is by all odds the commonest; it is the standard nightmare of the Arab; and it is the supreme boast of every poet that he has traveled long distances through dark and dreary wastes all alone.[2] Invariably darkness is given as the main source of terror (the heat and glare of the day, though nearly always mentioned, are given second place), and the culminating horror is almost always a "mist of darkness," a depressing mixture of dust, and clammy fog, which, added to the night, completes the confusion of any who wander in the waste.[3] Quite contrary to what one would expect, these dank mists are described by travelers in all parts of Arabia,[4] and al-Ajajj, one of the greatest of early desert poets, tells how a "mist of darkness" makes it impossible for him to continue a journey to Damascus.[5] In its nature and effect Lehi's "mist of darkness" (1 Nephi 8:23) conforms to this strange phenomenon most exactly.

When Lehi dreams of the vanity of the world, he sees "a large and spacious building," suspended in the air out of reach and full of smart and finely dressed people (1 Nephi 12:18; 8:26). That is exactly how the Bedouin of the desert, to whom the great stone houses of the city are an abomination, pictures the wicked world; and as the city Arabs still mock their desert cousins (whom they secretly envy) with every show of open contempt, so the well-dressed people in the big house "were in the attitude of mocking and pointing their fingers" (1 Nephi 8:27) at the poor little band of bedraggled wanderers, hungrily eating fruit from a tree, and duly abashed that their poverty should be put to open shame. One is reminded by Lehi's imagery of the great stone houses of the ancient Arabs, "ten- and twelve-story skyscrapers that . . . represent genuine survivals of ancient Babylonian architecture,"[6] with their windows beginning, for the sake of defense, fifty feet from the ground. At night these lighted windows would certainly give the effect of being suspended above the earth.

It is interesting that Joseph Smith, Sr., had almost the same dream, according to his wife, who took comfort in comparing the wanderings of her own family with those of "Father Lehi." But what is significant is not the resemblance of the two dreams but the totally different settings of the two; when the prophet's father dreamed himself lost in "this field [of] the world," he "could see nothing save dead, fallen timber," a picture which of course faithfully recalls his own frontier background.[7] When Dante, another westerner, sees himself lost in the midst of life's journey (one of the commonest and oldest of dreams, we repeat—a very classic among dreams) he is wandering through a dense, dark forest, the forest of his native Tuscany.

In a pleasanter vein Lehi sees "a large and spacious field, as if it had been a world" (1 Nephi 8:20) just as the Arab poet describes the world as a *maydān*, or large and spacious field.[8] When he dreams of a river, it is a true desert river, a clear stream a few yards wide with its source but a hundred paces away (1 Nephi 8:13-14)[9] or else a raging muddy wash, a *sayl* of "filthy water" that sweeps people away to their destruction (1 Nephi 8:32; 12:16; 15:27). In the year 960 A.D., according to Bar Hebraeus, a large band of pilgrims returning from Mekka "encamped in the bed of a brook in which water had not flowed for a long time. And during the night, whilst they were sleeping, a flood of water poured down upon them all, and it swept them and all their possessions out into the Great Sea, and they all perished."[10] Even a mounted rider if he is careless may be caught off guard and carried away by such a sudden spate of "head water," according to Doughty.[11] One of the worst places for these gully-washing torrents of liquid mud is in "the scarred and bare mountains which run parallel to the west coast of Arabia; . . . the rainstorms break against this long ridge and produce almost in a moment raging torrents—the Arabic *sail*, spate—which sweep away all obstacles without warning and with loss of life of man and cattle."[12] This was the very region through which Lehi travelled on his great trek.

The springhead and the *sayl*, such are the two and only types of "river" (for he calls them rivers) known to the desert Arab.[13] When Lehi dreams of people gone astray, they are lost in a trackless waste, "wandering in strange roads" (1 Nephi 8:23, 32) or blundering "into broad roads, that they perish and are lost" (1 Nephi 12:17) because of the "mist of darkness" (1 Nephi 8:23). Losing one's way is of course the fate that haunts every desert dweller sleeping and waking, and the Arab poets are full of the terror of "strange roads" and "broad ways."[14] To symbolize what is utterly inaccessible, Lehi is shown "a great and terrible gulf" (1 Nephi 12:18), "an awful gulf" (1 Nephi 15:28), a tremendous chasm with one's objective (the tree of life) maddeningly visible on the other side; all who have traveled in the desert know the feeling of utter helplessness and frustration at finding one's way suddenly cut off by one of those appalling canyons with perpendicular sides—nothing could be more abrupt, more absolute, more baffling to one's plans, and so will it be with the wicked in a day of reckoning.[15]

Wherever else one might find parallels to these things, in combination they could only come from a man who knew the desert. Rubah, one of the desert poets, describes in a single short poem the terror of the loneliness, the long journey, the mist of darkness (sultry and thick), the "awful gulf," the broad ways, and the paths that stray.[16] The Book of Mormon, in giving us not a few such clear and vivid snapshots (there are many more to come) of life in another world, furnishes picturesque but convincing proof of its own authenticity. Nephi's complaint, "they sought to take away my life, that they might leave me in the wilderness to be devoured by wild beasts" (1 Nephi 7:16), is ever in the mouth of the Arab poet, for to leave one's enemy lying in the desert to be devoured by wild beasts is standard and correct procedure when Arabs quarrel, and for all its popularity with the poets, no mere figure of speech.[17]

The Flight into the Wilderness

That a wealthy citizen of Jerusalem should leave the land of his inheritance at a moment's notice and with no more substantial incitement than a dream may seem at first blush highly improbable, to say the least. Yet Lehi had brooded long and anxiously over the fate of Jerusalem, praying "with all his heart, in behalf of his people" (1 Nephi 1:5), and when the dream came, he was prepared. Moreover in taking his sudden departure Lehi was doing not only the sensible but also the ordinary thing. From the earliest times to the present day the correct thing to do when going got rough in the cities and states of the Near East was simply to take off and seek the security of the desert. Sinuhe, a high official at the court of Amenemhet I, fearing a palace revolution on the death of the king, rushed impulsively out into the night and the desert, where he would have perished of thirst had he not been picked up by some friendly Arabs who traded with Egypt. His story, thirteen hundred years older than Lehi's, illustrates the ease with which men passed between the desert and the town, and shows us how natural was the impulse to take to the sands in a crisis. Had not Moses and the prophets, and even Father Abraham himself, sought safety from their enemies by flight into the desert? Had not the whole nation of Israel done the same in the beginning? But what makes Lehi's story ring true with perfect pitch is the recent discovery that those very leaders of the Jews at Jerusalem whose wickedness had obliged Lehi to leave the land while there was yet time, when *they* found the city on the verge of destruction and themselves faced with the consequences of their own folly, hid "in the wilds during the siege," and when all was lost fled to Egypt.[18] "Hiding in the wilds" was exactly what Lehi—and later anyone else who could escape—was doing.

The desert to which Sinuhe fled was the country south of Palestine, the classic hide-out land both of the Egyptians and the Jews, where "men of all conditions and nations . . . look to the Arab camp as a safe retreat and refuge."[19] While the Syrian desert is "the unenvied resort of defeated tribes,"[20] the proper home of the outcast, escapist, and discredited revolutionary was ever Edom and the south country, "the land of disoriented groups and of individual fugitives, where organized semi-nomad Arab tribes alternate with the flotsam and jetsam of sedentary society, with runaway slaves, bandits, and their descendants."[21] Even the great merchants who brought forth the civilized Nabataean state placed their confidence, says Diodorus, in their ability to disappear quickly and easily into the desert—like any common Bedouin.[22] So let us not suppose that Lehi was the first big merchant to take to the back-country with his worried family. Even in the present century Arab farmers and towndwellers, to flee the exactions of a tyrannical Turkish government, fled to the desert and adopted the life of wandering Bedouins,[23] and in recent years thousands of *fellaḥin*, raised to a life of farming, might have been seen eking out a miserable existence on the sands of the Syrian desert as the result of hasty and ill-advised flight from their homes.[24]

We have mentioned that "the Jews who were at Jerusalem" who finally got away when the city fell ended up in Egypt. Many of them settled far up the Nile, at Elephantine or Yeb.[25] This famous colony has been described as "but an eccentric deviation from the broad pathway of Hebrew history: it led nowhere, and had no influence on the development even of Egyptian Judaism."[26] In such words we might describe Lehi's own migration—an eccentric deviation breaking off completely from the main current of Jewish history, but, like the Elephantine settlement, preserving its own peculiar version of transplanted Judaism intact. The Elephantine story, by demonstrating the possibility of a development that scholars at first found inconceivable and were long reluctant to believe, confirms the possibility of just such an expedition as Lehi's. The Jews throughout history display, as Montgomery observes, a constant tendency to "revert to type" and go back to the desert, and Lehi was by no means the first or last Jew to do so.[27] Furthermore, it is not uncommon for rich town and country people and even poor farmers to take to the desert for a spell and enjoy from time to time a taste of nomad life, so that Lehi's behavior in turning Bedouin was thoroughly conventional and respectable. Of course, the people who take that sort of vacation are those who already have a good deal of experience in the desert way and have acquired a liking for it.[28]

As to the direction taken by Lehi's party the Book of Mormon is clear and specific. He took what we *now* know to have been the only possible way out, what with immediate danger threatening from the north, and the eastern and western lands held by opposing powers on the verge of war. Only the south desert, the one land where Israel's traders and merchants had felt at home through the centuries, remained open—even after Jerusalem fell this was so. And the one route into that desert was the great trade-road down the burning trough of the Arabah.[29] For a long time the party traveled south-southeast and then struck out almost due east over a particularly terrible desert and reached the sea at a point to be considered later. Nephi is careful to keep us informed of the main bearing of every stage of the journey, and never once does he mention a westerly or a northerly trend. The party traveled for eight years in but two main directions, without retracing their steps or doubling back, and many of their marches were long forced marches.

All this entirely excludes the Sinaitic Peninsula as the scene of their wanderings, and fits perfectly with a journey through the Arabian Peninsula. The slowest possible march "in a south-southeasterly direction" in Sinai would reach the sea and have to turn north within ten days; yet Lehi's people traveled "for many days," nay, months, in a south-southeasterly direction, keeping near the coast of the Red Sea all the while. Ten days take a foot traveler the entire length of that coast of Sinai which runs in a south-southeasterly direction—and what of the rest of the eight years?

What entirely excludes Sinai as the field of Lehi's journeyings is the total lack at all times of timber to build ships with, to say nothing of a lush and beautiful Land Bountiful. "It is quite possible," writes a present-day authority, "that, Solomon had to transport his ships, or the material for them, from the Mediterranean, for where on the shores of the Red Sea could timber be found for ship-building?"[30]

The desert into which Lehi first retreated and in which he made his first long camp has been known since Old Testament times as the *wilderness* par excellence. Thanks to the Bible, it is this very section of the earth's surface to which the word *wilderness* most closely applies, so that Nephi is using the word in its fullest correctness.[31] From 1 Nephi 8:4 and 7, we learn that by *wilderness* he means waste, i.e., desert, and not jungle. Today we call the region a desert, yet Woolley and Lawrence preferred the older word to designate this particular desert—the Wilderness of Zin. "The term 'wilderness' does not necessarily mean an uninhabitable waste," wrote Kenyon (thus associating the two words as Nephi does), "rather it means a country such as nomads may inhabit, with oases and wadies where crops may be reared."[32] So Lehi's wilderness had "more fertile parts" in which survival was possible (1 Nephi 16:16). The particular waste in which Lehi made his first camp is among the most uninviting deserts on earth; though some observers think the area enjoyed a little more rainfall in antiquity than it does today, all are agreed that the change of climate has not been considerable since prehistoric times—it was at best almost as bad then as it is now.[33] Even if Lehi took the main southern route down the Arabah, as he very probably did, since it was the direct road to the Red Sea, and a caravan way known to all the merchants, he would be moving through a desert so repelling that even the hardened Bedouins avoid it like the plague. Nor need we look there for any monuments of his passing: "The Egyptians, the Patriarchs, the Jews, the Romans, the Crusaders and the Arabs all passed over these tracks, and they have given us place-names and no more. Probably in their eyes the country was too detestable to merit further reference."[34] Detestable certainly describes the place in the eyes of Lehi's people, who "murmured" bitterly at being led into such a hell.

Tent People

The editors of the Book of Mormon have given a whole verse to Nephi's laconic statement, "And my father dwelt in a tent" (1 Nephi 2:15), and rightly so, since Nephi himself finds the fact very significant and refers constantly to his father's tent as the center of his universe.[35] To an Arab, "My father dwelt in a tent" says everything. "The present inhabitants of Palestine," writes Canaan, "like their forefathers, are of two classes: dwellers in villages and cities, and the Bedouin. As the life and habits of the one class differ from the those of the other, so do their houses differ. Houses in villages are built of durable material; . . . on the other hand, Bedouin dwellings, tents, are more fitted for nomadic life."[36] An ancient Arab poet boasts that his people are "the proud, the chivalrous people of the horse and camel, the dwellers-in-tents, and no miserable ox-drivers."[37] A Persian king but fifty years after the fall of Jerusalem boasts that all the civilized kings "as well as the Bedouin tent-dwellers brought their costly gifts and kissed my feet,"[38] thus making the same distinction as the later poet. One of the commonest oaths of the Arabs, Burckhardt reports, is "by the life of this tent and its owners," taken with one hand resting on the middle tent pole.[39] If a man's estate is to be declared void after his death, "the tent posts are torn up immediately after the man has expired, and the tent is demolished," while on the other hand "the erection of a new tent in the desert is an important event celebrated with feast and sacrifice."[40] And the cult of the tent was as important to the Hebrews as well. Indeed, the

Hebrew word for tent (*ohel*) and the Arabic word for family (*ahl*), were originally one and the same word.[41] "The Bedouin has a strong affection for his tent," says Canaan. "He will not exchange it with any stone house."[42] So Jacob was "a plain man, dwelling in tents" (Genesis 25:27), though, let us add, by no means in squalor: "Casual travelers in the Orient, who have seen only the filthy, wretched tents of the tribeless gypsy Bedouins . . . would be surprised, perhaps, at the spaciousness and simple luxury in the tent of a great desert *sheik*."[43]

So with the announcement that his "father dwelt in a tent," Nephi serves notice that he had assumed the desert way of life, as perforce he must for his journey. Any easterner would appreciate the significance and importance of the statement, which to us seems almost trivial. If Nephi seems to think of his father's tent as the hub of everything, he is simply expressing the view of any normal Bedouin, to whom the tent of the *sheikh* is the sheet anchor of existence.[44] "A white flag," we are told, "is sometimes hoisted above his tent to guide strangers and visitors. All visitors are led directly to the tent of the [*sheikh*]."[45] When Nephi urged the frightened Zoram to join the party in the desert, he said: "If thou wilt go down into the wilderness to my father thou shalt have place with us" (1 Nephi 4:34). The correctness of the proposal is attested not only by the proper role of Lehi in receiving members and guests into the tribe but also in the highly characteristic expression, "thou shalt *have place* with us." For since time immemorial the proper word of welcome to the stranger who enters one's tent has been *ahlan wa sahlan wa marḥaban*, literally (perhaps), "a family, a smooth place, and a wide place!"[46] Equivalent expressions are found in the Old Testament, as when Abraham invites his heavenly visitor to sit beneath his tree (Genesis 18:4), and here too such details are authentic touches of Bedouin life. But none of the Bible expressions are as typically "Arabic" as Nephi's invitation.

The Order of March

The Book of Mormon tells us a good deal about how Lehi and his people moved through the desert, and the report can now be checked against the firsthand accounts of life with the Arabs which the last one hundred years, and especially the last forty, have brought forth. All these would agree with Nephi that the keynote of life in Arabia is hardship: "Life is hard, a ceaseless struggle for existence against nature and man."[47] "It is no exaggeration," writes a present-day authority, "to say that the Bedouin is in an almost permanent state of starvation."[48] "Many times between their waterings," Doughty reports, "there is not a single pint of water left in the greatest *sheikh's* tent."[49] Palgrave's recollection is particularly impressive: "Then an insufficient halt for rest or sleep, at most of two or three hours, soon interrupted by the oft-repeated admonition, 'if we linger here we all die of thirst,' sounding in our ears, and then to remount our jaded beasts and push them on through the dark night amid the constant probability of attack and plunder from roving marauders . . . and about an hour before sunset we would stagger off our camels as best we might, to prepare an evening feast of precisely the same description as that of the forenoon, or more often, lest the smoke of our fire should give notice of some distant rover, to content ourselves with dry dates and half an hour's rest on the sand."[50] This, it is true, is marching under pressure, but the conditions—no fire, raw meat, "wad[ing] through much affliction" (Helaman 3:34), are exactly duplicated in the Book of Mormon.

Lehi's party is described as moving through the desert for a few days (three or four, one would estimate) and then camping "for the space of a time" (1 Nephi 16:17). This is exactly the way the Arabs move. Caravan speeds run between two and one-quarter and three and nine-tenths miles an hour, thirty miles being, according to

Cheesman, "a good average" for the day, and sixty miles being the absolute maximum.[51] "The usual estimate for a good day's march is reckoned by Arab writers at between twenty-eight and thirty miles: in special or favoured circumstances it might be near forty."[52] On the other hand, a day's slow journey for an "ass-nomad," moving much slower than camel-riders, is twenty miles.[53]

The number of days spent camping at any one place varies (as in the Book of Mormon) with circumstances. "From ten to twelve days is the average time a Bedouin encampment of ordinary size will remain on the same ground," according to Jennings-Bramley, who, however, observes, "I have known them stay in one spot for as long as five or six months."[54] The usual thing is to camp as long as possible in one place until "it is soiled by the beasts, and the multiplication of fleas becomes intolerable, and the surroundings afford no more pastureage, [then] the tents are pulled down and the men decamp."[55] "On the Syrian and Arabian plains," according to Burckhardt, "the Bedouins encamp in summer . . . near wells, where they remain often for a whole month."[56] Lehi's time schedule thus seems to be a fairly normal one, and the eight years he took to cross Arabia argue neither very fast nor very slow progress—the Banī Hilāl took twenty-seven years to go a not much greater distance. After reaching the seashore Lehi's people simply camped there "for the space of many days" (1 Nephi 17:7) until a revelation again put them in motion.

The Problem of Baggage

Were Lehi's party ass-nomads or camel-nomads? The latter, there can be no doubt. The times required it, and the Book of Mormon all but insists on it. But before turning to the evidence it would be well to correct the theory, sometimes propounded, that the party went on foot.

When the Lord appoints a man to a task, he gives him

the means of carrying it out, as Nephi himself observes, and to Lehi he had given ample means indeed. The sight of a rich merchant and his family setting out for the desert in a caravan even of some magnificence would never have excited the slightest comment from Lehi's neighbors. Burckhardt describes as a matter of course passing by the caravan of a rich merchant from Maskat in the deep desert: "He had ten camels to carry his women, his infant children, his servants, and his baggage."[57] Lehi would have been such a one. But for an elderly and aristocratic Hebrew to load himself, his wife, and his children with tents, utensils, weapons, food, and other supplies would have been as unthinkable then as now. "Without the camel," writes a modern authority, "it would be impossible for the nomads to carry their tents and furniture over the vast sandy spaces, where asses can pass only with difficulty and carry only a very small load."[58] The decisive clue is the fact that Lehi's party took grain with them and "all manner of seeds of every kind" (1 Nephi 8:1). The Arabs, as we shall see below, do this when they migrate in earnest, packing the seed in big, black 150 to 180-pound sacks, two to a camel. At the very least there has to be enough grain either to make a worth-while crop somewhere or to supply substantial food on the way—and who could carry such a load on his back? To pass through the heart of Arabia on the best camel in the world requires almost superhuman endurance—no need to make the thing ridiculous by carrying children, tents, books, food, furniture, weapons, and grain on one's back!

Raswan tells us that "camel breeders do not fear the waterless stretches of the desert as the sheep- and goat-raising Arabs do, and for that reason camel owners alone remain independent and free."[59] On the other hand, they are often in danger of starving, and when we read that Lehi's people were continually in such danger and supported themselves by hunting alone, so that a broken bow could mean death by starvation, we may be sure that they were camel-nomads without flocks, as indeed their hasty flight from Palestine requires. Among the listing of the stuff they took with them flocks are never mentioned, as of course they would be had they had such; the "flocks . . . of every kind" (Ether 1:41) of the Jaredites are always given first place in the description of their migration, and we may confidently assume that the silence of Nephi on this head indicates that his people did not travel as herdsmen.

But neither does Nephi mention camels. Why not? For the very reason that they receive no notice in many an Arabic poem which describes travel in the desert, simply because they are taken for granted. In the East the common words for travel *are* camel-words; thus *raḥal* and *safar*, the two basic words, both mean "to set out on a journey" and *also* "to saddle a camel," the presence of camels being inferred when no special mention of them is made. When I say I drove from Heber to Salt Lake, no one would think to ask "in a car?" though for all my hearers know I may have driven a chariot or a tricycle. In the same way when the Arab reports that he has journeyed in the desert he never adds "on a camel," for in his language "to travel" *means* to go by camel. Had Lehi's party gone afoot that would indeed have been a nine-days' wonder and something would have referred to it on every page—for such a thing was never seen nor heard of before or since his day. But when the camel is the only means of travel, it is as unnecessary to mention camels in describing a journey as it would be to specify that one sails the seas "in a ship." There is one episode, however, in which camels play a definite role in the Book of Mormon.

From their base camp in the valley of Lemuel, Lehi's sons made a flying trip back to Jerusalem. It was the young men alone who made the journey which turned out, as they expected (1 Nephi 3:5), to be a dangerous one. Now it is the established procedure among the Arabs for a few young men in a tribe to seek gain and glory by making quick raids on neighboring towns and tribes. On such expeditions they never take tents, for their transportation is limited, and speed is of the essence.[60] Nephi wants us to know that this trip to Jerusalem was no such raid, for they were going on legitimate business and took their *tents* with them (1 Nephi 3:9); they went boldly and openly in to Laban and stated their business. Only when he treated them as robbers were they forced to act as such, slinking about like true Bedouins outside the gates and entering the city only by night.

A typically Oriental episode of the story is the wild pursuit out of the city and into the desert—how many a filibuster by Bedouin braves in the town has ended that way! "You chase me and I chase you," is the essence of desert tactics according to Philby.[61] Of this exciting chase Nephi reports (1 Nephi 3:27), "we fled into the wilderness, and the servants of Laban did not *overtake* us, and we hid ourselves in the cavity of a rock." Note that they were pursued right *into* the wilderness, for upon reaching the desert they were not safe but had to hide under a rock. The young men might have fled a short distance through the town on foot, but fleeing "into the wilderness" was another matter; there they would have been quickly run down by mounted riders, unless they first escaped notice, but Nephi tells us that they hid only after they had outrun their pursuers, who failed to *overtake* them. The powerful and affluent military governor certainly had a fleet of steeds that could run down a camel, but in the sudden getaway of the brothers there would be no time to saddle them—an ancient Arab poet and king, Imrul-Qais, speaks of a phenomenal horse that "passed the night with saddle and bridle on him . . . without being sent to the stable."[62] But other horses, including Laban's, would need more attention and lose more time getting under way, and we can confidently assume that both pursuers and pursued rode the usual camels. As for the chance that Nephi and his brethren were mounted on horses, it is a remote one, for the horse cannot carry burdens in the desert, and even horse-raising Arabs seldom ride their animals on long journeys, but whenever possible lead them tethered to their camels, without riders or loads. Raswan gives many illustrations of this.

The use of camels is implied at every turn of the story of the mission to Laban: the otherwise insane carrying of tents, the trip down-country to bring back "exceedingly great" property (1 Nephi 3:25) to Laban's palace (hardly on their shoulders!), the flight into the open country and pursuit in the desert, and finally the long and necessarily hasty return trip (for they were marked men and possibly the direction of their take-off had been noted) to the secret base camp. Just as the Saints who had the means of avoiding it never crossed the plains on foot, so we would think Lehi's sons foolish indeed if they did not avail themselves of the common means of transportation that everyone was using—for camels were as common then as automobiles are today.

The Problem of Food

Not many years ago Professor Frankfort wrote of the south desert, "The secret of moving through its desolation has at all times been kept by the Bedawin."[63] Intrepid explorers of our own day have learned the secret, however, and Lehi knew of it too. Like a sudden flash of illumination comes the statement that Lehi by divine instruction "led us in the more fertile parts of the wilderness" (1 Nephi 16:16). Woolley and Lawrence describe such "more fertile parts" as "stretching over the flat floor of the plain in long lines like hedges." They are the depressions of dried-up watercourses, sometimes hundreds of miles long.[64] They furnish, according to Bertram Thomas, "the arteries of life in the steppe, the path of Badawin movement, the habitat of animals, by reason of the vegetation—scant though it is—which flourishes in their beds alone."[65] In Arabia it is this practice of following "the more fertile parts of the wilderness" (1 Nephi 16:16) that alone makes it possible for both men and animals to survive. Cheesman designates as "touring" the practice followed by men and beasts of moving from place to place in the desert as spots of fertility shift with the seasons.[66]

The Arab forager is everlastingly prowling, scouting, tracking, and spying; in fact, some believe that the original root of the names *Arab* and *Hebrew* is a combination of sounds meaning "to lie in ambush." "Every Bedawin is a sportsman both from taste and necessity," writes one observer, who explains how in large families some of the young men are detailed to spend all their time hunting.[67] Nephi and his brethren took over the business of full-time hunters and in that office betray the desert tradition of the family, for Nephi had brought a fine steel bow from home with him. Though we shall consider steel again in dealing with the sword of Laban, it should be noted here that a steel bow was not necessarily a solid piece of metal, any more than the Canaanites' "chariots of iron" (Joshua 17:16-18; Judges 1:19; 4:3) were solid iron, or than various implements mentioned in the Old Testament as being "of iron," e.g., carpenter's tools, pens, threshing instruments, were iron and only iron. It was in all probability a steel-ribbed bow, since it broke at about the same time that the wooden bows of his brothers "lost their springs" (1 Nephi 16:21). Only composite bows were used in Palestine, that is, bows of more than one piece, and a steel-backed bow would be called a steel bow just as an iron-trimmed chariot was called a "chariot of iron." Incidentally the founder of the Turkish Seljuk Dynasty of Iran was called Yaqaq, which means in Turkish, says our Arab informant, "a bow made out of iron."[68] The fact that "Iron Arrow" was a fairly common name among those people, and refers actually to an iron-headed arrow is a strong indication that the name Steelbow may also refer to a real weapon.

Hunting in the mountains of Arabia to this day is carried out on foot and without hawks or dogs; in classical times the hunter in this area was equipped with a bow and a sling—exactly like Nephi.[69] Nephi's discovery that the best hunting was only at "the top of the mountain" (1 Nephi 16:30) agrees with later experience, for the oryx is "a shy animal that travels far and fast over steppe and desert in search of food but retires ever to the almost inaccessible sand-mountains for safety."[70] In western Arabia the mountains are not sand but rock, and Burckhardt reports that "in these mountains between Medina and the sea, all the way northward (this is bound to include Lehi's area), mountain goats are met, and the leopards are not uncommon."[71] Julius Euting has left us vivid descriptions of the danger, excitement, and exhaustion that go with the hunting of the big game that abounds in these mountains, which are, by the way, very steep and rugged.[72]

Things looked black when Nephi broke his fine steel bow, for the wooden bows of his brothers had "lost their springs" (1 Nephi 16:21; note the peculiarly Semitic use of the plural for a noun of quality), and though skilled in the art of hunting, they knew little enough about bow-making, which is a skill reserved to specialists even among primitives. Incidentally, archery experts say that a good bow will keep its spring for about one hundred thousand shots; from which one might calculate that the party at the time of the crisis had been traveling anything from one to three years. It was of course out of the question to make the familiar composite bow, and was something of a marvel when Nephi "did make out of wood a bow" (1 Nephi 16:23), for the hunter, the most conservative of men, would never dream of changing from a composite to a simple bow. Though it sounds simple enough when we read about it, it was almost as great a feat for Nephi to make a bow as it was for him to build a ship, and he is justly proud of his achievement.

According to the ancient Arab writers, the only bow-wood obtainable in all Arabia was the *nab^c^* wood that grew only "amid the inaccessible and overhanging crags" of Mount Jasum and Mount Azd, which are situated in the very region where, if we follow the Book of Mormon, the broken bow incident occurred.[73] How many factors must be correctly conceived and correlated to make the apparently simple story of Nephi's bow ring true! The high mountain near the Red Sea at a considerable journey down the coast, the game on the peaks, hunting with bow and sling, the finding of bow-wood viewed as something of a miracle by the party—what are the chances of reproducing such a situation by mere guess work?

As for the grain which Lehi carried, it was not to be eaten on the journey, for it was "seed of every kind" (1 Nephi 16:11), a needless concern for variety unless it was meant to be sown. While "ordinary travellers scarcely ever carry grain for food" in the desert,[74] it is a common thing for migrating Bedouins to carry seed with them in the thought—sometimes very vague indeed—that possibly if the year is a good one, they might find a chance to sow a hasty crop. In Sinai, "the Bedouin yearly sow the beds of the wadies, but they do this with little hope of reaping a harvest more than once in every three or four years."[75] Lehi, looking for a promised land, would under no circumstances have set out without such provision for securing crops in his new home. In traveling, "the wheat is put in the black home-made goat's-hair sacks, *farde*(*t*). . . . The farde, the Heb. *sak* (Gen. 42:25) holds about 150 to 180 pounds of wheat. Two are put on a camel."[76] The mention of the custom in Genesis shows that it was ancient usage even in the time of Lehi.

4

Desert Ways and Places

Lehi's Altar

As his first act once his tent had been pitched for his first important camp, Lehi "built an altar of stones, and made an offering unto the Lord, and gave thanks to the Lord" (1 Nephi 2:7). It is for all the world as if he had been reading Robertson Smith: "The ordinary artificial mark of a Semitic sanctuary (Hebrew as well as Arabic, that is) [is] the sacrificial pillar, cairn, or rude altar . . . upon which sacrifices are presented to the god. . . . In Arabia . . . we find no proper altar but in its place a rude pillar or heap of stones beside which the victim is slain."[1] It was at this same "altar of stones" that Lehi and his family "did offer sacrifice and burnt offerings . . . and they gave thanks unto the God of Israel" (1 Nephi 5:9) upon the safe return of his sons from their dangerous expedition to Jerusalem. When Raswan reports, "A baby camel was brought up to Misha'il's tent as a sacrificial offer in honor of the safe return of Fuaz,"[2] we cannot help thinking of some such scene before the tent of Lehi on the safe return of his sons. This is what the Arabs call a *dhabīḥat-al-kasb*, a sacrifice to celebrate the successful return of warriors, hunters, and raiders to the camp. "This sacrifice," writes Jaussen, "is always in honor of an ancestor,"[3] and Nephi twice mentions the tribal ancestor Israel in his brief account. In the best desert manner Lehi immediately after the thanksgiving rites fell to examining the "spoils" (1 Nephi 5:10).

To this day the Bedouin makes sacrifice on every important occasion, not for magical and superstitious reasons, but because he "lives under the constant impression of a higher force that surrounds him."[4] St. Nilus, in the oldest known eyewitness account of life among the Arabs of the Tih, says, "they sacrifice on altars of crude stones piled together."[5] That Lehi's was such an altar would follow not only from the ancient law demanding uncut stones (Exodus 20:25), but also from the Book of Mormon expression "an altar of stones," which is not the same thing as "a stone altar." Such little heaps of stones, surviving from all ages, are still to be seen throughout the south desert.

Contacts in the Desert

The Book of Mormon makes no mention of Lehi's people meeting any other party in their eight years of wandering. Casual meetings with stray families of Bedouins then as now would merit no special attention, but how were they able to avoid any important contacts for eight years and some 2500 miles of wandering?

One illuminating "aside" by Nephi explains everything. It was only after they reached the seashore, he says, that his people were able to make fires without danger, "for the Lord had not hitherto suffered that we should make *much* fire, as we journeyed in the wilderness; for he said: I will make thy food become sweet, that ye cook it not; and I will also be your light in the wilderness" (1 Nephi 17:12-13). That tells all. "I remember well," writes Bertram Thomas, "taking part in a discussion upon the unhealthiness of campfires by night; we discontinued them forthwith in spite of the bitter cold."[6] Major Cheesman's guide would not even let him light a tiny lamp in order to jot down star readings, and they never dared build a fire on the open plain where it "would attract the attention of a prowling raiding party over long distances and invite a night attack."[7] Once in a while in a favorably sheltered depression "we dared to build a fire that could not be seen from a higher spot," writes Raswan.[8] That is, fires are not absolutely out of the question, but rare and risky—not *much* fire, was Lehi's rule. And fires in the daytime are almost as risky as at night: Palgrave tells how his party were forced, "lest the smoke of our fire should give notice to some distant rover, to content ourselves with dry dates," instead of cooked food.[9]

So of course no fire means raw food. And what is one to do if one's diet is meat? "Throughout the Desert," writes Burckhardt, "when a sheep or goat is killed, the persons present often eat the liver and kidney raw, adding to it a little salt. Some Arabs of Yemen are said to eat raw not only those parts, but likewise whole slices of flesh; thus resembling the Abyssinians and the Druses of Libanon [sic], who frequently indulge in raw meat, the latter to my own certain knowledge."[10] Nilus, writing fourteen centuries earlier, tells how the Bedouin of the Tih live on the flesh of wild animals, failing which "they slaughter a camel, one of their beasts of burden, and nourish themselves like animals from the raw meat," or else scorch the flesh quickly in a small fire to soften it sufficiently not to have to gnaw it "like dogs."[11] Only too well does this state of things match the grim economy of Lehi: "They did suffer much for the want of food" (1 Nephi 16:19); "we did live upon raw meat in the wilderness" (1 Nephi 17:2).

All this bears out the conviction, supported both by modern experience and the evidence of archaeology, that Lehi was moving through a dangerous world. In ancient times Jewish merchants traveling through the desert fell so often into the hands of Bedouin raiders that by the beginning of the Christian era their word for "captor" normally meant simply "Arab"![12] Arab inscriptions from Lehi's time show that "in the peninsula . . . there was constant unrest," even as in modern times.[13] Ordinary times in the desert are bad times when, in the words of one of the oldest Arab poets, "the honored man did not dare stay in the open country, and flight did not save the coward."[14] "A lonely life it is," writes Philby, ". . . a life of constant fear; . . . hunger is the rule of the desert."[15] Hunger, danger, loneliness, fear—Lehi's people knew them all.

Just what was the danger? "The Arab tribes are in a state of almost perpetual war against each other. . . . To surprise the enemy by a sudden attack, and to plunder a camp, are chief objects of both parties."[16] "Raiding to them is the spice of life. . . . Might is right, and man ever walks in fear for his life and possessions."[17] Lehi could ill afford to get embroiled in these perennial desert feuds, and yet he was everywhere a trespasser—the only way for him to stay out of trouble was to observe a rule which Thomas lays down for all travelers in the desert, even today: "An approaching party may be friend, but is always assumed to be foe."[18] In the words of the ancient poet Zuhair, "He who travels should consider his friend an enemy."[19] Nilus describes Bedouins on the march in the fifth century as possessed by the same jittery nervousness and unbearable tension that make the accounts of Cheesman, Philby, Thomas, Palgrave, Burckhardt, and the others such exciting reading: At the merest sign of an armed man, he says, his Bedu fled in alarm "as if seized by panic fear," and kept on fleeing, "for fear makes them exaggerate danger and causes them to imagine things far beyond reality, magnifying their dread in every instance."[20] Just so their modern descendants "live always under the impression that an invasion is on the way, and every suspicious shadow or movement on the horizon calls their attention," according to the astute Baldensperger. This almost hysterical state of apprehension is actually a prime condition of survival in the desert: "A Bedawy never tells his name," says the writer just quoted, "nor his tribe, nor his business, nor the whereabouts of his people, even if he is in a friendly district. . . . They are and must be very cautious; . . . a word out of season may bring death and destruction."[21] When the Banī Hilāl migrate, it is "under the darkness of the night, under the obscuring veil of the rain," bypassing settled places in darkness and in silence. What can better describe such a state of things than the Book of Mormon expression, "a lonesome and a solemn people" (Jacob 7:26)? Doughty said he had never met a "merry" man among the Arabs—and there is no humor in the Book of Mormon. This mood is hardly accidental: if the Hebrew gets his brooding qualities from his desert ancestors, why not the Lamanite?

Sir Richard Burton, one of the few individuals who has ever known both the American Indian and Bedouin Arab at first hand, was greatly impressed by their exact resemblance to each other, a resemblance so striking that he must warn his reader against attributing it to a common origin, explaining the perfect paralleling of temperament and behavior as due to "the almost absolute independence" of their way of life.[22] Yet many equally independent tribesmen in other parts of the world in no way resemble these two. One of the writer's best friends is a venerable but enterprising Lebanese, who has spent many years both among the Bedouins of the desert and the Indians of New Mexico as a peddler and trader; he avers that there is absolutely no difference between the two races so far as manners and customs are concerned. Arabs now living in Utah who have had some contact with Indians in the West, affirm the same thing with considerable emphasis. It is a nice problem for the sociologist, and the writer only mentions it because it has been brought to his attention innumerable times. There may be something to it.

Lehi's party, as we have noted, were like the Banī Hilāl trespassers wherever they walked. Every inch of the desert is claimed by some tribe or other that will demand the life of a trespasser.[23] "Marked boundaries do not exist, and it is natural that questions of ownership should be settled by fighting, which becomes an annual affair, while the looting of camels grows into a habit," according to Cheesman.[24] Hence the need for extreme caution and strict avoidance on Lehi's part: "In most cases," says Jennings-Bramley, "Arabs do not think it prudent to allow the raiders near enough to decide whether they are friendly or not," and he describes a typical meeting in the desert: "Both we and they were doing our best not to be seen."[25] Of course this sort of thing leads to comic situations, ignoble panic, and ridiculous anticlimaxes, but in a game of life and death one simply can't take chances, and Lehi was playing for the highest stakes. And so we are left with the picture of a wandering band sticking glumly to themselves for years on end, which, impossible as it seems to us, is a normal thing in the desert wastes, where the touchy, dangerous, unsocial Bedouin takes his stand as one of the most difficult, challenging, and fascinating creatures on earth.[26]

Family Affairs

But how do the members of such closed corporation hit it off among themselves? It is the domestic history that presents the real challenge to whoever would write a history of Bedouin life. To handle it convincingly would tax the knowledge of the best psychologist, and woe to him if he does not know the peculiar ways of the eastern desert, which surprise and trap the unwary westerner at every turn.

The ancient Hebrew family was a peculiar organization, self-sufficient and impatient of any authority beyond its own: "These are obviously the very conditions," writes Nowack, "which we can still observe today among the Beduins."[27] Thus, whether we turn to Hebrew or to Arabic sources for our information, the Book of Mormon must conform. Lehi feels no pangs of conscience at deserting Jerusalem, and when his sons think of home, it is specifically the land of their inheritance, their own family estate, for which they yearn. Not even Nephi evinces any loyalty to "the Jews who were at Jerusalem" (1 Nephi 2:13), split up as they were into squabbling interest-groups. Indeed,

Nephi speaks of his history as "an account . . . of my proceedings, and my reign and ministry" (1 Nephi 10:1), as if the wandering family recognized no government but that of its own head. This reminds one of the terms in which one of the earliest Bedouin poets, Ibn Kulthum, speaks of "many a chief of a tribe, whom they had crowned with the crown of authority and who protects those who seek refuge with him," as if every *sheikh* were truly a king.[28]

While Lehi lived, he was the *sheikh*, of course, and the relationship between him and his family as described by Nephi is accurate in the smallest detail. With the usual deft sureness and precision, the book shows Lehi leading—not ruling—his people by his persuasive eloquence and spiritual ascendency alone, while his murmuring sons follow along exactly in the manner of Philby's Bedouins—"an undercurrent of tension in our ranks all day," and great difficulty to "appease their evil, envious souls."[29] "We left Suwaykah," says Burton, "all of us in the crossest of humours. . . . So 'out of temper' were my companions, that at sunset, of the whole party, Omar Effendi was the only one who would eat supper. The rest sat upon the ground, pouting [and] grumbling. . . . Such a game at naughty children, I have seldom seen played even by Oriental men."[30]

The character and behavior of Laman and Lemuel conform to the normal pattern. How true to the Bedouin way are their long, bitter, brooding and dangerous outbreaks! How perfectly they resemble the Arabs of Lawrence, Doughty, Burton, and the rest in their sudden and complete changes of heart after their father has lectured them, fiery anger yielding for the moment to a great impulse to humility and an overwhelming repentance, only to be followed by renewed resentment and more unhappy wrangling! They cannot keep their discontent to themselves, but are everlastingly "murmuring": "The fact that all that happens in an encampment is known, that all may be said to be nearly related to each other, renders intrigue almost impossible."[31] "We were all one family and friendly eyes," Doughty recollects, but then describes the other side of the picture: "Arab children are ruled by entreaties. . . . I have known an ill-natured child lay a stick to the back of his good cherishing mother, . . . and the Arabs say, 'many is the ill-natured lad among us that, and he be strong enough, will beat his own father!'"[32] The fact that Laman and Lemuel were grown-up children did not help things. "The daily quarrels between parents and children in the Desert constitute the worst feature of the Bedouin character," says Burckhardt, and thus describes the usual source of the trouble: "The son, arrived at manhood, is too proud to ask his father for any cattle. . . . The father is hurt at finding that his son behaves with haughtiness towards him; and thus a breach is often made." The son, especially the eldest one, does not feel that he is getting what is coming to him and behaves like the spoiled child he is. The father's attitude is described by Doughty, telling how a great *sheikh* dealt with his son: "The boy, oftentimes disobedient, he upbraided, calling him his life's torment, Sheytan, only never menacing him, for that were far from a Beduin father's mind."[33] It is common, says Burckhardt, for mothers and sons to stick together in their frequent squabbles with the old man, in which the son "is often expelled from the paternal tent for vindicating his mother's cause."[34] Just so Sariah takes the part of her sons in chiding her own husband, making the same complaints against him that they did (1 Nephi 5:2-3), and she rates him roundly when she thinks he has been the cause of their undoing.

Is it any wonder that Laman and Lemuel worked off their pent-up frustration by beating their younger brother with a stick when they were once hiding in a cave? Every free man in the East carries a stick, the immemorial badge of independence and of authority; and every man asserts his authority over his inferiors by his stick, which "shows that the holder is a man of position, superior to the workman or day-labourers. The government officials, superior officers, tax-gatherers, and schoolmasters use this short rod to threaten—or if necessary to beat—their inferiors, whoever they may be." The usage is very ancient. "A blow for a slave," is the ancient maxim in Ahikar, and the proper designation of an underling is *ᶜabd-al-ᶜaṣa*, "stick-servant." This is exactly the sense in which Laman and Lemuel intended their little lesson to Nephi, for when the angel turned the tables he said to them, "Why do ye smite your younger brother with a rod? Know ye not that the Lord hath chosen *him* to be a ruler over *you*?" (1 Nephi 3:29). All that saved Nephi's life on one occasion was the pleading of a daughter of Ishmael and her mother—another authentic touch, since the proud Semite may yield only to the entreaties of a woman without losing face. Burton recalls how even robbers will spare a victim who appeals to them in the name of his wife, the daughter of his uncle.[35] Through it all, Laman, as the eldest son, is the nastiest actor: "When only one boy is in the family he is the tyrant, and his will dominates over all."[36] So we see Laman still thinking to dominate over all and driven mad that a younger brother should show superior talents. The rivalry between the sons of a *sheikh* "often leads to bloody tragedies in the *sheikh's* household,"[37] and Nephi had some narrow escapes.

The nature of Lehi's authority is clearly set forth in the Book of Mormon. Of the Arab *sheikh* we have noted Burkhardt's remark: "His commands would be treated with contempt; but deference is paid to his advice. . . . The real government of the Bedouins may be said to consist in the separate strength of their different families. . . . The Arab can only be persuaded by his own relations." The *sheikh*'s "orders are never obeyed, but his example is generally followed." This is especially so on the march; while the tribe is in motion the *sheikh* "assumes all responsibility and the whole power of government."[38] Yet in leading he gives no orders: when his tent is struck "it is the *raḥlah,*" and all the others without a word strike theirs; and "when the place of encampment is reached the *sheikh* puts his spear in the ground, and at once the tents are pitched."[39]

In the *sheikh*'s tent the councils of the tribe are held and all decisions concerning the journey are made (1 Nephi 9:1; 15:1-2), but "no *sheikh* or council of Arabs can condemn a man to death, or even inflict a punishment; it can only [when appealed to] impose a fine; it cannot even enforce the payment of this fine."[40] Why, then, if there was no power to compel them, did not Laman and Lemuel simply desert the camp and go off on their own, as discontented Arabs sometimes do?[41] As a matter of fact, they tried to do just that (1 Nephi 7:7), and in the end were prevented by the two things which, according to Philby, keep any wandering Bedouin party together—fear and greed. For they were greedy: they hoped for a promised land and when they reached the sea without finding it, their bitter complaint was, "Behold, these many years we have suffered in the wilderness, which time we might have enjoyed our possessions" (1 Nephi 17:21). And their position was precarious: Nephi pointed out to them the danger of returning to Jerusalem (1 Nephi 7:15), and where would they go if they deserted their father? As we have seen, with these people family was everything, and the Arab or Jew will stick to "his own people" because they are all he has in the world.[42] The family is the basic social organization, civil and religious, with the father at its head.[43] To be without tribe or family is to forfeit one's identity in the earth; nothing is more terrible than to be "cut off," and that is exactly the fate that is promised Laman and Lemuel if they rebel (1 Nephi 2:21). "Within his own country," says an Arab proverb, "the Bedouin is a lion; outside of it he is a dog."[44]

When the Lord has a task to be done, he picks a man

who is most suited for the work by temperament and training. When Moses fled into Midian, he traveled afoot in the very deserts through which he was later to lead the children of Israel, and he lived and married among the people of the desert in whose way of life he was to instruct his own people.[45] Lehi was no less prepared and qualified for his great task: richly endowed with means and experience, wise in the ways of the desert, firm, resourceful, cautious and unhurried, independent and not to be intimidated (1 Nephi 1:18-20; 2:1-4), never provoking though sorely provoked, he exemplifies what Philby has declared in a moving passage—that only the greatest strength of character in a leader can carry a party safely through a dangerous desert:

> For many days now I had endured the constant and inevitable friction of my own fixed and unalterable purpose and the solid weight of the innate national inertia thrown into the balance against me by the united body of my companions. Step by step we had progressed ever away from their home fires, but each step had been achieved only by the smallest margin as the momentum of a purposeful mind triumphed at each stage over the inert mass ever ready to recoil from any arduous objective.[46]

Those words might have been written to describe the achievement of Lehi. Had the Lord wished it, he could have transferred the whole party through the air; as it was, he apparently wanted them to do as much as possible on their own, with a minimum of miraculous intervention. Of all the righteous men in Jerusalem, Lehi alone was singled out for a task requiring a combination of qualifications and a measure of faith which few men have ever had. But though Lehi was no ordinary man, one fact about him should begin to emerge at this point of our study: that he was an actual flesh and blood person in a real situation, and no synthetic and overdrawn character of romantic fiction moving among the phantasmagoric stage properties that were once thought to represent the gorgeous East.

Characters and Complexions

Authorities on the East have often observed that the Arabic, and to a lesser extent the Jewish, character is remarkable for its two faces: on the one side the Semite is thoroughly proud and noble, the soul of honor, the impeccable family man, the true friend, faithful to death; and on the other, the low and cunning tramp, the sly assassin, dangerous companion and unpredictable rogue. Every page of Doughty reflects this strange paradox of the desert character, which has received its classic treatment in the third chapter of Lawrence's *Seven Pillars of Wisdom*: pure gold mixed with the basest dross and all within a single family.[47] And where can one find a better illustration of that than in Lehi's own household? For that matter, it comes near to being the *leitmotif* of the Book of Mormon.

This amazing *coincidentia oppositorum* is the clash of black and white. With the Arabs, to be white of countenance is to be blessed and to be black of countenance is to be cursed; there are parallel expressions in Hebrew and Egyptian. And what of Lehi's people? It is most significant that the curse against the Lamanites is the very same as that commonly held in the East to blight the sons of Ishmael, who appear to the light-skinned people of the towns as "a dark and loathsome, and a filthy people, full of idleness and all manner of abominations, . . . an idle people, full of mischief and subtlety," etc. (1 Nephi 12:23; 2 Nephi 5:24). It is noteworthy that all the descendants of the Book of Mormon Ishmael fall under the curse (Alma 3:7), as if their Bedouin ancestry predisposed them to it. The Book of Mormon always mentions the curse of the dark skin in connection with and as part of a larger picture: "*After* they had dwindled in unbelief they *became* a dark, and loathsome, and a filthy people," etc. "Because of the cursing which was upon them they did become an idle people . . . and did seek in the wilderness for beasts of prey" (2 Nephi 5:24). The statement that "*God* did cause a skin of blackness to come upon them" (2 Nephi 5:21) describes the result, not the method, which is described elsewhere. Thus we are told (Alma 3:13, 14, 18) that while the fallen people "set the mark upon *themselves*," it was none the less God who was marking them: "I will set a mark upon them," etc. So natural and human was the process that it suggested nothing miraculous to the ordinary observer, and "the Amlicites knew not that they were fulfilling the words of God when they began to mark *themselves*; . . . it was expedient that the curse should fall upon them" (Alma 3:18). Here God places his mark on people as a curse, yet it is an artificial mark which they actually place upon themselves. The mark was not a racial thing but was acquired by "whosoever suffered himself to be led away by the Lamanites" (Alma 3:10); Alma moreover defines a Nephite as anyone observing "the tradition of their fathers" (Alma 3:11). Which makes the difference between Nephite and Lamanite a cultural, not a racial, one. Does this also apply to the dark skin? Note that the dark skin is never mentioned alone but always as attending a generally depraved way of life, which also is described as the direct result of the curse. When the Lamanites become "white" again, it is by living among the Nephites as Nephites, i.e., adopting the Nephite way of life (3 Nephi 2:15-16). The cultural picture may not be the whole story of the dark skin of the Lamanites, but it is an important part of that story and is given great emphasis by the Book of Mormon itself. There is nowhere any mention of red skin, incidentally, but only of black (or dark) and white, the terms being used as the Arabs use them.

Place Names in the Desert

The stream at which he made his first camp Lehi named after his eldest son; the valley, after his second son (1 Nephi

2:8). The oasis at which his party made their next important camp "we did call . . . Shazer" (1 Nephi 16:13). The fruitful land by the sea "we called Bountiful," while the sea itself "we called Irreantum" (1 Nephi 17:5).

By what right do these people rename streams and valleys to suit themselves? No westerner would tolerate such arrogance. But Lehi is not interested in western taste; he is following a good old Oriental custom. Among the laws "which no Bedouin would dream of transgressing," the first, according to Jennings-Bramley, is that "any water you may discover, either in your own territory or in the territory of another tribe, is named after you."[48] So it happens that in Arabia a great *wady* (valley) will have different names at different points along its course, a respectable number of names being "all used for one and the same valley. . . . One and the same place may have several names, and the *wadi* running close to the same, or the mountain connected with it, will naturally be called differently by members of different clans," according to Canaan,[49] who tells how the Arabs "often coin a new name for a locality for which they have never used a proper name, or whose name they do not know," the name given being usually that of some person. However, names thus bestowed by wandering tribesmen "are neither generally known or commonly used," so that we need not expect any of Lehi's place names to survive.[50]

Speaking of the desert "below the Negeb proper," i.e., the general area of Lehi's first camp, Woolley and Lawrence report "peaks and ridges that have different names among the different Arab tribes, and from different sides,"[51] and of the nearby Tih Palmer says, "In every locality, each individual object, whether rock, mountain, ravine, or valley, has its appropriate name,"[52] while Raswan recalls how "miraculously each hill and dale bore a name."[53] But how reliable are such names? Philby recounts a typical case: "Zayid and 'Ali seemed a little vague about the nomenclature of these parts, and it was only by the irritating process of continual questioning and sifting their often inconsistent and contradictory answers that I was able in the end to piece together the topography of the region."[54] Farther east Cheesman ran into the same difficulty: "I pointed out that this was the third different hill to which he had given the same name. He knew that, was the reply, but that was how they named them."[55] The irresponsible custom of renaming everything on the spot seems to go back to the earliest times, and "probably, as often as not, the Israelites named for themselves their own camps, or unconsciously confounded a native name in their carelessness."[56] Yet in spite of its undoubted antiquity, only the most recent explorers have commented on this strange practice, which seems to have escaped the notice of travelers until explorers in our own times started to make maps.

Even more whimsical and senseless to a westerner must appear the behavior of Lehi in naming a river after one son and its valley after another. But the Arabs don't think that way. In the Mahra country, for example, "as is commonly the case in these mountains, the water bears a different name from the wadi."[57] Likewise we might suppose that after he had named the river after his first-born the location of the camp beside its waters would be given, as any westerner would give it, with reference to the river. Instead, the Book of Mormon follows the Arabic system of designating the camp not by the name of the river (which may easily dry up sometime), but by the name of the valley (1 Nephi 10:16; 16:6).

Another surprise: Nephi more than once refers to the river of Laman as "flowing into the fountain of the Red Sea" (1 Nephi 2:9). Since when is the Red Sea a fountain, forsooth? In the first place we should note that Nephi does not call the Red Sea a fountain but speaks of a body of water as a "fountain *of* the Red Sea." To what can he be referring? "In Hebrew," writes Albright, "the word *yam* means '(large) river' and 'fresh water lake' as well as 'sea' in the English sense. In our case we cannot, however, be sure whether the designation *yam* came originally from inland, referring to pure fresh water as the source of life, or . . . it referred to the Mediterranean as the main source of Canaanite livelihood."[58] In the former case *fountain* is the best translation of the word, and it is certainly in this "inland" sense that Nephi uses it, for he employs a totally different expression, as we shall see, when speaking of the ocean. The Nile and the Euphrates were anciently called *yams,* and this has been explained as "probably a kind of poetic hyperbole, founded upon the fact that they annually overflowed their banks."[59] Now the average width of the Gulf of 'Aqaba is only about twelve miles, and Musil reports that one can look right across it and "see on the Sinai Peninsula not only the mountains of the southern part of the peninsula, but also the plain extending north. . . . To the South we had a view of the greater part of the at-Tihama (southern Sinai) shore."[60]

From the Arabian side, then, the long northeastern extension of the Red Sea for over a hundred miles, that is, the sector where Lehi's party possibly first came upon the sea (1 Nephi 2:5), is not an open sea at all, and is not the Red Sea; it is a broad and elongated sheet of water like the Nile and Euphrates at flood, and like them it is not closed water—not a great lake—but opens out to the sea at its mouth, flowing out through two channels about five miles wide each. A glance at the map will show that there is a northwestern extension of the Red Sea also, closely resembling the one on the northeast. This western arm anciently had the mysterious and much-discussed name of *Yam Suph,* "Sea (or fountain) of Weeds (or rushes)." If *it* was called a *yam,* what is more natural than that its twin gulf to the east should bear the same designation? The latter certainly was what the ancients, by Albright's definition, called a *yam,* the word having, whether applied to salt water or fresh, the basic meaning of *source* or *fountain*. When Lehi's party first saw this body of water, it was a feeder of the Red Sea, with the spring torrents pouring into it (1 Nephi 2:9), a *yam*, that is, in the very sense that the Nile and the Euphrates at flood were *yams*.

When the travelers reached the ocean proper, "we beheld the sea," Nephi recalls, "which we called Irreantum, which, being interpreted, is many waters" (1 Nephi 17:5). But why did they not simply call it the sea and be done? Obviously because there was no name in their language to designate this particular sea. The ancients regularly resort to epithets when speaking of the outer oceans, as the "Great Green" of the Egyptians and the "Great Deep" of the Hebrews. In Coptic, the last form of Egyptian, the Red Sea proper was called *fayum nehah* (*phiom n̄hah*), literally "many waters." If one wanted to speculate, it would be easy to trace Irreantum back to some derivation containing Egyptian *wr* (great) and *n.t* (Copt. *nout* "standing water"), or to identify the final *-um* with the common (Eg., Copt., Heb.) *yem, yam, yum,* "sea" and the rest of the word with Coptic *ir-n-ahte* "great or many." But we need not go so far. It is enough to know that in Lehi's day the ocean was designated by epithets, and that the sea to the east was called "many waters" by the Egyptians.[61]

The first important stop after Lehi's party had left their base camp was at a place they called *Shazer* (1 Nephi 16:13-14). The name is intriguing. The combination *shajer* is quite common in Palestinian place names; it is a collective meaning "trees," and many Arabs (especially in Egypt) pronounce it *shazher*. It appears in *Thoghret-as-Sajur* (the Pass of Trees), which is the ancient *Shaghur,* written *Segor* in the sixth century.[62] It may be confused with Shaghur "seepage," which is held to be identical with Shihor, the "black river" of Joshua 19:36.[63] This last takes in western Palestine the form *Sozura,* suggesting the name of a famous water hole in South Arabia,[64] called *Shisur* by Thomas and *Shisar* by Philby.[65] It is a "tiny copse" and one of the loneliest spots in all the world.[66] So we have *Shihor, Shaghur, Sajur, Saghir, Segor* (even *Zoar*), *Shajar, Sozura, Shisur, and Shisar,* all connected somehow or other and denoting either seepage—a weak but reliable water supply—or a clump of trees. Whichever one prefers, Lehi's people could hardly have picked a better name for their first suitable stopping place than *Shazer*.

When Ishmael died on the journey, he "was buried in the place which was called Nahom" (1 Nephi 16:34). Note that this is not "*a* place which *we* called Nahom," but *the* place which *was* so called, a desert burial ground. Jaussen reports that though Bedouins sometimes bury the dead where they die, many carry the remains great distances to bury them.[67] The Arabic root NHM has the basic meaning of "to sigh or moan," and occurs nearly always in the third form, "to sigh or moan with another." The Hebrew *Nahum,* "comfort," is related, but that is not the form given in the Book of Mormon. At this place, we are told, "the daughters of Ishmael did mourn exceedingly," and are reminded that among the desert Arabs mourning rites are a monopoly of the women.[68]

A Note on Rivers

Before leaving the subject of waters, it would be well to note that Nephi's mention of a river in a most desolate part of Arabia has caused a good deal of quite unnecessary eyebrow-raising. Though Hogarth says that Arabia "probably never had a true river in all its immense area,"[69] later authorities, including Philby, are convinced that the peninsula has supported some quite respectable rivers even in historic times. The point to notice, however, is that Lehi made his discovery in the spring of the year, for Nephi's story begins "in the commencement of the first year of the reign of Zedekiah" (1 Nephi 1:4), and moves very rapidly; with the Jews and "in the Bible throughout the 'first month' always refers to the first spring month."[70] In the spring the desert mountains are full of rushing torrents. The very fact that Nephi uses the term "a river of water" (1 Nephi 2:6), to say nothing of Lehi's ecstasies at the sight of it, shows that they are used to thinking in terms of *dry* rivers—the "rivers of sand" of the East.[71] The Biblical expression "rivers of water" illustrates the point nicely, for the word for "river" in this case is none of the conventional ones but the rare *aphe*, meaning gully or channel (e.g., Ezekiel 32:6; 35:8); in one of the instances where "rivers of waters" are mentioned in the Bible, the river is actually dried up (Joel 1:20), in another they contain not water but also wine and milk (Joel 3:18), and in a third (Song of Solomon 5:12) the proper rendering, as in many modern translations, is "water-brooks." One only speaks of "rivers of water" in a country where rivers do not run all the time. But in the spring it is by no means unusual to find rivers in the regions through which Lehi was moving, as a few examples will show.

"We . . . descended . . . into Wady Waleh. Here was a beautiful seil, quite a little river, dashing over the rocky bed and filled with fish. . . . The stream is a very pretty one, . . . bordered by thickets of flowering oleanders. Here and there it narrows into a deep rushing torrent."[72] Describing the great wall that runs, like our Hurricane fault in Utah, all along the east side of the Dead Sea, the Arabah, and the Red Sea, an earlier traveler says: "Farther south the country is absolutely impassable, as huge gorges one thousand to fifteen hundred feet deep, and nearly a mile wide in some places [compare Lehi's "awful" chasm! (1 Nephi 15:28)], are broken by the great torrents flowing in winter over perpendicular precipices into the sea."[73] The sea is the Dead Sea, but the same conditions continue all down the great wall to "the borders which are near the [Red Sea]" (1 Nephi 2:8). One is reminded of how impressed Lehi was when he saw the river of Laman flowing "into the fountain of the Red Sea" (1 Nephi 2:9). On the desert road to Petra in the springtime "there are several broad streams to pass, the fording of which creates a pleasant little excitement."[74] A party traveling farther north reports, "We presently came upon the deep Wady 'Allan, which here cuts the plain in two. How delightful was the splash and gurgle of the living water rushing over its rocky bed in the fierce heat of that Syrian day!"[75]

Given the right season of the year, then—and the Book of Mormon is obliging enough to give it—one need not be surprised at rivers in northwestern Arabia. It was this seasonal phenomenon that led Ptolemy to place a river between Yambu and Meccah with perfect correctness.[76]

That invaluable researcher and indefatigable sleuth, Ariel L. Crowley, has suggested with considerable astuteness that the river of Laman was a very different kind of stream from the "rivers of water" of which we have been speaking, being nothing less than Necho's canal from the Nile to the Red Sea.[77] The greater part of Brother Crowley's study is devoted to proving that there was such a canal, but that is no issue, since it is not disputed. What we cannot believe is that the big ditch was Laman's river, and that for a number of reasons of which we need here give only two.

First, while noting that Nephi's account of the exodus "is so precisely worded that it bears the stamp of deliberate, careful phrasing," Crowley fails to note that nothing is more precise and specific than Nephi's report on the *direction* of the march, and that, as we have seen, he never mentions a westerly direction, which must have been taken to reach the place. Brother Crowley assumes that "into the wilderness" (1 Nephi 2:2) means by the "Wilderness Way" to Egypt, first "for the sake of hypothesis," then, without proof, as a fact.[78] There is no expression commoner in the East than "into the wilderness," which of course is not restricted to any such area. The last place in the world to flee from the notice of men would be to the border of Egypt, which at all times in ancient history was very heavily fortified and closely guarded (see the Story of Sinuhe); and Lehi as a member of the *anti*-Egyptian party would be the last man in the world to seek refuge in Egypt.

Second, Crowley calls Necho's canal a "mighty stream," and says that it lay "at the ancient crossroads of continents, perhaps as well-known as any place on earth in 600 B.C."[79] Then why wasn't it known to Lehi? It was the greatest engineering triumph of the age, the most important purely commercial waterway in the world; it lay astride the most travelled highway of antiquity if not of history; reached by a few days' journey from Jerusalem over a level coastal plain, it was the only great river anywhere near Jerusalem except for the Nile, of which it was a branch, and yet "the stream was *unknown* to Lehi [!], otherwise it is improbable that he would have given it a new name. In this very fact," says Crowley, "lies confirmation of the recent creation of the stream."[80] Just how long does it take news to travel in the East? The canal was at least ten years old, it had taken years to build, a wonder of the world, an inestimable boon to world trade, less than two hundred miles from Lehi's doorstep by a main highway, and yet at a time of ceaseless and feverish coming and going between Egypt and Palestine, neither Lehi, the great merchant with his sound Egyptian education, nor his enterprising and ambitious sons, had ever heard of it! It is impossible to believe that Lehi did not know that if one traveled towards Egypt and came across a *mighty* stream in a perfectly empty desert, it would not be some unknown and undiscovered watercourse but really quite an important one. If anyone knew about Necho's canal, it was Lehi. But we agree with Crowley that the river of Laman was obviously *not* known to him. Therefore the two cannot have been the same. "No river answering the description of Nephi could have escaped historical notice in profane works," says Crowley.[81] Why not? It escaped Lehi's notice, steeped as he was in the lore of Egyptians and Jews. It cannot therefore have been an important stream, let alone one of the most remarkable on earth, or Lehi would have known about it. Nor does Nephi ever say or imply that it was a great river; it was not a waterway at all, but a "river of water," which is a very different thing.

5

The City and the Sand

Lehi the Poet

The powerful speech by which alone Lehi kept his rebellious sons in line is a gift demanded of every real *sheikh* in the desert, and indeed, against the proud and touchy Bedouins that is the only weapon the *sheikh* possesses, for as we have seen he may not use force. The true leader, says an ancient Arab poetess, "was not one to keep silent when the contest of words began." When the men assemble in the chief's tent to take counsel together, the leader "address[es] the whole assembly with a succession of wise counsels intermingled with opportune proverbs," exactly in the manner of Lehi with his endless parables. People of any other country hearing them speak, says our informant, "would simply suppose them filled with a supernatural gift."[1] "Poetical exclamations . . . rose all around me," Burton recalls, "showing how deeply tinged with imagination becomes the language of the Arab under the influence of strong passion or religious enthusiasm."[2] Let us visit the tent of Lehi: "I returned to the tent of my father," says Nephi, "and . . . I beheld my brethren, and they were disputing one with another concerning the things which my father had spoken unto them . . . and . . . after I had received strength I spake unto my brethren" (1 Nephi 15:1-2, 6). "And . . . after I, Nephi, had made an end of speaking to my brethren . . . they did humble themselves before the Lord" (1 Nephi 16:1-5). Great is the power of speech among the desert people, and if Lehi's language sounds strangely exclamatory and high-flown to us, it is because it is of the ancient pattern, "by the Spirit of the Lord which was in our father" (1 Nephi 15:12).

Moreover, Lehi was a poet, and there is no more remarkable passage in the Book of Mormon than the eloquent little verses which he on one memorable occasion addressed to his wayward sons.

It was just after the first camp had been pitched, with due care for the performance of the proper thanksgiving rites at the "altar of stones" (1 Nephi 2:7), that Lehi, being then free to survey the scene more at his leisure (for among the desert people it is the women who make and break camp, though the *sheikh* must officiate in the sacrifice), proceeded, as was his right, to name the river after his first-born and the valley after his second son (1 Nephi 2:6-8, 14). The men examined the terrain more closely, as Arabs always do after pitching camp in a place where they expect to spend some time, and discovered that the river "emptied into the fountain of the Red Sea," at a point "near the mouth thereof" (1 Nephi 2:8-9), which suggests the Gulf of Aqaba at a point not far above the Straits of Tiran. When Lehi beheld the view, perhaps from the sides of Mt. Musafa or Mt. Mendisha,[3] he turned to his two elder sons and recited his remarkable verses. Nephi seems to have been standing by, for he takes most careful note of the circumstance:

> And when my father saw that the waters of the river emptied into the fountain of the Red Sea, he spake unto Laman, saying: O that thou mightest be like unto this river, continually running into the fountain of all righteousness!
>
> And he also spake unto Lemuel: O that thou mightest be like unto this valley, firm and steadfast, and immovable in keeping the commandments of the Lord! (1 Nephi 2:9-10).

No subject has been more intensively studied over a greater number of years than that of primitive Semitic poetry, and nowhere could one find a more perfect illustration of the points that are now agreed upon as to the nature and form of the original article than in this brief account of Nephi's.

First there is the occasion: It was the sight of the river flowing into the gulf which inspired Lehi to address his sons. In a famous study, Goldziher pointed out that the earliest desert poems ever mentioned are "those *Quellenlieder* (songs composed to fresh water) which, according to the record of St. Nilus, the ancient Arabs used to intone after having refreshed and washed themselves in some fountain of running water discovered in the course of a long journeying."[4] Nilus' own account is a vivid picture of what Lehi's party went through:

> The next day . . . after making their way as is usual in the desert by devious routes, wandering over the difficult terrain, forced to turn aside now this way, now that, circumventing mountains, stumbling over rough, broken ground through all but impenetrable passes, they beheld in the far distance a spot of green in the desert; and striving to reach the vegetation by which the oasis might provide a camp or even sustain a settlement for some of them [we are reading *nomadikon* for the senseless *monadikon*], as they conjecture, they turned their eyes towards it as a storm-tossed pilot views the harbor. Upon reaching it, they found that the spot did not disappoint their expectations, and that their wishful fantasies had not led them to false hopes. For the water was abundant, clean to the sight, and sweet to the taste, so that it was a question whether the eye or the mouth was the more rejoiced. Moreover, there was adequate forage for the animals; so they unloaded the camels and let them out to graze freely. For themselves, they could not let the water alone, drinking, splashing, and bathing as if they could not revel in it enough. So they recited songs in its praise [the river's], and composed hymns to the spring.[5]

Ibn Qutayba, in a famous work on Arabic poetry,

quoted a great desert poet, Abu Sakhr, as saying that nothing on earth brings verses so readily to mind as the sight of running water and wild places.[6] This applies not only to springs, of course, but to all running water. Thomas recounts how his Arabs upon reaching the Umm al-Hait hailed it with a song in praise of the "continuous and flowing rain," whose bounty filled the bed of the *wady*, "flowing along between sand and stream course."[7] Just so Lehi holds up as the most admirable of examples "this river, continually running"; for to the people of the desert there is no more miraculous and lovely thing on earth than continually running water. In the most stirring episode of Saint-Exupery's *Wind, Sand, and Stars*, the Arab chiefs who view the wonders of Paris with stolid indifference burst into cries of devout rapture at the sight of a torrent in the Alps.[8] When the Banī Hilāl stopped at their first oasis, the beauty of it and the green vegetation reminded them again of the homeland they had left, "and they wept greatly remembering it."[9] It was precisely because Laman and Lemuel were loud in lamenting the loss of their pleasant "land of Jerusalem . . . and their precious things" (1 Nephi 2:11), that their father was moved to address them on this particular occasion.

If the earliest desert poems were songs inspired by the fair sight of running water, no one today knows the *form* they took. That can only be conjectured from the earliest known form of Semitic verse. This is the *saj*ᶜ, a short exhortation or injunction spoken with such solemnity and fervor as to fall into a sort of chant. Examples would be magical incantations, curses, and the formal pronouncements of teachers, priests, and judges. From the earliest times the *saj*ᶜ was the form in which inspiration and revelation announced themselves.[10] Though the speaker of the *saj*ᶜ did not aim consciously at metrical form, his words were necessarily more than mere prose, and were received by their hearers as poetry. The *saj*ᶜ had the effect, we are told, of overawing the hearer completely, and was considered absolutely binding on the person to whom it was addressed, its aim being to compel action.[11]

Lehi's words to his sons take just this form of short, solemn, rhythmical appeal. The fact that the speech to Laman exactly matches that to his brother shows that we have here such a formal utterance as the *saj*ᶜ. The proudest boast of the desert poet is, "I utter a verse and after it its brother," for the consummation of the poetic art was to have two verses perfectly parallel in form and content. Few ever achieved this, and Ibn Qutayba observes that the usual verse is followed not by a "brother" but at best by a "cousin."[12] Yet Lehi seems to have carried it off. Of the moral fervor and didactic intent of his recitation there can be no doubt; the fact that Nephi recounts the episode in a record in which there is, as he says, only room for great essentials, shows what a deep impression it made upon him.

In addressing his sons in what looks like a little song, Lehi is doing just what Isaiah does (1 Nephi 5:1-7) when he speaks to Israel in a *shirat dodi,* "a friendly chant," a popular song about a vine which, once the hearer's attention has been won, turns into a very serious moral tirade.[13] On another occasion, as we have noted, he employs the popular figure of the olive tree. The stock opening line of the old desert poems is, "O my two beloved ones! (or friends)," an introduction which, says Ibn Qutayba, should be avoided, "since only the ancients knew how to use it properly, uniting a gentle and natural manner with the grandiose and magnificent."[14] Lehi's poem is an example of what is meant: he addresses his two sons separately but each with the peculiar and typical Arabic vocative "O that thou . . . !" (*Yā laytaka*), and describes the river and valley in terms of unsurpassed brevity and simplicity and in the vague and sweeping manner of the real desert poets, of whom Burton says, "there is a dreaminess of idea and a haze thrown over the object, infinitely attractive, but indescribable."[15] Lehi's language is of this simple, noble, but hazy kind.

According to Richter, the best possible example of the primitive Arabic *qasīda* (the name given to the oldest actual poetry of the desert) is furnished by those old poems in which one's beloved is compared to a land "in which abundant streams flow down . . . with rushing and swirling, so that the water overflows every evening continually."[16] Here the "continually flowing" water is compared to the person addressed, as in Lehi's "song" to Laman. The original *qasīda*, the same authority avers, was built around the beseeching (*werbenden*, hence the name *qaṣīda*) motif, not necessarily erotic in origin, as was once thought, but dealing rather with praise of virtue in general (*Tugendlob*).[17] Ibn Qutayba even claims that the introductory love theme was merely a device to gain attention of male listeners and was not at all the real stuff of the poem.[18] The standard pattern is a simple one: (a) the poet's attention is arrested by some impressive natural phenomenon, usually running water; (b) this leads him to recite a few words in its praise, drawing it to the attention of a beloved companion of the way, and (c) making it an object lesson for the latter, who is urged to be like it. Burton gives a good example: at the sight of the Wady al-Akik the nomad poet is moved to exclaim,

> O my friend, this is Akik, then stand by it,
> Endeavoring to be distracted by love,
> if not really a lover.[19]

This seems to be some sort of love song, albeit a peculiar one, and some have claimed that all the old *qaṣīdas* were such.[20] But Burton and his Arabs know the real meaning, "the esoteric meaning of this couplet," as he calls it, which quite escapes the western reader and is to be interpreted:

> Man! This is a lovely portion of God's creation:
> Then stand by it, and here learn to love

the perfections of thy Supreme Friend.[21]

Compare this with Lehi's appeal to Lemuel:

O that thou mightest be like unto this valley,
firm and steadfast,
And immovable in keeping the commandments
of the Lord! (1 Nephi 2:10).

Note the remarkable parallel. In each case the poet, wandering in the desert with his friends, is moved by the sight of a pleasant valley, a large *wady* with water in it; he calls the attention of his beloved companion to the view, and appeals to him to learn a lesson from the valley and "stand by it," firm and unshakable in the love of the ways of the Lord. Let us briefly list the exacting conditions fulfilled by Nephi's account of his father's *qaṣīdas* and demanded of the true and authentic poet of the earliest period:

(1) They are *Brunnen-* or *Quellenlieder*, as the Germans call them, that is, songs inspired by the sight of water gushing from a spring or running down a valley.

(2) They are addressed to one or (usually) two traveling companions.

(3) They praise the beauty and the excellence of the scene, calling it to the attention of the hearer as an object lesson.

(4) The hearer is urged to be like the thing he beholds.[22]

(5) The poems are recited extempore on the spot and with great feeling.

(6) They are very short, each couplet being a complete poem in itself.[23]

(7) One verse must be followed by its "brother," making a perfectly matched pair.

Here we have beyond any doubt all the elements of a situation of which no westerner in 1830 had the remotest conception. Lehi stands before us as something of a poet, as well as a great prophet and leader, and that is as it should be. "The poetic art of David," says Professor Montgomery, "has its complement in the early Arabic poets . . . some of whom themselves were kings."[24]

It has often been said that there is no real poetry in the Book of Mormon – no real English poetry, that is. Of course not; there is no Italian or Russian poetry, either, for Lehi did not compose in those languages. Whenever Semitic poetry is translated into a modern language, if any attempt at all is made to retain the original meanings, the result is pretty awful. The Psalms are beautiful in English, for example, because the translators were very largely ignorant of the fine points of what they were reading, and so wrote a free and uninhibited English.[25] But accuracy is the first and last aim of our Book of Mormon text, and if there were any good poetry in the book it would give just cause for suspicion, for Burton, even while praising the matchless genius of the desert poets, is careful to point out that they are utterly "destitute of the poetic taste, *as we define it*."[26] To Lehi's "literary" critics we need only reply that Nephi is not supposed to be writing good English poetry, and that they might with equal justice maintain that there is no good literature in Mutanabbi or the *Kitāb-al-Aghānī* because, forsooth, none of the innumerable poems contained in them has ever been done into great or even good English verse – they cannot be and still contain any of their original form or content. Yet those who know these books best insist that they represent the high point not only in Arabic but also in all lyric poetry.

As if to prove that no westerner could possibly have dreamed up Nephi's account, we are challenged by the remarkable expression, "like unto this valley, firm and steadfast, and immovable" (1 Nephi 2:10). Who west of Suez would ever think of such an image? At the very least the proofreader should have caught such a howler, which should certainly have been corrected in subsequent editions. For we, of course, know all about everlasting *hills* and immovable mountains, the moving of which is the best-known illustration of the infinite power of faith, but who ever heard of a steadfast valley? The Arabs, to be sure. For them the valley, and not the mountain, is the symbol of permanence. It is not the mountain of refuge to which they flee, but the valley of refuge. The great depressions that run for hundreds of miles across the Arabian peninsula pass for the most part through plains devoid of mountains. It is in these ancient riverbeds alone that water, vegetation, and animal life are to be found when all else is desolation. They alone offer men and animals escape from their enemies and deliverance from death by hunger and thirst. The qualities of firmness and steadfastness, of reliable protection, refreshment, and sure refuge when all else fails, which other nations attribute naturally to mountains, the Arabs attribute to valleys.[27] So the ancient Zohair describes a party like Lehi's:

> And when they went down to the water, blue and still in its depression, they laid down their walking-sticks like one who has reached a permanent resting-place.[28]

Adventure in Jerusalem

Nephi and his brothers made two trips back to Jerusalem. The second was only to "the land of Jerusalem" (1 Nephi 7:2) to pick up Ishmael. The fact that this was a simple and uncomplicated mission at a time when things would have been very hot for the brethren in the city itself (where they had been chased by Laban's police on their former expedition and would be instantly recognized) implies that Ishmael, like Lehi, lived well out in the country (1 Nephi 7:2-5). But the first mission was an exciting and dangerous assignment in the city itself. Though it was no mere raid, as we have seen, the men taking their tents with them and going up quite openly, they were expecting trouble and drew lots to see who should go in to Laban. The record tells of hiding without the walls, daring exploits in the dark streets, mad pursuits, dangerous masquerading, desperate deeds, and bitter quarrels—a typical Oriental romance, one might say, but typical because such things actually do, and always did, happen in Eastern cities.

It has ever been an established and conventional bit of gallantry for some Bedouin bravo with a price on his head to risk his life by walking right through a city under the noses of the police in broad daylight—a very theatrical gesture but one which my Arab friends assure me has been done a thousand times. It was while reading the Banī Hilāl epic that the writer was first impressed by the close resemblance of the behavior of Lehi's sons on that quick trip to Jerusalem to that of the young braves of the Banī Hilāl when they would visit a city under like circumstances. The tales of the wanderings of the 'Amer tribe tell the same story—camping without the walls, drawing lots to see who would take a chance, sneaking into the city and making a getaway through the midnight streets[29]—it is all in the Book of Mormon and all quite authentic.

Thoroughly typical also is the hiding out of the young men in caves near the city while they waited for Laban's henchmen to cool off and debated with Oriental heat and passion their next move (1 Nephi 3:27-28). Since the *Palestine Exploration Fund Quarterly* started to appear many years ago, its readers have been treated to a constant flow of official reports on newly-discovered caves in and near Jerusalem. The country is peppered with them; for the area southwest of the city, "it is difficult to give an account of the principal excavations of this type (of caves) without appearing to use the language of exaggeration. . . . To attempt a descriptive catalogue of these caves would be altogether futile. The mere labor of searching the hills for examples . . . would be almost endless."[30] Farther out, the Beit Jibrin area "contains an innumerable number of artificial caves,"[31] and the deserts of Tih and Moab swarm with them.[32] Many of these caves, being artificial, are younger than Lehi's time, but many are also older and have been used at all times as hiding places.[33] But who in America knew of these hiding places a hundred years ago?

The purpose of the first return trip to Jerusalem was the procuring of certain records which were written on bronze plates (the Book of Mormon like the Bible always uses "brass" for what we call bronze—a word that has become current only since its translation). Lehi had a dream in which he was commanded to get these records which, as he already knew, were kept at the house of one Laban. Nephi does not know exactly the reason for this and assumes, incorrectly as it turned out, that the object was to "preserve unto our children the language of our fathers" (1 Nephi 3:19).[34] It is interesting that the Banī Hilāl in setting out for their great trek felt it necessary to keep a record of their *fathers* and to add to it as they went, "so that the memory of it might remain for future generations."[35] The keeping of such a *daftar*, as it was called, was also known to other wandering tribes.

But what were the records doing at Laban's house, and who was Laban anyway?

Dealings with Laban

For ages the cities of Palestine and Syria had been more or less under the rule of military governors, of native blood but, in theory at least, answerable to Egypt. "These commandants (called *rabis* in the Amarna letters) were subordinate to the city-princes (*chazan*), who commonly address them as 'Brother' or 'Father.' "[36] They were by and large a sordid lot of careerists whose authority depended on constant deception and intrigue, though they regarded their offices as hereditary and sometimes styled themselves kings. In the Amarna letters we find these men raiding each other's caravans, accusing each other of unpaid debts and broken promises, mutually denouncing each other as traitors to Egypt, and generally displaying the usual time-honored traits of the high official in the East seeking before all things to increase his private fortune. The Lachish letters show that such men were still the lords of creation in Lehi's day—the commanders of the towns around Jerusalem were still acting in closest cooperation with Egypt in military matters, depending on the prestige of Egypt to bolster their corrupt power, and still behaving as groveling and unscrupulous timeservers.[37]

One of the main functions of any governor in the East has always been to hear petitions, and the established practice has ever been to rob the petitioners (or anyone else) wherever possible. The Eloquent Peasant story of fifteen centuries before Lehi and the innumerable Tales of the Qadis of fifteen centuries after him are all part of the same picture, and Laban fits into that picture as if it were drawn to set off his portrait.

> And Laman went in unto the house of Laban, and he talked with him as he sat in his house.
>
> And he desired of Laban the records which were engraven upon the plates of brass, which contained the genealogy of my father.
>
> And . . . Laban was angry, and thrust him out from his presence; and he would not that he should have the records. Wherefore, he said unto him: Behold thou art a robber, and I will slay thee.
>
> But Laman fled out of his presence, and told the things which Laban had done, unto us (1 Nephi 3:11-14).

Later the brothers returned to Laban laden with their family treasure, foolishly hoping to buy the plates from him. They might have known what would happen:

> And it came to pass that when Laban saw our property, and that it was exceedingly great, he did lust after it, insomuch that he thrust us out, and sent his servants to slay us, that he might obtain our property.

> And it came to pass that we did flee before the servants of Laban, and we were obliged to leave behind our property, and it fell into the hands of Laban (1 Nephi 3:25-26).

Compare this with the now classic story of Wenamon's interview with the rapacious Zakar Baal, governor of Byblos, almost exactly five hundred years before. The Egyptian entered the great man's house and "found him sitting in his upper chamber, leaning his back against a window," even as Laman accosted Laban "as he sat in his house" (1 Nephi 3:11). When his visitor desired of the merchant prince and prince of merchants that he part with some cedar logs, the latter flew into a temper and accused him of being a thief ("Behold thou art a robber!" says Laban in 1 Nephi 3:13), demanding that he produce his credentials. Zakar Baal then "had the journal of his fathers brought in, and he had them read it before [him]," from which it is plain that the important records of the city were actually stored at his house and kept on tablets. From this ancient "journal of his fathers," the prince proved to Wenamon that his ancestors had never taken orders from Egypt, and though the envoy softened his host somewhat by reminding him that Ammon, the lord of the universe, rules over all kings, the hard-dealing official "thrust him out" and later even sent his servants after him—not, however, to slay him, but with the more generous afterthought of bringing him something in the way of refreshment as he sat sorrowing. With cynical politeness the prince offered to show Wenamon the graves of some other Egyptian envoys whose missions had not been too successful, and when the business deal was finally completed, Zakar Baal, on a legal technicality, turned his guest over to the mercies of a pirate fleet lurking outside the harbor.[38] And all the time he smiled and bowed, for after all Wenamon was an Egyptian official, whereas Lehi's sons lost their bargaining power when they lost their fortune. The Laban story is an eloquent commentary of the ripeness of Jerusalem for destruction.

A few deft and telling touches resurrect the pompous Laban with photographic perfection. We learn in passing that he commanded a garrison of fifty, that he met in full ceremonial armor with "the elders of the Jews" (1 Nephi 4:22) for secret consultations by night, that he had control of a treasury, that he was of the old aristocracy, being a distant relative to Lehi himself, that he probably held his job because of his ancestors, since he hardly received it by merit, that his house was the storing place of very old records, that he was a large man, short-tempered, crafty, and dangerous, and to the bargain cruel, greedy, unscrupulous, weak, and given to drink. All of which makes him a *Rabu* to the life, the very model of an Oriental pasha. He is cut from the same cloth as Jaush, his contemporary and probably his successor as "military governor of this whole region, in control of the defenses along the western frontier of Judah, and an intermediary with the authorities of Jerusalem," or as Hoshaiah, "apparently the leader of the military company situated at some outpost near the main road from Jerusalem to the coast," whose character was one of "fawning servility."[39]

As to the garrison of fifty, it seems pitifully small for a great city. It would have been just as easy for the author of 1 Nephi to have said "fifty thousand," and made it really impressive. Yet even the older brothers, though they wish to emphasize Laban's great power, mention only fifty (1 Nephi 3:31), and it is Nephi in answering them who says that the Lord is "mightier than Laban and his fifty," and adds, "or even than his tens of thousands" (1 Nephi 4:1). As a high military commander Laban would have his tens of thousands in the field, but such an array is of no concern to Laman and Lemuel: it is the "fifty" they must look out for, the regular, permanent garrison of Jerusalem. The number fifty suits perfectly with the Amarna picture where the military forces are always so surprisingly small and a garrison of thirty to eighty men is thought adequate even for big cities. It is strikingly vindicated in a letter of Nebuchadnezzar, Lehi's contemporary, wherein the great king orders: "As to the fifties who were under your orders, those gone to the rear, or fugitives return them to the ranks." Commenting on this, Offord says, "In these days it is interesting to note the indication here, that in the Babylonian army a platoon contained fifty men;"[40] also, we might add, that it was called a "fifty," – hence, "Laban and his fifty" (1 Nephi 4:1). Of course, companies of fifty are mentioned in the Bible, along with tens and hundreds, etc., but not as garrisons of great cities and not as *the* standard military unit of this time. Laban, like Hoshaiah of Lachish, had a single company of soldiers under him as the permanent garrison, and like Jaush (his possible successor) worked in close cooperation with the authorities in Jerusalem.

Returning by night in a third attempt to get the records, Nephi stumbled upon the prostrate form of Laban, lying dead drunk in the deserted street (1 Nephi 4:7). The commander had been (so his servant later told Nephi) in conference with "the elders of the Jews . . . out by night among them" (1 Nephi 4:22), and was wearing his full dress armor. What a world of inference in this! We sense the gravity of the situation in Jerusalem which "the elders" are still trying to conceal; we hear the suppressed excitement of Zoram's urgent talk as he and Nephi hasten through the streets to the city gates (1 Nephi 4:27), and from Zoram's willingness to change sides and leave the city we can be sure that he, as Laban's secretary,[41] knew how badly things were going. From the Lachish letters it is clear that informed parties in Jerusalem were quite aware of the critical state of things at Jerusalem, even while the *sarim*, "the elders," were working with all their might to suppress every sign of criticism and disaffection. How could they take counsel to provide for the defense of the city and their own interests without exciting alarm or giving rise to general rumors and misgivings? By holding their meetings in secret, of course, such midnight sessions of civil and military leaders as Laban had just been attending.

With great reluctance, but urged persistently by "the voice of the Spirit" (1 Nephi 4:18), Nephi took Laban's own sword and cut off his head with it. This episode is viewed with horror and incredulity by people who recently approved and applauded the far less merciful slaughter of far more innocent men on the islands of the Pacific. Samual ibn Adiyt, the most famous Jewish poet of Arabia in ancient times, won undying fame in the East by allowing his son to be cruelly put to death before his eyes rather than give up some costly armor which had been entrusted to his care by a friend.[42] The story, true or not, is a reminder that eastern and western standards are not the same, and that the callousness of Americans in many matters of personal relationships would shock Arabs far more than anything they do shocks us. The Book of Mormon is no more than the Bible confined to mild and pleasant episodes; it is for the most part a sad and grievous tale of human folly. No one seems more disturbed by the demise of Laban, however, than Nephi himself, who takes great pains to explain his position (1 Nephi 4:10-18). First he was "constrained by the Spirit" to kill Laban, but he said in his heart that he had never shed human blood and became sick at the thought: "I shrunk and would that I might not slay him" (1 Nephi 4:10). The Spirit spoke again, and to its promptings Nephi adds his own reasons: "I also *knew* that he had sought to take away mine own life; yea, and he would not hearken unto the commandments of the Lord; and he also had taken away our property" (1 Nephi 4:11). But this was still not enough; the Spirit spoke again, explaining the Lord's reasons and assuring Nephi that he would be in the right; to which Nephi appends yet more arguments of his own, remembering the promise that his people would prosper only by keeping the commandments of the Lord, "and I also *thought* that they could not keep the commandments . . . save they should have the law" (1 Nephi 4:15), which the dangerous and criminal Laban alone kept them from having. "And again, I knew that the Lord had delivered Laban into my hands for this cause. . . . *Therefore* I did obey the voice of the Spirit" (1 Nephi 4:17-18).

At long last Nephi finally did the deed, of which he is careful to clear himself, putting the responsibility for the whole thing on the Lord. If the Book of Mormon were a work of fiction, nothing would be easier than to have Laban already dead when Nephi found him or simply to omit an episode which obviously distressed the writer quite as much as it does the reader, though the slaying of Laban is no more reprehensible than was the beheading of the unconscious Goliath.

From time to time the claim is put forth, that the story of Laban's death is absurd, if not impossible. It is said that Nephi could not have killed Laban and made his escape. Those who are familiar with night patroling in wartime, however, will see in Nephi's tale a convincing and realistic account. In the first place, the higher critics are apparently not aware that the lighting of city streets, except for festivals, is a blessing unknown to ages other than our own. Hundreds of passages might be cited from ancient writers, classical and Oriental, to show that in times gone by the streets of even the biggest towns were perfectly dark at night, and very dangerous. To move about late at night without lamp bearers and armed guards was to risk almost certain assault. In the famous trial of Alcibiades for the mutilation of the Hermes, we have the testimony of one witness who, all alone, beheld by moonlight the midnight depredations of a drunken band in the heart of downtown Athens, from which it is clear that the streets of the greatest city in the western world were unlighted, deserted, and dangerous at night. In times of social unrest the streets at night were virtually given over to the underworld, as they were in some European cities during the blackouts of the late war. The extreme narrowness of ancient streets made their blackout doubly effective. From the Greek and Roman comedy and from the poets we learn how heavily barred and closely guarded the doors of private houses had to be at night, and archaeology has shown us eastern cities in which apparently not a single house window opened onto the public street, as few do even today at ground level. East and West, the inmates simply shut themselves in at night as if in a besieged fortress. Even in Shakespeare's day we see the comical terror of the night watch passing through the streets at hours when all honest people are behind doors. In a word, the streets of any ancient city after sundown were a perfect setting for the committing of deeds of violence without fear of detection.

It was very late when Nephi came upon Laban (1 Nephi 4:5, 22); the streets were deserted and dark. Let the reader imagine what he would do if he were on patrol near enemy headquarters during a blackout and stumbled on the unconscious form of some notoriously bloodthirsty enemy general. By the brutal code of war the foe has no claim to a formal trial, and it is now or never. Laban was wearing armor, so the only chance of dispatching him quickly, painlessly, and safely was to cut off his head—the conventional treatment of criminals in the East, where beheading has always been by the sword, and where an executioner would be fined for failing to decapitate his victim at one clean stroke. Nephi drew the sharp, heavy weapon and stood over Laban for a long time, debating his course (1 Nephi 4:9-18). He was an expert hunter and a powerful man: with due care such a one could do a quick and efficient job and avoid getting much blood on himself. But why should he worry about that? There was not one chance in a thousand of meeting any honest citizen, and in the dark no one would notice the blood anyway. What they *would* notice would be the armor that Nephi put on, and which, like the sword, could easily be wiped clean. The donning of the armor was the natural and the shrewd thing for Nephi to do. A number of instances from the last war could be cited to show that a spy in the enemy camp is never so safe as when he is wearing the insignia of a *high* military official—provided he does not hang around too long, and Nephi had no intention of doing that. No one dares challenge big brass too closely (least of all a grim and hot-tempered Laban); their business is at all times "top secret," and their uniform gives them complete freedom to come and to go unquestioned.

Nephi tells us that he was "led by the Spirit" (1 Nephi 4:6). He was not taking impossible chances, but being in a tight place he followed the surest formula of those who have successfully carried off ticklish assignments. His audacity and speed were rewarded, and he was clear of the town before anything was discovered. In his whole exploit there is nothing in the least improbable.

How Nephi disguised himself in the clothes of Laban and tricked Laban's servant into admitting him to the treasury is an authentic bit of Oriental romance, and of history as well. One need but think of Sir Richard Burton's amazingly audacious masquerades in the East, carried on in broad daylight and for months on end with perfect success, to realize that such a thing is entirely possible. When Zoram, the servant, discovered that it was not his master with whom he had been discussing the highly secret doings of the elders as they walked to the outskirts of the city, he was seized with terror, as well he might be. In such a situation there was only one thing Nephi could possibly have done, both to spare Zoram and to avoid giving alarm—and no westerner could have guessed what it was. Nephi, a powerful fellow, held the terrified Zoram in a vice-like grip long enough to swear a solemn oath in his ear, "as the Lord liveth, and as I live" (1 Nephi 4:32), that he would not harm him if he would listen. Zoram immediately relaxed, and Nephi swore another oath to him that he would be a free man if he would join the party: "Therefore, if thou wilt go down into the wilderness to my father thou shalt have place with us" (1 Nephi 4:34).

We have already considered the correctness of the expressions "go down," and "have place," as well as the necessity of having Zoram address himself to no one but Nephi's father. What astonishes the western reader is the miraculous effect of Nephi's oath on Zoram, who upon hearing a few conventional words promptly becomes tractable, while as for the brothers, as soon as Zoram "made an oath unto us . . . that he would tarry with us from that time forth . . . our fears did cease concerning him" (1 Nephi 4:35, 37).

The reaction of both parties makes sense when one realizes that the oath is the one thing that is most sacred and inviolable among the desert people: "Hardly will an Arab break this oath, even if his life be in jeopardy,"[43] for "there is nothing stronger, and nothing more sacred than the oath among the nomads," and even among the city Arabs, if it be exacted under special conditions.[44] But not every oath will do: to be most binding and solemn an oath should be by the *life* of something, even if it be but a blade of grass; the only oath more awful than "by my life" or (less commonly) "by the life of my head," is the *wa ḥayat Allah*, "by the life of God," or "as the Lord liveth," the Arabic equivalent of the ancient Hebrew *ḥai Elohim*.[45] Today it is glibly employed by the city riffraff, but anciently it was an awful thing, as it still is among the desert people: "I confirmed my answer in the Beduin wise," says Doughty. "By his life . . . he said, . . . 'Well, swear by the life of Ullah (God)!' . . . I answered, . . . and thus even the nomads use, in a greater occasion, but they say, *By the life of thee*, in a little matter."[46] So we see that the one and only way that Nephi could have pacified the struggling Zoram in an instant was to utter the one oath that no man would dream of breaking, the most solemn of all oaths to the Semite: "as the Lord liveth, and as I live" (1 Nephi 4:32).

6

Lehi the Winner

A Word about Plates

We have seen how the ruler of Byblos, to score a point in bargaining with Wenamon, had his family records and accounts brought out and read to him. In the Amarna tablets, the *Rabu* of one Palestinian city writes to a neighboring prince: "But now behold [note the Book of Mormon style] the king causeth that his true city should go from his hand; let the king search in the tablets which are kept in the house of his father, and learn whether the one who rules Gubla has been his true servant."[1] Here as in Byblos the records were kept at the house of the ruling family; even in distant Rome in the time of Lehi the records from which the later annals were composed seem to have been preserved on tablets in the houses of the leading families.[2] At that time the practice seems to have been general around the Mediterranean. Where the record was one of real importance, plates of copper, bronze, or even more precious metal were used instead of the usual wooden, lead, or clay tablets. One of the most recent finds of this type from Palestine is "a metal tablet of copper or bronze" in Hebrew, dating from the twelfth century B.C., containing a message "of entirely secular, profane character," but "which must have seemed important enough to be engraved on the durable, though 'impractical,' material of metal."[3] More precious documents, such as the famous treaty of 1287 between the kings of Egypt and the Hittites, were kept on silver plates, and the royal record of the deeds of Darius deserved nothing less than gold, and have received considerable notice from Mormon writers. The mysterious "reformed Egyptian" texts from Byblos are on bronze plates, and the Demotic Chronicle of Egypt was kept originally on plates. There is an interesting account in Idrisi (1226 A.D.) of the opening of the tomb of Mycerinus in the third of the three great pyramids. The writer reports that all that was found in the tomb was a blue sarcophagus containing "the decayed remains of a man, but no treasures, excepting some golden tablets inscribed with characters of a language which nobody could understand." The tablets were used to pay the workmen, and the gold in each of them was worth about two hundred dollars.[4] We leave the reader to speculate on what might have been written on those plates of gold which one of the greatest of Pharaohs apparently regarded as the greatest treasure with which he could be buried.

From an unexpected direction comes new and possibly significant light on the subject of record-plates. Of recent years a considerable number of copper plates, inscribed, perforated, and linked together on metal rings, have turned up in India. We may take as typical (except that they are narrower than most) the Kesaribeda Plates: "The set consists of three copper plates strung together on a copper ring. . . . The circumference and diameter of the ring are about 7.4 [inches] and 2 [inches] respectively. . . . The plates measure roughly 7.5 [inches] in length and [one-fifth of an inch] in breadth each. The corners are rounded off. . . . The plates contain to their proper right hand a hole having a diameter of 1/5 [inch] for the ring to pass through." All plates are written on both sides.[5] The date of these plates is about 324 A.D. The contents, a charter of royalty, state the conditions under which the land shall be governed.

Farther east, but still within the sphere of Indian culture, inscribed plates of the same type, but which no one can read anymore, are handed down "from father to son" as ancient charms of supernatural origin,[6] showing how the idea of authority and sacredness clings to the plates long after men have lost the ability to read them. Among the Karens, such a plate, formed of two kinds of plates welded together back to back, the one of copper and the other apparently of gold, was actually "the talisman by which the chief held his power over the people,"[7] which means that the right to rule the land was attendant upon the possession of these plates—possibly because the plates actually were originally a royal charter.

Now Hither India seems to be far removed indeed from the cultural world of Lehi, yet the ancient and modern writing of the area was actually derived from Aramaic and Phoenician forms, taken ultimately from the Egyptian.[8] Since the oldest writing known in India (not counting the prehistoric glyphs of Mohenjo-Daro, etc.) is that found on the plates, it is at least probable that the writing and the plates were introduced at the same time, and that the people who introduced the Semitic letters into the area kept their records on plates bound together with rings, the form being preserved by the Indians themselves in their oldest and most sacred records. The case of the Karens is particularly interesting because those people have displayed such astonishing cultural affinities with the Jews that some observers have even claimed them to be of Jewish origin.[9] If that is so, their history may have paralleled Lehi's in more ways than one. Many chapters of the Diaspora remain to be written. But what we want to point out here is that the knowledge and use of metal plates for the keeping of important records is beginning to emerge as a general practice throughout the ancient world. It will not be long before men forget that in Joseph Smith's day the prophet was mocked and derided for his description of the plates more than anything else.

Nephi was much impressed by Laban's sword: "The hilt thereof was of pure gold, and the workmanship thereof was exceedingly fine, and . . . the blade thereof was of the most precious steel"(1 Nephi 4:9). Such ceremonial swords and daggers with hilts of finely worked gold have been common in the Near East throughout historic times. Many exemplars from Egypt and Babylonia repose in our museums,[10] but none is more famous or more beautiful than the fine steel dagger with its hilt of pure gold and finest workmanship, that was found on the person of the youthful King Tutankhamen.[11] It has even been suggested that this dagger was one of those two sent many years before by King Dushratta of the Mitanni to the then reigning Pharaoh as the most royal of gifts and described in a contemporary document as having hilts of gold and blades of steel.[12] Nephi's term "precious steel" is interesting, for in his day real steel was far more precious than gold, being made possibly of meteoric iron and of superlative quality. The famous Damascus blades, of the finest steel the world has ever seen, were always made of meteoric iron, according to Jacob—an indication of very ancient origin.[13] Even in modern Palestine swords and daggers have been "mostly of Damascus or Egyptian manufacture."[14] No Arab prince to this day is ever seen in native dress without his *khanjar,* the long curved dagger of Damascus steel with its gorgeous hilt of gold. These ceremonial weapons are often heirlooms of great antiquity and immense value. At any time from the Amarna period (15th century B.C.) to the present, then, Laban would be required by the etiquette of the aristocratic East to carry just such a weapon as Nephi describes.

The End of the Desert

In desert travel, the experts tell us, one day is depressingly like another. For thousands of years the language of the desert has remained virtually unchanged, employing the same words and expressions without alteration from century to century, because the things they describe have never changed. With perfect right Margoliouth uses the epic of the Banī Hilāl to illustrate the migrations of the Children of Israel, thousands of years before them: "They do not migrate haphazardly" but send out scouts, and before making any move they are careful to determine the will of heaven by "various omens and auguries." That is just as true of Lehi's people, with their young men ceaselessly scouting and hunting. As to learning the will of heaven, what better device than the marvelous Liahona? The name suggests so many possible Hebrew and Egyptian interpretations (it is, "being interpreted, a compass," Alma 37:38) that one man's guess is as good as another's, and it does not concern us here since, as a miraculous thing, it has no parallel in everyday life. Such a parallel may easily be found on the other hand to Nephi's comment on the marvelous way in which the women seemed to thrive on the hard Bedouin way of life (1 Nephi 17:2), for this phenomenon has always impressed visitors among the Arabs, where, says Burton, "between the extremes of fierceness and sensibility, the weaker sex, remedying its great want, power, raises itself by courage, physical as well as moral."[15]

There is no reason for Nephi to give us in his greatly abbreviated history a day-by-day account of a long and monotonous journey through the sands; he has given us a clear general picture, as we have seen, of the ill temper, the exhaustion, and the danger that make up the common tale of desert travel, and there is little more to tell than that. But he cannot conceal the excitement and delight of the journey's end.

After traveling a vast distance in a south-southeasterly direction (1 Nephi 16:13, 33), the party struck off almost due eastward through the worst desert of all, where they "did wade through much affliction," to emerge in a state of almost complete exhaustion into a totally unexpected paradise by the sea. There is such a paradise in the Qara Mountains on the southern coast of Arabia. To reach it by moving "nearly eastward" (1 Nephi 17:1) from the Red

Sea coast, one would have to turn east on the nineteenth parallel. In *The Improvement Era* for September 1950 the present writer published a map in which his main concern was to make Lehi reach the sea in the forested sector of the Hadhramaut, and no other consideration dictated his sketching of the map. He foolishly overlooked the fact that Dr. John A. Widtsoe had published in the *Era* some months previously what purports to be a "Revelation to Joseph the Seer," in which it is stated that Lehi's party "traveled nearly a south, southeast direction until they came to the nineteenth degree of north latitude; then nearly east to the sea of Arabia."[16] By an interesting coincidence, the route shown in the author's map turned east exactly at the nineteenth parallel. This correlation of data from two totally different sources is a strong indication that both are correct. The only other possible route would have been down the *western* shore of the Red Sea from Necho's canal, and on such a course one cannot turn eastward until passing the tenth parallel, and then it is not the Arabian Sea that one finds but the Indian Ocean. Along with this, certain other rigorous conditions must be fulfilled which can only be met on the south coast of Arabia.

Of the Qara Mountains which lie in that limited sector of the coast of south Arabia which Lehi *must* have reached if he turned east at the nineteenth parallel, Bertram Thomas, one of the few Europeans who has ever seen them, writes:

> What a glorious place! Mountains three thousand feet high basking above a tropical ocean, their seaward slopes velvety with waving jungle, their roofs fragrant with rolling yellow meadows, beyond which the mountains slope northwards to a red sandstone steppe. . . . Great was my delight when in 1928 I suddenly came upon it all from out of the arid wastes of the southern borderlands.[17]

Captain Thomas (whom Lowell Thomas calls "the

greatest living explorer") goes on to describe the aromatic shrubs of the place, the wooded valleys, "the hazy rim of the distant sea lifted beyond the mountains rolling down to it," and the wondrous beauty of the "sylvan scenes" that opened to the view as he passed down through the lush forests to the sea.[18]

Compare this with Nephi's picture,

> And we did come to the land which we called Bountiful, because of its much fruit and also wild honey. . . . And we beheld the sea . . . and notwithstanding we had suffered many afflictions and much difficulty, yea, even so much that we cannot write them all, we were exceedingly rejoiced when we came to the seashore; and we called the place Bountiful, because of its much fruit. . . . And . . . the voice of the Lord came unto me, saying: Arise and get thee into the mountain (1 Nephi 17:5-7).

It is virtually the same scene: the mountains, the rich woodlands with timber for ships, the rolling yellow meadow a paradise for bees, the view of the sea beyond, and above all the joyful relief at the sudden emergence from the "red sandstone steppe," one of the worst deserts on earth. Thomas, of course, was not interested in finding honey, but for those who must live permanently in the desert there is no greater treasure than a find of honey, as a great number of roots and derivative words in the Arabic vocabulary make clear.[19] Much the same description might suit the mountains of Oman farther east and lying on the twenty-fifth parallel, the discovery of which came as a great surprise in 1838.[20] When in 1843 von Wrede gave a glowing description of the mountains of the Hadramaut to which Lehi came, the great von Humboldt and, following him, of course, the whole learned world, simply refused to believe him.[21] Thomas' delectable mountains were unknown to the west until less than twenty-five years ago. Though "the southern coasts of Arabia have admirable

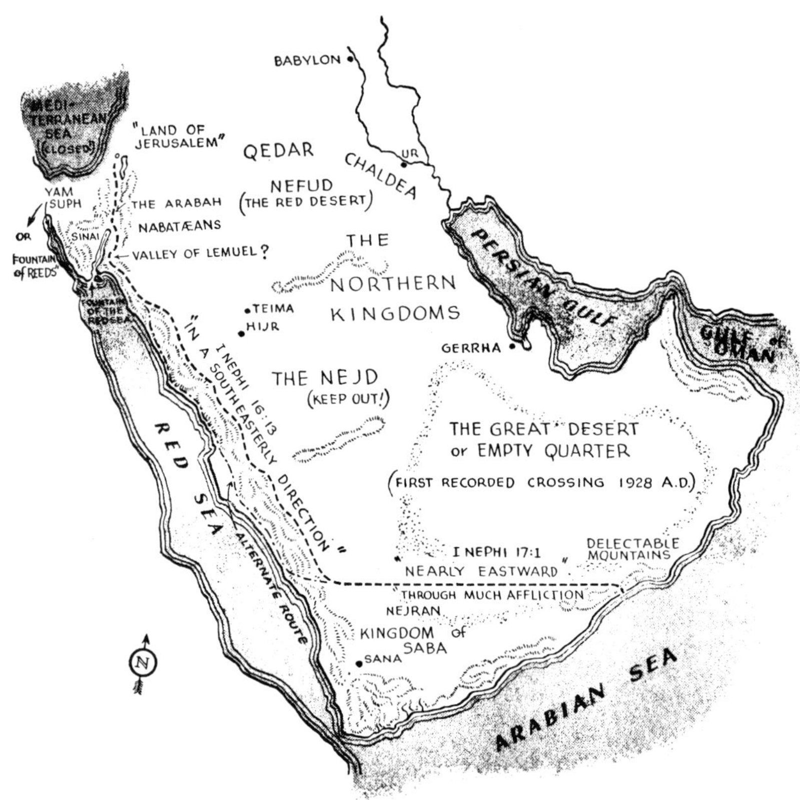

harbors," they appear not to have been used, with a few possible exceptions, until well after the time of Christ.[22]

Watching Lehi's travel-worn band wending its way down the pleasant valleys to the sea, one is moved to reflect that they have come an unconscionably long way just to build a ship. Well, let the reader suggest some other route. The best guide to Arabia at the time of the writing of the Book of Mormon imagined forests and lakes in the center of the peninsula, while insisting that the whole coastline was "a rocky wall . . . as dismal and barren as can be: not a blade of grass or a green thing" to be found.[23] The Book of Mormon reverses the picture and has Lehi avoid the heart of the continent to discover smiling woodlands on the south coast. Where else could he have found his timber on all the coast of Arabia? "It is quite possible," writes a present-day authority, "that Solomon has to transport his ships, or the material for them, from the Mediterranean, for where on the shores of the Red Sea could timber be found for ship-building?"[24]

And by what other route could Lehi have reached his happy shore? To the north lay enemy country, the Mediterranean was a world of closed harbors and closed seas, as dangerous as in the days of Wenamon, who was repeatedly stopped by enemies and pirates, the deserts to the east of Jerusalem swarmed with hostile and warring tribes, north and central Arabia were the classic grazing and fighting grounds of the Arabs, and so crisscrossed with trade routes in the time of Ptolemy "that there appears little left of the inaccessible desert. . . . 'In general Ptolemy knows of no desert.' "[25]

Egypt offered no escape to one marked as an enemy by the pro-Egyptian party. Only one way lay open, the hardest and wildest, through the mountains that border the Red Sea and then due east over the western extension of the terrible "Empty Quarter" where the party saw so much affliction. They had to turn east when they did because the whole southwest corner of the peninsula comprised the kingdom of the Sabaeans, probably the strongest, richest, and most thickly settled state Arabia has ever had.

So, long and painful though it was, Lehi's itinerary turns out to have been actually the shortest and safest, if not the only one he could have taken. On the shore of the Arabian Sea the story of Lehi in the Desert properly ends. Though this time has been but a preliminary telling, still there is enough to justify certain reflections by way of summary.

Lehi on the Witness Stand

We have never been very much interested in "proving" the Book of Mormon; for us its divine provenance has always been an article of faith, and its historical aspects by far the *least* important thing about it. But "the world" insists that it is a gross and stupid forgery, a barefaced fraud perpetrated by an ignorant rustic who could hardly write his name. They have made the charge; let them prove it. That should be a very easy thing to do if they are right, a mere matter of riffling through a few pages and pointing out the swarming errors, since the accused has committed himself in no uncertain terms and at unsparing length. The nature of the document he pretends to be translating is so singular, and the conditions it must fulfil so unique and exacting, that its composer must certainly be convicted at a glance if he is lying. On the other hand, if his writing shows *any tendency at all* to conform to the peculiar conditions prescribed, its critics must be put to a good deal of explaining, and if it shows a *constant tendency* to conform to those difficult conditions, its critics will be bankrupt. We believe that this little study, tentative and limited as it is, nonetheless indicates such a tendency beyond reasonable doubt.

What has been proved? Simply that everything which the book of 1 Nephi says happened really *could* have happened. Not that it *did* happen: to prove that is neither necessary nor possible. Unique events in history can never be reconstructed with certainty; but characteristic related events—manners, customs, rituals, etc., things that happen not just once but again and again in familiar patterns—may be the object of almost absolute certainty. Hence they, and not particular events, are the hardest things to fake; in testing forgeries and identifying documents it is the general pattern that is all-important. This principle is well illustrated in Cheesman's criticism of Palgrave. Though the latter's descriptions of Hufhuf are so full of "sheer inaccuracy" and "blazing indiscretion" as to appear almost pure fabrications, and though "Palgrave's map of Hufhuf is so full of inaccuracies that I have not been able even to orient it," Cheesman nonetheless concludes that "The picture Palgrave painted of Hufhuf, its gardens, its archways, and its industries and people, . . . could only have been composed by an eyewitness." With all its imperfections the general picture presents objects that would not have been mentioned if they had not been seen. "It is only too easy," writes the same author, "however careful one may be, to fall into little inaccuracies in an endeavor to put color into one's description of a country, and it is easier still, as I found, to come behind and point out the shortcomings of a predecessor."[26] This is a powerful argument in favor of the sober and detailed account of Nephi, whose mistakes of detail we could pardon if we could discover them. In talking about Lehi in the Desert we have, as it were, put the old patriarch on the stand as a witness in the case of Joseph Smith versus the World. Smith has been accused (and how!) of fraudulent practices, and Lehi is a witness for the defense. He claims to have spent years in certain parts of the Near East about 2550 years ago. Is he telling the truth?

Generations of shrewd and determined prosecutors have failed to shake Lehi's testimony or catch him contradicting himself. That should be enough to satisfy the most critical. But now, behold, out of the East come new witnesses—Captain Hoshaiah of Lachish and a host of sunburned explorers returned from Lehi's deserts to tell us what life there is like; the ancient poets of the Arabs, crates and crates of exhibits A to Z, seals, inscriptions, letters, artifacts from Lehi's own homeland. Whoever dreamed that Lehi would one day be confronted with eyewitnesses to the very scenes he claims he saw? In the light of all this new evidence, the defense asks that the case be reopened.

So Lehi and the new-found witnesses are cross-examined together and their answers compared. The questions come thick and fast: What is your name? Don't you know there is no such personal name? (A shard is produced from Lehi's time and it bears the name *Lehi,* not an uncommon one.) Where did you live at the time? What do you mean, "the land of Jerusalem"? Don't you mean the city? (Defense produces an ancient letter showing that the territory around the city was all known as the land of Jerusalem.) Who governed Jerusalem? What kind of men were they? What did you do to turn them against you? Where did you get this great wealth your son talks about? How did you happen to learn Egyptian—wasn't that a waste of time? Why didn't you learn Babylonian, a language much nearer to your own? What was all the trouble about in your family? I have quite a list of names here—your purported family and descendants: Do you expect the court to believe these are genuine? If this is a genuine list, why does it contain no *Baal* names? You say you had dreams: about what? A river? What kind of river? What is this weird "mist of darkness"? Did you ever see anything like it when you were awake? (Dozens of witnesses testify.) Don't you think a dream is pretty slim pretext for leaving your home and country? In which direction did you flee? How could you build up a big caravan without being apprehended? What did you take with you? How did you travel—on foot? How did you manage to survive with women and children in a terrible desert? How did you escape being killed off by raiders? Don't you know that desert was very dangerous? What did you eat? Did you march continually? When you camped, what was the first thing you did? What kind of altar? What sort of game did you hunt? Where? How? Who did the hunting? Your son made a bow, you say; where in desolate Arabia could he find wood for that? What right had you to go around giving new names to places? Do you think any sane person would give a river and its valley different names? (Roar of protest from Arabs in the audience.) Whoever called the Red Sea a fountain? Don't you know there are no rivers in Arabia? This little speech you gave your sons on the river bank—isn't it a bit overdone? (More protest from the Bedouins.) Don't you think it rather silly to describe a valley as "firm and steadfast"? Where did your sons stay when they went back to Jerusalem? What about this cave? Aren't metal plates rather clumsy writing material to keep records on? Aren't fifty men a ridiculously small garrison for a city like Jerusalem? You describe nocturnal meetings between the elders and the commandant: Wouldn't it be much more sensible to hold meetings in the daytime? Do you want the court to believe that you actually carried grain with you on this long and exhausting journey? Are you trying to tell the court that you found a paradise on the southernmost rim of the most desolate land on earth?

And so on, and so on. The reader may add to the list of searching questions at will—there are well over a hundred possibilities indicated in our study, and most of them such questions as *no one on earth* could have answered correctly 120 years ago. The writer of 1 Nephi was confronted by a hundred delicately interrelated problems of extreme difficulty. The probability of coming up with a plausible statement by mere guesswork once or twice is dim enough, but the chances of repeating the performance a hundred times in rapid succession are infinitely remote. The world through which Lehi wandered was to the westerner of 1830 a quaking bog without a visible inch of footing, lost in impenetrable fog; the best Bible students were hopelessly misinformed even about Palestine. Scientific study of the Holy Land began with Edward Robinson in 1838, yet forty years later a leading authority writes: "Few countries are more traveled in than Palestine; and in few are the manners and customs of the people less known."[27] The official statement of the Palestine Exploration Fund ten years later was, "There is scarcely anything definite known about [the desert of the Wandering]."[28] The Bible itself, instead of clearing up problems, is the main cause for the "great discrepancies" in the reports of observers, according to Palmer.[29] The classic example of this is Dr. H. Clay Turnbull's *Kadesh Barnea*, recommended by high authorities in 1884 as the standard work on the south desert and "accepted by biblical geographers as the authority on the district," right down to our own day, when Woolley and Lawrence explored the area and discovered that this infallible guidebook was simply "fantastic."[30] As to Clarke's work on the same region, published a year after Trumbull's, the same critics content themselves with remarking: "We will not print comments on this."[31] As late as 1935 Colonel Newcombe could write: "I had several books on the subject of the Wanderings, but nearly all were written by idealistic but very inexperienced visitors. . . . Most of these books had entirely missed the truth from lack of knowledge of the country or understanding of the Beduin mind. Each seemed to exaggerate grossly his own little theory at the expense of any one else's."[32] So let no one suppose that access to the Bible would have made easy the task of composing the story of Lehi—it would only have complicated matters. Yet we find our guide confident and sure-footed, never retracing his steps to change his course, never hesitating a moment or seeking refuge in noncommittal vaporings, never begging to be excused or falling back on the old appeal to be understood in a "religious" sense only, never moving behind a smoke screen or becoming consciously or unconsciously confusing or involved.

Some Simple Tests

The present treatment of the Lehi story leaves much to be desired (*we* can afford to crave the reader's indulgence for using the term *Jew* too loosely or engaging in rather fuzzy speculation on language), but if only a fraction of our information has been sound, 1 Nephi cannot possibly be explained on the grounds of mere coincidence. To illustrate this, let the reader make a simple test. Let him sit down to write a history of life, let us say, in Tibet in the middle of the eleventh century A.D. Let him construct his story wholly on the basis of what he happens to know right now about Tibet in the eleventh century—that will fairly represent what was known about ancient Arabia in 1830, i.e., that there was such a place and that it was very mysterious and romantic. In composing your Tibetan fantasy you will enjoy one great advantage: since the canvas is an absolute blank, you are free to fill it with anything that strikes your fancy. So you should have no trouble in getting "smoothly launched into your narrative"—which Mrs. Brodie seems to think was the only obstacle confronting the author of the Book of Mormon. But there will be other obstacles, for in your chronicle of old Tibet we must insist that you scrupulously observe a number of annoying conditions: (1) you must never make any absurd, impossible or contradictory statement; (2) when you are finished, you must make no changes in the text—the first edition must stand forever; (3) you must give out that your "smooth narrative" is not fiction but true, nay, sacred history; (4) you must invite the ablest orientalists to examine the text with care, and strive diligently to see that your book gets into the hands of all those most eager and most competent to expose every flaw in it. The "author" of the Book of Mormon observes all these terrifying rules most scrupulously.

In your Tibetan epic you might get something right by happy accident once in a while but don't expect it. You may console yourself by turning to any good historical novel dealing with the ancient world and marking with a red pencil every anachronism, incongruity, and inaccuracy in the book. The result is carnage, but be merciful! To realize what difficulties confront the creative historian, one has but to contemplate the laborious production of the Book of Mormon's latest critics. It was all too easy for the present author, lacking the unfair advantage of either wit or learning, to show where Mrs. Brodie in composing a history of events but a hundred years old contradicted *herself* again and again.[33]

A Victor Hugo or an Anatole France can tell a convincing story when he is near to his own land and time, but let any writer, even the most learned, slip back a couple of thousand years and a few thousand miles around the globe, and he finds himself in a treacherous terrain from which the only escape lies in taking to the wings of fantasy. It is not particular details so much as the general background and atmosphere of their stories that oblige Messrs. White and Douglas to wink knowingly and tell us it's all in fun. Any handbook of Greek or Roman antiquities can supply a writer with all the accurate detail he can possibly use, but no writer yet has succeeded in integrating a mass of such stuff into a simple, natural, and flawless whole. Thornton Wilder and Naomi Mitchison neatly avoid the pitfalls of historical reconstruction by concentrating on such timeless things as mountains, seas, and human emotions, and so make their tales convincing. But Nephi enjoys no such artistic luxuries or immunities; it is history he is writing, and he imparts his information in such simple, effortless, and matter-of-fact discourse that the reader easily overlooks the vast amount of detail that is woven into the natural and uncomplicated pattern. What writer of historical fiction has ever remotely approached such an achievement?

But haven't we been decidedly partial in dealing with Lehi? Of course we have. We are the counsel for the defense. Our witnesses have all been of our own choosing, but no one can deny that they are competent and unprejudiced. We invited the prosecution to examine them. To date they have not done so, but instead have brought their own witnesses into court, up-to-date intellectuals who can tell us just exactly what the accused was *thinking* when he wrote the Book of Mormon. Such evidence is not evidence at all—it is bad science, bad history, and even bad newspaper reporting and would be rejected by any court in the land. But it might impress the half-educated jury, and that is its purpose. We can best explain the new trend in Book of Mormon criticism by a little parable.

A young man once long ago claimed he had found a large diamond in his field as he was ploughing. He put the stone on display to the public free of charge, and everyone took sides. A psychologist showed, by citing some famous case studies, that the young man was suffering from a well-known form of delusion. An historian showed that other men have also claimed to have found diamonds in fields and been deceived. A geologist proved that there were no diamonds in the area but only quartz: the young man had been fooled by a quartz. When asked to inspect the stone itself, the geologist declined with a weary, tolerant smile and a kindly shake of the head. An English professor showed that the young man in describing his stone used the very same language that others had used in describing uncut diamonds: he was, therefore, simply speaking the common language of his time. A sociologist showed that only three out of 177 florists' assistants in four major cities believed the stone was genuine. A clergyman wrote a book to show that it was not the young man but someone else who had found the stone.

Finally an indigent jeweler named Snite pointed out that since the stone was still available for examination the answer to the question of whether it was a diamond or not had absolutely nothing to do with who found it, or whether the finder was honest or sane, or who believed him, or whether he would know a diamond from a brick, or whether diamonds had ever been found in fields, or whether people had ever been fooled by quartz or glass, but was to be answered simply and solely by putting the stone to certain well-known tests for diamonds. Experts on diamonds were called in. Some of them declared it genuine. The others made nervous jokes about it and declared that they could not very well jeopardize their dignity and reputations by appearing to take the thing too seriously. To hide the bad impression thus made, someone came out with the theory that the stone was really a synthetic diamond, very skilfully made, but a fake just the same. The objection to this is that the production of a good synthetic diamond 120 years ago would have been an even more remarkable feat than the finding of a real one.

The moral of this story is that the testimony brought out by the prosecution, however learned, has been to date entirely irrelevant and immaterial. It is hardly necessary to observe that it is also incompetent, since it is highly argumentative and based entirely on conclusions of the witnesses, who have furthermore already made up their minds, on other grounds, that the accused is guilty.

Another thing, the prosecution must prove their case to the hilt: it is not enough to show, even if they could, that there are mistakes in the Book of Mormon, for all humans make mistakes; what they must explain is how the "author" of the book happened to get so many things right. Eighty-odd years of zealous searching by the Palestine Exploration Fund have brought to light little or nothing proving the Exodus; to this day "of the story of . . . Saul, David, Solomon, or even of their existence, there is no trace whatever outside of Palestine." Yet this shortage of evidence by no means disproves the Bible. We should not have been disappointed or surprised to find all the records completely silent on matters relevant to the Book of Mormon; yet they have been far from that. If a man makes a mistake in solving a very complex mathematical problem, that proves nothing as to his ability as a mathematician, for the greatest make slips. But if he shows a correct solution for the problem, it is impossible to explain away his success as an accident, and we must recognize him, whoever he is, as a bona fide mathematician. So it is with the author of 1 Nephi: If we could find mistakes in his work, we could readily explain and forgive them, but when he keeps coming up with the right answer time after time, we can only accept his own explanation of how he does it.

One significant aspect of the story of Lehi in the Desert must not be overlooked. It is wholly, from beginning to end, a history of the Old World. There is in it not so much as a hint of the "Noble Red Man." Nothing in it ever betrays the slightest suspicion that the drama is going to end in the New World. Lehi's people thought they had found their promised land in Bountiful by the sea and were horribly upset when Nephi, who himself had thought the project impossible (1 Nephi 17:8-9), undertook by special instruction to build a ship.

From what oriental romance, then, was the book of 1 Nephi stolen? Compare it with any attempts to seize the letter and the spirit of the glamorous East, from Voltaire to Grillparzer, nay, with the soberest oriental histories of the time, and it will immediately become apparent how unreal, extravagant, overdone, and stereotyped they all are, and how scrupulously Nephi has avoided all the pitfalls into which even the best scholars were sure to fall. There is no point at all to the question: Who wrote the Book of Mormon? It would have been quite as impossible for the most learned man alive in 1830 to have written the book as it was for Joseph Smith. And whoever would account for the Book of Mormon by any theory suggested so far—save one—must completely rule out the first forty pages.

Notes

Chapter 1: The Troubled Orient

1. William F. Albright, *Archaeology and the Religion of Israel* (Baltimore: Johns Hopkins University Press, 1942), 62.

2. Ibid., 63.

3. Jens D. C. Lieblein, *Handel und Schiffahrt auf dem rothen Meere in alten Zeiten* (Leipzig: Christiania, 1886; reprinted Amsterdam: Meridian, 1971), 8.

4. Albright, *Archaeology and the Religion of Israel,* 63.

5. Henry G. Tomkins, "Egyptology and the Bible," *PEFQ* (1884), 54.

6. "Though archaeological research goes back over a century in Palestine and Syria, it is only since 1920 that our material has become sufficiently extensive and clearly enough interpreted to be of really decisive value." Albright, *Archaeology and the Religion of Israel,* 37.

7. J. W. Jack, "The Lachish Letters—Their Date and Import," *PEFQ* (1938), 165.

8. On his conversations with Arabs, Nibley noted in his original version of "Lehi in the Desert," published as a series in the *Improvement Era,* that "the author has consulted extensively with modern Arabs, Syrians, Iraqians, Lebanese, Egyptians, etc., and after fifteen years of searching is ready to declare Mr. Mose Kader of Provo, Utah, a true Bedouin. The same adventurous spirit that brought this remarkable man to settle on a solitary farm near the mouth of Rock Canyon drove him from his father's farm near Jerusalem in his youth, to spend many years with the Bedouins of the desert; and the same tenacious conservatism that has enabled him to rear a family as strict Moslems a thousand miles from any other Moslems has kept fresh his memory of days in the desert in the olden times before World War I. On fine points he is a marvelous informant." Hugh W. Nibley, "Lehi in the Desert," *IE* 53 (1950): 15. Nibley further noted that "in 1932 Mr. Kader returned to Palestine to get himself a wife. Though she has not, like her husband, traveled in the desert, Mrs. Kader's knowledge of the customs of Palestine is encyclopedic, and she has the uncanny memory of one who has never been handicapped with a knowledge of reading and writing," ibid., 70, n. 8.

9. J. A. Knudtzon, *Die El-Amarna-Tafeln* (Leipzig: Hinrich, 1915; reprinted Aalen: Zeller, 1964) 1:864-67, 872-77, tablets 287 and 289; for Bet-Ninib, ibid., 1:876-77, tablet 290, lines 15-16.

10. See Albrecht Alt, "Die syrische Staatenwelt vor dem Einbruch der

Assyrer," *ZDMG* 88 (1934): 247; and Wilhelm Nowack, *Lehrbuch der hebräischen Archäologie* (Freiburg i/B: Mohr, 1894), 149.

11. The parallel development of Athens embracing many small communities is described by Georg Busolt, Adolf Bauer & Iwan Müller, *Die griechischen Staats-, Kriegs-, und Privataltertürmer* (Nördlingen: Beck, 1887), 106-7.

12. "To go down" in the Book of Mormon means to travel away from Jerusalem (1 Nephi 4:33-35), while "to go up to the land" is to return to Jerusalem (1 Nephi 3:9, 7:15). The Egyptian word *ha,* "to go down," when applied to travel means "to go to Egypt." Adolf Erman & Hermann Grapow, *Wörterbuch der Aegyptischen Sprache,* 5 vols. (Leipzig: Hinrich, 1929), 2:472. So in the Old Testament he "went down into Egypt" (Genesis 12:10), and "up to Jerusalem . . . up out of the land of Egypt" (1 Kings 12:28). In the Lachish letters, "Down went the commander . . . to Egypt." Harry Torczyner, *The Lachish Letters* (London: Oxford University Press, 1938), 1:51 (letter 3). The elevation of Jerusalem was well appreciated by the Jews, as was the lowness of Egypt, and this fact lies behind the use of these expressions, always correct in the Book of Mormon. On the other hand, in the Book of Mormon one simply goes "unto" a house within the city (1 Nephi 3:4, 11), so that when the brothers "went down to the land of our inheritance . . . and after . . . went up again unto the house of Laban" (1 Nephi 3: 22-23), it is perfectly clear that their property included land as well as a house and necessarily lay outside the city, as the terms "down" and "up" attest.

13. Nowack, *Lehrbuch der hebräischen Archäologie,* 300-4. Quote is on 304.

14. Jack, "The Lachish Letters—Their Date and Import," 175-77. Cf. William F. Albright, "A Brief History of Judah from the Days of Josiah to Alexander the Great," *BA* 9 (February 1946): 4.

15. Jack, "The Lachish Letters—Their Date and Import," 175-77.

16. For a recent summary of the international situation around 600 B.C., besides the studies cited, see John Bright, "A New Letter in Aramaic, Written to a Pharaoh of Egypt," *BA* 12 (February 1949): 46-52.

17. James H. Breasted, *A History of Egypt,* 2nd ed. (New York: Scribner, 1951), 577. "The artists no longer work only for the court and the temples; they had now to fill orders for for a wealthy bourgeoisie." Alexandre Moret, *Histoire de l'Orient* (Paris: Presses Universitaires, 1941), 2:728.

18. Albright, *Archaeology and the Religion of Israel,* 69; Eduard Meyer, *Geschichte des Altertums,* 2nd ed. (Stuttgart: Cotta, 1928), vol. 2, pt. 1, p. 98.

19. Meyer, *Geschichte des Altertums* (Stuttgart: Cotta, 1909), vol. 1, pt. 2, p. 260; (1928) vol. 2, pt. 1, pp. 98, 135. The "prince kings" of Tyre and Sidon "accumulated great wealth and could afford the benefits of

Egyptian culture," in their business of transporting the goods of the princes of Syria and Palestine, whose "figs, wine, honey, oil, fruit trees, corn and cattle," were the source of their wealth. George Steindorff, *Egypt* (New York: Augustin, 1943), 64. For the economy of the great Palestine estates, see Philip J. Baldensperger, "The Immovable East," *PEFQ* (1908), 290-98, and (1918), 121.

20. Jack, "The Lachish Letters—Their Date and Import," 177.

21. Albright, "A Brief History of Judah from the Days of Josiah to Alexander the Great," 6.

22. Ibid.

23. Ibid.

24. William F. Albright, "The Seal of Eliakim and the Latest Preexilic History of Judah, With Some Observations on Ezekiel," *JBL* 51 (1932): 93-95.

25. Jack, "The Lachish Letters—Their Date and Import," 178.

26. The theory of D. L. Risdon as discussed by Arthur Keith, "The Men of Lachish," *PEFQ* (1940), 7-12.

27. James L. Starkey, "Lachish as Illustrating Bible History," *PEFQ* (1937), 177-78; Alan Rowe, "Excavations at Beisan During the 1927 Season," *PEFQ* (1928), 73-90; Richard D. Barnett, "Phoenician and Syrian Ivory Carving," *PEFQ* (1939), 4-5, 7; J. W. Crowfoot and Grace M. Crowfoot, "The Ivories from Samaria," *PEFQ* (1933), 7, 18, 21; Charles C. Torrey, "A Hebrew Seal from the Reign of Ahaz," *BASOR* 79 (October 1940): 27-28; Bright, "A New Letter in Aramaic, Written to a Pharaoh of Egypt," 46-48; H. Louis Ginsberg, "An Aramaic Contemporary of the Lachish Letters," *BASOR* 3 (October 1948): 24-27.

28. Abraham S. Yahuda, *The Accuracy of the Bible* (London: Heinemann, 1934), xxix; Stephen L. Caiger, *Bible and Spade* (London: Oxford University Press, 1936), 83-84, 91-92. Since the days of the Pan-Babylonian school, "the pendulum of theory of origins has . . . swung westwards to Egypt." James A. Montgomery, *Arabia and the Bible* (Philadelphia: University of Pennsylvania Press, 1934), 1.

29. Archibald H. Sayce, "The Jerusalem Sealings on Jar Handles," *PEFQ* (1927), 216; J. Garrow Duncan, "Fifth Quarterly Report on the Excavation of the Eastern Hill of Jerusalem," *PEFQ* (1925), 18-20.

30. "Already in the days of the kings of Egypt their fathers had built that temple in Yeb." Arthur E. Cowley, *Aramaic Papyri of the Fifth Century B.C.* (Oxford: Clarendon, 1923), 120. These papyri "have shed undreamed light on some of the darkest areas of Jewish history," says Albright, *Archaeology and the Religion of Israel,* 41.

31. Yahuda, *The Accuracy of the Bible,* xxix-xxx; see especially by the same author, *The Language of the Pentateuch in its Relation to Egypt* (London: Oxford University Press, 1933), 1:xxxii-xxxv.

32. William F. Albright, "The Egyptian Empire in Asia in the Twenty-first Century B.C.," *JPOS* 8 (1928): 226-30; cf. William F. Albright, "Palestine in the Earliest Historical Period," *JPOS* 2 (1922): 110-38.

33. David G. Hogarth, "Egyptian Empire in Asia," *JEA* 1 (1914): 9-12.

34. Breasted, *A History of Egypt*, 516, 518, 526, 529, 580; Harry R. H. Hall, "The Eclipse of Egypt," and "The Restoration of Egypt," *Cambridge Ancient History* (New York: Macmillan, 1925) 3:256-57, 261, 295-99.

35. Hogarth, "Egyptian Empire in Asia," 13-14. Even the Davidic state owed its administrative organization largely to Egyptian models." Albright, *Archaeology and the Religion of Israel*, 108; the same writer discussed the weakness of Egypt in the later period in "Egypt and the Early History of the Negeb," *JPOS* 4 (1924): 144-46.

36. For the first quotation, Henri Frankfort, "Egypt and Syria in the First Intermediate Period," *JEA* 12 (1926): 96; for the second, Moret, *Histoire de l'Orient* 2:787.

37. Meyer, *Geschichte des Altertums*, vol. 2, pt. 1, pp. 132-33; Hogarth, "Egyptian Empire in Asia," 12.

38. Jack, "The Lachish Letters—Their Date and Import," 177.

39. Meyer, *Geschichte des Altertums*, vol. 1, pt. 2, pp. 297-99; Meyer notes that variants *Ja'bqhr* and *Ja'pqhr* and others also appear. He associates these names with the god Ja'qob. See especially, William F. Albright, *Vocalization of the Egyptian Syllabic Orthography* (New Haven: American Oriental Society, 1934).

40. Abraham S. Yahuda, *The Language of the Pentateuch in Its Relation to Egypt* (London: Oxford University Press, 1933), 51.

41. E. A. Wallis Budge, *Papyrus of Ani* (New York: Putnam, 1913) 1:50.

42. Theodor Nöldeke, *Die semitischen Sprachen* (Leipzig: Tauchnitz, 1899), 34.

43. Torczyner, *The Lachish Letters*, 15.

44. Raymond O. Faulkner, "The Bremner-Rhind Papyrus," *JEA* 23 (1937): 10; Elias J. Bickerman, "The Colophon of the Greek Book of Esther," *JBL* 63 (1944): 339-62, shows that the tradition of the colophon was carefully preserved in Egypt; Francis L. Griffith, "The Teaching of Amenophis the Son of Kanakht, Papyrus B.M. 10474," *JEA* 12 (1926): 195.

45. The formula *iw-f-pw* concludes the Story of Sinuhe and the Maxims of the Sages Ptahotep and Kagemeni. Kurt Sethe, *Aegyptische Lesestücke* (Leipzig: Hinrich, 1924), 17, 42, 43, and *Erläuterungen zu den Aegyptischen Lesestücken* (Leipzig: Hinrich, 1927), 21, 58, 61. "That is its end" concludes the Teaching of Amenophis. Griffith, "The Teaching of Amenophis the Son of Kanakht, Papyrus B.M. 10474," 225.

46. Alan H. Gardiner, "New Literary Works from Ancient Egypt," *JEA* 1 (1914): 25; the work quoted here had Palestine connections, ibid., 30.

47. Meyer, *Geschichte des Altertums,* vol. 1, pt. 2, p. 176.

48. The Teaching of Amenophis is addressed: "For his son, the youngest of his children, little compared to his relations." Then follows a long text presenting a number of surprising parallels to the book of Proverbs and a remarkable one to Psalms 1, the righteous man being compared to a fruitful tree. Griffith, "The Teaching of Amenophis the Son of Kanakht, Papyrus B.M. 10474," 197. Compare this with 2 Nephi 2 and 3. Lehi's description of fruit as "white" (1 Nephi 8:11) is a typical Egyptianism. See Erman & Grapow, *Wörterbuch der Aegyptischen Sprache* 3:206-7, 211-12.

49. Meyer, *Geschichte des Altertums,* vol. 1, pt. 2, p. 274; Albright, *Archaeology and the Religion of Israel,* 21; David C. Simpson, "The Hebrew Book of Proverbs and the Teaching of Amenophis," *JEA* 12 (1926): 232.

50. August von Gall, *Basileia tou Theou* (Heidelberg: Winter, 1926), 65-68.

51. Ibid., 49-55.

52. The following comparisons between the Book of Mormon and ancient Egypt first appeared in Hugh W. Nibley, "The Book of Mormon as a Mirror of the East," *IE* 51 (April 1948): 202-4 , 249-51; reprinted *IE* 73 (November 1970): 15-20, 122-25. That article began with this introduction: " 'The average man,' wrote the great A. E. Housman, 'believes that the text of ancient authors is generally sound, not because he has acquainted himself with the elements of the problem, but because he would feel uncomfortable if he did not believe it.' The Book of Mormon has enjoyed no such popular support. Indeed, the 'average man' would like nothing better than to see it thoroughly exposed once and for all; it has made him feel uncomfortable for over a century. What is holding up the show? For one thing, the Book of Mormon is immune to attack from the West. No matter how much archaeological evidence may pile up one way or the other, the fact remains that the Book of Mormon never claims to be telling the story of all the people who ever lived in the western hemisphere. Even within its own limited compass it is, as Professor Sidney B. Sperry has shown, for the greater part 'a minority report' and does not deal with various branches of several groups that came from the Old World. Thus, where research in America may conceivably bring forth a wealth of evidence to support the Book of Mormon, no findings can be taken as unequivocal evidence against it. It is a far different story when our book presumes to invade the soil of the East, giving specific names, places, and dates. Here any imposter of the 1820s would be on dangerous ground indeed. No better handle could be asked

for unsparing and rigorous criticism than the outright commitments of the Book of Mormon on matters Egyptian. By harping on the peculiar neo-Egyptian language of the Nephites, by furnishing a list of their personal and place names, by pretending to describe political conflicts originating in the Old World, the author of the Book of Mormon plays right into the hands of modern critics. For the Near East of 600 B.C. is no longer the twilight zone of gorgeous mysteries it was in the days of Joseph Smith. Any fabrication by him or even his most learned contemporary would necessarily appear today as a mass of blunders in which some accidental resemblance of truth might be detected once, but hardly twice. Does the author or translator of the book display any knowledge concerning that part of the world in which it claims to have had its origin? That is the question. By way of answer—a mere opening edge as it were—we shall briefly discuss a few short years in Book of Mormon history, that stormy time during which the system of rule by judges passed through some of those severe tests which finally proved its undoing. We shall match the story step by step with a number of Old World parallels, and after a few general observations let the reader decide for himself just what significance should be attributed to these parallels."

53. Hall, "The Eclipse of Egypt," 268.

54. Budge calls it *Heriher* in his 1925 edition of *The Mummy* as against his earlier reading *Her-Heru* in his 1893 edition. See E. A. Wallis Budge, *The Mummy* (London: Cambridge University Press, 1925), 103, and *The Mummy* (London: Cambridge University Press, 1893), 52. It is read *Hurhor* in *ZASA* 20 (1882): 149B, Plate II, Fig. V.7A; *Her-Hor* by Alfred Wiedemann, "Beiträge zur Ägyptischen Geschichte" *ZASA* 23 (1885): 83 ; and *Hrihor* by Breasted, *A History of Egypt* (New York: Scribner, 1912), 513, 519-21. We are following the most recent study, that of Moret, who calls it *Herihor*. Moret, *Histoire de l'Orient* 2:591.

55. Moret, *Histoire de l'Orient* 2:569.

56. Herbert E. Winlock, "The Eleventh Egyptian Dynasty," *JNES* 2 (1942): 256, 266.

57. Ibid., 266.

58. Moret, *Histoire de l'Orient* 2:518.

59. On the alternate readings Ammon-Amon, see Alan H. Gardiner, *Egyptian Grammar* (London: Oxford University Press, 1950), 435.

60. Moret, *Histoire de l'Orient* 1:437-39, 2:567-69; see generally, Walter Wolf, "Vorläufer der Reformation Echnatons," *ZASA* 59 (1924) : 109-19; Hans Bonnet, "Zum Verständnis des Synkretismus," *ZASA* 75 (1939): 45-46.

61. Winlock, "The Eleventh Egyptian Dynasty," 250; Moret, *Histoire de l'Orient* 1:209, 436-38.

62. The original magazine version of this material included the fol-

lowing elaboration: "This colony at Elphantine may have been very ancient, since according to Egyptian records it had been the custom of the people of Palestine and Syria from time immemorial to seek refuge in Egypt and settle in such communities. It is conceded, at any rate, that the colony is a good deal older than the Hebrew records which came from it in the fifth century B.C.; possibly it dates from the middle of the seventh century. James H. Breasted, *Ancient Records of Egypt* (Chicago: University of Chicago Press, 1906) 3:27. Harry R. H. Hall, *Cambridge Ancient History* (New York: Macmillan, 1925) 3:294. This would make it old in the time of Lehi and furnish a possible explanation for the strange tendency of Book of Mormon names to be concentrated in Upper Egypt."

63. For a striking parallel to the Book of Mormon account, see Hall, "The Eclipse of Egypt," 254.

64. Knudtzon, *Die El-Amarna-Tafeln* 1:528-29, tablet 122; 1:562-63, tablet 132; notes in 2:1222, and index in 2:1566.

65. Lists of priest-kings are reproduced in *ZASA* 20 (1882): 149B, plate II, fig. V. 7A.

66. Harry R. H. Hall, "The Ethiopians and Assyrians in Egypt," *Cambridge Ancient History* (New York: Macmillan, 1925) 3:273.

67. Wilhelm Spiegelberg, "Der Stratege Pamenches," *ZASA* 57 (1922): 88-92. Compare the Amarna name *Pa-kha-am-na-ta,* in Knudtzon, *Die El-Amarna-Tafeln* 2:1566, governor of Amurru under Egypt.

68. At this point in the magazine version, the following additional information was given: "For the Egyptian chief priests Pachom, Pamenchi, Pakybis, and Panaš (Spiegelberg, "Der Stratege Pamenches," 91), we have no Book of Mormon parallel, but from the Nephite list we must not omit the name of Pachus, since, though I have not found it in the limited documents at my disposal, it is perfectly good Egyptian (meaning 'he—Amon—is praised'), both elements occurring frequently in Egyptian proper names. Winlock, "The Eleventh Egyptian Dynasty," 275, finds Egyptian commoners at Thebes with names *Hesem, Hesi.*

69. Knudtzon, *Die El-Amarna-Tafeln* 1:951, tablets 336 and 337, and index in 2:1562.

70. Albright, *Vocalization of Egyptian Syllabic Orthography,* 67, list 22, B-4.

Chapter 2: Men of the East

1. The Egyptian names may be found in Hermann Ranke, *Die Ägyptischen Personennamen* (Glückstadt: Augustin, 1935); Jens D. C. Lieblein, *Dictionnaire de noms hiéroglyphiques* (Christiania: Brögger & Christie, 1871); J. A. Knudtzon, *Die El-Amarna-Tafeln* (Leipzig: Hinrich, 1915; reprinted Aalen: Zeller, 1964) 2:1555-83; and scattered throughout the *JEA.*

2. Knudtzon, *Die El-Amarna-Tafeln* 2:1561.

3. Ranke, *Die Ägyptischen Personennamen*, 412, lines 8 and 9.

4. Ibid., 252, line 15.

5. Wilhelm Spiegelberg, "The God Panepi," *JEA* 12 (1926): 35.

6. Alan H. Gardiner, *Egyptian Grammar* (London: Oxford University Press, 1950), 437.

7. Hugh W. Nibley, "The Book of Mormon as a Mirror of the East," *IE* 51 (1948): 249. In 1948, the following had been said: "It requires no great effort of the imagination to detect a sort of parallelism between the two short listings. But aren't we using unjustified violence when we simply take the names at random and place them side by side? That is just what is most remarkable; we did pick names at random, and we had the whole Near East to draw on, with Egyptian names by no means predominating numerically in the lists before us. Yet the only Old World names that match those in the Book of Mormon episode all come from Egypt, nay, from one particular section of Egypt, in the far south, where from an indefinite date, but at least as early as the mid-seventh century, a Jewish colony flourished. What is more, all these names belong to the later dynasties, after the decline. The Book of Mormon tells us that Lehi was a rich merchant, who, though he 'dwelt in Jerusalem all his days,' enjoyed an Egyptian education and culture, which he endeavored to transmit to his children. The book continually refers to the double culture of the people of Lehi: Hebrew to the core, but proud of their Egyptian heritage. 'Egyptian civilization was one to be admired and aped,' writes Harry R. H. Hall, speaking of Lehi's own land and time. The only non-Hebraic names to enjoy prominence among the Nephites should, by the Book of Mormon's own account, be Egyptian, and such is found to be the case." After discussing the names Sam and Ammon, as in the text above, the 1948 article then concluded: "To return to our question: What did Joseph Smith, translator of the Book of Mormon, know about the Old World? So much seems certain, that he knew:

"(1) A number of typically Egyptian names, queer-sounding words in no way resembling Hebrew or any other language known to the world of Joseph Smith's time.

"(2) He knew the sort of plot and setting in which those names would figure in the Old World and seems quite at home on the Egyptian scene.

"(3) He gives a clear and correct picture of cultural relationships between Egypt and Israel, with due emphasis on its essentially commerical nature, in the remarkably convincing picture of Lehi—a typical merchant prince of the seventh century B.C. The picture of life in the ancient east which the Book of Mormon allows us to reconstruct is the more wonderful in the light of those fantastic conceptions of the gorgeous East which bedizened the heads of even the best scholars at the time the book came forth. The whole field of Book of Mormon names still awaits the careful study it deserves—the purpose of the present sketch being merely to indicate that such a study will prove anything but a blind alley. As a parting example of the validity of this claim, we cite a principle stated by Albright: 'The loss of the ending *on* is quite common in Palestinian place-names.' William F. Albright, *The Vocalization of the Egyptian Syllabic Orthography* (New Haven: American Oriental Society, 1934) 10:12. In Egyptian or 'reformed' Egyptian such an ending would be preserved, and so we have Book of Mormon place-names Emron, Heshlon, Jashon, Moron, Morianton, etc. It is no small feat, as was demonstrated in Harold Lundstrom, 'Original Words of the Book of Mormon,' *IE* 51 (February 1948): 85, simply to have picked a lot of strange and original names out of the air. But what shall we say of the man who was able to pick the *right* ones?"

8. William F. Albright, "A Brief History of Judah from the Days of Josiah to Alexander the Great," *BA* 9 (February 1946): 4-5.

9. E. C. Briggs, *Saints Herald* (21 June 1884), 396-97.

10. William F. Albright, "King Joiachim in Exile," *BA* 5 (December 1942): 51.

11. Harry Torczyner, *The Lachish Letters* (London: Oxford University Press, 1938) 1:198. We are following the spelling used in Torczyner's text rather than the transliterations in his list.

12. R. A. Stewart Macalister, "The Craftsmen's Guild of the Tribe of Judah," *PEFQ* (1905), 333.

13. Ephraim A. Speiser, "Introduction to Hurrian," *AASOR* 20 (1941): 216 (index). But Jens D. C. Lieblein, *Handel und Schiffahrt auf dem rothen Meere in alten Zeiten* (Leipzig: Christiania, 1886; reprinted Amsterdam: Meridian, 1971), 143-44, finds the name *Anti* in the far south, around the Red Sea.

14. Other references to Egypto-Hittite names are found in Sidney Smith, "Kizzuwadna," *JEA* 10 (1924): 108; Anton L. Mayer & John Garstang, "Kizzuwadna and Other Hittite States," *JEA* 11 (1925): 24 (Cadyanda), 26 (Kumani); Gerald A. Wainwright, "Keftiu," *JEA* 17 (1931): 27-29, 43 (Sandon), 35, 38, 40 (Achish).

15. Emil O. Forrer, "The Hittites in Palestine II," PEFQ (1937), 100.

16. Robert H. Pfeiffer, "Hebrews and Greeks Before Alexander," *JBL* 56 (1937): 91-95, 101; William F. Albright, "A Colony of Cretan Mercenaries on the Coast of the Negeb," *JPOS* 1 (1921): 187-94; Joseph G. Milne, "Trade Between Greece and Egypt Before Alexander the Great," *JEA* 25 (1939): 178; F. B. Welch, "The Influence of the Aegean Civilization on South Palestine," *PEFQ* (1900), 342-50. At Tel-el-Hesy, just west of Lachish, "the Greek influence begins at 700 [B.C.], and continues to the top of the town." William M. F. Petrie, in *PEFQ* (1890), 235. Nelson Glueck, "Ostraca from Elath," *BASOR* 80 (December 1940): 3.

17. Eduard Meyer, *Geschichte des Altertums*, 2nd ed. (Stuttgart: Cotta, 1928), vol. 2, pt. 1, p. 553.

18. Joseph Offord , "Further Illustrations of the Elephantine Aramaic Jewish Papyri," *PEFQ* (1917), 127.

19. William F. Albright, *Archaeology and the Religion of Israel* (Baltimore: Johns Hopkins University Press, 1942), 160.

20. David S. Margoliouth, *The Relations between Arabs and Israel Prior to the Rise of Islam*, Schweich Lectures (London: Oxford University Press, 1924), 13.

21. Harry R. H. Hall, "The Eclipse of Egypt," *Cambridge Ancient History* (New York: Macmillan, 1925) 3:256, 269, 292.

22. Meyer, *Geschichte des Altertums* (Stuttgart: Cotta, 1909), vol. 1, pt. 2, p. 156; Hall, "The Eclipse of Egypt," 256.

23. James L. Montgomery, *Arabia and the Bible* (Philadelphia: University of Pennsylvania Press, 1934), 52; second quote is on 18.

24. The danger of preparing for an expedition in the city is obvious, since the curiosity aroused leads to dangerous questions and may have far-reaching effects. See generally, Bertram Thomas, *Arabia Felix* (New York: Scribner, 1932), 36; for an account of preparations and activities at the "base camp," see ibid., 112-13; Harry S. J. B. Philby, *The Empty Quarter* (New York: Holt, 1933), 9-13.

25. Arthur E. Cowley, *Aramaic Papyri of the Fifth Century B.C.* (Oxford: Clarendon, 1923), 226 (col. 14, 1, 208).

26. To this day there are farmers in Palestine who spend much of their time living in tents on the desert; our friend Mose Kader was of this class. See George E. Kirk, "The Negev or the Southern Desert of Palestine," *PEFQ* (1941), 60. On the other hand, H. H. Kitchener, "Major Kitchener's Report," *PEFQ* (1884), 206, noticed tent-dwelling Arabs, true Bedouins, sowing barley on the land around Gaza. Of the Moahib Arabs Doughty writes: "Their harvest up, they strike the hamlets of tents, and with their cattle go forth to wander as nomads," Charles M. Doughty, *Travels in Arabia Deserta* (London: Cape, 1926) 1:276. Carl R. Raswan, *Drinkers of the Wind* (New York: Creative Age Press, 1942), describes at length the easy coming and going between desert and city, rich Arabs of the town often going out to spend a season or a few hours on the sands. See also J. W. Crowfoot and Grace M. Crowfoot, "The Ivories from Samaria," *PEFQ* (1933), 24. Nearly a contemporary of Lehi is "the Arabian chief who camped in the outskirts of Jerusalem at Nehemiah's time and bore the good North Arabic name of Geshem (Jusham)." Nabih A. Faris, ed., *The Arab Heritage* (New Jersey: Princeton University Press, 1944), 35.

27. Montgomery, *Arabia and the Bible*, 23; the Montgomery quote earlier in the paragraph is on 185; see also Eduard Meyer, *Die Israeliten und ihre*

Nachbarstämme (Halle, 1906; reprinted Darmstadt: Wissenschaftliche Buchgesellschaft, 1967), 209-561.

28. Margoliouth, *The Relations between Arabs and Israel Prior to the Rise of Islam,* 25; Montgomery, *Arabia and the Bible,* 186; Philip J. Baldensperger, "The Immovable East," *PEFQ* (1922), 163, and (1926), 93-97. This is not to say that the patriarchs were "primitives," for "we are learning to think of the immigrants not as nomads in the savage or semi-savage state, but as colonists carrying with them to their new homes the memories of a developed political organization, with usages and practices, having a history behind them." Margoliouth, *The Relations between Arabs and Israel Prior to the Rise of Islam,* 25. See also, Edouard P. Dhorme, "Le Pays de Job," *RB* 8 (1911): 102-7; George A. Barton, "The Original Home of the Story of Job," *JBL* 31 (1912): 63.

29. Baldensperger, "The Immovable East," *PEFQ* (1923), 176.

30. William F. Albright, "Recent Progress in North-Canaanite Research," *BASOR* 70 (April 1938): 21.

31. Margoliouth, *The Relations between Arabs and Israel Prior to the Rise of Islam,* 5, 8; Theodor Nöldeke, *Die semitischen Sprachen* (Leipzig: Tauchnitz, 1899), 52, 57; Meyer, *Die Israeliten und ihre Nachbarstämme,* 305-7 .

32. Montgomery, *Arabia and the Bible,* 53, citing Duncan B. MacDonald, *The Hebrew Literary Genius* (Princeton: Princeton University Press, 1933), 26-27.

33. "I do not think that there is much doubt that the Hebrews were what we should call Arabs, using the term in its widest sense." Alfred Guillaume, "The Habiru, the Hebrews, and the Arabs," *PEFQ* (1946), 65-67.

34. Albright, "Recent Progress in North-Canaanite Research," 21.

35. Guillaume, "The Habiru, the Hebrews, and the Arabs," 64-85; Stephen L. Caiger, *Bible and Spade* (London: Oxford University Press, 1936), 84-85.

36. Montgomery, *Arabia and the Bible,* 47.

37. William F. Albright, *Vocalization of Egyptian Syllabic Orthography* (New Haven: American Oriental Society, 1934), 50 (ch. 10, C, line 12).

38. Abraham Bergman, "The Israelite Tribe of Half-Manasseh," *JPOS* 16 (1936): 225, 228, 249; Moses H. Segal, "The Settlement of Manasseh East of the Jordan," *PEFQ* (1918), 124.

39. It has been suggested that Ammon, like his competitor Aton, was originally from Syria-Palestine, a theory that has somewhat to recommend it, expecially since Wainwright has shown the pre-historic Palestinian associations of Min of Coptos (the original Amon). Gerald A. Wainwright, "The Emblem of Min," *JEA* 17 (1931): 185-95; and Gerald A. Wainwright, "Letopolis," *JEA* 18 (1932): 161-63.

40. Albright, *Archaeology and the Religion of Israel,* 171.

41. In the 1950 magazine version, Nibley noted: "This three-cornered culture is an established pattern in that part of the world where the caravans of Egypt and Israel pass each other, guided through the sands by those men of the desert who were the immemorial go-between of the two civilizations." Hugh W. Nibley, "Lehi in the Desert," *IE* 53 (1950): 155. "The natural character of the Bedu tribes has always been to act as a kind of intermediary people, with no fixed politics." Baldensperger, "The Immovable East," *PEFQ* (1925), 85. Even today "the 'Arishiye(t) Bedus on the Egyptian frontier carry goods by land from Gaza to Egypt and vice versa. They are a peculiar intermediate-class; they practice commerce and agriculture and are camel rearers." Ibid. , *PEFQ* (1922), 161. Cf. John L. Burckhardt, *Notes on the Bedouins and Wahábys* (London: Colburn & Bently, 1831), 1:9, 26-27, 30-31, 275-76. In the sixth century B.C. the Arabs took Gaza, the northern anchor of the Egyptian trade line. Herodotus, *Histories* III, 5; III, 7; III, 91; William F. Albright, "Egypt and the Early History of the Negeb," *JPOS* 4 (1924): 130. Arab merchants, enriched by the three-cornered trade founded the Nabataean state. Kirk, "The Negev or the Southern Desert of Palestine," 62. At all times the Palestine-Egyptian trade was the main, if not the only source of wealth to these people. Taufik Canaan, "Byzantine Caravan Routes in the Negeb," *JPOS* 2 (1922): 144. On the antiquity of the three-cornered trade, see Lieblein, *Handel und Schiffahrt auf dem rothen Meere in alten Zeiten*, 76, 134-36; William J. T. Phythian-Adams, "Israel in the Arabah," *PEFQ* (1941), 61-62; Stewart Perowne, "Note on I Kings, Chapter X, 1-13," *PEFQ* (1939), 201; Albright, "Egypt and the Early History of the Negeb," 130-32.

42. Montgomery, *Arabia and the Bible*, 5.

43. Baldensperger, "The Immovable East," *PEFQ* (1925), 85, and (1922), 161; Burckhardt, *Notes on the Bedouins and Wahábys* 1:9, 26-27, 30-31; Kirk, "The Negev or the Southern Desert of Palestine," 62; Canaan, "Byzantine Caravan Routes in the Negeb," 144; Phythian-Adams, "Israel in the Arabah," *PEFQ* (1933), 143; Perowne, "Notes on I Kings, Chapter X, 1- 13," 201; Albright, "Egypt and the Early History of the Negeb," 131-41. Of the ties between the Bedouins and the merchants and farmers of Palestine and Egypt, Warren says: "Anybody who takes the trouble to investigate and understand these relationships will find it comparatively easy to make arrangements with tribes in the desert, however far they may be." Charles Warren, "Notes on Arabia Petraea and the Country Lying between Egypt and Palestine," *PEFQ* (1887), 45, n. 23. From the beginning the Jews were forced by their geographical position to deal with Arabs and to engage in trade, see Elias Auerbach, *Wüste und Gelobtes Land*, 2 vols. (Berlin: Schocken, 1932).

44. Thus "the Arabs of the south, though settled at their bases, were

indomitable travelers and merchants." Guillaume, "The Habiru, the Hebrews, and the Arabs," 67. There is nothing to prevent Lehi, though settled at his base, from being an indomitable traveler, unless one interprets 1 Nephi 1:4 to mean that he never set foot outside the city from the day of his birth—a palpable absurdity.

45. Montgomery, *Arabia and the Bible,* 12.

46. Margoliouth, *The Relations between Arabs and Israel Prior to the Rise of Islam,* 29; Guillaume, "The Habiru, the Hebrews, and the Arabs," 84-85.

47. Meyer, *Die Israeliten und ihre Nachbarstämme,* 302.

48. John Zeller, "The Bedawin," *PEFQ* (1901), 198.

49. The writer's attention was called by Professor Sperry to a statement attributed to Joseph Smith, that Ishmael was of Ephraim, and that his sons married Lehi's Daughters. G. D. Watt & J. V. Long, reporters, *Journal of Discourses* (Liverpool: Cannon/London: LDS Book Depot, 1862; reprinted Los Angeles: Gartner, 1956), 23:184, discussed in Sidney B. Sperry, "Did Father Lehi Have Daughters Who Married the Sons of Ishmael?" *IE* 55 (September 1952): 642. Ephraim, like Manasseh, was of the desert.

50. Meyer, *Die Israeliten und ihre Nachbarstämme,* 322-23.

51. Ibid., 322.

52. Paul Haupt, "Heb. leḥi, cheek, and lo[a], jaw," *JBL* 33 (1914): 290-95. Cf. Judges 15:17, 19.

53. Glueck, "Ostraca from Elath," 5-6, fig. 2.

54. Edward H. Palmer, "Arabic and English Name Lists," in *Survey of Western Palestine* (London: Palestinian Exploration Fund, 1881) 8:358.

55. Eliezer ben Yahuda, "The Edomite Language," *JPOS* 1 (1921): 113-15; Montgomery, *Arabia and the Bible,* 171, notes that there was an Arabic Massa tribe, but "there is no Hebrew king Lemuel."

56. C. Clermont-Ganneau, "The Arabs in Palestine," in *Survey of Western Palestine, Special Papers* (London: Palestine Exploration Fund, 1881) 4:325.

57. Claude R. Conder, "Moslem Mukams," in *Survey of Western Palestine, Special Papers* (London: Palestine Exploration Fund, 1881), 4:272.

58. Palmer, "Arabic and English Name Lists," 17, 40, 66.

59. Adolf Reifenberg, "A Hebrew Shekel of the Fifth Century B.C.," *PEFQ* (1943), 102; Albright, *Archaeology and the Religion of Israel,* 113. Among the children of those contemporaries of Lehi who fled to Egypt, Persian, Babylonian and "even Arabian names may be suspected," though they remained good Jews. Samuel A. Cook, "The Jews of Syene in the Fifth Century B.C.," *PEFQ* (1907), 68-73.

Chapter 3: Into The Desert

1. W. E. Jennings-Bramley, "The Bedouin of the Sinaitic Peninsula," *PEFQ* (1906), 106, and (1907), 281.

2. Frank E. Johnson, tr., *Al-Muʿallaqāt* (Bombay: Education Society's Steam Press, 1893), 17-18, lines 46-49; 42-44, lines 34, 40-41; 106-7, lines 40-43; 175-76, lines 25-28; W. Ahlwardt, *Sammlungen alter arabischer Dichter* (Berlin: Reuther & Reichard, 1903); in vol. 2, nos. 3:21-38; 5:58-63; 12:24-26; 15:40-49; 22:1-45; 30:9-11*; 31:47-80*; 40:51-69*; in vol. 3 , nos. 1; 10:37-56; 16:28-44; 18:33-44; 25:91-115; 27:29-36; 31:1-26; 33:48-77; 34:9-36; 40:1-14; 54:57-77; 55:34-66; 58:44-65. All passages starred in vol. 2, and all passages given in vol. 3, refer to unpleasant mists in the desert. Other poets are cited in Carl Brockelmann, *Geschichte der arabischen Litteratur* (Leiden: Brill, 1943), 10, 16-17, 19-22, 54, 91.

3. The entire section on "Travel," in Kabir al-Din Ahmad & Gholam Rabbani, eds., *The Diwán Hammásah of Abu Tammam* (Calcutta: n.p., 1856), 206-9, is taken up with the exhaustion and terror of travel in the dark. The mist of darkness is mentioned in nearly all passages given in the preceding footnote.

4. In the country lying between Egypt and Palestine, according to Charles Warren, "Notes on Arabia Petraea and the Country Lying between Egypt and Palestine," *PEFQ* (1887), 44, "during November, December, and March, there are often dense mists. . . . These mists depend upon the wind, and often alternate with intense droughts." Harry S. J. B. Philby, *The Empty Quarter* (New York: Holt, 1933), 96, 134, 183, reports the same phenomenon in the most desert part of South Arabia: "A thick mist descended upon and blotted out the landscape after sunrise. . . . Everything was grimed with sand and the sun was feeble in the extreme. . . . A light, clammy northern breeze gently fanned a thick damp mist."

5. Ahlwardt, *Sammlungen alter arabischer Dichter,* 2, no. 1.

6. Edward J. Byng, *The World of the Arabs* (Boston: Little, Brown, 1944), 64-65.

7. Lucy Mack Smith, *History of Joseph Smith* (Salt Lake City: Bookcraft, 1958), 47-50. The dream is not to be minutely examined, since it is only Mother Smith's memory of a dream reported to her 34 years before; see "Introduction," vii and ix.

8. Thus al-Buḥturī, cited in Brockelmann, *Geschichte der arabischen Litteratur,* 88; cf. Lebid, cited in ibid., 55. *Maydān* means both "large, spacious field," and "an ample life" in Arabic.

9. "The scenery of a desert oasis, with its rivers springing miraculously from nowhere and emptying themselves again perhaps in the

desert sands." James L. Montgomery, *Arabia and the Bible* (Philadelphia: University of Pennsylvania Press, 1934), 6.

10. E. A. Wallis Budge, *The Chronography of Bar Hebraeus* (London: Oxford University Press, 1932) 1:167.

11. Charles M. Doughty, *Travels in Arabia Deserta* (London: Cape, 1926), 2:229.

12. Montgomery, *Arabia and the Bible,* 85.

13. "Our 'river' is an imperfect way of conveying the idea," but since we have no other word in English, the Book of Mormon must use it. Richard F. Burton, *Pilgrimage to Al-Medinah and Meccah* (London: Tylston & Edwards, 1893) 1:250, n. 2.

14. E.g., Al-ᶜAjjāj, in Ahlwardt, *Sammlungen alter arabischer Dichter,* 2, no. 1; Theodor Nöldeke, *Delectus Veterum Carminum Arabicorum* (Berlin, 1890), 111; Psalm 1:6 is another example.

15. For the presence of such canyons in Lehi's deserts, see Burton, *Pilgrimage to Al-Medinah and Meccah* 1:207, describing "titanic walls, lofty donjons, huge projecting bastions, and moats full of deep shade." See "A Note on Rivers" in the text below.

16. In Ahlwardt, *Sammlungen alter arabischer Dichter* 3, no. 1.

17. Nöldeke, *Delectus Veterum Carminum Arabicorum,* 95; Brockelmann, *Geschichte der arabischen Litteratur,* 19, 21; Johnson, *Al-Muᶜallaqāt,* 188, line 61.

18. William F. Albright, "A Brief History of Judah from the Days of Josiah to Alexander the Great," *BA* 9 (February 1946): 4.

19. Philip J. Baldensperger, "The Immovable East," *PEFQ* (1922), 170-71.

20. C. Leonard Woolley and Thomas E. Lawrence, *The Wilderness of Zin* (London: Cape, 1936), 34.

21. William F. Albright, *Archaeology and the Religion of Israel* (Baltimore: Johns Hopkins Press, 1942), 101.

22. *Diodorus* XIX, 94, 100.

23. Antonin Jaussen, "Mélanges," *RB* 3 (1906): 95.

24. In Nibley's magazine version of this material, he continued: "As far as Lehi's flight into the wilderness is concerned, the Book of Mormon shows flawless judgment in every detail: the manner of his flight is strictly in keeping with the best conventions, and he takes what we know now was the only possible direction he could have taken." Hugh W. Nibley, "Lehi in the Desert," *IE* 53 (1950): 202. At this date it is plain that all other routes of escape would be closed; the intimate danger would be, of course, from the north. See John L. Myres, "God and the Danger from the North in Ezekiel," *PEFQ* (1932), 213-15. While the south desert remained open to the end, some Jewish settlements there actually

"appear to have escaped destruction" altogether. Albright, "A Brief History of Judah from the Days of Josiah to Alexander the Great," 6.

25. Albright, "A Brief History of Judah from the Days of Josiah to Alexander the Great," 4-5. The earlier version of "Lehi and the Desert," 202, noted, "It is in that region that we located in a previous article in the *Era* some important Book of Mormon names, not realizing at the time that those names belonged to the descendants of Lehi's own contemporaries." Hugh W. Nibley, "The Book of Mormon as a Mirror of the East," *IE* 51 (1948): 202-4.

26. Stephen L. Caiger, *Bible and Spade* (London: Oxford University Press, 1936), 188.

27. Montgomery, *Arabia and the Bible,* 15.

28. Carl R. Raswan, *Drinkers of the Wind* (New York: Creative Age Press, 1942), illustrates this meeting of town and desert.

29. "The Hebrew stock had its original kinship with the tribes to the east and south of Palestine-Syria, and especially southwards. . . . The one line of maritime venture pursued by Judan policy was the development of the Red Sea route (e.g., I Kings 9:26ff); that is, the commercial prospects of the state looked towards Arabia," Montgomery, *Arabia and the Bible,* 12, 51-52, 185.

30. Stewart Perowne, "Notes on I Kings, Chapter X, 1-1 3," *PEFQ* (1939), 200.

31. David S. Margoliouth, *The Relations between Arabs and Israel Prior to the Rise of Islam,* Schweich Lectures (London: Oxford University Press, 1924), 47.

32. Woolley & Lawrence, *The Wilderness of Zin,* 11.

33. "It is, we think, both natural and correct to assume that at all periods in man's history the southern desert has been very much the desert that it is to-day." Ibid., 36.

34. Ibid., 37.

35. 1 Nephi 2:6, 3:1, 4:38, 7:5, 7:21, 9:1, 10:16, 16:6.

36. Taufik Canaan, "The Palestinian Arab House," *JPOS* 12 (1932): 225.

37. Georg Jacob, *Altarabisches Beduinenleben* (Berlin: Mayer & Müller, 1897), 226.

38. Caiger, *Bible and Spade,* 181.

39. John L. Burckhardt, *Notes on the Bedouins and Wahábys* (London: Colburn & Bently, 1831; reprinted New York: Johnson Reprint, 1967) 1:127.

40. Jaussen, "Mélanges," 93-94. If a woman wants to divorce her husband, she simply turns over his tent. Jacob, *Altarabisches Beduinenleben,* 212.

41. Philip J. Baldensperger, "Tent Life," *PEFQ* (1923), 179.

42. Canaan, "The Palestinian Arab House," *JPOS* 13 (1933): 57.

43. William B. Seabrook, *Adventures in Arabia* (New York: Harcourt, 1927), 6; cf. Grace M. Crowfoot, "The Tent Beautiful," *PEFQ* (1945), 34-46.

44. "Those in the neighboring booths watch when the day is light, to see if the shaykh's hareem yet strike his tent; and, seeing this, it is the rahla." Doughty, *Travels in Arabia Deserta,* 1:257. In the same way, when the sheikh pitches his tent, all without discussion, follow suit, the chief's tent being as it were the tabernacle that leads them through the wilderness. It will be recalled that the Liahona was found at the door of Lehi's tent. It is notable that even the richest sheikh "has never more than one tent," according to Burckhardt, *Notes on the Bedouins and Wahábys* 1:42, speaking of the Aneze. Nibley concluded in his magazine version: "It is not uncommon in the East for rich town and country people to take to the desert for a spell, so Lehi was by no means doing the impossible or unusual thing; only the people who do so are of course those who already have had a good deal of experience in the desert way and have acquired a taste for it." Hugh W. Nibley, "Lehi in the Desert," 276. Thus a well-to-do sheikh "spends the winter in his 'house of stone' and the summer in his 'house of hair.' " Jaussen, "Mélanges," 95.

45. Canaan, "The Palestinian Arab House," *JPOS* 13 (1933): 55.

46. Frederic D. Thornton, *Elementary Arabic* (Cambridge: Cambridge University Press, 1943), 156.

47. Max von Oppenheim, *Die Beduinen* (Leipzig: Harrassowitz, 1939) 1:28.

48. Claude S. Jarvis, "The Desert Yesterday and To-day," *PEFQ* (1937), 122.

49. Doughty, *Travels in Arabia Deserta* 1:259.

50. William G. Palgrave, *Narrative of a Year's Journey Through Central and Eastern Arabia* (London: Macmillan, 1865), 1:12-13.

51. Robert E. Cheesman, *In Unknown Arabia* (London: Macmillan, 1926), 27, 52.

52. William J. T. Phythian-Adams, "The Mount of God," *PEFQ* (1930), 199.

53. Albright, *Archaeology and the Religion of Israel,* 97.

54. Jennings-Bramley, "The Bedouin of the Sinaitic Peninsula," *PEFQ* (1907), 30.

55. Baldensperger, "The Immovable East," *PEFQ* (1923), 180.

56. Burckhardt, *Notes on the Bedouins and Wahábys,* 1:227-28.

57. John L. Burckhardt, *Travels in Arabia* (London: Colburn, 1829; reprinted London: Cass, 1968), 402.

58. Baldensperger, "The Immovable East," *PEFQ* (1922), 163.

59. Raswan, *Drinkers of the Wind,* 129.

60. Burckhardt, *Notes on the Bedouins and Wahábys,* 1:157-60.

61. Philby, *The Empty Quarter,* 229-30.

62. Johnson, *Al-Muᶜallaqāt,* 26.

63. Henri Frankfort, "Egypt and Syria in the First Intermediate Period," *JEA* 12 (1926): 81.

64. Woolley & Lawrence, *The Wilderness of Zin,* 32.

65. Bertram Thomas, *Arabia Felix* (New York: Scribner, 1932), 141.

66. Cheesman, *In Unknown Arabia,* 338-39.

67. W. E. Jennings-Bramley, "Sport among the Bedawin," *PEFQ* (1900), 369.

68. Ibn ᶜAli al-Husaynī, *Akhbār 'al-Dawla al-Saljūqiyya* (Lahore: University of the Panjab, 1933), 1.

69. Baldensperger, "The Immovable East," *PEFQ* (1925), 82-90.

70. Philby, *The Empty Quarter,* 249.

71. Burckhardt, *Travels in Arabia,* 403.

72. Julius Euting, *Tagebuch einer Reise in Inner-Arabien* (Leiden, 1892) 2:76-80, 92-93.

73. Jacob, *Altarabisches Beduinenleben,* 131-33. Mt. Jasum is in the Mecca area; Mt. Azd in the Serat Mountains is farther south but also near the coast.

74. Jennings-Bramley, "The Bedouin of the Sinaitic Peninsula," *PEFQ* (1907), 284.

75. Ibid., *PEFQ* (1914), 9.

76. Baldensperger, "The Immovable East," *PEFQ* (1923), 181.

Chapter 4: Desert Ways and Places

1. W. Robertson Smith, *The Religion of the Semites,* Burnett Lectures (London: Black, 1907), 200-201.

2. Carl R. Raswan, *Drinkers of the Wind* (New York: Creative Age Press, 1942), 237.

3. Antonin Jaussen, "Mélanges," *RB* 3 (1906): 109.

4. Ibid., 110.

5. Nilus, *Narratio (Narrations)* 3, in *PG* 79:612.

6. Bertram Thomas, *Arabia Felix* (New York: Scribner, 1936), 137.

7. Robert E. Cheesman, *In Unknown Arabia* (London: Macmillan, 1926), 228-29, 234, 240-41, 280.

8. Raswan, *Drinkers of the Wind,* 200.

9. William G. Palgrave, *Narrative of a Year's Journey Through Central and Eastern Arabia* (London: Macmillan, 1865), 1:13.

10. John L. Burckhardt, *Notes on the Bedouins and Wahábys* (London: Colburn & Bently, 1831; reprinted New York: Johnson Reprint, 1967), 1:242.

11. Nilus, *Narrations* 3, in *PG* 79:612.

12. David S. Margoliouth, *The Relations between Arabs and Israel Prior to the Rise of Islam,* Schweich Lectures (London: Oxford University Press, 1924), 57.

13. Ibid., 54.

14. Frank E. Johnson, tr., *Al-Muʿallaqāt* (Bombay: Education Society's Steam Press, 1893), 218, line 38.

15. Harry S. J. B. Philby, *The Empty Quarter* (New York: Holt, 1933), 27.

16. Burckhardt, *Notes on the Bedouins and Wahábys,* 1:133.

17. Thomas, *Arabia Felix,* 142.

18. Ibid., 172-73.

19. Johnson, *Al-Muʿallaqāt,* 87, line 58.

20. Nilus, *Narrations* 6, in *PG* 79:669.

21. Philip J. Baldensperger, "The Immovable East," *PEFQ* (1925), 81; second quote is from *PEFQ* (1922), 168-69.

22. Richard F. Burton, *Pilgrimage to Al-Medinah and Meccah* (London: Tylston & Edwards, 1893), 2:118.

23. Hence it is regarded as an honorable and courageous act to camp outside of one's own tribal domain. Georg Jacob, *Altarabisches Beduinenleben* (Berlin: Mayer & Müller, 1897), 211.

24. Cheesman, *In Unknown Arabia,* 24. In Nibley's original magazine article, he also noted: "After a raid a whole tribe will go in to hiding to avoid reprisals," Hugh W. Nibley, "Lehi in the Desert," *IE* 53 (1950): 383. W. E. Jennings-Bramley, "The Bedouin of the Sinaitic Peninsula," *PEFQ* (1912), 16, states that "not a soul was to be seen, for the Debur were in temporary hiding, having come home from a successful raid, and the victims might daily expect to return the compliment."

25. Jennings-Bramley, "The Bedouin of the Sinaitic Peninsula," *PEFQ* (1908), 31, 36.

26. On the anti-social nature of the Arab, see Baldensperger, "The Immovable East," *PEFQ* (1922), 168-70; Antonin Jaussen, "Chronique," *RB* 3 (1906): 443; Edward H. Palmer, *Desert of the Exodus* (Cambridge: Deighton, Bell, 1871) 1:79-81.

27. Wilhelm Nowack, *Lehrbuch der hebräischen Archäologie* (Freiburg i/B: Mohr, 1894), 152.

28. Johnson, *Al-Muʿallaqāt,* 139, line 30.

29. Philby, *The Empty Quarter,* 219.

30. Burton, *Pilgrimage to Al-Medinah and Meccah,* 1:276.

31. Jennings-Bramley, "The Bedouin of the Sinaitic Peninsula," *PEFQ* (1905), 213.

32. Charles M. Doughty, *Travels in Arabia Deserta* (New York: Random House, 1936), 1:272, 282-83.

33. Burckhardt, *Notes on the Bedouins and Wahábys*, 1:354; Doughty, *Travels in Arabia Deserta*, 1:258 .

34. Burckhardt, *Notes on the Bedouins and Wahábys*, 1:114.

35. Burton, *Pilgrimage to Al-Medinah and Meccah*, 2:102.

36. Philip J. Baldensperger, "Women in the East," *PEFQ* (1901), 75.

37. Max von Oppenheim, *Die Beduinen* (Leipzig: Harrassowitz, 1939), 1:30.

38. Burckhardt, *Notes on the Bedouins and Wahábys*, 1:116-17; Jaussen, "Chronique," *RB* 12 (1903): 107-8; Oppenheim, *Die Beduinen*, 1:30.

39. John Zeller, "The Bedawin," *PEFQ* (1901), 194; Jaussen, "Mélanges," *RB* 12 (1903): 254.

40. Jennings-Bramley, "The Bedouin of the Sinaitic Peninsula," 217.

41. H. H. Kitchener, "Major Kitchener's Report," *PEFQ* (1884), 215.

42. Eliahu Epstein, "Bedouin of the Negeb," *PEFQ* (1939), 61-64; Baldensperger, "The Immovable East," *PEFQ* (1906), 14. "The tyranny of relations is more severe . . . than the descent of the Indian sword," says the ancient poet Ṭarafah. Johnson, *Al-Muᶜallaqāt*, 57, line 81.

43. Nowack, *Lehrbuch der hebräischen Archäologie*, 154; Jacob, *Altarabisches Benduinenleben*, 212.

44. Jaussen, "Chronique," *RB* 12 (1903): 109.

45. Philby, *The Empty Quarter*, 216.

46. Ibid.

47. Thomas E. Lawrence, *Seven Pillars of Wisdom* (New York: Garden City Publishing, 1938), ch. 3.

48. Jennings-Bramley, "The Bedouin of the Sinaitic Peninsula," *PEFQ* (1908), 257.

49. Taufik Canaan, "Studies in the Topography and Folklore of Petra," *JPOS* 9 (1929): 139; cf. David G. Hogarth, *The Penetration of Arabia* (London: Lawrence & Bullen, 1904), 162.

50. Canaan, "Studies in the Topography and Folklore of Petra," 140. This is the standard work on desert place names. Burton, *Pilgrimage to Al-Medinah and Meccah* 1:250, n. 3: "A folio volume would not contain a three months' collection" of such names, so numerous are they.

51. C. Leonard Woolley & Thomas E. Lawrence, *The Wilderness of Zin* (London: Cape, 1936), 70.

52. Palmer, *Desert of the Exodus*, 1:20.

53. Raswan, *Drinkers of the Wind*, 131.

54. Philby, *The Empty Quarter,* 39.

55. Cheesman, *In Unknown Arabia,* 261.

56. Woolley & Lawrence, *The Wilderness of Zin,* 86-87; cf. Claude R. Conder, "Lieut. Claude R. Conder's Reports, XXXII," *PEFQ* (1875), 126.

57. Thomas, *Arabia Felix,* 50-51.

58. William F . Albright, *Archaeology and the Religion of Israel* (Baltimore: Johns Hopkins Press, 1942), 149.

59. Joseph Offord, "The Red Sea," *PEFQ* (1920), 179.

60. As cited by William J. T. Phythian-Adams, "The Mount of God," *PEFQ* (1939), 204.

61. Wilhelm Spiegelberg, *Koptisches Handwörterbuch,* 204, 258.

62. Claude R. Conder, *Survey of Eastern Palestine* (London: Palestine Exploration Fund, 1889), 1:239, 241; Edward H. Palmer, "Arabic and English Name Lists," in *Survey of Western Palestine* (London: Palestine Exploration Fund, 1881), 8:116, 134. Another transliteration of the Arabic is *Thughrat-al-Shajar.*

63. Claude R. Conder, "Notes on the Language of the Native Peasantry in Palestine," *PEFQ* (1876), 134; Edward H. Palmer, *The Survey of Western Palestine, Name Lists* (London: Palestine Exploration Fund, 1881), 29, 93.

64. Claude R. Conder and H. H. Kitchener, "Memoirs of the Topography, Orography, Hydrography and Archaeology," in *Survey of Western Palestine* (London: Palestine Exploration Fund, 1881), 2:169.

65. Thomas, *Arabia Felix,* 136-37; Philby, *The Empty Quarter,* 231.

66. Thomas, *Arabia Felix,* 136-37.

67. Jaussen, "Chronique," *RB* 10 (1901): 607.

68. Ibid.; Taufik Canaan, "Unwritten Laws Affecting the Arab Women of Palestine," *JPOS* 11 (1931): 189: "In funeral processions women may not mix with men. . . . When the burial is over the women assemble alone. . . . In visiting the tomb . . . they always go alone." Cf. Baldensperger, "Women in the East," 83; and Burckhardt, *Notes on the Bedouins and Wahábys,* 1:101: "At the moment of a man's death, his wives, daughters, and female relations unite in cries of lamentation." Among the Jews the men play a more prominent part in mourning rites, and even professional male mourners were not unknown. Nowack, *Lehrbuch der hebräischen Archäologie,* 196. Both the root *nhm* (groan, suffer, complain) and the similar root *nḥm* (sigh, mourn, console) are relevant here.

69. Hogarth, *The Penetration of Arabia,* 3.

70. Abraham S. Yahuda, *The Accuracy of the Bible,* (London: Heinemann, 1934), 201.

71. Cf. Burton, *Pilgrimage to Al-Medinah and Meccah,* 2:72.

72. Edward H. Palmer, "The Desert of the Tíh and the Country of Moab," in *Survey of Western Palestine, Special Papers* (London: Palestine Exploration Fund, 1881), 4:67.

73. Conder, "Lieut. Claude R. Conder's Reports, XXXII," 130.

74. Gray Hill, "A Journey to Petra—1896," *PEFQ* (1897), 144.

75. W. Ewing, "A Journey in the Hauran," *PEFQ* (1895), 175.

76. Burton, *Pilgrimage to Al-Medinah and Meccah,* 2:154.

77. Ariel L. Crowley, "Lehi's River Laman," *IE* 47 (1944): 14-15, 56, 59-61.

78. Ibid., 15, 56.

79. Ibid., 15, 61.

80. Ibid., 61 (emphasis added).

81. Ibid., 15.

Chapter 5: The City and the Sand

1. Philip J . Baldensperger, "The Immovable East," *PEFQ* (1925), 81.

2. Richard F. Burton, *Pilgrimage to Al-Medinah and Meccah* (London: Tylston & Edwards, 1893), 1:280.

3. The river would flow between these two elevations, as indicated on maps of the area. The valley seems to be commodious enough. We suggest an investigation: from the most ancient times it has been the custom of travelers in the desert to inscribe their names on rocks at places where they have camped. "We find now hundreds of these inscriptions." Theodor Nöldeke, *Die semitischen Sprachen* (Leipzig: Tauchnitz, 1899), 37. It is almost certain that Lehi's people left their marks at the more important stopping places.

4. Ignac Goldziher, *Abhandlungen zur arabischen Philologie* (Leiden, 1896), 1:58.

5. Nilus, *Narratio* (*Narrations*) 5, in *PG* 79:648.

6. Ibn Qutayba, *Introduction au livre de la poesie et des poetes (Muqaddamatu Kitab-ish-Shiʿre wa sh-Shuʿara)* (Paris: l'Association Guillaume Budé, 1947), 18.

7. Bertram Thomas, *Arabia Felix* (New York: Scribner, 1932), 153.

8. Antoine de San Exupéry, *Wind, Sand and Stars* (New York: Harcourt, Brace, 1967), 104.

9. *Kitāb Taghrībat Banī Hilāl* (Damascus: Hashim), 54.

10. Goldziher, *Abhandlu ngen zur arabischen Philologie* 1:67-71.

11. Ibid., 1:59, 72 -75.

12. Ibn Qutayba, *Introduction au livre de la poesie et des poetes,* 25; cf. Goldziher, *Abhandlungen zur arabischen Philologie* 1:74.

13. Pierre Cersoy, "L'apologue de la vigne," *RB* 8 (1899): 40-47.

14. Emmanuel Cosquin, "Le livre de Tobie et 'L'histoire du sage Ahikar,' " *RB* 8 (1899): 54-55.

15. "I cannot well explain the effect of Arab poetry on one who has not visited the Desert." Burton, *Pilgrimage to Al-Medinah and Meccah,* 2:99.

16. Gustav Richter, "Zur Entstehungsgeschichte der altarabischen Qaside," *ZDMG* 92 (1938): 557-58. The passage cited is from 'Antara.

17. Ibid., 563-65.

18. Ibn Qutayba, *Introduction au livre de la poesie et des poetes,* 13.

19. Burton, *Pilgrimage to Al-Medinah and Meccah,* 1:278.

20. Carl Brockelmann, *Geschichte der arabischen Litteratur* (Leiden: Brill, 1943), 16.

21. Burton, *Pilgrimage to Al-Medinah and Meccah,* 1:278, n. 3.

22. Richter, "Zur Entstehungsgeschichte der altarabischen Qaside," 557-58.

23. Brockelmann, *Geschichte der arabischen Litteratur,* 12.

24. James L. Montgomery, *Arabia and the Bible* (Philadelphia: University of Pennsylvania Press, 1934), 21.

25. Even the whole interpretation of the 23rd Psalm is now being questioned.

26. Burton, *Pilgrimage to Al-Medinah and Meccah,* 2:98.

27. See "The Problem of Food" discussed in the text above.

28. Frank E. Johnson, tr., *Al-Muʿallaqāt* (Bombay: Education Society's Steam Press, 1893), 71, line 13.

29. J. Dissard, "Les migrations et les vicissitudes de la Tribu des 'Amer," *RB* 2 (1905): 411-16.

30. Frederick J. Bliss & R. A. Stewart Macalister, *Excavations in Palestine* (London: Palestine Exploration Fund, 1902), 204.

31. Ibid., 269.

32. Edward H. Palmer, "The Desert of the Tíh and the Country of Moab," in *Survey of Western Palestine, Special Papers* (London: Palestine Exploration Fund, 1881), 4:19-21.

33. Bliss & Macalister, *Excavations in Palestine,* 266-67; W. F. Birch, "Hiding-Places in Canaan," *PEFQ* (1884), 61-70, also (1880), 235, and (1881), 323-24.

34. As a matter of fact, that language was not preserved even in antiquity, and when the time came for the record to fulfill its great purpose of bearing witness to the world, it had to be translated by the gift and power of God. Of this purpose Nephi at the time knew nothing.

35. *Kitāb Taghrībaht Banī Hilāl,* 14.

36. Eduard Meyer, *Geschichte des Altertums,* 2nd ed. (Stuttgart: Cotta, 1928), vol. 2, pt. 1, p. 137.

37. J. W. Jack, " The Lachish Letters—Their Date and Import," *PEFQ* (1938), 168.

38. The Wenamon story may be found in James H. Breasted, *A History of Egypt,* 2nd ed. (New York: Scribner, 1951), 513-18; James Baikie, *The History of the Pharaohs* (London: Black, 1926), 285-87; James H. Breasted, "The Decline and Fall of the Egyptian Empire," *Cambridge Ancient History* (Cambridge University Press, 1931), 2:193-94. More recently, Hans Goedicke, *The Report of Wenamun* (Baltimore: Johns Hopkins University Press, 1975).

39. Jack, "The Lachish Letters—Their Date and Import," 168.

40. Joseph Offord, "Archaeological Notes on Jewish Antiquities," *PEFQ* (1916), 148.

41. William F. Albright, "The Seal of Eliakim and the Latest Preexilic History of Judah, With Some Observations on Ezekiel," *JBL* 51 (1932): 79-83, shows that the title "servant" in Jerusalem at this time meant something like "official representative" and was an honorable rather than a degrading title.

42. Brockelmann, *Geschichte der arabischen Litteratur,* 34.

43. W. Ewing, "A Journey in the Hauran," *PEFQ* (1895), 173.

44. Antonin Jaussen, "Mélanges," *RB* 12 (1903): 259; cf. C. Clermont-Ganneau, "The Arabs of Palestine," in *Survey Western Palestine, Special Papers* (London: Palestine Exploration Fund, 1881), 4:327.

45. Clermont-Ganneau, "The Arabs of Palestine," 326-27; Baldensperger, *PEFQ* (1910), 261.

46. Charles M. Doughty, *Travels in Arabia Deserta* (New York: Random House, 1936), 2:27.

Chapter 6: Lehi the Winner

1. J. A. Knudtzon, *Die El-Amarna-Tafeln* (Leipzig: Hinrich, 1915; reprinted Aalen: Zeller, 1964) 1:372-73, tablet 74.

2. Livy, *Ab Urbe Condita (From the Founding of the City)* VIII, 40, 4; cf. IV, 16, 3 ; kept on "boards" (tabulae, *pinakes*) or sacred tablets (*en hierais deltois*), Dionysius of Halicarnassus, *Roman Antiquities* I, 73, 1; I, 74, 3-5.

3. Julian Obermann, "An Early Phoenician Political Document," *JBL* 58 (1939): 229-31. Albright calls it a "a Hebrew letter of the twelfth century" on a copper or bronze plate. William F. Albright, "A Hebrew Letter of the Twelfth Century," *BASOR* 73 (February 1939): 9-13.

4. The Idrisi passage is quoted at length by E. A. Wallis Budge, *The Book of the Dead* (New York: Dover, 1967), xix, n. 3.

5. G. Ramadas, "Kesaribeda Copper Plate," *Journal of Bihar Research Society* 34 (1948): 32; 34-35 lists besides these the Mattapad plates of Damodaravarman 6 3/8" by 1 1/2"; the Kauteru plates of Vijayaskandavarman 5 1/2" by 4/5"; the Peddavegi plates of Salankayan a Nandivarman 6 4/5" by 2 1/10"; the Koroshanda copper plates of Visakharvarma 7 1/2" by 2"; the Chikulla plates of Vikramendravarma 7 1/8" by 2 1/4"; the Komarti plates of Chandavarma 7 1/2" to 7 5/8" by 2 1/4" to 2 3/8".

6. Alonzo Bunker, "On a Karen Inscription-Plate," *JAOS* 10 (1872): 172-77.

7. It was 6 3/16" by 2 1/ 8". Ibid., 175.

8. See Fritz Hommel, *Ethnologie und Geographie des alten Orients* (Munich: Beck, 1926), 201-3.

9. E. B. Cross, "The Karens," *JAOS* 4 (1854): 308.

10. Eduard Meyer, *Geschichte des Altertums,* 2nd ed. (Stuttgart: Cotta, 1928), vol. 2, pt. 1, p. 205; R. Maxwell Hyslop, et al., "An Archaeological Survey of the Plain of Jabbul, 1939," *PEFQ* (1942), 23, plate VII, fig. 14; An iron ceremonial weapon found recently had a finely worked handle of copper and gold. Theodore H. Gaster, "On an Iron Axe from Ugarit," *PEFQ* (1943), 57-58.

11. Gerald A. Wainwright, "The Coming of Iron," *Antiquity* 10 (1936): 17-18.

12. Ibid.

13. Georg Jacob, *Altarabisches Beduinenleben,* (Berlin: Mayer & Müller, 1897), 151-52.

14. Philip J. Baldensperger, "The Immovable East," *PEFQ* (1903), 168. Nibley continued in his magazine article: "The general question of steel in the ancient world is still unsettled. The Babylonians distinguished between *eru* (cf. our 'ore'), meaning iron, lead, or copper, and 'shining *eru,*' " which meant copper or steel". Fr. Lenormant, 'Les noms de l'Arain et du Cuivre . . . ,' *Biblical Archaeological Society Transactions* 5 (1876): 344-45. In Egypt a like distinction was made between ordinary iron, which was not only known but actually used for utensils as early as the Old Kingdom, and that type of iron known as *tehazet,* which some interpret as asiatic iron. Felix von Luschan, "Eisentechnik in Afrika," *Zeitschrift für Ethnologie* 41 (1909): 47. Another type, *benipe,* is 'iron from heaven,' i.e., either meteoric iron or, as Von Luschan believed, 'sky-colored metal' (Metall von Himmelsfarbe), ibid., 48, which may well have been steel. Ceremonial swords in very old Egyptian tomb painting are colored blue to represent either iron or steel, according to the same authority, ibid., 49. While the problem of the origin and age of iron and steel remains unsolved, every step in the last forty years has been in the

direction of proving a much greater antiquity and much more widespread use of those metals than was formerly believed to be possible." Hugh W. Nibley, "Lehi in the Desert," *IE* 53 (1950): 707.

15. Richard F. Burton, *Pilgrimage to Al-Medinah and Meccah* (London: Tylston & Edwards, 1893) 2:94, 141-42.

16. John A. Widtsoe, "Is Book of Mormon Geography Known?" *IE* 53 (1950): 547.

17. Bertram Thomas, *Arabia Felix* (New York: Scribner, 1932), 48-49.

18. Ibid., 48.

19. Burton, *Pilgrimage to Al-Medinah and Meccah,* 2:130.

20. David G. Hogarth, *The Penetration of Arabia* (London: Lawrence & Bullen, 1904), 137-39.

21. Ibid., 148-50.

22. James L. Montgomery, *Arabia and the Bible* (Philadelphia: University of Pennsylvania Press, 1934), 71, 74 .

23. Josiah Conder, *A Popular Description of Arabia,* Modern Traveller Series (London: Duncan, 1926), 9, 14-15, 348-49.

24. Stewart Perowne, "Notes on I Kings, Chapter X, 1-13," *PEFQ* (1939), 200.

25. Montgomery, *Arabia and the Bible,* 75.

26. Robert E. Cheesman, *In Unknown Arabia* (London: Macmillan, 1926), 67-71.

27. C. Clermont-Ganneau, "The Arabs in Palestine," *PEFQ* (1875), 202.

28. Edward H. Palmer, "The Desert of the Tíh and the Country of Moab," in *Survey of Western Palestine, Special Papers* (London: Palestine Exploration Fund, 1881), 4:73.

29. Edward H. Palmer, *The Desert of the Exodus* (Cambridge: Deighton, Bell, 1871), 2.

30. Charles M. Watson, "The Desert of the Wanderings," *PEFQ* (1914), 18-23; C. Leonard Woolley & Thomas E. Lawrence, *The Wilderness of Zin* (London: Cape, 1936), 71-72.

31. Woolley & Lawrence, *The Wilderness of Zin,* 73, n. 1.

32. S. F. Newcombe, "T. E. Lawrence—Personal Reminiscences," *PEFQ* (1935), 110-11.

33. See further Hugh W. Nibley, *No Ma'am, That's Not History* (Salt Lake City: Bookcraft, 1946).

Part 2
The World of the Jaredites

1

A Twilight World

Author's note: The epistolary form of this series of articles is the style in which the writer most commonly expounds his views. Although "Professor F." to whom these letters are addressed is a purely fictitious anthropologist in an eastern university, he is typical of many a real correspondent, and the letters themselves are no less typical. If "F." seems unduly meek and teachable, that is because with the limited space at our disposal it would be folly to engage in long and needless controversies.

The Problem[1]

My dear Professor F.:

I warned you that you would find the Book of Mormon full of strange and puzzling things. Please don't hesitate to tell me what you think; above all, there is no need to be concerned about offending my religious sensibilities. The Book of Mormon is tough; it thrives on investigation; you may kick it around like a football, as many have done; and I promise you it will wear you out long before you ever make a dent in it.

As to your first objection, you say that you are disturbed by the apparent attempt of the Book of Mormon to trace the origin of our Indian tribes to a single city in the Near East and to a time as recent as 600 B.C. This would seem to you to be a much too simple and limited explanation for everything. It seems so to me, too. But since you have only begun your reading of the Book of Mormon, my urgent advice to you is, read on! There is a great surprise awaiting you in the next to last book. Far from being oversimplified, this strange history is extremely varied and complicated. As you know, the missionaries in the early days of the Church recommended the Book of Mormon to the world as "a history of the Indians," Indians being one of the few subjects on which Americans in general possessed some information and on which their interest could be easily aroused. But as a matter of fact, the Book of Mormon is not so much a history of the Indians as of their distant ancestors—people as different from them in many things as our Anglo-Saxon forefathers are from us. The story of the Indians only begins where the Book of Mormon ends: before that it deals largely with those great city-building nations of the south, about whom you know much more than I do.

But before the Book of Mormon ever approaches your glamorous field, it has a good deal to say about another culture, one that has been much studied in our day and can still be examined at first hand, namely (of all things) that of the desert Arabs, which is brought before our eyes in First Nephi with a vividness and clarity which, I believe, say much for the authenticity of the record. The same book also gives us a glimpse into the life of the prosperous and civilized "Jews at Jerusalem" in the days of Zedekiah, briefer but no less clear and specific than the picture of life in the desert.

Already, you see, this remarkable document offers to impart information on no less than *four* widely divergent cultures. I leave it to you whether an accurate description of any one of them, with the possible exception of some Indian tribes, would have been possible from source materials available in the days of Joseph Smith. But it is to the culture number *five* that I would now call your attention. The last history in the Book of Mormon, which goes under the title of the book of Ether, is even more wonderful in my opinion than the first. It takes us into the twilight world of proto-history where the dim half-described shadow-empires of Asia are only in our day beginning to take on recognizable form. As you know, my constitutional weakness for whatever is vague and fuzzy has drawn me irresistibly to this dangerous area, and I have been guilty of a number of lengthy articles on matters that sensible people hold to be unsearchable. You are free to laugh at this, but if you think *I* am trespassing, what would you say of a man who tried to give an account of life in that prehistoric world from what was known of it 120 years ago!

With the same unfaltering and unhurried step that led us across the sands of Arabia (and you must agree that that was a marvelous performance), the author of the Book of Mormon now conducts us into a world so remote, so utterly different from anything within the scope of the Biblical or classical student, that if we would follow him, we must acquire a whole new gear and tackle for the journey. I think we are agreed that it would take a great deal of training for anyone to acquire the background necessary to compose First Nephi. Now imagine any man insane enough to try after such colossal exertions to write *another* such story, of equal length and detail but this time about a totally different race of people, living in an age far removed from the other and in a wholly different geographical setting! As far as I know, not even Joseph Smith ever called anyone's attention to this prodigious feat; we all take it for granted. Yet you will soon see that the author of Ether could have obtained precious little help from any materials used in writing First Nephi. On the contrary, the former experience could only tend to embarrass any attempt at a new history, which would call for an entirely new training and preparation.

What the author of Ether has to supply is not a new plot but all new props and scenery. Every century sees its wars, treaties, migrations, and so forth, but always in a different setting; so that the test of an historical document lies, as we have so often insisted, not in the story it tells but in the casual details that only an eyewitness could have seen. The story of Jared and the story of Lehi have the same theme, the familiar one of the righteous man who leads his people out of a doomed and wicked world. There is nothing original in that: it is also the story of Noah, Enoch, Abraham, Moses, "The Church in the Wilderness," and, for that matter, the restored Church. But what a setting! What strange institutions and practices! How shall we ever be able to check up on such recondite stuff? It is going to require a bit of doing, and so I would advise you to prepare yourself for a long siege.

As you know, it is my unfortunate habit either to write appallingly long letters (twenty pages yet) or none at all. Since you have set this off by accusing the Book of Mormon of proposing an oversimplified story of the Indians, I am not going to let go of your throbbing wrist until, Hamlet-like, I have forced you to look upon a number of strange and disturbing pictures. Had the Jaredites lived in a vacuum, their story would today be beyond the reach of criticism. But they did not live in a vacuum: the book of Ether tells us that they continued in the New World the customs and vices that had flourished in the Old. If, then, we can only find out what people were up to in the homeland at that early day, we will have our "control" for the Ether story. That, as you will recall, is the way we handled the problem of Lehi in the Desert—found out what was going on in the world that Nephi was supposed to be describing and then compared the data with what Nephi had to tell us. The task of checking up on Lehi's activities was greatly simplified by the fact that the Bedouins of Arabia do things in our day much as they did them in his. What we find in Central Asia—Jared's country—are customs equally stable.

"But," I can hear you snorting, "what about the evidence?" It is one thing, I will admit, to read Arabic, and another to lisp the chaste Mongolian. From the isolation of Utah it is not possible to do more than skim the top of our materials; but if you will hasten to consult the bibliographies of such standard works as McGovern and Vernadsky, you will see that even they have hardly done more. Until someone appears who is competent to deal with the difficult documents—a classicist who is also a Sinologist, an Indologian, an expert on Semitics, Turkish, Slavic, and what-not, in short, another Vambery—we must be content to base our speculations on the limited materials within our control. Our whole justification is that these are adequate, as in the case of Lehi, to prove what we want to prove, no more. And what are we going to prove? That certain strange and unfamiliar things described in Ether actually could have taken place as described, because they actually *did* take place—characteristically and repeatedly—in those very cultural areas in which, according to the Book of Mormon, the Jaredites acquired their culture and civilization.

And what are those "materials" to which we have been so darkly alluding? They come in periods. To illustrate, let us say that there is a peculiar custom—of the royal court or the hunt, for example—described in Ether. We find the same custom described by modern travelers in Central Asia (source number one); Christian and Moslem merchants, geographers, and missionaries report the same peculiar custom in the same region in the Middle Ages (source number two); next we move back another seven or eight hundred years and behold: the spies and ambassadors of the Byzantine court describe the same custom (source number three, and so on), for which we are now beginning to feel a measure of respect! Moving back through the centuries, we find that classical historians from Cassiodorus to Herodotus, a full thousand years apart, mention the same custom, and then slipping back another fifteen hundred to two thousand years we read about it in the records of the Assyrians and Babylonians. Last of all, the Russian archaeologists find evidence for the same thing in prehistoric times. From these many points of reference we may project, as it were, a smooth curve right back to the Jaredites, and safely assume that when the book of Ether describes the very institutions depicted in these records of early Asia it is on solid ground. In each instance, however, you will have to be the judge, for all we can give at the present interval is a sampling of the evidence. You may have to wait thirty years for the rest of it.

Please note that we are limiting our curiosity to *the sort of thing that happened*. The exact time and place of any specific event are no concern of ours. Such matters are always open to dispute, and in the case of the Jaredites they don't begin to come within guessing distance. Bear in mind that these people lived in a realm far removed from the current of world history; in a dateless age they took their culture from the common source and thereafter were on their own until they disappeared from the earth. What difference whether they had a battle in one spot or another—in one year or another? The important thing is that they did have battles and, for our purpose, that those battles followed patterns of warfare peculiar to central Asia. We specialize in patterns.

The first chapter of our Ether text gives us warning not to be dogmatic about chronology. In the genealogical list of thirty names running back to "the great tower" the word "descendant" occurs, once where several generations may be spanned (Ether 1:23; 10:9), and twice interchangeably with the word "son" (Ether 1:6, 16; cf. 10:31; 11:23). As you know, in Hebrew and other languages "son" and "descendant" are both rendered by one very common word. One and the same word describes a modern Jew and Father Isaac as "sons" of Abraham—the word is understood differently in each case, but is *not* written differently. A person confined to a written text would have no means of knowing when *ben* should be taken to mean "son" in a literal sense and when it means merely "descendant." The ancient Hebrews knew perfectly well when to make the distinction: like the Arabs and Maoris they kept their records in their heads, and in mentioning a particular patriarch, it was assumed that the hearer was familiar with his line down to his next important descendant, the written lists being a mere outline to establish connections between particular lines—the name of a patriarch was enough to indicate his line, which did not have to be written out in full. Sir Leonard Woolley has some interesting things to say on this subject in his book *Abraham*. Now Ether proves, at least to Latter-day Saints, that "son" and "descendant" were both used in the ancient genealogies, which thus do not present an unbroken father-to-son relationship. We are told that the genealogy in Ether belongs to the second part of a record and that "the first part of this record . . . is had among the Jews" (Ether 1:3). So we may regard the Old Testament genealogies as the earlier part of this same list and are thus faced with the possibility, long suspected by many, that in Biblical genealogies *ben* must sometimes be read "son" and sometimes "descendant," though men have long since lost the knowledge that enabled the ancient ruler to make the necessary distinction. The result is, of course, that our Biblical genealogies as we read them today may be much too short.

Incidentally, the genealogy in Ether, chapter one, explains why neither the brother of Jared nor his children are ever named. (We are not even told how many sons he had, though Jared's own sons are listed by name.) This once puzzled me, since the brother of Jared is by all odds the most important character in the book. It is, of course, because "he that wrote this" is a direct descendant of Jared (Ether 1:2, 32), and not of Jared's brother, and is giving the history of his own line only.

To get involved in Andree's eighty-eight versions of

the Flood story, or the sixty-four conflicting accounts of the dispersion listed by von Schwarz, might jeopardize the terseness and brevity that give our little notes their gem-like quality. Let us consign such matters to the decent obscurity of a footnote.[2] As long as you insist on having the evidence for everything, by the way, you cannot object to an occasional reference in small print. The trouble with the Babel story is that we are told so little. A few short enigmatic verses in Genesis are not enough in themselves to justify the dogmatic reconstructions and wild surmises that have raged about the tower. Ether has the support of the latest conclusions, based on Genesis 10, that when the tower was built, the people had already been "spread abroad in the earth after the deluge" for some time.[3] It is interesting that all accounts are very vague as to where the human family lived *before* the flood, the best version, that of Berossos, reporting that "the flood survivors are 'lost,' and have to be told by a divine revelation where they are."[4]

When our source describes a particular region as "*that quarter* where there never had man been" (Ether 2:5), the implication is that men had certainly been in other quarters. Moreover, Jared's people were reluctant to leave their homes, and when they were finally "driven out of the land," they took with them flocks, herds, and seeds of every kind, together with the knowledge and skills (they even took books with them) necessary to establish a great civilization—all these things being the necessary products of a long-established and widespread economy. Civilization meets us full-blown, nay, decadent, in the pages of Ether. One looks in vain for very many signs of evolution in the Book of Mormon. This is a red rag to the social scientists, I know, but that is only because social scientists don't read the historical documents, which, if they only knew it, are the inexhaustible field notes and lab notes of the human race. To those whose view of the world comes from questionnaires and textbooks, it seems incredible that the early dynastic civilization of Sumer, for example, should be so far ahead of later cultures that "compared with it everything that comes later seems almost decadent; the handicrafts must have reached an astounding perfection."[5] It is hard to believe that the great Babylonian civilization throughout the many centuries in which it flourished was merely coasting, sponging off the achievements of a much earlier civilization which by all rights should have been "primitive"; yet that is exactly the picture that Meissner gives us in his great study.[6] It is against the rules that those artistic attainments for which Egypt is most noted—the matchless portraits, the wonderful stone vessels, the exquisite weaving—should reach their peak at the very dawn of Egyptian history, in the predynastic period, yet such is the case. It is in the earliest dynasties, and not in the later ones, that technical perfection and artistic taste of the Egyptians in jewelry, furniture, ceramics, etc., are most "advanced." "Here is a very odd thing," a British authority recently commented. "In literature the best in each kind comes first, comes suddenly and never comes again. This is a disturbing, uncomfortable, unacceptable idea to people who take their doctrine of evolution over-simply. But I think it must be admitted to be true. Of the very greatest things in each sort of literature, the masterpiece is unprecedented, unique, never challenged or approached henceforth."[7] More impressive is the report of the Egyptologist Siegfried Schott: "Time and again in the development of Egyptian culture the monuments of a new epoch present something heretofore unknown in a state of completely developed perfection." He lists as such items the sudden appearance of the Pyramid Texts, "the surprising emergence of temple architecture and its mural decorations, without any prior forms to indicate an earlier development," the buildings of Zoser at Sakkara, the great pyramids themselves, and the temple reliefs which display a complete mastery of medium and style on their first appearance.[8] Are not the earliest paintings of the human race to this day unexcelled? Please note that we are only able to pass judgment on those things which happen to have survived from those remote ages: We assume that those people were crude and primitive in all *other* things, until some of those other things turn up and show them to be far ahead of us. We must admit, for example, that the stone chipping of certain paleolithic hunters has never been equaled since their day; it so happens that stone implements are all that have survived from those people—have we any right to deny them perfection of other things? Is there any reason for supposing that their wood or leather work was inferior? Anyone with a modern education will tell you without hesitation that the earliest weaving of our ancestors *must* have been very crude indeed. But when, contrary to all expectations, some of the cloth was actually found, the French experts gave it careful examination and declared it the equal of the very finest stuff we are capable of producing today.[9] The only weapons that have survived from prehistoric times are far more suited for their purpose than a modern rifle. The deadliest of all hunting weapons remains to this day the stone-headed (not steel-headed) arrow. In my recent labors on the marked arrows I had occasion to assemble an impressive amount of evidence on this head.[10] Eyre has recently supplied a good deal of evidence to prove that our "primitive" ancestors enjoyed a good deal more security, comfort, and pleasure in life than we do.[11] Moreover, as an anthropologist you know perfectly well that backward and primitive people may have mental powers equaling or excelling our own—look at Elkin's Australian aborigines or, if they are too far away, I can lead you to some Indians who in some things can make us feel like cretins. If it would not take us too far afield, I could show you that the dogma of the evolutionary advancement of the human race as a whole is nothing but an impressive diploma which the nineteenth century awarded—*summa cum laude*—to itself. Modern man is a self-certified genius who, having pinned the blue ribbon on his own lapel, proceeds to hand out all the other awards according as the various candidates are more or less like *him*.

"Yes," I can hear you say, "but there must have been a long evolution behind all these early achievements." Which is for you to prove, not assume, if you are a scientist. What is certain to date is (a) that their evolutionary background has not been discovered, and (b) that there is no record of *subsequent* improvement through all these thousands of years. So let the biologists talk of evolution; for the historian it has no meaning. Indeed Professor Van der Meer, perhaps the foremost living student of ancient chronology, can only regret "the influence of a theory of evolutionism which has been dragged so unfortunately into the study of ancient history."[12]

By now I imagine I have got you into such a state that you would refuse to read farther even if I had the time to write more. I leave you now with a promise of coming attractions, pending your willingness to carry on the discussion. Be so good as to indicate your reactions to all these words, and I shall conduct myself accordingly.

The Tower[13]

Dear Professor F.:

In reply to my sustained blast of the 17th of this month, you tax me with a "naive and gullible acceptance of the Tower of Babel story." I knew you would. Most people believe quite naively that Lincoln wrote the Gettysburg Address, but their totally uncritical acceptance of the fact does not prevent it from being true. You may accept any story naively or you may take it critically. What would you say if I were to accuse you of being very simple and gullible in *rejecting* the story of the tower? The cornerstone of "sound scholarship" in our day is the comfortable doctrine that the answer *no* can never be quite as wrong as the answer *yes*, a proposition which to my knowledge has never been demonstrated. Excuse me if I seem recalcitrant, but I find it odd that the one skill most appreciated and rewarded in those circles where one hears everlastingly of "the inquiring mind" and the importance of "finding out for one's self" is the gift and power of taking things for granted. Even our Latter-day Saint intellectuals are convinced that the way to impress the Gentiles is not to acquire a mastery of their critical tools (how few even know Latin!), but simply to defer in all things to their opinions.

Think back, my good man, to the first act of recorded history. What meets our gaze as the curtain rises? People everywhere building towers. And why are they building towers? To get to heaven. The tower was, to use the Babylonian formula, the *markas shame u irsitim,* the "binding-place of heaven and earth," where alone one could establish contact with the upper and lower worlds.[14] That goes not only for Babylonia but also for the whole ancient world, as I have pointed out at merciless length in my recent study on the "Hierocentric State."[15] The towers were artificial mountains, as any textbook will tell you, and no temple-complex could be without one. The labors of Dombart, Jeremias, Andrae, Burrows, and others will spare us the pains of showing you these towers scattered everywhere throughout the old world as a means of helping men get to heaven.[16] The legends concerning them are legion, but they all fall into the same pattern: In the beginning an ambitious race of men tried to get to heaven by climbing a mountain or tower; they failed and then set out to conquer the world. A thoroughly typical version of the story is a variant found in Jewish and Christian apocryphal writers in which the sons of Seth (the angels, in some versions), eager to regain the paradise Adam had lost, went up on to Mount Hermon, and there lived lives of religious asceticism, calling themselves "the Watchers" and "the Sons of Elohim." It was an attempt to establish the heavenly order, and it failed, the embittered colony descending the mountain to break the covenant, marry the daughters of Cain, and beget a race of "men notorious for murders and robberies." Determined to possess the earth if they could not possess heaven, the men of the mountain denied that they had failed, faked the priesthood, and forced the inhabitants of the earth to accept the kings they put over them.[17] This story you will recognize as an obvious variant of the extremely ancient and widespread Mad Hunter cycle, which I treated in an article on the origin of the state.[18] The Mad Hunter, you will recall, claimed to be the rightful ruler of the universe, challenged God to an archery contest, and built a great tower from which he hoped to shoot his arrows into heaven. Sir James Frazer has collected a large number of American Indian versions of the story to illustrate Old World parallels, for the tale is met with among primitive hunters throughout the world.[19]

In Genesis 10:4 we read that Nimrod, the "mighty hunter against the Lord,"[20] founded the kingdom of Babel, and in the next chapter that Babel was the name of the tower built to reach to heaven. This Nimrod seems to be the original arch-type of the Mad Hunter.[21] His name is for the Jews at all times the very symbol of rebellion against God and of usurped authority; he it was "who became a hunter of men," established false priesthood and false kingship in the earth in imitation of God's rule and "made all men to sin."[22] A very early Christian writing tells how Noah's descendants waged bitter war among themselves after his death, to see who should possess his kingship; finally one of the blood of Ham prevailed, and from him the Egyptians, Babylonians, and Persians derive their priesthood and kingship. "From the race of Ham," says the text, "came one through the magical (as opposed to the holy) succession named Nimrod, who was a giant against the Lord . . . whom the Greeks call Zoroaster and who ruled the world, forcing all men by his false magical arts to recognize his authority."[23] The Chronicon Paschale reports a widespread tradition that this giant who built Babylon was not only the first king of Persia, the earthly Cosmocrator, but also the first man to teach the killing and eating of beasts, a belief also expressed in the Koran.[24] There is another common tradition that Nimrod's crown was a fake, and that he ruled without right in the earth over all the sons of Noah, and they were all under his power and counsel; while he did not go in the ways of the Lord, and was more wicked than all the men that were before him.[25] The antiquity of these stories may be judged from an early Babylonian account of a wicked king who first mingled "small and great . . . on the mound" and caused them to sin, earning for himself the title of "king of the noble mound" (cf. the tower), "god of lawlessness," god of no government.[26] In the very earliest Indo-European traditions this person is Dahhak, "The type of the *dregvant*, the man of the Lie and king of mad-men," who sat on the throne for a thousand years and forced all men to subscribe their names in the book of the Dragon, thus making them subject to him.[27] This recalls the very ancient tradition that when Seth succeeded Adam in the priesthood, he ordered a special record to be kept, which was called the Book of Life and which was concealed from the sons of Cain. The Dragon's Book was an imitation of this.[28] There is a constant tendency in ancient records to confuse Jemshid, the founder of the earthly kingship and the father of the human race, not with Adam, but with the false Adam or usurper.[29]

In the book of Ether the name of Nimrod is attached to "the valley which was northward," and which led "into that quarter where there never had man been" (Ether 2:2, 5), which suits very well with the legendary character of Nimrod as the Mad Hunter of the Steppes. The name of Nimrod has always baffled philologians, who have never been able to locate it—though Kraeling now accepts Eduard Meyer's much-doubted theory that the name is Egypto-Lybian, which suits well with our own belief regarding the curse of Ham[30]—but at the end of the last century the explorer and scholar Emin found that name attached to legends (mostly of the Mad Hunter variety) and place names in the region of Lake Van, the great valley system due north of upper Mesopotamia.[31] Now I am not insisting for a minute that the legendary Nimrod ever existed. As I told you before, I am only interested in the *type* of thing that happened, and after having examined hundreds of legends from all parts of the ancient world, all telling substantially the same story, I think that anyone would find it difficult, in view of the evidence, to deny that there was some common event behind them. It seems to have been a *single* event, moreover.

How so? I said above that we find mounds, towers, and accompanying rituals throughout the whole ancient world; now I will go further and say that these mounds and towers and the great cult-complexes that go with them were not so many independent local inventions but actually imitations derived ultimately from a single original. Every great national shrine of antiquity had a founding legend of how in the beginning it was brought through the air from some mysterious faraway land. And this faraway land always turns out to have been in central Asia. Our Norse Othinn came from the giants' land to the east, the Greek national cult from the land of the Hyperboreans, far to the northeast of Greece; people of the Near East looked to a mysterious white mountain of the North as the seat of their primordial cult, the Chinese to the paradise or mountain of the West, and so forth. You may list the various founding legends and trace them back at your leisure to a single point of origin.[32] I find it strange that the founding father and *summus deus* of each nation of antiquity is somewhere declared to be a fraud and an impostor, a wandering tramp from afar whose claims to supreme authority cannot stand a too careful examination. Think of Prometheus' challenge to Zeus, of Loki's blackmailing of Othinn, of the dubious "Justification of Osiris," of the terror of almighty Anu when Tiamat challenges his authority, and so forth.[33] Run down these legends, and you will find in every case that the usurper comes from Central Asia. Even Isaiah (Isaiah 14:12-14) recalls that in the beginning the adversary himself set up his throne "upon the Mountain of the assembly in the regions of the North," and there pretended to be "like the Most High." For all this a single origin is indicated; whether historical or ritual makes little difference.

There is one aspect of the Nimrod cycle that is too interesting to pass by, especially for an anthropologist. That is the tradition of the stolen garment.

The Stolen Garment

Nimrod claimed his kingship on the ground of victory over his enemies;[34] his priesthood, however, he claimed by virtue of possessing "the garment of Adam." The legends of the Jews assure us that it was by virtue of owning this garment that Nimrod was able to claim power to rule over the whole earth, and that he sat in his tower while men came and worshiped him.[35] The Apocryphal writers, Jewish and Christian, have a good deal to say about this garment. To quote one of them: "the garments of skin which God made for Adam and his wife, when they went out of the garden, were given . . . after the death of Adam . . . to Enoch"; hence they passed to Methusaleh, and then to Noah, from whom Ham stole them as the people were leaving the ark. Ham's grandson Nimrod obtained them from his father Cush.[36] As for the *legitimate* inheritance of this clothing, a very old fragment recently discovered says that Michael "disrobed Enoch of his earthly garments, and put on him his angelic clothing," taking him into the presence of God.[37] This garment of Enoch was supposed to be the very garment of skins that John the Baptist wore, called by the early Christians "the garment of Elias."[38] An Arabic "Life of John the Baptist" says that Gabriel brought it to John from heaven as "the garment of Elijah"; "it went back," says John Chrysostom, "to the beginning of the world, to the times before which Adam required covering. Thus it was the symbol of repentance."[39] Others believed it was the same garment that Herod and later the Romans put under lock and key when they wished to prevent the people from putting it on a candidate of their own choice, and tell how the Jews tried to seize the garment by force and put it on John the Baptist, thus making him, instead of Herod, their high priest.[40] Whatever its origin, the wearing of a garment of repentance, symbolic of life of man in his fallen state, was known to the most ancient Christians and practiced by certain ultra-conservative cults down to modern times.[41]

Incidentally the story of the stolen garment as told by the old rabbis, including the great Eleazer, calls for an entirely different rendering of the strange story in Genesis 9 from the version in our King James Bible. They seemed to think that the *ᶜerwath* of Genesis 9:22 did not mean "nakedness" at all, but should be given its primary root meaning of "skin covering." Read thus, we are to understand that Ham took the garment of his father while he was sleeping and showed it to his brethren, Shem and Japheth, who took a pattern or copy of it (*salmah*) or else a woven garment like it (*simlah*) which they put upon their own shoulders, returning the skin garment to their father. Upon awaking, Noah recognized the priesthood of two sons but cursed the son who tried to rob him of his garment. By an extremely common type of substitution, the *simlah* of Genesis 9:23 could very easily stand for an original *tsimlah*, a copy, imitation, pattern, or by an equally common type of transposition for *Salmah*, a garment or mantle, as in Micah 2:8. Even as it stands *simlah* means only a woven garment and can hardly refer to the original skin article. This is, apparently, the source of the widespread legend that Ham stole the garment of Noah and claimed to possess the priesthood by virtue of his illegal insignia. Ham's descendants, Cush and Nimrod—both Africans, though Nimrod in his wandering moved to Asia[42]—made the same claim. It is interesting that according to certain ancient scriptures which the Latter-day Saints claim have been restored by revelation in our own age, Pharaoh (who represents the Afro-Asian line of Cush-Nimrod) was blessed as to the kingship but cursed as to the priesthood, and he offered Abraham the privilege of wearing his own royal insignia in hope that Abraham would return the compliment by allowing Pharaoh to wear his priestly ones (Abraham 1:26-27). According to a very old tradition, Pharaoh coveted the priesthood of Moses exactly as his ancestor Nimrod did that of Abraham, and it was said that the Pharaohs of Egypt dressed in a skin garment "to show that their origin was older than time itself."[43]

According to the Talmud, Nimrod's "great success in hunting was due to the fact that he wore the coat of skin which God made for Adam and Eve."[44] There is a tradition that Nimrod, becoming jealous of the rival hunter Esau (so much for chronology!), lay in ambush for him but was defeated by Esau, who cut off his head and "took the valuable garments of Nimrod, . . . with which Nimrod prevailed over the whole land (or earth!), and he ran and concealed them in his house." These garments, says the report, were nothing less than the birthright which Esau later sold to Jacob.[45]

Two significant conclusions come from all this: (1) that any historical reconstruction of what actually happened is out of the question, what has come down to us being a mass of conflicting legends and reports, and (2) that these conflicting legends and reports nevertheless agree on certain main points, that they are very old, and were considered by the most learned Jews to present matters of great importance, whose significance escaped later ages. The priests and kings of antiquity certainly wore such garments,[46] and the skin garment was often imitated in woven materials[47]; in fact, the skin garment was itself held to be a substitute for a still older garment made of the leaves of the *ficus religiosus*.[48]

I make no apology for conducting you into these lost bypaths of the past. You have often proclaimed it your professional obligation to be interested in all things, and especially the unusual. Still there is such a thing as going too far, and it is high time I was showing you what a sober, factual, and common-sense document the book of Ether really is. Let us return to Babel.

2

Departure

The Dispersion

The book of Ether, depicting the uprooting and scattering from the tower of a numerous population, shows them going forth not individually but in groups, and not merely family groups but groups of friends and associates: "thy friends and their families, and the friends of Jared and their families" (Ether 1:41). There was no point in having Jared's language unconfounded if there was to be no one he could talk to, and his brother cried to the Lord that his friends might also retain the language. The same, however, would apply to any other language: If every individual were to speak a tongue all of his own and so go off entirely by himself, the races would have been not merely scattered but quite annihilated.[1] We must not fall into the old vice of reading into the scripture things that are not there. There is nothing said in our text about every man suddenly speaking a new language. We are told in the book of Ether that languages were confounded with and *by* the "confounding" of the people: "Cry unto the Lord," says Jared (Ether 1:34), "that he will not confound us that we may not understand our *words*" (italics added). The statement is significant for more than one thing. How can it possibly be said that "*we* may not understand *our* words"? Words we cannot understand may be nonsense syllables or may be in some foreign language, but in either case they are not *our* words. The only way we can fail to understand our own words is to have words that are actually ours change their meaning among us. That is exactly what happens when people, and hence languages, are either "confounded," that is, mixed up, or scattered. In Ether's account, the confounding of *people* is not to be separated from the confounding of their languages; they are, and have always been, one and the same process: the Lord, we are told (Ether 1:35-37), "did not confound the language of Jared; and Jared and his brother were not confounded . . . and the Lord had compassion upon their friends and their families also, that they were not confounded." That "confound" as used in the book of Ether is meant to have its true and proper meaning of "to pour together," "to mix up together," is clear from the prophecy in Ether 13:8, that "the remnant of the house of Joseph shall be built upon this land; . . . and they shall no more be confounded," the word here meaning mixed up with other people, culturally, linguistically, or otherwise.

Yet another important biblical expression receives welcome elucidation from our text: though Ether says nothing about "the whole earth" being "of one language and one speech" (Genesis 11:1), he does give us an interesting hint as to how those words may be taken. Just as "son" and "descendant" are the same word in Hebrew and so may easily be confused by translators (who in fact have no way of knowing, save from the context, in which sense the word is to be understood), so "earth" and "land" are the same word, the well-known *eretz*. In view of the fact that the book of Ether, speaking only of the Jaredites, notes that "there were none of the fair sons and daughters upon the face of the whole earth who repented of their sins" (Ether 13:17), it would seem that the common "whole earth" (*kol ha-aretz*) of the Old Testament need not always be taken to mean the entire globe. Certainly it is quite as legitimate to think of the days of Peleg as the time when, as the old Jewish writers describe it, "the children of Noah began to divide the earth among themselves,"[2] as, without the least authority, to visualize the drifting of the continents or the rending apart of the terrestrial globe. A reader's first reaction to an ancient and fragmentary text usually becomes a lifelong credo, though research and revelation have combined in latter days to discredit this obvious and easy solution of the mysteries. The book of Ether, like First Nephi, is, when we come to examine it, heavily weighted in the direction of sober and factual history and was never meant to be a springboard for the imagination; for example, our record does not attribute the scattering of the people, as one might innocently suppose it does, to the confusion of tongues. After the brother of Jared had been assured that he and his people and their language would not be confounded, the question of whether they would be driven out of the land still remained to be answered: That was another issue, and it is obvious that the language they spoke had as little to do with driving them out of the land as it did with determining their destination. It was something else that drove the reluctant Jaredites from their homes. What could have forced them to leave? History to be sober and factual need not deal with the dull, normal, and everyday. The confounding and scattering of the people of the tower was no slow working out of the historical process. It was sudden and terrible, and the book of Ether gives the clearest possible indication of what caused it.

But this introduces a theme on which it is impossible for me to speak with brevity. Let us consign it to a later communication.

A Note on the Weather[3]

Dear F.:

It is gratifying to know that you have at last read the book of Ether and found that it is not, in spite of its name, "chloroform in print." The thing to which you are now objecting, "the extravagant and overdone account of how they crossed the ocean," is the very thing to which my last letter was leading. We ended, you will recall, with the observation that it must have been something terrific that drove the Jaredites out of the land. What was it?

The *burans* of central Asia are terrible at all times. Ancient and modern travelers tell almost unbelievable but uniform tales of those appalling winds which almost daily shift vast masses of sand, dust, and even gravel from one part of the continent to another.[4] The great loess deposits on the eastern and western fringes of the vast area bear witness to even more dreadful dust storms that accompanied the drying up of the land after the glacial epoch. But it is when the world's weather gets out of hand, as it has a number of times in the course of history, that the blowing sands of Asia bring mighty empires to ruin, bury great cities almost overnight, and scatter the tribes in all directions to overrun and submerge the more favored civilizations of the east and west. The weather of Asia is the great central driving mechanism of world history. It is only in recent years that men have begun to correlate the great migrations of history, with their attendant wars and revolutions, with those major weather crises such as the great wind and drought of 2300-2200 B.C. and the world floods of 1300 B.C., which we now know to have taken place in the course of recorded history.[5] So hypnotized have students of society become by the ease and directness with which an evolutionary rule-of-thumb may be applied to all the contingencies of life, that the raging of the elements and the crash of empires go unheeded in their graphs and handbooks. With examples gross as earth before them, they still disdain to recognize anything as cheaply sensational as plagues and earthquakes, nor will they acknowledge the frightening speed with which the scenes of world history are shifted.

Sir Aurel Stein in his book *Lou-Lan* has described the deserted houses and streets of that city standing exactly as they did fourteen centuries ago, when their inhabitants were driven forth by drought so sudden and severe that neither the wood of the fruit trees nor the most delicate fabrics have rotted since then.[6] The mighty city of Etsina was just as suddenly deserted six hundred years ago, and not found until 1909: "All natural life died. The trees of the forest threw themselves to the ground [referring, of course, to the terrible winds] . . . and storms arose which soon buried the country in sand." To this day the trees remain undecayed, "like sun-dried mummies, dead, naked and grey. . . . Over a vast area, once shady forest, they lay in thousands. . . . We passed other ruins of deserted strong-holds, and with strange sensations dug up objects that no human being had touched for more than six hundred years."[7] The same traveler who reports these things was to witness the recurrence of this familiar Asiatic tragedy with his own eyes:

> Once we came upon an abandoned Sart village, where newly thrown-up dams and uncompleted excavations bore witness to the departed population's desperate struggle to retain the vanishing water. . . . But a day had come when there was no more water to be had. The animals stood by the watering places and sought in vain for moisture, the women wept in the houses, and the men gathered in the mosque to pray to Allah for the miracle which alone could save their many homes. [Cf. Ether 1:38.] But no miracle happened; the village got no water, and in the last extremity of famine the people had thrown their most indispensable possessions on to the remaining horses and donkeys and hastily left their homes and the lands of their fathers to follow their *aksakal* [village elder, cf. the brother of Jared] out into the parched country around on a desperate search for water.[8]

The fate of the unhappy wanderers is thus described: "Later on we sometimes met with small parties of these former agricultural villagers, who now drifted about out on the steppes as unhappy nomads. The fugitives had been obliged to divide into small groups, since no one water-hole could accommodate them all."[9]

Is not this the story of the dispersion in miniature? You

know the story of how the ancestors of the Etruscans were driven out of Asia Minor by drought and moved to the west, hunting for a promised land. It is not merely water these people were looking for, but a better land, above all, a better grazing land. In the epic of the Banī Hilāl we are shown how one of the greatest of Arab tribes was driven from their homes by seven years of hot winds, and how they sought a promised land, first in Central Asia and then in Morocco. It was when the rest of the world was smitten with famine that Egypt became the refuge of the patriarchs, for "there was corn in Egypt." As you know, there are two classic points or centers of radiation from which all the great migrations of antiquity took their beginning—the heart of Asia and (to a far lesser degree) the Arabian desert. Is it not remarkable that the migrations of the Book of Mormon take their departure from these same two centers?

You must get over the idea that history moves at a slow, even, majestic pace. It does not. The sudden calamity that overtook an Asian village in 1927 has struck repeatedly in the past, dispersing the inhabitants of mighty capitals to become wanderers on the earth, and "when the storm laid itself to rest, the flying sands solidified again and the terrified nomads found the whole face of nature changed into new shapes."[10] And of all the many cities and empires dispersed by a sudden puff of burning air, Babel, *the* city of the tower, has left behind the richest deposit of legend and tradition.

Eusebius in his *Chronicon,* which has surprisingly proved one of the most reliable sources of early oriental history, cites the Sibyl to the effect that "when all men were of one tongue, some of them built a high tower so as to mount up to heaven, but God destroyed the tower by mighty winds."[11] Two centuries earlier Theophilus of Antioch gave a fuller version of the story, quoting the Sibyl in verse: "After the cataclysm cities and kings had a new beginning, in this manner. The first city of all was Babylon, . . . and one by the name of Nimrod became its king. . . . Since at that time men tended to become scattered, they took counsel of themselves and not of the Lord, to build a city and a tower the top of which would reach to heaven, so that their own name might be glorified. . . . Thus speaks the Sybil: But when the threats of the great God were fulfilled of which he had warned mortal men at the time, they built a tower in the Assyrian land. They all once spoke the same language and wanted to mount up to the starry heavens. But forthwith the Immortal One laid great stress upon the blasts, so that the wind overthrew the mighty tower, and drove mortals to strive with one another. And when the tower had fallen, the languages of men were divided up into many dialects, so that the earth became filled with different kingdoms of men."[12] The Book of Jubilees (second century B.C.) tells how "the Lord sent a mighty wind against the tower and overthrew it upon the earth, and behold it was between Asshur and Babylon in the land of Shinar, and they called its name 'Overthrow.' "[13] The zealous and learned Persian antiquary Tha'labi (d. A.D. 1030) records the report that the people were scattered from the tower by an awful drought, accompanied by winds of such velocity as actually to blow down the tower.[14] "And forty years after the Tower was finished," says Bar Hebraeus, who collected a vast amount of lore in central Asia in the thirteenth century, "God sent a wind and the Tower was overturned and Nemrodh died in it."[15] The picture of violent atmospheric disturbances accompanied by social upheavals, the scattering of tribes, and the changing of languages cannot but go back to some real experience; not only is it the sort of thing one would expect, but it is also definitely known to have happened time and time again—there is no reason for doubting that a great city called Babel once long ago suffered the same fate as the people of 'Ad and Thamud, of Lou Lan, Etsingol, or the Nasamonians.[16]

But what of the Book of Mormon? In striking contrast to the story of Lehi, where the only terrors met on the journey by land and sea were the normal and familiar ones, including a typhoon, we have in the history of the Jaredite migration a very freakish state of things. The Lord commanded Nephi to build "a ship"—an ordinary ship, which his brothers felt sure he would never be able to finish. Yet the ship was finished, and the family set sail. Nephi's brethren, for all their mocking, apparently had no scornful comments to make on the type of ship he was building. From which we conclude that it was, as it is repeatedly called, simply "a ship," though, as a landsman, Nephi needed special guidance (1 Nephi 17:8). Now, Lehi's people had to cross at least twice and probably three or four times as much water as the Jaredites, and an ordinary ship sufficed for their purpose. But Jared's ships were altogether unusual vessels. The Lord gave the builder special instructions for every detail. They had to be submersible and yet ride very lightly on the surface of the waves. "They were small and they were light upon the water," yet built to stand terrific pressure: "exceedingly tight," "tight like unto a dish," with special sealed vent holes that could not be opened when the water pressure on the outside was greater than the air pressure within. The Lord explained why it would be necessary to build such peculiar vessels: because he was about to loose winds of incredible violence that would make the crossing a frightful ordeal at best: any windows, he warns, will be dashed to pieces; fire will be out of the question; "ye shall be as a whale in the midst of the sea; for the mountain waves shall dash upon you. . . . Ye cannot cross this great deep save I prepare you against the waves of the sea, and the winds which have gone forth, and the floods which shall come. Therefore what will ye that I should prepare for you that ye may have light when ye are swallowed up in the depths of the sea?" (Ether 2:23-25). This was no normal crossing and no brief passing storm: "The wind did *never cease* to blow towards the promised land while they were upon the waters" (Ether 6:8)—"the Lord God caused that there should be a furious wind blow upon the face of the waters; . . . they were *many times* buried in the depths of the sea, because of the mountain waves which broke upon them, and also the great and terrible tempests which were caused by the fierceness of the *wind*" (Ether 6:5-6; italics added). It is perfectly clear from our account that the party was to spend a good deal of time below the surface of the sea! Of course such phenomenal and continual winds cannot have been a mere local disturbance, and we may confidently assume that the book of Ether is reporting the same super-winds that are said to have accompanied and possibly caused the destruction of the tower.

In so many words, the book of Ether tells us that at the time of the dispersion the world was swept by winds of colossal violence. There are three main sources for checking on this: (1) the old traditions of the tower, which almost always mention the winds, (2) the studies of the paleoclimatologists which correlated with historical records show that the world has repeatedly passed through catastrophic climatic changes within the last 6,000 years, e.g. the great world drought and windstorms of cir. 2200 B.C., the terrible drought of 1000 B.C., the equally violent floods of 1300 B.C. and the *Fimbulwinter* of 850 B.C. etc.,[17] and (3) actual historical records of places that have suffered the same fate as Babel, showing that to be not a fantastic but actually a characteristic occurrence in world history. A good example of such historical records is Qazwini's *Cosmography*, which tells how in the Middle Ages the great dome of Bagdad, which "dome was the symbol (*'alam*) of Bagdad, and the crown of the country, and the principal achievement of the sons of Abbas," collapsed during a great windstorm. Scholars have often pointed out that the Tower of Babel was just such a symbol of the power and unity of its builders (Genesis 11:4).[18]

Not only does the Bible not mention the winds, but the Book of Mormon itself does so casually, albeit quite specifically, by way of explaining why the Jaredite ships were built as they were and in describing the sea voyage. This very casualness is a strong argument for the authenticity of the record.

The Way Out[19]

Dear F.:

From the plain of Shinear the Jaredites moved northward into a valley named after Nimrod, the mighty hunter, and thence "into that quarter where there never had man been" (Ether 2:5). This would take them into the land of great broad valleys where the Tigris, Euphrates, Kura, and Araks rivers have their headwaters, a "hub of radiating valleys and routes to which the Euphrates owes its importance as a highway of commercial and military penetration."[20] The frequent occurrence of the name of Nimrod in this area, which we have already noted, may not be without genuine significance, for no historical phenomenon has been more thoroughly demonstrated than the extreme tenacity of place names. In many instances place names still in use among illiterate peasants or nomads have been proved to go back to prehistoric times.

Whether the party moved east or west from the valley of Nimrod is not a major issue, though a number of things favor an eastern course.[21] For one thing, there is the great length of the journey: "for this many years we have been in the wilderness" (Ether 3:3); such a situation calls not only for vast expanses to wander in, but a terrain favorable to cattle-raising nomads and a region "in which there never had man been," conditions to which the Asiatic rather than the European areas conform. But most revealing is the report that "the wind did never cease to blow towards the promised land, while they were upon the waters; and thus they were driven forth before the wind" (Ether 6:8). Now whether the Jaredites sailed from eastern or western shores, they would necessarily have to cross the ocean between the thirtieth and sixtieth parallels north, where the prevailing winds are westerly right around the world. Since the cause of these winds is tied up with the revolution of the earth and the relative coolness of the polar regions, it may be assumed that the same winds prevailed in Jared's time as in ours. Of course, one cannot be too dogmatic on such a point, for weather has changed through the ages, and freak storms do occur; yet the extreme *steadiness* of the wind strongly suggests prevailing westerlies and a North Pacific crossing, since it would have meant a headwind all the way had the voyagers attempted the Atlantic. The length of the sea journey, 344 days, tells us nothing, since the vessels, though driven before the wind, apparently did not use sails: the almost perpetual hurricane conditions would have made sails impossible even if they had had them. But the fact that the party spent almost a year on the water even with the winds behind them certainly suggests the Pacific, and recalls many tales of Chinese junks that through the centuries have been driven helplessly before the wind to end up after a year or so at sea stranded on the beaches of our West Coast.[22] Then too, we must not forget that a mountain of "exceeding height" stood near the point of Jaredite embarkation (Ether 3:1), and that there is no such mountain on the Atlantic seaboard of Europe, as there are at many points on the Asiatic shore.

But east or west, from the Baltic to the Pacific, "from the Gobi desert and the border of Korea to the Lower Danube and the Carpathian Mountains," a single way of life has prevailed since the dawn of history, conditioned by a remarkably uniform type of terrain.[23] A number of authoritative studies in the so-called Art of the Steppes, and the excavations of the Russians in recent years have confirmed the most extravagant speculations on the extent, antiquity, and uniformity of the steppe cultures. The newly discovered Kelteminarian culture, for example, would seem to bind together all the major languages of Europe and central Asia in a single, vast, prehistoric continuum that embraces not only the Indo-European family but the Turanian as well and even the ancient non-Aryan languages of India.[24] Asia is the classic land of wandering tribes and nations, with a common type of culture and society which, as we shall see, is perfectly exemplified by the Jaredites.

Only the book of Ether sees the now dry and dusty landscapes under peculiar conditions: "And it came to pass that they did travel in the wilderness, and did build barges, in which they did cross many waters, being directed continually by the hand of the Lord. And the Lord would not suffer that they should stop beyond *the sea* in the wilderness, but he would that they should come forth even unto the land of promise" (Ether 2:6-7; italics added). The crossing of many waters under continual direction comes as a surprise, "the sea" in question being apparently but one —though the most formidable—of many waters to be crossed. Now it is a fact that in ancient times the plains of Asia were covered with "many waters," which have now disappeared but are recorded as existing well down into historic times; they were of course far more abundant in Jared's time. Even as late as Herodotus, the land of the Scythians (the region into which Jared's people first advanced) presented formidable water barriers to migration: "The face of the country may have differed considerably from what it is now," says Vernadsky, "the rivers were much deeper and many lakes were still left from the glacial age which later turned into swamps."[25] Indeed, Pumpelly's theory of the development of civilization from oasis cultures rests on the assumed existence of vast inland seas, now vanished, but well attested even as late as the Chinese annals, which speak of "expansive bodies of water of which Lob-nor and other shrunken lakes and brackish tarns are the withered survivals."[26] The steady and continual drying up of the Asiatic "heartland" since the end of the last ice age is one of the basic facts of history and is even looked upon by some experts as the mainspring of world history. But it is a relatively recent discovery. Whoever wrote the book of Ether showed remarkable foresight in mentioning waters rather than deserts along the migrants' way, for most of the deserts are of very recent origin, while nearly all the ancient waters have completely vanished. We need only remind ourselves that Sven Hedin has discovered that there are lakes which actually *move* in Central Asia!

3

Jared on the Steppes

The Moving Host

Ether's account of "crossing the plains" is an Asiatic idyll. Nothing essential is missing. First of all, the steppe is darkened by "flocks, both male and female, of every kind," and if we look more closely fowl, fish, even bees, and "seed of the earth of every kind" are not wanting. Moreover the brother of Jared was instructed to admit to his company anyone whom he felt like taking: "also Jared thy brother and his family; and also thy friends and their families, and the friends of Jared and their families" (Ether 1:41). Here is another striking contrast with the Lehi story: unlike the people of the sands, these ancients do not form their societies on the basis of blood relationship—the friends of Jared and the friends of his brother are two separate groups, as they would not be if they were relatives. Apparently whoever is a friend is a supporter and member of the tribe, and this rule, significantly enough, has been a basic law of Asiatic society from the earliest recorded times, when the formula "I counted them among my people" was applied to whatever people a king could subdue, regardless of race or language.[1]

All these families with their herds and their baggage moved through the valleys and out over the plains with the intent and expectation of becoming "a great nation" and finding a promised land; in all of which they are typical Asiatic nomads of the old school, as a few examples should make clear.

Ammianus Marcellinus, writing in the fourth century A.D., describes the Alans on the march as resembling "a moving city." All the people of Asia migrate in the same way, he explains, driving vast herds before them as they go, mounted on the backs of beasts, with their families and household effects following along on great ox-drawn wagons. In spite of their wealth of cattle, says Ammianus, the people hunt and plunder as they go.[2] The Huns, who defeated and supplanted the Alans, kept the same customs, as in turn did their successors, and so on,[3] until in the thirteen century William of Rubruck, traveling as a spy and observer for Louis IX of France, uses almost the very words of Ammianus: "On the next day we met with the carts of the Scacatai laden with houses, and I thought that a mighty city came to meet me. I wondered also at the huge droves of oxen, and horses, and at the flocks of sheep."[4] In the present century Pumpelly describes how "a thousand Kirghiz families descended from the passes round about, with their long camel trains caparisoned and rich-laden with nomadic wealth, and each caravan with its flocks of sheep and goats, herds of camels and cattle and horses."[5] Note that the herds of all these people consist of every type of animal—to us an almost inconceivable mix-up: "flocks of every kind," says Ether, who seems to know what he is talking about. If you want to move backward in the time scale, you will find at an age far more remote from Ammianus than he is from our own, the annals of the Assyrian kings swarming with the same huge herds of cattle, sheep, horses, camels, and human beings, all mixed up together and moving across the plains either as prisoners of mighty conquerors or as seekers after escape and security in some promised land.[6] It is a touching and tragic picture, that of the wandering tribes ever seeking for new homelands—promised lands where they might settle and become "mighty nations." Almost without exception these people, however terrible they may appear to us or to the weaker tribes that lay in their way, were actually refugees who had been driven from their native farms and pastures by the pressure of still other tribes who in the end had been forced to move by the common necessity which the weather imposes from time to time on the users of marginal and sub-marginal grasslands.[7]

If the Jaredites mixed their cattle, they also seem to have mixed their professions, and you might well ask, what were they: hunters, herdsmen, or farmers? You might ask the same of any normal Asiatic society and get the same answer: They are all three. McGovern repeatedly points out that the tribes of the steppes have at all times been hunters, herdsmen, and farmers all at once.[8] And in my recent studies on the state I have shown that they were the original city builders to the bargain. All the tribes we have just mentioned, for example, were expert hunters, though none lacked animals in plenty. Typical is the case of the Manchu-Solons who when murrain destroyed their herds took to farming, yet they "plough no more than hunger compels them to, and in years when game is plentiful they do not plough at all,"[9] that is, they are hunters, cattlemen, or cultivators as conditions require or permit. Let us be careful, then, not to oversimplify our picture of what life was like in the first civilizations and dream up Cecil B. DeMille ideas about "primitive" conditions that never existed.

It is a remarkable thing that mention of flocks of *any* kind is conspicuously absent from the history of Lehi, though that story is told in considerable detail. What an astonishing contrast! The one group hastening away from Jerusalem in secrecy to live a life of hunting and hiding in the desert and almost dying of starvation, and the other accepting volunteers, as it were, from all sides, moving out in a sort of massive front, driving innumerable beasts before them and carrying everything from libraries to hives of bees and tanks of fish! It would be hard to conceive of two more diametrically opposite types of migration, yet each fits perfectly with the customs and usages recorded throughout history for the part of the world to which the Book of Mormon assigns it.

But how could the Jaredites have carried all that stuff with them? The same way other Asiatics have always done—in wagons. And such wagons! "Measuring once the breadth between the wheel ruts of one of their carts," William of Rubruck reports, "I found it to be twenty feet over. . . . I counted twenty-two oxen in one team, drawing a house upon a cart . . . the axletree of the cart was of huge size, like the mast of a ship."[10] Marco Polo saw the houses of the Tartars mounted "upon a sort of cart with four wheels."[11] Seventeen hundred years before Marco Polo, Xenophon beheld enormous wagons on the plains of Asia, drawn by eight yokes of oxen,[12] and yet a thousand years earlier we have reports of how the Philistines rolled into Palestine with their families and their possessions loaded on huge, solid-wheeled affairs drawn by four oxen.[13] To this day the archaic type of wagon has survived in the immense ceremonial wagons of India and the huge cars in which such plainsmen as the Buriats carry their gods across the steppes.[14] But can we say the wagon is possibly as old as the Jaredites?

In all probability it is. We now have a few samples of such high antiquity as to come within hailing distance of the flood itself, and these vehicles have already acquired the form and perfection which they are to keep without major alteration for thousands of years to come. The teams and wagons from the royal tombs at Ur, the el-Agar chariot found in 1937, the Khafaje car, prehistoric wagon tracks everywhere, all point to the great antiquity and central Asiatic origin of the wagon.[15] The last-named vehicle, dating from the fourth millennium B.C., was horse-drawn and justifies Gertrud Hermes in her conclusion that the horse was not only known "but actually used, at least in some places, as a draught animal with war chariots" at a surprisingly early date.[16]

H. G. Wells once wrote a vivid description of how a primitive man swinging from a branch one day landed to his surprise on the back of a grazing horse that happened to walk under his tree. Such an event, he believes, would account most logically for the discovery of the art of riding. Perhaps it would, but that is not the way it happened according to the present-day consensus, which is that "driving everywhere preceded riding." Nay, McGovern tells how at a relatively recent date "the Scythians and Sarmatians hit upon the brilliant and original notion of mounting the animal they had long been accustomed to drive."[17] It is generally agreed that ox-drawn vehicles were older than horse-drawn, but both go back to the fourth millennium B.C., and though it would have been possible for the Jaredites to go afoot, as the Mongols themselves did as late as the sixth century B.C., it would *not* have been possible for them in such circumstances to have carried bird cages, beehives, and tanks of fish with them. There is not the slightest objection to their using wagons, especially since they had no shortage of beasts to pull them.

Concerning Deseret[18]

My dear Professor F.:

By all odds the most interesting and attractive passenger in Jared's company is *deseret*, the honeybee. We cannot pass this creature by without a glance at its name and possible significance, for our text betrays an interest in *deseret* that goes far beyond respect for the feat of transporting insects, remarkable though that is. The word *deseret*, we are told (Ether 2:3), "by interpretation is a honeybee," the word plainly coming from the Jaredite language, since Ether (or Moroni) must interpret it. Now it is a remarkable coincidence that the word *deseret*, or something very close to it, enjoyed a position of ritual prominence among the founders of the classical Egyptian civilization, who associated it very closely with the symbol of the bee.

The people, the authors of the so-called Second Civilization, seem to have entered Egypt from the northeast as part of the same great outward expansion of peoples that sent the makers of the classical Babylonian civilization into Mesopotamia.[19] Thus we have the founders of the two main parent civilizations of antiquity entering their new homelands at approximately the same time from some common center—apparently the same center from which the Jaredites also took their departure, but more of this later. What concerns us here is that the Egyptian pioneers carried with them a fully developed cult and symbolism from their Asiatic home.[20] Chief among their cult objects would seem to be the bee, for the land they first settled in Egypt was forever after known as "the land of the bee," and was designated in hieroglyphic by the picture of a bee, while every king of Egypt "in his capacity of 'King of Upper and Lower Egypt' " bore the title, "he who belongs to the sedge and the bee."[21]

From the first, students of hieroglyphic were puzzled as to what sound value should be given to the bee-picture.[22] By the New Kingdom, according to Sethe, the Egyptians themselves had forgotten the original word,[23] and Grapow designates the bee-title of honor as "unreadable."[24] Is it not strange that such a common and very important word should have been forgotten? What happened? Something not at all unusual in the history of cult and ritual, namely the deliberate avoidance or prohibition of the sacred word. We know that the bee sign was not always written down, but in its place the picture of the Red Crown, the majesty of Lower Egypt was sometimes "substituted . . . for superstitious reasons."[25] If we do not know the original name of the bee, we do know the name of this Red Crown—the name it bore when it was substituted for the bee. The name was *dsrt* (the vowels are not known, but we can be sure they were all short); the "s" in *dsrt* had a heavy sound, perhaps best represented by "sh," but designated by a special character—an "s" with a tiny wedge above it by which the Egyptians designated both their land and crown they served. Now when the crown appears in place of the bee, it is sometimes called *bit* "bee,"[26] yet the bee, though the exact equivalent of the crown, is never by the same principle called *dsrt*. This certainly suggests deliberate avoidance, especially since *dsrt* also means "red," a word peculiarly applicable to bees. If the Egyptians were reluctant to draw the picture of the bee "for superstitious reasons," they would certainly hesitate to pronounce its true name. As meaning "red" the word could be safely uttered, but never as meaning "bee." A familiar parallel immediately comes to mind. To this day no one knows how the Hebrew name of God, YHWH, is to be pronounced, because no good Jew would dare to pronounce it even if he knew, but instead when he sees the written word always substitutes another word, *Adonai*, in its place to avoid uttering the awful sound of the Name. Yet the combination of sounds HWH is a common verb root in Hebrew and as such used all the time. There are other examples of such substitution in Hebrew, and there must have been many in hieroglyphic which, as Kees points out, is really a kind of double talk.

That the Egyptians deliberately avoided calling the bee *deseret* while applying the name to things symbolized by it and even substituted for it is further indicated by another remarkable fact. The bee symbol spread in other directions from its original home, wherever that was, enjoying a prominent place in the royal mysteries of the Hittites, turning up in that living archive of prehistory, the *Kalevala*, and even surviving in the Easter rites of certain nations. In all of these the bee is the agent through which the dead king or hero is resurrected from the dead, and it is in this connection that the bee also figures in the Egyptian rites.[27] Now the original "deseret" people, the founders of the Second Civilization, "the intellectuals of On," claimed that their king, and he alone, possessed the secret of resurrection. That, in fact, was the cornerstone of their religion; it was nothing less than "the king's secret," the power over death by which he held his authority both among men and in the hereafter.[28] If the bee had any part in the profoundly secret royal resurrection rites of the Old Kingdom—and how else can we account for its presence in later and more popular versions of the same rites?—it is plain why its real name and office were carefully concealed from the world. Furthermore, that the *dsrt*-crown is the "bee-crown" is, I believe, clearly indicated by the most prominent feature of the crown, namely the long antenna that protrudes from the base of it and which in the oldest drawings is not elaborately curled, as later, but exactly resembles the extremely long and prominent antennae on the earliest hieroglyphic bees. Some entomologists have maintained that the bee-sign is not a bee at all, but a hornet, and certain Egyptologists have accordingly read it as such; this makes the business even more mysterious, however, since it leaves the honey-loving Egyptians without a word for bee, indicating a perfect censorship of the name. I am personally persuaded that the archaic and ritual designation of the bee was *deseret*, a "word of power" too sacred to be entrusted to the vulgar, being one of the keys to "the king's secret."

In certain editions of the Book of Mormon, though not the first, the word *deseret* is capitalized, for the editors have recognized that it is really a title, "which by interpretation is a honeybee," as distinct from the "swarms of bees" which also went along. In that case one might be justified, though we will not insist on it, in seeing in Deseret the national symbol or as it were the totem of Jared's people,[29] since the author of our record seems to attach unusual importance to it. Through the prehistoric haze we seem dimly to descry the tribes moving outward from a common center somewhere to the north of Mesopotamia to plant a common civilization in various regions of the earth. "All the major migrations without exception," writes Eduard Meyer, "which repeatedly in the course of world history have changed the face of the European-Asiatic continent . . . have moved into the distant regions of the west from a point in Central Asia."[30] And of all these great waves of expansion the most important moved under the aegis of the life-giving bee.

We need not resort to speculation, however, to make out an interesting case for *deseret*. Let us list the known facts and let it go at that. (1) The Jaredites in their wanderings took with them "a honeybee" which they called in their language *deseret*, as well as "hives of bees." (2) The founders of the Second Civilization of Egypt had the bee as the symbol of their land, their king, and their empire, to all of which they applied the designation *deseret*, or something very close to it.[31] (3) Though they never called the bee itself *dsrt*, the sign which is often "for superstitious reasons" written in its place is so designated. (4) The bee sign was always regarded by the Egyptians as very sacred: "As a determinative," says Sethe, "it is significant to note that it is always placed *before* any of the others."[32] As is well known, such priority is the prerogative of the holiest objects only in the writing of hieroglyphic. Its extreme sacredness and its role in top-secret ritual amply explain, nay, all but demand, that suppression of its true name in the reading of texts.

To come down to modern times, it is to say the least a very picturesque coincidence that when the Lord's people migrated to a promised land in these latter days, they called the land Deseret and took for the symbol of their society and their government the honeybee. The book of Ether is of course directly responsible for this, but it is hard to see how the book can have produced such a striking repetition of history without itself having a real historical basis. When a historical record of any period names persons and institutions that actually existed, it is always assumed that the record insofar as those things are concerned has authentic ties with the past. Both *deseret* and the honeybee seem quite at home in the twilight world of prehistory, alternately concealing and explaining each other, but never very far apart. The numerous ties and parallels that in the end must clear up the matter still await investigation. Suffice it for the present to show that such evidence does exist.

As a naturalist you will no doubt protest at this point that the bee was unknown in ancient America, having first been introduced into the New World by the white man in the seventeenth century. There are seven references to bees or honey in the Book of Mormon, and without exception they all belong to the Old World. Lehi's wanderers, starved for sweets, gloried as Arabs always do in the discovery of honey—but that was in Arabia. The Jaredites carried hives of bees from Babel into the wilderness for a journey of many years, but there is no mention of bees in the cargo of their ships (Ether 5:4)—a significant omission, since our author elsewhere goes out of his way to mention them. The survival of the word *bee* in the New World after the bees themselves had been left behind is a phenomenon having many parallels in the history of language, but the Book of Mormon nowhere mentions bees or honey as existing in the Western Hemisphere.

Early Asiatic and Jaredite Civilization: a General View

A few lines above I suggested that the Jaredites were but one of "various tribes moving outward in all directions from a common center . . . to plant a common protohistoric civilization in various regions of the earth." I was thinking in terms of the latest researches, and it did not occur to me at the time that the picture of the great dispersion is exactly that depicted in the Bible and Book of

Mormon. If we are to believe these, a single civilization was spread throughout the world in the beginning, and historians have now learned that such was actually the case. Scholars no longer argue as to whether Egypt or Mesopotamia was the true founder of civilization, for we now know that both were derived from a common source, "a world civilization, spread over an immense area and by no means localized in the Orient." With the finding of the royal cemeteries at Ur scholars began to suspect that both Egypt and Babylonia took their civilization "from an unknown common source," which "in the beginning at least," united all the civilizations of the world in a single world civilization, of which all subsequent civilizations are but variations on a theme.[33] In my recent studies on the origin of the super-state I have tried to show that the original heart and center of this world civilization is to be located somewhere in central Asia, from which the conquering hordes have periodically spilled over into the provincial or peripheral areas of India, China, Egypt, and Europe, there to establish kingly and priestly dynasties. And now it would seem that the New World must be included in this Asiatic system, for Professor Frankfort reports that "in such striking cases as the early Chinese bronze, or the design of Mexican sculpture or of the Northwest American Indians, one must reckon to a greater extent than most of us were hitherto prepared to admit, with the possibility of diffusion from Eastern Europe and the Middle East."[34] A few years ago this would have been high treason to American archaeologists. Now it serves as another indication of the unity of world civilization which we are beginning to realize was as characteristic of ancient as of modern history.

In the case of the Nephites, it was possible to locate exactly the Old World centers of culture from which their civilization sprang. Can we do the same for the Jaredites? I think so, for they came from that region that served in ancient times as a veritable martialing area for world invasions. That is where their culture belongs and where it fits. It is still too early to attempt a detailed picture of life in the days of the dispersion. "The archaeology of nomad central Asia is still in its infancy, . . ." writes G. N. Roerich; "a new branch of historical science is coming into being, the object of which will be to formulate laws that will build up the nomad state and to study the remains of a great forgotten past."[35] But the general picture begins to take form. Let me quickly sketch for you the rough outline.

The basic fact is space—vast expanses of grassland, woods, and mountains, where hunters and herdsmen have ranged since time immemorial, trespassing on each other's territory, raiding each other's settlements, stealing each other's cattle, grimly escaping and pursuing each other by turns. In good times the tribes multiply and there is crowding; in bad times they are forced to invade each other's lands in search of grass. The result is chronic chaos, a condition which has been a standing challenge to the genius and ambition of men with a talent for leadership. Periodically the Great Man appears in Asia to unite his own jangling tribesmen in fanatical devotion to himself, subdue his neighbors one after another, and finally by crushing a great coalition bring all resistance to an end, and at last bring "peace and order" to the world. The endless expanse of the steppes and the lack of any natural boundaries call for statesmanship in the grand manner, both the concept and techniques of empire being in fact of Asiatic origin. For a time one mind nearly succeeds in ruling the world, but a quick reckoning comes when the Great Man dies. In a wild scramble for the throne among his ambitious relatives the world-empire promptly collapses: Space, the force that produced the super-state, now destroys it by allowing disgruntled and scheming heirs and pretenders to go off by themselves to distant regions and found new states with the hope in time of absorbing all the others and restoring world dominion. The chaos of the steppes is not the primitive disorder of small savage tribes accidentally colliding from time to time in their wanderings. It is rather, and always has been, a shrewd game of chess, played by men of boundless ambition and formidable intellect with mighty armies at their disposal.[36]

Now to return to the Jaredites. Their whole history is the tale of a fierce and unrelenting struggle for power. The book of Ether is a typical ancient chronicle, a military and political history relieved by casual references to the wealth and splendor of kings. You will note that the whole structure of Jaredite history hangs on a succession of strong men, most of them rather terrible figures. Few annals of equal terseness and brevity are freighted with an equal burden of wickedness. The pages of Ether are dark with intrigue and violence, strictly of the Asiatic brand. When a rival for the kingdom is bested, he goes off by himself in the wilderness and bides his time while gathering an "army of outcasts." This is done by "drawing off" men to himself through lavish bestowal of gifts and bribes. The forces thus won are retained by the taking of terrible oaths. When the aspirant to the throne finally becomes strong enough to dispose of his rivals by assassination, revolution, or a pitched battle, the former bandit and outlaw becomes king and has to deal in turn with a new crop of rebels and pretenders. It is exactly as if one were reading Arabshah's grim and depressing *Life of Timur*, the biography of a typical Asiatic conqueror, with its dark allusions to the supernatural and especially to the works of the devil. It is a strange, savage picture of nightmare politics that the book of Ether paints, but it is historically a profoundly true picture. Take a few examples from the Old World.

In the oldest records of the race we find the supreme god, founder of the state and cult, "winning his way to the throne by battle, often by violence against family predecessors, which generally involves horrific and obscene in-

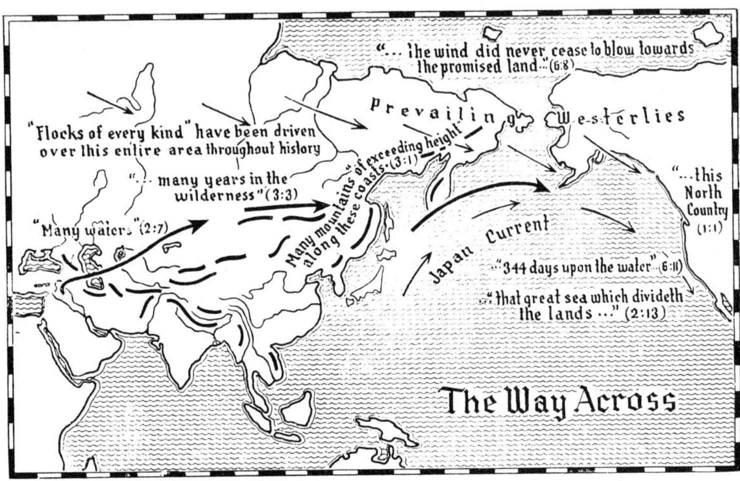

cidents."[37] The "abominations of the ancients" about which Ether has a good deal to say are thus seen to have a respectable antiquity. There is now ample reason for believing that the oldest empires known to us were by no means the first, and that the familiar processes go back to prehistoric times: "Empires must have been formed and destroyed then as they were to be later on."[38] Such empires "were not the result of gradual expansion or development but rapidly became enormous empires under the leadership of a single great man," McGovern observes, "and under the reign of his successors slowly but surely declined," though in many cases they "disintegrate immediately after the death of their founders."[39]

The fugitive who gathers forces in the wilderness[40] by "drawing off" people from his rival is a strictly conventional figure on the steppes. That is the way every great conqueror begins. Lu Fang, "the leader of a small military band, half soldiers, half bandits," nearly won the Hunnish and Chinese empires for himself two thousand years ago, and would have done so had not some of his own ambitious officers deserted him just as he had deserted others.[41] It was after cheating his brother of the throne that Attila "sought to subdue the foremost nations of the world,"[42] and after his death two of his descendants went out into the wilderness, and there gathered about them "armies of outcasts," each hoping to win back the world empire for himself.[43] You will remember that Jenghiz Khan lived for years as an outcast and a bandit as he gathered around him the forces that were to conquer all his rivals, and that those forces were actually "drawn off" from the armies of the rivals themselves. Under the nomad system, "the leaders, the *bagadurs* and *noyans*, strove to become independent, by attracting subjects and followers of their own."[44] The great rulers of Asia have regularly passed from the risky station of bandit chief to the hardly less risky one of world monarch—and back again, in a world where "every man was filled with the desire to become an independent prince," and every prince to become lord of all.[45] "The boldest . . . adventurers flocked eagerly to the banner of the new and successful chieftain of their race," in the beginning as in our own day, when all the youth of central Asia rallied to the standard of the fifteen-year-old Ma Chung-ying as he "calmly worked out a plan for the conquest of the whole world."[46]

Not only is the Jaredite practice of seeking to "draw off" to one's own side the followers of a rival while building up an army in the wilderness in the best Asiatic tradition, but the method of doing it is likewise in the best accepted tradition.[47] Thus Akish bound his followers around the nucleus of his family (the Asiatic conquerors are fanatically family conscious) by lavish gifts, for "the people of Akish were desirous for gain, even as Akish was desirous for power; wherefore, the sons of Akish did offer them money, by which means they drew away the more part of the people after them" (Ether 9:11). It was the sons of Jenghiz

Khan, you will remember, who did most of his campaigning for him, and from the very beginning the secret of his power was the huge heap of precious things that always stood near his throne and from which, after the immemorial custom of the steppes, he rewarded all who joined him.[48] In the sixth century Menander, a Roman ambassador to the court of the Grand Khan, beheld five hundred wagons full of gold, silver, and silken garments, that accompanied the monarch on his wanderings,[49] for "the ancient law of the Khans" was that none enters the presence of the ruler empty-handed nor departs hence unrewarded.[50] The pattern of steppe imperialism, according to Vernadsky, begins with "accumulated wealth in the hands of some able chieftain," which enables him to expand his popularity among neighboring clans.[51] All observers of the Asiatic system have commented on the dedicated zeal with which the men of the steppes devote themselves to two objectives—power and gain. They are inseparable, of course, and each begets the other, but nowhere is all government put on such a frankly mercenary basis as in Asia, where the most venal ambassadors of the West have been embarrassed equally by the frankness and the astuteness of their Asiatic hosts to whom all life is simply a business deal. That this quality is peculiar to Jaredite society appears from the fact that the twin motives of power and gain receive far more attention in the book of Ether than anywhere else in the Book of Mormon, as a glance at the concordance will show.

But if the ambitious chieftain gains adherents by bribery, he keeps them by oaths. The oath is the cornerstone of the Asiatic state of the Jaredite. Akish again furnishes an excellent example:

> And it came to pass that Akish gathered in unto the house of Jared all his kinsfolk, and said unto them: Will ye swear unto me that ye will be faithful unto me in the thing which I shall desire of you?

> And it came to pass that they all sware unto him, by the God of heaven, and also by the heavens, and also by the earth, and by their heads, that whoso should vary from the assistance which Akish desired should lose his head. . . .
>
> And Akish did administer unto them the oaths which were given by them of old who also sought power, which had been handed down even from Cain (Ether 8:13-15).

Note that these terrible oaths are traced back explicitly to the Old World. The very oldest texts in "the oldest language in the world," according to Hommel, are incantations "having the stereotyped conclusion: 'let it be sworn (or conjured) by the name of heaven, let it be sworn by the name of earth!' "[52] From the flood of documents that have come forth of recent years to teach us the ways of men at the dawn of history, it is apparent that oaths, conspiracies, and combinations were the established order of things from the beginning. What better illustration of this could one ask than the great Babylonian New Year's hymn, the "Enuma Elish," in which Tiamat, aiming at the rule of the universe, "draws off" the gods to her side, so that "they conspire unceasingly night and day" against the rightful ruler, and "gather themselves together in a host to make battle." When he heard the news, the true king sat upon his throne "grim and silent, without saying a word," then "He smote his thigh, he bit his lips, controlled his voice," and finally gave the order to assemble his army—which by formal acclamation took the oath of allegiance to its leader Marduk.[53] This story, which goes back to the beginning of things (the actual text comes from the first Babylonian dynasty),[54] is no mere primitive fantasy: it is the authentic and familiar picture of the great khan who learns that a relative and a rival is raising an army against him in the wilderness.

The story of the rise and career of any great conqueror

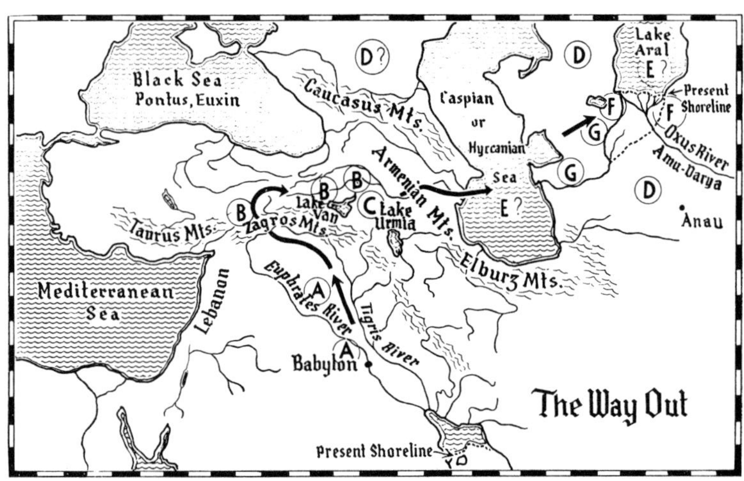

A. The Land of Shinear, where the Great Tower was. (P. Dhorme, in *Rev. Biblique* [1928]: 509-511). Ether 1:33.
B. "The valley which was northward" (2:1). (The northern headwaters of the Euphrates "command a hub of radiating valleys and travel routes, to which the Euphrates owes its importance as a highway of commercial and military penetration." A. Moret, *Hist. de l'Orient* 1:306).
C. "And the name of the valley was Nimrod" (2:1). Nimrod country: home of Nimrod place-names and legends. (N. Emin).
D. "That quarter where there never had man been" (2:5). Anau, once thought to be the oldest city in the world, was originally built in a wilderness.
E. "The sea in the wilderness" (2:7). Both the Aral and Caspian Seas were much larger in ancient times than they are today.
F. "Many waters" (2:6). The Turanian plain was anciently full of lakes, marshes, and streams. The Oxus Delta was a vast lake.
G. Ancient course of the Oxus (as recently as the time of Alexander), now dried up.

is a long catalog of terrible oaths taken and broken. The most solemn of these oaths are sealed by the drinking of blood, as when "the King of the Commains . . . caused the [Emperor of Constantinople] and their people . . . to be blooded, and each drank alternately of the other's blood."[55] The study of the oldest annals of Asia conducts us, as does the study of the oldest languages, into a world of oaths and covenants.[56] And why should this be so? The explanation is simple, for the purpose of the oath is to *bind*—the Egyptian word for "oath," to give one example, is simply *ankh*, originally a "knot." In a world of vast open spaces and limited population, where wandering nomads may take independence for themselves by hunting beasts or driving cattle over limitless grasslands, how can men be bound to any spot or leader? They must be tied by oaths, because there is no other way of holding them. Of course every effort was made to render the oath as binding, that is, as terrible, as possible, and of course such oaths were broken whenever convenient. The ease with which men of the steppes can pass from one camp to another has always kept their kings in a state of suspicious alert, so that Asiatic monarchy is at all times enveloped in a stifling—and very Jareditish—atmosphere of suspicion and intrigue.

Mithra rules, says the *Avesta*, by virtue of his ten thousand spies, which make him alone of all kings undeceivable.[57] This is the institution of "the King's eyes" and "the King's ears," perfected by the Persians and inherited by the monarchs of many lands. The success of any conspiracy against such watchful royalty depends therefore on secrecy and surprise before all else, and so we have as the unfailing adjunct and nemesis of Asiatic kingship the secret society, investing all life with a paralyzing sense of insecurity, as Hoernes notes, and overthrowing dynasties and empires in a single night.[58] Asia's gift to the world has many times saved the world from Asia's rule, for how many an Assyrian, Persian, or Mongol conqueror has had to turn his back on the West just as he stood on the verge of world conquest, to quench the fires of rebellion set by the secret conspiracies of relatives behind his back! The normal constitution of Asiatic empire, write Huart and Delaporte, is "despotism tempered by dethronement and assassination," in which the clergy play the leading role.[59] For better or for worse, every ruler of the steppes, however great his personal power and prestige, has to reckon on the presence of a class of ambitious and powerful priests—usually shamans. Even Jenghiz Khan, the mightiest of them all, was nearly pushed from his throne by an ambitious high priest, and at the dawn of history more than one such high priest seized the rule for himself.[60] The case of the brother of Shared, whose "high priest murdered him as he sat upon his throne" (Ether 14:9), is, then, thoroughly typical, and that by no mere coincidence. For we are not only told that the system was inherited "from them of old" and perpetuated by the same methods of secret societies, family compacts, bribes, oaths, assassinations, etc., as in the Old World, but we are given a clear image of the physical background of the whole thing.

We are told, for example, how a son of King Akish, enraged at his father for the inhuman death of his brother by starvation (how typical!), went out and joined the growing hosts of the deposed King Omer, who since he had been overthrown by a "secret combination of Akish and his friends" had been dwelling in tents and gathering strength for a comeback (Ether 9:3, 9). Note the apparent fluidity of Jaredite society—the possibility of large parties of people wandering here and there over a sparsely settled continent. Note also how closely conditions "upon the face of this north country" duplicate those prevailing in the same latitudes on the other side of the world, where much the same landscape also prevails. This, we shall see later, is very significant, for it plainly points to the possible origin of much of the Indian way of life among the hunters and nomads of Asia at a very early date: the very thesis that has so often been thrown up as the strongest argument against the Book of Mormon is first propounded by the Book of Mormon itself! But more of this later.

4

Jaredite Culture: Splendor and Shame

A World of Jails

The Jaredites, like their Asiatic relatives and unlike the Nephites, were thoroughgoing monarchists, and their monarchy is the well-known Asiatic despotism lacking none of the trimmings. Where could one find a more perfect thumbnail portrait of the typical Asiatic overlord than in the four verses that describe the reign of Riplakish? (Ether 10:5-8). The lechery and cruelty, the magnificence and the oppression are all there. That sort of thing was well known in Joseph Smith's day—after all, *Hajji Baba* came out in 1824—but the book of Ether goes far beyond the conventional picture to show us institutions quite alien to the experience of Western people.

Such is the practice, mentioned many times in the book, of keeping a king prisoner throughout his entire lifetime, allowing him to beget and raise a family in captivity, even though the sons thus brought up would be almost sure to seek vengeance for their parent and power for themselves upon coming of age. Thus Kib was taken captive by his own son, begot yet other children in captivity, and died of old age, still a prisoner. To avenge Kib, his son Shule overcame the unfilial Corihor whom, however, he allowed to continue in power in the kingdom! Shule in turn was taken prisoner by Corihor's son Noah, only to be kidnapped from his prison and restored to power by his own sons. And so on: "Seth . . . did dwell in captivity all his days; . . . Moron dwelt in captivity all the remainder of his days; and he begat Coriantor. And it came to pass that

Coriantor dwelt in captivity all his days. And [he] begat Ether, and he died, having dwelt in captivity all his days."[1] It seems to us a perfectly ridiculous system, yet it is in accordance with the immemorial Asiatic usage. Thus when Baidu and Kaijatu disputed the throne of Asia, the advisers of the latter when he gained ascendency declared: "It is right that he [Baidu] should be yoked under service, and that he should be kept in bondage for the whole period of his life, so that his hand can never be stretched out to kill or commit any injury." Kaijatu failed to heed this advice, to his sorrow, for presently his brother staged a coup and put *him* in a tower for the rest of his days, but refused to kill him.[2] The expression "yoked under service" reminds us that in the book of Ether kings are made to "*serve* many years in captivity" (Ether 8:3; 10:15; 10:30). Benjamin of Tudela tells how the khalif, the spiritual ruler of all western Asia, arranged for "the brothers and other members of the khalif's family" to live lives of ease, luxury, and security: "Every one of them possesses a palace within that of the khalif, *but they are all fettered by chains of iron*, and a special officer is appointed over every household to prevent their rising in rebellion against the great king."[3] Jenghiz Khan during his earlier career was put in stocks and carried about with the court of a rival prince as a permanent prisoner—his escape was almost superhuman. His descendant Timur and his wife were also made permanent prisoners and kept in a cowshed by a rival ruler.[4] In an emergency the shah of Persia was unable to come to the same Timur's aid as an ally because, he explained, "his nephew Mansur had robbed him of his army and thrown him into prison"—yet he was able to write letters.[5] When Izzudin overcame his brother Alluddin in their fight for the Seljuk empire, he locked him up in prison; but when at the end of seven years Izzudin died, his brother was immediately released and put on the throne without a dissenting voice—he had been kept behind bars all that time just as a precaution![6]

It was the custom of Turkish kings, as was long doubted by scholars but has recently been proved, to allow their defeated rivals to sit upon their thrones by day, but lock them up in iron cages for the night![7] These lords of the steppes, like the Mamluke ruler who brought an upstart general to heel by having him hauled to court in a cage,[8] were following in the footsteps of much earlier kings. Sennacherib reports of no less a rival than the king of Babylonia that "they threw him fettered into a cage and brought him before me. I tied him up in the middle gate of Nineveh, like a pig."[9] And of the king of Arabia, Assurbanipal says: "I put him into a kennel. With jackals (?) and dogs I tied him up and made him guard the gate of Nineveh."[10] Moving back to the earliest records of all, we find a large class of legends all over the ancient world telling how a victorious god in the beginning bound and imprisoned his rebellious relatives—not killing them, since they partook of his own divine nature; the earliest myths of Zeus and Osiris at once come to mind.[11] You will notice that the imprisoned kings in Ether are all jailed by their relatives.

Related to the permanent confinement of kings is the institution of forced labor in prisons. Riplakish "did obtain all his fine work, yea, even his fine gold he did cause to be refined in prison; and all manner of fine workmanship he did cause to be wrought in prison" (Ether 10:7). Work in prison, we are told, was the alternative to paying ruinous taxes (Ether 10:6). Much the same system was used by the Assyrians from the beginning: Tiglath Pileser III tells how, "I laid tribute and taxes upon them; . . . [their horses, their mules,] their camels, their cattle and their sheep (and) workmen without number I carried away. . . . All the skilled artisans I shrewdly used to best advantage. Feudal dues, forced labor, and overseers I imposed upon the land of Nairi."[12] Note the combination of dues and forced labor—the same as in Ether. Even kings are made to serve, as we have seen was the case among the Jaredites: "The kings, their rulers, I brought in submission to my feet and imposed taskwork."[13] The later rulers of Asia continued the tradition, the Scythians considering all people their slaves, and their Parthian successors binding the inhabitants of huge areas to labor on their great work farms.[14] While in western Asia, Alaric and Attila treated all men as their bound serfs,[15] to the east the Wei conquerors kept a million captives working for a hundred years in caves to produce "all manner of fine workmanship."[16] "In a house erected for the purpose," says Marco Polo, describing how it is done in one part of Asia, "every artisan is obliged to work for one day in the week for his majesty's service."[17] Each relative of the Great Khan "received a certain number of skilled workmen, artisans, artists and so on, who were at his entire disposal and whom he made settle where he liked."[18] Tamerlane kept such artists, especially goldsmiths and glass workers, for himself, forcing them to settle in prison camps at Samarkand in much the way Assur-Nazir-Pal had bound down the Aramaean workers 3000 years before.[19] Even in our own day the Ja Lama forced everyone who fell into his power, "Tibetan officials, . . . Mongol pilgrims, lamas, . . . Chinese traders, . . . Kirghiz headmen," as well as an innumerable host of soldiers and peasants "to work erecting buildings and constructing towers and walls" to his glory.[20]

We must not overlook the ambitious building programs of the Jaredite kings, for nothing is more typical of the earliest rulers of the East, where even the prehistoric legends harp upon building with a notable persistence.[21] Coriantumr "did build many mighty cities," (Ether 9:23); the magnificent Riplakish "did build many spacious buildings" (Ether 10:5), and Morianton "built up many cities, and the people became exceedingly rich . . . in buildings" (Ether 10:12). It is a strange thing that warlike and nomadic kings should display a passion for building, but it is a fact in Asia as in America: "Cities sprang up like mushrooms in honor of the ruling Khan, most of them remaining unfinished and falling speedily into decay. Armies of handicraftsmen would be assembled for the purpose [another Jaredite practice]; . . . then the Khan would perish and of the intended glory nothing would remain but a heap of ruins."[22] A silly and wasteful procedure that often led to financial ruin and revolution, as we learn from the pages of Bar Hebraeus and also from the Book of Mormon example of Riplakish (Ether 10:5-8): "He did have many wives and concubines, and did lay that upon men's shoulders which was grievous to be borne; yea, he did tax them with heavy taxes; and with the taxes he did build many spacious buildings, . . . and . . . the people did rise up in rebellion against him, . . . insomuch that Riplakish was killed, and his descendants were driven out of the land." I have discussed this strange passion for building in a recent article, but what I want to call attention to here is the exact resemblance of the Jaredite practice to that in the Old World. Incidentally, the wives and concubines are an important part of the picture, for they provided the main item of expense and the main cause of financial ruin among the rulers of the steppes, where the rule was that every king displayed his wealth and power by the number of his wives and concubines, each one of which had to possess a complete camp and court of her own.[23]

The particular care and expense bestowed upon the royal throne of Riplakish (Ether 10:6) is another authentic touch. The plan of the royal throne was said to have been revealed to Gudea, the famous patesi of Lagash, from heaven, and at all times there was a widespread belief in Asia that there could be only one true throne in the world, and that any unauthorized person who attempted to sit upon it would suffer grave injury.[24] The importance of the throne[25] is well illustrated in the story of how the Mongol Baidu was "led into error by the flatterers, and he became proud and magnified himself. . . . He sent and had brought the great throne which was in Tabriz, . . . and he planted it in the neighborhood of Aughan, and he went up and sat upon it, and he imagined that henceforth his kingdom was assured."[26] Very famous is the story of how Merdawij of Persia, seeking to assume the title and glory of the King of the Universe in the ninth century, erected a golden throne after the pattern of the ancient Persian monarchs, and foolishly believed that it was the throne that gave him majesty.[27] Of the throne of the Grand Khan, Carpini writes: "There was also a lofty stage built of boards, where the emperor's throne was placed, being very curiously wrought out of ivory, wherein also was gold and precious stones, and there were certain stairs to ascend to it. And it was round at the back."[28] Something of that sort was the "exceedingly beautiful throne" of Riplakish, for it can be shown that the thrones of old wherever found, whether dragon throne, peacock throne, griffon throne, or even the Roman *sella curulis*, all go back to the old central Asiatic pattern.[29]

The Salome Episode

There is one tale of intrigue in the book of Ether that presents very ancient and widespread (though but recently discovered) parallels. That is the story of Jared's daughter. This was a later Jared who rebelled against his father, "did flatter many people, because of his cunning words, until he had gained half of the kingdom. . . . [And] did carry away his father into captivity" after defeating him in battle, "and did make him serve in captivity" (Ether 8:2-3). In captivity the king raised other sons who finally turned the tables on their faithless brother and beat his forces in a night skirmish. They spared his life on his promise to give up the kingdom, but they failed to count on Jared's daughter, an ambitious girl who had read, or at least asked her father if *he* had read "in the records which our fathers brought across the great deep," a very instructive account

The Throne of Darius, depicting among other things Darius himself sitting upon the throne. An inscription on the throne reads: "Behold the representation of those who bear my throne, and you shall know how great is the number of the lands which Darius the King has seized." Compare this with the "exceedingly beautiful throne" of Riplakish (Ether 10:6) and the oppressive means by which he got it.

of those devices by which the men of old got "kingdoms and great glory."

> Hath he not read the record which our fathers brought across the great deep? Behold, is there not an account concerning them of old, that they *by their secret* plans did obtain kingdoms and great glory?
>
> And now, therefore, let my father send for Akish, the son of Kimnor; and behold, I am fair, and I will dance before him, and I will please him, that he will desire me to wife; wherefore if he shall desire of thee that ye shall

> give unto him me to wife, then shall ye say, I will give her if ye will bring unto me the head of my father, the king (Ether 8:9-10).

Historically, the whole point of this story is that it is highly unoriginal. It is supposed to be. The damsel asks her father if he has read "the record" and refers him to a particular account therein describing how "they of old . . . did obtain kingdoms." In accordance with this she then outlines a course of action which makes it clear just what the "account" was about. It dealt with a pattern of action (for "kingdoms" is in the plural) in which a princess dances before a romantic stranger, wins his heart, and induces him to behead the ruling king, marry her, and mount the throne. The sinister daughter of Jared works the plan for all it is worth. Having got her grandfather beheaded and her father on the throne, she proceeds to marry the murderer Akish, who presently having "sworn by the oath of the ancients [the old system again] . . . obtained the head of his father-in-law, as he sat on his throne" (Ether 9:5). And who put him up to this new crime? "It was the daughter of Jared who put it into *his* heart to search up these things of old; and Jared put it into the heart of Akish" (Ether 8:17). At first she influenced Akish through her father Jared, but after Akish became her husband he would of course act directly under her influence to dispatch the next rival. According to the ancient pattern (for Ether insists that it all goes back to "the ancients") Akish as soon as his successor became apparent would be marked as the next victim, and surely enough we find him so suspicious of *his* son that he locks him up in prison and starves him to death; but there were other sons, and so "there began to be a war between the sons of Akish and Akish," ending in the complete ruin of the kingdom (Ether 9:12). Many years later the old evil was revived by Heth, who "began to embrace the secret plans again of old," dethroned his father, "slew him with his own sword; and he did reign in his stead" (Ether 9:26-27).

This is indeed a strange and terrible tradition of throne succession, yet there is no better attested tradition in the early world than the ritual of the dancing princess (represented by the *salme* priestess of the Babylonians, hence the name *Salome*) who wins the heart of a stranger and induces him to marry her, behead the old king, and mount the throne. I once collected a huge dossier on this awful woman and even read a paper on her at an annual meeting of the American Historical Association.[30] You find out all about the sordid triangle of the old king, the challenger, and the dancing beauty from Frazer, Jane Harrison, Altheim, B. Schweitzer, Farnell, and any number of folklorists.[31] The thing to note especially is that there actually seems to have been a succession rite of great antiquity that followed this pattern. It is the story behind the rites at Olympia and the Ara Sacra and the wanton and shocking dances of the ritual hierodules throughout the ancient world.[32] Though it is not without actual historical parallels, as when in A.D. 998 the sister of the khalif obtained as a gift the head of the ruler of Syria,[33] the episode of the dancing princess is at all times essentially a ritual, and the name of Salome is perhaps no accident, for her story is anything but unique. Certainly the book of Ether is on the soundest possible ground in attributing the behavior of the daughter of Jared to the inspiration of ritual texts—secret directories on the art of deposing an aging king. The Jaredite version, incidentally, is quite different from the Salome story of the Bible, but is identical with many earlier accounts that have come down to us in the oldest records of civilization.

Steel, Glass, and Silk

Before coming to grips with the grim and depressing military annals that make up the bulk of Jaredite history, as of all ancient history, it will be our pleasant duty to consider briefly the few casual references contained in the

Book of Mormon to the material culture of this strange nation.

A few years ago your loudest objection to the Jaredite history would most certainly have been its careless references to iron and even steel (Ether 7:9) in an age when iron and steel were supposedly undreamed of. Today the protest must be rather feeble, even in those quarters "still under the influence of a theory of evolutionism which has been dragged so unfortunately in the study of ancient history."[34] Nothing better illustrates the hopelessness of trying to apply the neat, convenient, mechanical rule of progress to history than the present-day status of the metal ages. Let me refer you to Wainwright's recent study on "The Coming of Iron." There you will learn that the use of iron is as primitive as that of any other metal: "In using scraps of meteoric iron while still in the Chalcolithic Age the predynastic Egyptians were in no way unusual. The Eskimos did so, though otherwise only in the Bone Age, as did the neolithic Indians of Ohio. The Sumerians of Ur were at that time in the early Bronze Age though later they relapsed into the Copper Age."[35] The possibility of relapse is very significant—there is no reason why other nations cannot go backwards as well as the Sumerians. But scraps of meteoric iron were not the only prehistoric source, for "it now transpires that, though not interested in it, man was able at an extremely early date to smelt his own iron from its ores and manufacture it into weapons."[36] But how can any men have made such a great discovery or perpetuated such a difficult art without being interested in it? We can only believe that there were somewhere people who *were* interested in it, and such people, as we shall presently see, actually dwelt in the original home of the Jaredites. Certainly there is no longer any reason for denying the Jaredites iron if they wanted it. A Mesopotamian knife blade "not of meteoric origin" and set in a handle has been dated with certainty to the twenty-eighth century

B.C.; iron from the Great Pyramid goes back to 2900 B.C. and "might perhaps have been smelted from an ore."[37] Yet the Egyptians, far from specializing in iron, never paid much attention to the stuff except in their primitive rituals—the last place we would expect to find it if it were a late invention. While Wainwright himself found iron beads at Gerzah in Egypt that "date to about 3,500 or earlier, . . . actually Egypt was the last country of the Near East to enter the Iron Age, and then under an intensification of northern influences."[38] In fact by 1000 B.C., "Egypt still keeps on in the Bronze Age."[39] Having proved that the working of iron is as old as civilization, the Egyptians then go on to prove that civilization is perfectly free to ignore it, to the dismay of the evolutionists. It was the Asiatics who really made the most of iron. As early as 1925 B.C., a Hittite king had a throne of iron, and in Hittite temple inventories "iron is the common metal, *not* the bronze to which one is accustomed in other lands of the Near East."[40] If we move farther east, into the region in which the Jaredites took their rise, we find the manufacture of iron so far advanced by the Amarna period that the local monarch can send to the king of Egypt two splendid daggers "whose blade is of *khabalkinu*," the word being usually translated as "steel."[41] Though the translation is not absolutely certain, literary references to steel are very ancient. The *Zend Avesta* refers constantly to steel, and steel comes before iron in the four ages of Zarathustra,[42] reminding one of the Vedic doctrine that the heaven was created out of steel and that steel was the "sky-blue metal" of the earliest Egyptians and Babylonians.[43] The legends of the tribes of Asia are full of iron and steel birds, arrows, and other magic articles, and the founder of the Seljuk dynasty of Iran was, as we have noted, called Iron- or Steel-Bow.[44] The working of iron is practised in central Asia even by primitive tribes, and Marco Polo speaks of them as mining "steel," rather than iron.[45] Where "steel" may be taken to mean any form of very tough iron, the correct chemical formula for it is found in steel objects from Ras Shamra, dating back to the fourteenth century B.C.[46] If we would trace the stuff back to its place and time of origin, we should in all probability find ourselves at home with the Jaredites, for theirs was the land of Tubal-cain, "the far northwest corner of Mesopotamia," which, Wainwright observes in approving the account in Genesis 4:22, is "the oldest land where we know stores of manufactured iron were kept and distributed to the world."[47] It is to this region and not to Egypt that we must look for the earliest as well as the best types of ancient iron work, even though the Egyptians knew iron by 3500 B.C. at least.

The example of iron, steel, and bronze is instructive. They are not evolved by imperceptible degrees to conquer the world in steady progressive triumph through the ages, but appear fully developed to be used in one place and forbidden in another, thrive in one age and be given up in the next.[48] The same applies to another product attributed to the Jaredites and believed until recent years to have been a relatively late invention. In Joseph Smith's day and long after there was not a scholar who did not accept Pliny's account of the origin of glass without question.[49] I used to be perplexed by the fact that the reference in Ether 2:33 to "windows . . . [that] will be dashed *in pieces*" (emphasis added) can only refer to glass windows, since no other kind would be waterproof and still be windows, and they would have to be brittle to be dashed "in pieces." Moreover, Moroni, in actually referring to "transparent glass" in Ether 3:1, is probably following Ether. This would make the invention of glass far older than anyone dreamed it was until the recent finding of such objects as Egyptian glass beads from "the end of the third millennium B.C."[50] and "plaques of turquoise blue glass of excellent quality" in the possession of one of the very earliest queens of Egypt.[51] "Very little . . . is known," writes Newberry, "about the early history of glass," though that history "can indeed be traced back to prehistoric times, for glass beads have been found in prehistoric graves."[52] We need not be surprised if the occurrences of glass objects before the sixteenth century B.C. "are few and far between,"[53] for glass rots, like wood, and it is a wonder that any of it at all survives from remote antiquity. There is all the difference in the world, moreover, between few glass objects and none at all. One clot of ruddy dirt is all we have to show that the Mesopotamians were using iron knives at the very beginning of the third millennium B.C.—but that is all we need. Likewise the earliest *dated* piece of glass known comes from the time of Amenhotep I; yet under his immediate successors glass vases appear that indicate an advanced technique in glass working: "they reveal the art in a high state of proficiency; that must be the outcome of a long series of experiments," writes Newberry.[54]

The finding of the oldest glass and ironwork in Egypt is not a tribute to the superior civilization of the Egyptians at all, but rather to the superior preservative qualities of their dry sands. We have seen that the Egyptians cared very little for iron, which was really at home in the land of Tubal-Cain. The same would seem to be true of glass. The myths and folklore of the oldest stratum of Asiatic legend (the swan-maiden and arrow-chain cycles, for example) are full of glass mountains, glass palaces, and glass windows. In one extremely archaic and widespread legend the Shamir-bird (it goes by many names), seeking to enter the chamber of the queen of the underworld, breaks his wings on the glass pane of her window when he tries to fly through it. The glass mountain of the northern legends and the glass palace of the immense Sheba cycle I have shown in another study to be variants of this. "Glaze and vitreous paste," so close to glass that its absence in the same region comes as a surprise, were "known and widely used in Egypt and Mesopotamia from the fourth millennium B.C. onwards."[55] But such stuff, applied to clay objects, has a far better chance of leaving a trace of itself than does pure glass which simply disintegrates in damp soil—a process which I have often had opportunity to observe in ancient Greek trash heaps. This easily accounts for the scarcity of glass remains outside of Egypt. We now realize that the scholars who categorically deny Marco Polo's claim to have seen colored glass windows at the court of the Grand Khan spoke too soon. A contemporary of Marco "mentions that the windows of some of the yachts or barges had plate glass" in China, but the commentator who cites this authority adds that "the manufacture was probably European."[56] It is interesting that the earliest use of window glass in the Far East was for ship windows, but the fact that glass was scarce in China does not make this European glass, for it was not Europe but central Asia that excelled in glass production. A Chinese observer in central Asia in 1221 was impressed by the great native industry, which produced among other things windows of clear glass.[57] We have noted the Great Khans had a special interest in goldsmiths and glass workers.

If glass and iron perish, what shall we say of silk? The "fine twined linen" of the Jaredites (Ether 10:24) offers no serious problem, since as I pointed out in an earlier letter, scraps of the finest linen have actually survived at prehistoric sites in the Old World. But the same verse speaks of silk. Since few substances suffer more complete oxidation than silk, it is not surprising that the only evidence we have of its early existence is written records. But these are sufficient to allow the Jaredites the luxury of their silken garments, if any credence is to be placed in the claims cited in the *Encyclopedia Britannica* that silk was worn in China in the first half of the third millennium B.C. and in India as early as 4000 B.C.[58] The priority of India over China suggests a central distribution point for both of them, which would of course be central Asia, and indeed Khotan in central Asia was the great center of the Middle Ages. The making of silk on Greek islands at a very early date, and a legend of the Minoan Daedalus reported by Apollodorus which can only refer to silk culture, strongly indicate Asia rather than China as the prehistoric distribution center of the knowledge of silk in the world.

The Animal Kingdom

Like metal and glass, the animals of old have long been misrepresented by the settled preconceptions of the antiquarians. Up until five years ago—and perhaps still—the very best archaeologists were convinced that the camel was not known in Egypt until Greek and Roman times, and dismissed the Biblical account of Abraham's camels (Genesis 12:16) as the crudest of blunders. Yet J. P. Free has been able to demonstrate the continued existence and use of the animal in Egypt right down from prehistoric times to the present, and that on the basis of evidence within the reach of any conscientious student.[59] We know that the horse, like the iron with which it is so often associated in conventional history, did not appear on the scene in just one place to spread gradually and steadily throughout the world, but was repeatedly introduced into the primitive Indo-Germanic culture-area, filtering in, so to speak, again and again.[60] While certain prehistoric peoples (e.g., at Anau) had the ox and the horse before either the dog or the goat, others (like the Erteboellian) had the dog long before the others. "It is rather remarkable," writes McGovern, "that we find no specific reference to the camel among the Scythians and Sarmatians, although . . . its existence and usefulness must have been known."[61] The moral is that we can never be too sure. Any naturalist would assume that the elephant has been extinct in western Asia for hundreds of thousands of years, for all the evidence the creature has left of itself: it is from written history alone that we receive the assurances that large herds of elephants roamed the temperate lands of Syria and the upper Euphrates as late as the XVIII Egyptian dynasty, when the Pharaohs hunted them there for sport, and that elephants were used by the war-lords of central Asia well into the Middle Ages.[62] In late antiquity the wild variety disappear without trace, due perhaps to a change in world climate. I think it quite significant that the Book of Mormon associates elephants only with the Jaredites, since there is no apparent reason why they should not have been as common in the fifth as in the fifteenth century B.C. All we know is that they became extinct in large parts of Asia somewhere between those dates, as they did likewise in the New World, to follow the Book of Mormon, leaving only the written records of men to testify of their existence.

"They have plenty of iron, *accarum, and andanicum,*" says Marco Polo of the people of Kobian. "Here they make mirrors of highly polished steel, of large size and very handsome." The thing to note here is not primarily the advanced state of steelworking in Central Asia, though that as we have seen is significant, but the fact that no one knows for sure what *accarum* and *andanicum* are. Marco knew, of course, but since the things didn't exist in Europe there was no western word for them and so all he could do was to call them by their only names. It is just so with the *cureloms and cumoms* of Ether 9:19. These animals were unknown to the Nephites, and so Moroni leaves the words untranslated, or else though known to the Nephites, they are out of our experience so that *our* language has no name to call them by. They were simply breeds of those "many other kinds of animals which were useful for the food of man" (Ether 9:18). The history of the breeding of "animals which were useful for man" is an extremely complex one; to trace even such conspicuous breeds as the Arabian horse, the dromedary, or the ox is still quite impossible.[63] Travelers in central Asia both from Europe and the Far East always comment on the peculiar breeds of animals they find there—camels with two humps (which are really no more like the Arabian camels than a llama is like a sheep), big-tailed sheep, and strange varieties of oxen and horses, for none of which it is possible for the travelers to find words in their own languages.[64] So they call *dromedaries* and Bactrian camels both "camels" and *kulans* "horses," just as no doubt the Book of Mormon designates as sheep and cattle breeds that we would hardly recognize. I find it most reassuring that the book of Ether, taking us to archaic times, insists on complicating things by telling about animals plainly extinct in Nephite days and breeds that we cannot identify.

The description of how people were driven out of a land by a plague of serpents that then "hedge up the way that the people could not pass" (Ether 9:31-35) may put a strain on your scientific credulity. I hasten to relieve it. Pompey the Great, we are told, could not get his army into Hyrcania because the way was barred by snakes along the Araxes, a stream that still swarms with the creatures.[65] One of the chief philanthropic activities of the Persian magi was to make war on the snakes—a duty which must go back to a time when the race was sorely pressed by them.[66] The Absurtitani were said to have been driven from their country by snakes, and Esarhaddon of Assyria recalls the horror and danger of a march by his army through a land "of serpents and scorpions, with which the plain was covered as with ants."[67] In the thirteenth century A.D. Shah Sadrudin set his heart on the building of a capital which should surpass all other cities in splendor; yet the project had to be abandoned after enormous expense when during a period of drought the place so swarmed with serpents that no one could live in it.[68] It is interesting in this connection that the plague of serpents in Ether is described as following upon a period of extreme drought (Ether 9:30).

In the tenth chapter of Ether we read how great hunting expeditions were undertaken in the days of King Lib into the rich game country of the south "to hunt food for the people of the land" (Ether 10:19). Westerners are prone to think of hunting as a very individualistic activity; indeed, Oppenheimer insists that hunters operate "always either in small groups or alone." But that is not the way the ancient Asiatics hunted. According to Odoric and William, the Mongols always hunted in great *battues*, thousands of soldiers driving the game towards the center of a great ring where the king and his court would take their pick of the animals.[69] That was the normal way of provisioning an army and a nation in Asia as Xenophon describes it seventeen centuries before Carpini.[70] Thousands of years before Xenophon, a predynastic Egyptian carved a green slate palette on which he depicted an army of beaters forming a great ring around a panicked confusion of animals being driven towards a round enclosure in the center. It is the royal hunt, Jaredite fashion, at the dawn of history.[71] In these great hunts the king was always the leader, as among the Jaredites: "And Lib also himself became a great hunter" (Ether 10:19). "Kings must be hunters," and every royal court must have its hunting preserve in imitation of the early rulers of Asia who invariably set aside vast tracts of land as animal refuges where habitation was forbidden.[72] Here the Book of Mormon confronts us with a truly astounding scoop: "And they did preserve the land southward for a wilderness, to get game. And the whole face of the land northward was covered with inhabitants" (Ether 10:21). The picture of the old Asiatic hunting economy is complete in all its essentials, and correct on all points.

5

They Take Up the Sword

The Great Open Spaces[1]

My dear Professor F.:

If my insistent harping on central Asia annoys you, let me remind you again that the book of Ether gives us no choice. It never lets us forget that what the Jaredite kings did was a conscious imitation and unbroken continuation of the ways of "the ancients," of "them of old" on the other side of the water. This, incidentally, is another indication that we are not to regard the Jaredite migration as taking place immediately after the flood, for the fall of the tower saw the destruction of an ancient and established order. The Jaredites left their homeland driving great herds of cattle before them in the immemorial Asiatic manner, and even if they had never been nomads before, they certainly lived the life of the steppes during those many years before they set sail (Ether 3:3), and when they embarked, they crammed all they could of their beasts into their small boats, "flocks and herds" and other beasts (Ether 6:4), and upon reaching the New World continued to cultivate "all manner of cattle, of oxen, and cows, and of sheep" just as their ancestors had in the old country (Ether 9:18). Nothing could be better calculated to keep the Old World ways alive than those notoriously conservative secret societies which Ether always traces back to "the oaths of the ancients" and which at all times have exerted a fatal attraction on the men of Asia. We have already noted that such secret abominations are the necessary product of society in which social ties may be easily broken. The political history of the Jaredites clearly betrays in all its aspects the ways of the "space people."

Jaredite history in the New World was formally inaugurated by a general assembly and census of the entire nation (Ether 6:19), a thoroughly Asiatic practice which goes back to the days of prehistoric hunters and which lies at the root of all ancient political organization, as I have demonstrated in a number of articles.[2] Strictly in accordance with the ancient pattern, this assembly was the occasion for the choosing of a king, and the establishment of a dynasty, which as the brother of Jared clearly foresaw, could only lead straight to the slough of Old World intrigue and turmoil from which the Jaredites had already been once delivered (Ether 6:23). He was right, for presently one Corihor "rebelled against his father, and went over and dwelt in the land of Nehor; . . . and . . . drew away many people after him" (Ether 7:4). Then he went back to the land of Moron and captured his father, but was subdued by his righteous brother Shule who achieved an ambition of every Asiatic monarch to "spread his kingdom upon all the face of the land" (Ether 7:11).[3] Shule then gave his capable brother and erstwhile rival "power in his kingdom" (Ether 7:13), a surprising but quite authentic touch, from which it appears that emirs shared in the immense task of ruling the empire, as in Asia. Shule's grandson "rebelled against his father, and came and dwelt in the land of Heth," drawing people away until he had gained half the kingdom (Ether 8:2). His deposed father "departed out of the land with his family, and traveled many days" to reach the place where later the Nephites were to be destroyed; from there he continued eastward until he reached the sea (Ether 9:3), where he lived in tents and was joined in time by other refugees from his distracted kingdom (Ether 9:9), where civil war had reduced the population almost to zero—another Asiatic touch as we shall see. Years later, when the royal brothers Shared and Coriantumr fought for the kingdom, the latter beat his brother, "did pursue him to the wilderness of Akish," where the two armies raided each other by night and "did lay siege to the wilderness," until Coriantumr emerged victor, chased his brother's successor to the seashore only to be beaten in turn and pursued back to the wilderness of Akish, taking "all the people with him as he fled before Lib" (Ether 14:15). More battles and another pursuit to the coast (Ether 14:26), thence to the waters of Ripliancum, then southward to camp in Ogath, thence to the Hill Ramah for the showdown.

This sampling should give you a picture of the peculiar warfare of the Jaredites, a war of motion with no set frontiers, great armies sweeping over the continent in flight or pursuit, making the most of space by continually falling back on this or that "wilderness," setting up rival camps for a period of a year or two, while dissenting groups or individuals join themselves to one army or another. It is Asia all over again, and it calls for a geographical note.

The North American continent is a rough copy of the Asiatic, with tundra and forest in the north giving way to open grasslands, deserts, and finally tropical jungles in the south. The main difference is that in Asia everything is bigger: the forests and plains seem never ending; the deserts are wider, hotter and drier; the mountains far higher and more forbidding; the jungles deeper and more dangerous; the rivers wider and deeper. And yet these formidable barriers have not prevented the rapid and ceaseless marches and countermarches of mighty armies in every age. One of the earliest of Aryan texts is the prayer: "May we go smoothly along the roads, find good pathways in the mountains, run easily through the forests, and cross happily the rivers!"[4] During one campaign, we are told, the army of Juji "was separated by only about 1,200 miles" from the main body of Mongols.[5] That should give some idea of the distances covered by these hordes that would winter in the plains of France or Hungary and make their summer camps in the Altai or on the Onon River almost within sight of the North Pacific. It was not all flat plains, either, for the kings of the steppes extended their rule time and again to China, India, Persia, Asia Minor, Europe, and Siberia, which meant regularly traversing the greatest deserts, highest mountains, and widest rivers on earth.

The Asiatic state consists of two main elements, on the one hand a sedentary populace living in oasis-cities and bringing the arts, industry, and agriculture to sometimes astonishing peaks of perfection, and on the other hand a migratory ruler, moving at the head of his warlike host—a tribal army of conquerors with his own tribe and family as its nucleus—ever marching from city to city and from castle to castle over burning wastes or freezing mountain passes to overawe the world, stifle rebellion, and above all curtail the ambitions of any possible rival to world dominion.[6] This army is a moving nation, with its wives and children—the Mongols when they left their families behind inaugurated a radical change in steppe warfare, achieving a speed and mobility that quickly paralyzed the slower-moving hordes of their rivals, who still observed the old-fashioned custom of marching with their families and household effects. The Hyksos in the eighteenth century B.C., and the People of the Sea 500 years later were just such nations on the march—a devastating army, but an army carrying all their goods and families along with them as they sought new lands to settle, sweeping "off the inhabitants of the land, all who would not join with them," exactly in the Jaredite manner (Ether 14:27).[7] At all times among the people of the steppes "the nation and the army are one and the same; the lord of the clan or rex becoming duke or *vovoid*" in battle.[8] This is certainly the case with the Jaredites, whose kings are before everything leaders in the field, and who go to battle "with their wives and their children—both men, women, and children being armed with weapons of war, having shields, and breastplates, and being clothed after the manner of war" (Ether

15:15). The armor deserves mention, since it is now known that armor is another central Asiatic invention of great antiquity, borrowed in later times by Europe and the Far East, but reaching a high state of perfection on the steppes in prehistoric times.[9]

Since the Jaredite kings with their migratory armies were constantly on the move in the best Asiatic manner, is there any reason why they should not have covered Asiatic distances? Then why all the fuss about Cumorah? From the Narrow Neck of Land to New York state is a distance that staggers us, but for Juji or Timur it would be a milk-run. Because *we* think of journeys in terms of hours or days at the most, we are liable to forget that people who never stop moving think of space not in terms of time but of stages, and that when it is broken down into stages the longest route on earth becomes negotiable even to the most primitive means of transportation—in a word, distance is no object. A glance at the map will show that the vast extent of territory possibly covered by the Jaredites is really rather moderate by Asiatic standards. The Brigham Young Academy Expedition of 1900 went from Provo to Panama in a remarkably short time, though poorly equipped by any standards.[10]

When King Omer was overthrown by his son Jared he had to travel "many days" before he was beyond the reach of the usurper who had seized a kingdom that was "spread upon all the face of the land" (Ether 9:3; 7:11). In fact he fled as far as he possibly could, to regions which were to become the classic hiding and fighting grounds of the latest Jaredites. It is in the field that we must seek the bones and burial mounds of the Jaredites, but not in their cities. Just as the great structures of the Mongols, among the noblest buildings on earth, are to be found in the south and west, far from the primordial hunting and fighting grounds of the tribes, so the great monuments of Jaredite civilization abound in the lands of the south that they first settled rather than in the wilderness of the last great battles. One of the strange paradoxes of history is that the nomads of the steppes were perhaps the greatest builders of all time, though their normal type of "city" was "more suggestive of an ordo-like tent-city than a town in the usual sense."[11] In the lands that the Mongol conquers he builds Taj Mahals and Jehols, but in his own lands the "winds clean up the place which he has soiled, the pastures which his flocks have cropped grow greener than ever, and Nature promptly repairs all the mischief he has done to her clean orderliness,"[12] and so "mighty nomad empires rose and vanished into the unknown" without a trace.[13] The thing to note is that in the Asiatic pattern camp culture, which leaves no mark behind, and city culture have been characteristically sponsored by the *same* tribes and rulers since the beginning of history. That people should live as nomads and yet build great cities is no more contradictory than that they should be both hunters and farmers or both herdsmen and merchants at one and the same time. But from the first men have preferred to practise hunting, grazing, and farming in special areas set aside for the purpose, a custom duly observed by the Jaredites, as we have seen (Ether 10:19-21).[14] A study of the old Asiatic system will provide a ready explanation for any apparent difficulties in locating Cumorah in lands far from the Jaredite center.

The normal life of Asia is one of chaos, violence, and insecurity produced by constant warring between the tribes and rivalry among ambitious men within them. From time to time a super-man appears who, first gaining complete control of one tribe, ruthlessly crushes his neighbors one by one, forcing the survivors to make common cause against him and form a great coalition; a final showdown in which this coalition is either destroyed or victorious in a great "battle of the nations" decides the fate of the world for generations to come. If the great man wins, the world knows a period of enforced peace and unity under the absolute sway of one iron will. At any moment in his career the world-conqueror has to face one particular rival, his most dangerous rival of the hour, against whom his whole attention is directed with passionate personal hatred and dedicated fury. This can be shown from almost any page of the life of any would-be cosmocrat from Sargon to Hitler. It is the leitmotif of Jaredite history as well, which whenever it becomes coherent crystallizes about the person of some dreadful but competent warrior pitted against an equally alarming rival. While "Coriantumr dwelt with his army in the wilderness for the space of two years, in which he did receive strength to his army," his opponent Shared "also received strength to his army" through the operation of "secret combination." Later Coriantumr pitched his tents by the Hill Ramah and spent four years "gathering together the people" (Ether 14:7-8; 15:11-14). Just so Jenghiz Khan hid out in the wilderness for two years recruiting an army against his relative Wang Khan, who was doing the same thing, and later devoted four years to building up an army to meet the emperor of Khwarizm, who worked feverishly to build up *his* army, each doing everything in his power to "draw off" his enemy's supporters to his own side.[15]

This system of "drawing off" is, as we have noted before, very ancient in Asia. There is even a special Arabic word for it—*jadhab*. "From whom shall I take away . . . the awful sovereignty?" asks Mithra in the *Avesta*, which is full of legendary heroes who draw off each other's followers.[16] The gathering of rival forces is regularly accompanied, as in the Book of Mormon, by exchange of personal letters between the chiefs and the sending of formal challenges: "Let the Shanyu come to the south and either meet the emperor in open battle or else become a subject and pay reverence to the Imperial throne" is a typical example.[17] Jealousy and ambition, says Xenophon, are the essence of Asiatic kingship, which is an intensely personal thing; he describes how Croesus and Cyrus each devoted every ounce of energy and treasure gathering together huge conglomerate armies to fight it out for the rule of all Asia.[18] How intensely personal this rivalry was has been recounted in the unforgettable pages of Herodotus. In the Egyptian annals Pharaoh alone is the only victor and the only hero, and the issue of every war is simply his personal argument with the opposing monarch.[19] Every king of Babylonia or Assyria performs all of his tremendous feats single-handed, as the monuments explain, and makes it a point to report that his majesty personally dispatched the rival king: "In the midst of that battle my own hand captured Kashtilash, the Kassite king." "Against [the king] himself, at the point of the spear, unto the setting of the sun I waged battle."[20] This last vividly recalls the Book of Mormon picture of Shiz and Coriantumr hacking away at each other until nightfall (Ether 15:20-29). The actual exploits of a Sargon, Cyrus, Thothmes III, or Rameses II, moreover, give us to understand that the personal combat between kings was no mere hollow boast but actually took place.

Since every war was a personal combat between two kings, it was customary for them to challenge each other to single combat. The king of the Scythians sent his challenge to the king of the Massagetae and also to the great Darius, whose father exchanged challenges with an earlier queen of the Massagetae; the king of the Visigoths challenged the Emperor Honorius to single combat as King Lazarus of Servia did Amurath the Turk, and so on.[21] I need not point out at this date that the whole system of chivalric etiquette originates on the steppes of Asia. The Great Khans when their rivals were captured in battle would personally behead them, as Chinese generals still do other Chinese generals.[22] Queen Tomyris not only beheaded Cyrus, according to the legend, but mad with hatred sloshed his head around in a skin filled with blood.[23]

It was common among the rulers of the steppes to convert the skull of a personal enemy into a drinking cup, as the emperor of the Bulgars did with the skull of the Emperor Nicephorus, and the king of the Hiung-nu did of the top-piece of the ruler of Iran. The ancient Ukrainians would take their oaths by drinking blood from such vessels.[24] The Assyrian rulers collect the skins of rival monarchs, as the Ja Lama did in our own day.[25]

We have dwelt at unsavory length on these gory details because it is necessary to explain what the book of Ether is about. The grim ferocity with which the rulers of Asia concentrate all their wrath against the person of a rival king belongs to the Jaredite tradition: "And it came to pass that Coriantumr was exceedingly angry with Shared, and he went against him . . . to battle; and they did meet in great anger" (Ether 13:27). And "when Shiz had received his epistle, he wrote an epistle unto Coriantumr, that if he would give himself up, *that he might slay him with his own sword,* that he would spare the lives of the people" (Ether 15:5). During the battle that ensued, "Shiz arose, and also his men, and he swore in his wrath that he would slay Coriantumr, or he would perish by the sword" (Ether 15:28). What these men seek before everything else is not power or victory but a settlement with a personal rival.

Wars of Extermination

Both Shiz and Coriantumr as they moved about on their endless campaigns "swept off the inhabitants before them, all they that would not join them" (Ether 14:17). This is the classic Asiatic method of forced recruiting: "If the neighbouring province to that which they invade will not aid them," says an eyewitness of the Tartar technique, "they waste it, and with the inhabitants, whom they take with them, they proceed to fight against the other province. They place their captives in the front of the battle, and if they fight not courageously put them to the sword."[26] In such a way the Asiatic war-lords from the beginning "[swept] the earth before [them]" like Shiz (Ether 14:18), and like the Communist hordes of our day, forcing all that lay in their path to become part of them. "I counted them among my people," says the Assyrian conqueror of one nation after another, and this ancient formula would seem to go back to our old friend Nimrod, whom popular superstition saw reincarnated in Jenghiz Khan as he "became a mighty hunter," according to Carpini. "He learned to steal men, and to take them for prey. He ranged into other countries taking as many captives as he could, and joining them to himself," as Nimrod had done by awful oaths.[27] This system of "sweeping the earth" explains how it was possible for small and obscure Asiatic tribes to rise very quickly to be conquerors of all Asia and most of Europe: The tribe that gave its name to the conquering hordes was merely the nucleus of an army which snowballed into a world-army by forced recruiting of all it met.

A great deal has been written about the calculated *Schrecklichkeit* of the great conquerors, especially Jenghiz Khan, whose practices have been condoned by recent biographers on the grounds that there is no better weapon than terror to soften up opposition, provoke early surrender, and thus save lives. Certainly terror is the keynote of Asiatic warfare in which its "contempt for human life,"[28] and the boast of an Assyrian king might be echoed by many an ancient and modern successor: "I marched victoriously, like a mad dog, spreading terror, and I met no conqueror."[29] Being a mad dog seems to us a poor thing to boast of, but the terror was carefully calculated. Shiz would have understood, as in his pursuit of Coriantumr "he did slay both women and children, and he did burn the cities. And there went a fear of Shiz throughout all the land; yea, a cry went forth throughout the land—Who can stand before the army of Shiz? Behold, he sweepeth the earth before him!" (Ether 14:17-18). When Coriantumr gained a victory, it was his turn to be the terror of the earth, and "the people began to be frightened, and began to flee before the armies of Coriantumr" (Ether 14:27).

An important by-product of the Asiatic-Jaredite system of rallying armies and absorbing nations is an efflorescence of robber bands on all the face of the land. All who will not join the great armies are put to death, as we have seen, but what of those who escape? They are naturally outlaws, having no allegiance to any king and hence no rights or claims to protection. To survive, these people band themselves together, and since all are deserters whose heads are forfeit, their behavior becomes very dangerous. Asia has at all times swarmed with robber bands, exactly as did this continent under the Jaredites, and from time to time these robber bands have formed coalitions strong enough to ruin states and overturn thrones. After wars between the Mongols and Mamlukes had exhausted all their resources and brought ruin to many lands, soldiers from both sides banded together in robber armies, gathered up the outcasts in the deserts and mountains, and came near to conquering all of western Asia.[30] The pages of Bar Hebraeus swarm with these robber bands and good descriptions of how they operate. Whenever central governments became weakened by wars and corruption, bands of robbers would appear as if out of the earth, as when early in the ninth century the robber Omar became the terror of all the Near East and joining forces with the robber chief Nasir in the north "began to destroy the world."[31]

Just as robber bands often formed the nucleus of world-conquering armies (some Chinese emperors had whole armies composed of "bad young men"), so those world armies, once beaten, promptly broke up into robber bands again, while their leader, lately a world ruler, would find himself again nothing but a bandit chief.[32] The years during which Justinian and Chosroes were locked in deadly rivalry for the rule of the world saw the rise in western Asia of a motley array of robber gangs numbering 12,000 men, who brought complete ruin upon a large part of the civilized world; in this time of panic and insecurity "great schism fell upon the Arabs (i.e., the inhabitants) and in every quarter a man rose up who did not agree with his companion."[33] This typical and recurrent state of things vividly recalls the awful days of the Jaredite robbers, when every man slept on his sword to guard his property from every other man—and still had it stolen (Ether 14:1-2). We need not dwell on the pathological aspects of Asiatic warfare—the hideous disguises, the bloody oaths, the insane yells, the pyramids of heads and all that. In *Taras Bulba*, Gogol describes the Kazakh hordes as going quite insane in battle or, as Ether puts it (Ether 15:22): "They were drunken with anger, even as a man who is drunken with wine." One unpleasant aspect of the business worthy of mention is the universal custom of scalp collecting, at all times practised with zeal on the steppes of Asia as in America.[34] It was actually the custom for Asiatic conquerors at all times to pose as incarnations of the devil.[35]

The insane wars of the Jaredite chiefs ended in the complete annihilation of both sides, with the kings the last to go. The same thing had almost happened earlier in the days of Akish, when a civil war between him and his sons reduced the population to thirty (Ether 9:12). This all seems improbable to us, but two circumstances peculiar to Asiatic warfare explain why the phenomenon is by no means without parallel: (1) Since every war is strictly a personal contest between kings, the battle *must* continue until one of the kings falls or is taken. (2) And yet things are so arranged that the king must be very *last* to fall, the whole army existing for the sole purpose of defending his person. This is clearly seen in the game of chess, in which all pieces are expendable except the king, who can never be taken. "The *shah* in chess," writes M. E. Moghadam, "is *not* killed and does *not die*. The game is terminated when the *shah* is *pressed to a position from which he cannot escape*. This is in line with all good traditions of chess playing, and back of it the tradition of capturing the king in war rather than slaying him whenever this could be accomplished."[36] You will recall the many instances in the book of Ether in which kings were kept in prison for many years but not killed. In the code of medieval chivalry, taken over from central Asia, the person of the king is sacred, and all others must perish in his defense. After the battle the victor may do what he will with his rival—and infinitely ingenious tortures were sometimes devised for the final reckoning—but as long as the war went on, the king could not die, for whenever he did die, the war was over, no matter how strong his surviving forces. Even so, Shiz was willing to spare *all* of Coriantumr's subjects if he could only behead Coriantumr with his own sword. In that case, of course, the subjects would become his own. The circle of warriors, "large and mighty men as to the strength of men" (Ether 15:26) that fought around their kings to the last man, represent that same ancient institution, the sacred "shieldwall," which our own Norse ancestors took over from Asia and which meets us again and again in the wars of the tribes, in which on more than one occasion the king actually *was* the last to perish. So let no one think the final chapter of Ether is at all fanciful or overdrawn. Wars of extermination are a standard institution in the history of Asia.

To cite a few examples, when Jenghiz Khan overcame the great Merkit nation he left only *one* man alive—the brother of his favorite wife.[37] The Assyrian kings would systematically annihilate every living thing in the lands they conquered, sowing fields with salt, like the Romans, and flooding the sites of cities they destroyed to convert them into uninhabitable wastelands.[38] In cities of a million inhabitants the Mongols left not a dog or a cat alive, and they converted vast provinces into complete deserts.[39] The great island of Cyprus was an uninhabited waste for seven years after the Turkomans took it.[40] The Goths in a single battle entirely exterminated the Sciri[41] as the Huns did the Scythians and Alans, and as the Mongols did the Tartars.[42] The Mongols themselves met retribution in 1732 when their own kinsmen, the Manchus, wiped out nine-tenths of the Oret Mongols in a Chinese-inspired project aimed at the complete obliteration of *both* sides.[43] Such mutual suicides of nations were not uncommon: the Kin and the Hsia Hsia, the two greatest empires of their day and as closely related in blood as were the people of Shiz and Coriantumr, engaged in fifteen years of warfare that wiped out eighteen million people—a figure that makes Ether's two million (Ether 15:2) look rather paltry. Incidentally, the wars of Jenghiz Khan cost China alone forty million lives![44] The Hunnish Jao Dynasty of the North and the Dsin Empire of the South almost achieved mutual quietus during a civil war in which "neither side was willing to make peace until the other was completely crushed." In the first century B.C. the Huns divided to follow two brothers, Jiji and Huhansie. Twenty years of war followed, and the deadlock was only broken when in 43 B.C. Jiji's people in despair finally fled west in the best Jaredite manner, leaving "vast stretches of land bare and deserted" behind them.[45]

This sort of history should convince the most skeptical that the book of Ether is not exaggerating in what it tells us either of what happened or of the scale of events. The whole picture is a conservative one by Asiatic standards, but by the same standards completely authentic.

What the Jaredites left behind was a land littered with bones, for "so swift and speedy was the war," that "the whole face of the land was covered with the bodies of the dead" (Ether 14:21), and a generation later "their bones lay scattered in the land northward" (Omni 1:22). A medieval traveler, passing Kiev years after the great wars between the Mongol and Russian hordes, reports: "When we were traveling through this country, we found an innumerable multitude of dead men's skulls and bones lying upon the earth." Far away, in Commania and Cangle, "we found many skulls and bones lying upon the ground like cattle-dung." All the living inhabitants, he notes, were reduced to slavery.[46] Where burial was at all possible after these great battles, the only practical procedure was to heap up the bodies in great piles and cover them up with earth, "erecting great tumuli over them." The entire Naiman nation was thus buried after its destruction.[47] Joinville, traveling a whole year through Asia to reach the court of "the cham of Tartary," saw all along the road of Tartar conquest "large mounds of bones."[48] A careful comparison of the prehistoric mounds of Asia and America is in order, but not very likely for years to come.

Jaredite Survivors?[49]

The first rule of historical criticism in dealing with the Book of Mormon or any other ancient text is, never oversimplify. For all its simple and straightforward narrative style, this history is packed as few others are with a staggering wealth of detail that completely escapes the casual reader. The whole Book of Mormon is a condensation, and a masterly one; it will take years simply to unravel the thousands of cunning inferences and implications that are wound around its most matter-of-fact statements. Only laziness and vanity lead the student to the early conviction that he has the final answers on what the Book of Mormon contains. "It is the constitutional disposition of mankind," said Joseph Smith, "to set up stakes and set bounds to the works and ways of the Almighty. . . . Why be so certain that you comprehend the things of God, when all things with you are so uncertain?"[50] These words apply equally to the wildest revivalist and the ablest scientist. Tertullian taught that anything which is not specifically stated in the Bible to have occurred in the past must actually be assumed *not* to have happened at all. Even the most opinionated

Bible student today would not limit himself so strictly; but granted that we may go farther than Tertullian, how far may we go? Nothing in the restored gospel was more offensive to the Christian world than its insistence on going much too far to suit the *Christian* world, and daring to speak of doctrines and events not mentioned in the Bible at all.

For example, Brigham Young states, in the face of long centuries of misinterpretation of Genesis 1:14: "How long the starry heavens have been in existence we cannot say; how long they will continue to be we cannot say. How long there will be air, water, earth; how long the elements will endure, in their present combinations it is not for us to say. Our religion teaches us that there never was a time when they (the physical elements) were not, and there never will be a time when they will cease to be; they are here and will be hereafter."[51] Obviously the implications of such statements are highly offensive to many good Christians. Six months before his death the Prophet Joseph Smith declared: "I have tried for a number of years to get the minds of the Saints prepared to receive the things of God; but we frequently see some of them, after suffering all they have for the work of God, will fly to pieces like glass as soon as anything comes that is contrary to their traditions."[52] Of what traditions is he speaking? Not infant damnation, or baptism by sprinkling, or Neoplatonic ideas about God, for such things the Saints had left behind. The traditionalism to which he refers is clear from another address given by the Prophet at about the same time, when he said, "I suppose I am not allowed to go into an investigation of anything that is not contained in the Bible. If I do, I think there are so many over-wise men here, that they would cry 'treason' and put me to death. So I will go to the old Bible and turn commentator today."[53] Notice that good members of the Church are charged with two follies: (1) taking the Bible as the only possible source of knowledge, and (2) interpreting the Bible strictly in the light of their own limited experience.

Turning to the Book of Mormon, is it not possible there also to fall into the old sectarian vice of oversimplifying? Are there not many Latter-day Saints who will insist that every American of pre-Columbian descent must be a Lamanite because, forsooth, there were once Nephites and Lamanites, and the Nephites were destroyed? Yet the Book of Mormon itself makes such an interpretation impossible. The Nephites were destroyed, we are told, but it is pertinent to the case of the Jaredites to ask, what does the Book of Mormon mean by "destroyed"? The word is to be taken, as are so many other key words in the book, in its primary and original sense: "to unbuild; to separate violently into its constituent parts; to break up the structure." To destroy is to wreck the structure, not to annihilate the parts. Thus in 1 Nephi 17:31 we read of Israel in Moses' day that, "According to his word he did destroy them; and according to his word he did lead them," bringing them together *after* they had been "destroyed," i.e., scattered, and needed a leader. "As one generation hath been destroyed among the Jews," according to 2 Nephi 25:9, "even so they have been destroyed from generation to generation according to their iniquities." A complete slaughter of any one generation would of course be the end of their history altogether, but that is not what "destroyed" means. Of the Jews at Jerusalem Nephi says (1 Nephi 17:43), "I know that the day must shortly come that they must be destroyed, save only a few." Later, "after the Messiah hath arisen from the dead . . . behold, Jerusalem shall be destroyed again" (2 Nephi 25:14). In these two cases what actually happened was that the Jews were all scattered "save a few only" that remained in the land. The Israelites upon entering the Promised Land, we are told, drove out "the children of the land, yea, unto the scattering them to destruction" (1 Nephi 17:32). Here it is plainly stated that the destruction of the Canaanites was their scattering—as is known to have been the case. Likewise of the Nephites: "and after thy seed shall be destroyed, and dwindle in unbelief, and also the seed of thy brethren, behold these things shall be hid up" (1 Nephi 13:35), where both Nephites and Lamanites dwindle in unbelief *after* they have been destroyed.

Only once in the Book of Mormon do we read of a case of annihilation, when we are specifically told that "every living soul of the Ammonihahites was destroyed" (Alma 16:9), where not only the social structure but each individual is undone. In other instances the Lord promises that he will not utterly destroy the descendants of Lehi's youngest son, Joseph (2 Nephi 3:3), or of Lemuel (2 Nephi 4:9), and even Nephi is told that God "will not suffer that the Gentiles will utterly destroy the mixture of thy seed which are among thy brethren" (1 Nephi 13:30), even though the promise and fulfillment were that the Nephites should be "destroyed" (Ether 8:21), and even though Moroni can say: "there is none, save it be Lamanites" (Ether 4:3).

So when we read that the Jaredites "were destroyed by the hand of the Lord upon the face of this north country" in the very first verse of Ether, we are to understand that the nation was smashed and dispersed, but not that the catastrophic final battle was necessarily the whole story. The first thing that occurs to King Mosiah on the discovery of the twenty-four gold plates was, "perhaps they will give us a knowledge of the remnants of the people who have been destroyed, from whence this record came" (Mosiah 8:12), showing that whether anyone survived or not, for Mosiah at least it was perfectly possible for *remnants* of a people to exist *after* that people had been "destroyed." But did not Ether prophesy that "every soul should be destroyed save it were only Coriantumr?" (Ether 13:21). Every soul of what? Specifically of "his kingdom . . . and all his household." Ether himself, hiding out in a cave, was not included in the number, and neither were other inhabitants of the continent—Nephites, Lamanites, and Mulekites that were actually living here at the time of the Jaredite destruction. Neither were renegade Jaredites, wandering far and wide beyond the confines of the kingdom. That there were such renegades will appear from a number of things.

6

A Permanent Heritage

Nephites with Jaredite Names

In the first place, a number of undeniably Jaredite names turn up from time to time among the Nephites. Such a striking coincidence calls for investigation, for it can hardly have been an accident. From the Book of Mormon we learn that the Jaredites and Nephites spoke entirely different languages, and even a cursory search will show that Jaredite proper names have a peculiar ring of their own. Their most characteristic feature is the ending in -m. This is called *mimation* and is actually found among the most ancient languages of the Near East, where it was followed by the later *nunation,* or ending in -n, the most characteristic feature of classical Arabic and also of Nephite proper names, as we noted above.[1] The correct use and sequence of mimation and nunation in the Book of Mormon speaks strongly for the authenticity of the record, for the principle is a relatively recent discovery in philology. It may be illustrated by the only Jaredite common nouns known to us, *curelom* and *cumom,* and the only adjective, *shelem,* applied to a mountain "because of its exceeding height" (Ether 3:1). It is interesting that the original meaning of the best known of Semitic roots, *SALAM,* may be "a high place" (Arabic *sullam,* ladder, stairway, elevation) with the idea of safety, and hence peace, as a secondary derivation.

But it is the proper names that concern us here. When out of the short list of Jaredite names preserved to us, a respectable percentage turn up as Nephite names as well, it is high time to ask, is this one case where the author of the Book of Mormon has slipped up, or is there something significant about those Nephites who bear Jaredite names? The answer is a surprise: Virtually all of these men have Mulekite backgrounds and lead subversive movements against the Nephite state and religion! The significance of this will appear at once if we consider that the only case of definite overlapping between the Jaredite and Nephite peoples is provided in the episode of Coriantumr and the Mulekites.

Coriantumr, the last Jaredite chief, spent the last nine months of his life among the Mulekites. These people had left Jerusalem eleven years after Lehi did and therefore three years after Lehi's people had already settled in the New World. We are told that "Coriantumr was *discovered by* the people of Zarahemla" (Omni 1:21, emphasis added). Since Coriantumr had been very badly wounded and with not a soul to help him, he could not have got very far; the fact that he lingered only nine months after his rescue implies as much, though it does not necessarily prove it. But the evidence strongly suggests that the Mulekites "discovered" Coriantumr shortly after the last Jaredite battle, and hence that they had been on the continent for quite a while, though some years fewer than the Nephites. The overlap between the Mulekite and Jaredite cultures was at least nine months long, and may have extended over many years. At any rate we have proof that the Jaredites made a permanent cultural impression on the Nephites *through Mulek*, for centuries after the destruction of the Jaredite nation we find a Nephite bearing the name of Coriantumr, and learn that this man was a descendant of Zarahemla, the illustrious leader of the Mulekites. This shows the Jaredite influence reaching the Nephites through Mulekite channels, which is exactly what one would expect. The name had been preserved either in the royal family (Coriantumr the Jaredite would have been the guest of the chief) or in the records—most likely the former, since people do not as a rule go to written histories for their names, while nothing is more persistent than personal names, most of those we use today being at least a thousand years old.

The first land settled by the Jaredites was Moron, a name still borne by one of the last Jaredite kings. Now the Nephite land "in the borders, by the seashore on the edge of the wilderness was called by them Moroni," and anyone with a rudimentary knowledge of the Near East will instantly recognize Moroni as meaning "belonging to Moron," or "of Moron," the old *-i* ending being the most familiar and unchanging suffix from the oldest Egyptian and Babylonian to modern Arabic, and always having the same signification of relationship. Both the time—the very end of Jaredite history—and the place—the outer borderland—agree in bringing the two names *Moron* and *Moroni* together in a cultural overlap. A parallel case is that of Morianton, the name of an early Jaredite king and also of a land on the coast settled by a Nephite of the same name about 72 B.C. In this case the man might well have taken his name from the land he colonized, as ancient conquerors used to (e.g., Africanus, Germanicus, etc.), being named for the old Jaredite coastland which he resettled. The survival of Jaredite place names is further indicated by the Hill Shim. The ten-year-old Mormon was told that he would be able to find that hill when he grew up, though it lay in another part of the country, because it would be called Shim (Mormon 1:3), which shows that it actually went by its Jaredite name among the Nephites. For it is probable that Moroni is giving the hill its Jaredite name in Ether 9:3, since it is his practice to use Jaredite names in describing itineraries, and the very next name on the list after Shim is undoubtedly Jaredite. Another Jaredite place name, Nehor, given to the wilderness into which the first Jaredite rebel withdrew, as well as to a city built in that region, was borne by a notorious Nephite apostate.

Noah[2] was a Jaredite king, and another Noah was a

Nephite king. The name may be authentic Jaredite, for aside from the original Biblical character "Noah" "does not recur elsewhere in Hebrew either alone or as a component part of a name," according to C. L. Woolley, but is "Harrian," coming from the country north of Babylonia,[3] i.e., the original Jaredite home. Noah's priest Alma betrays a mixture of culture if not of blood; his stamping ground was the Mulekite country, and two of his grandsons bore the Jaredite names of Shiblon and Corianton (Alma 31:7). Though Corihor was the grandson of the first Jaredite king, the name was borne by a Jaredite of the last generation, when it may have been taken over by the Nephites as Korihor.

Considering how few Jaredite names we have, it seems clear, then, that we have here a definite overlapping of the two cultures. What clinches the matter is the fact that our Nephites with Jaredite names all have Mulekite background and connections. That the Mulekite-Jaredite background represented a definite cultural tradition among the Nephites and was consciously cultivated is, I believe, very clearly shown in the *behavior* of men with Jaredite names. Five out of the six whose names are definitely Jaredite betray strong anti-Nephite leanings, and the sixth one, Shiblon, was only saved from the ranks of such rebels because an angel converted his anti-Nephite father. Of the others, Morianton sought to lead a great body of people back into the wilderness; Coriantumr was a notorious apostate and subversive; Korihor rebelled against the church and state and tried to inaugurate a mass uprising; Nehor actually succeeded in setting up a rival system of religion and government in opposition to the Nephite rulers, and was only stopped when he was executed for murdering a righteous judge; King Noah, perhaps of mixed Mulekite descent, horrified the Nephites by introducing the ways of the old Jaredite kings—oppressive taxation, whoredoms, and abominations, "elegant and spacious buildings," the pursuit of his opponents into the wilderness, priestly colleges and ritual hierodules, and all the rest. We have here two opposing ways of life, with strong indication that all the popular support is by no means on the side of the Nephites. That the name of the prize rebel of them all, Gadianton, is not found in the short Jaredite list is not to be wondered at, but we only need to compare it with such titles as Morianton and Corianton to realize that it is good Jaredite.

There is nothing in the Book of Mormon that shows *direct* contact between the Nephites and the Jaredites. There is always a go-between—the Mulekites, who, as the story of the elder Coriantumr shows, were the nearest neighbors to the Jaredites and separated, as we learn from Mosiah's accunt, by a considerable distance from the Nephites. Everything points to the absorption of a good deal of Jaredite culture by the people of Zarahemla shortly after their arrival: The tradition of a very Jaredite pattern of behavior and dissent against Nephite rule by men of Mulekite background bearing Jaredite names makes the case pretty clear. The dropping of the name Jaredites by their mixed descendants has many historical parallels. Thus the Hurrians lost their name so quickly and completely when they mixed with the Hittites that until recent years it was doubted that there ever were such people; yet we now know that it was the Hurrians, ranging over the vast back country to the north, that supplied the Hittites with their ruling class and their tradition of empire. Such a role may the scattered and nomad Jaredites of the last days have played in contact with the more civilized but less aggressive people of Zarahemla, completely losing their Jaredite identity but still given away, as are the Hurrians, by the strange names of their leaders. Incidentally, the fact that Nephite weights and measures bear *Jaredite* names indicates long cultural overlap.

The Hiders

Decisive, I believe, in determining the ultimate fate of the Jaredites is the fact they were past masters at dodging and hiding. Their history begins with Nimrah and Omer hiding in the wilderness and ends with Shiz and Coriantumr and Ether himself doing the same. Are we to believe of such people that when "part of them fled to the army of Shiz, and a part of them fled to the army of Coriantumr" (Ether 14:20), none of them attempted to flee to the wilderness? Or that no one *tried* to get away when "the cry went throughout the land" that Shiz was approaching, sweeping the earth before him? (Ether 15:18). Or that no one *succeeded* in escaping when "the people began to be frightened, and began to flee before the armies of Coriantumr"? (Ether 15:27). When we read that the wild hosts "swept off the inhabitants *before* them, all they that would not join them" (Ether 14:27, emphasis added), the picture is that of people doing their best to get out of the way, the classic picture of those who "flee to the mountains" or break for the woods on the approach of the Assyrian king, the Mongol hordes, or the modern Chinese general.[4] In Asia the escapees often formed themselves for survival into formidable warlike tribes (the modern Goloks are such), and carried on a tradition and style of warfare remarkably like that of the North American Indians.[5] Centuries of wars of annihilation have given the people of central Asia "a great heritage of the hiding instinct, and only by using and cultivating this have they avoided extermination."[6] As we have seen, this valuable instinct was zealously cultivated among the Jaredites, and nowhere is there any indication that none made their escape, either during the final war or at an earlier time.

When Shiz and Coriantumr attempted a universal *levee en masse* it was not the work of four weeks to bring their armies together, but of *four years*, which argues an outstanding lack of patriotic passion among the people in general. Such levees took just as long in Asia (e.g., those of Jenghiz Khan and the king of Khwarazm), and for the obvious reason that the people were very widely scattered, out of touch with the central governments, reluctant to cooperate in an enterprise in which they had nothing to gain but wounds. The same situation is clearly suggested in Ether 15:14: "They were for the space of four years gathering together the people, that they might get all who were upon the face of the land, and that they might receive all the strength which it was possible that they could receive." Note the purpose clause: We are not told that they achieved their goal, but only that they tried; in the next verse the statement "when they were all gathered together" is simply a general remark (it is a favorite expression with Homer) that could be made of any group no matter how large or how small.

On top of this, the established Jaredite practice of simply refusing to join any army and living as robbers or "band of outcasts" would have made it very hard to keep the people in line even after the big armies had sucked them in. Ether finds it worthy of note that great numbers actually stuck it out to the end and can only attribute their behavior in *not* deserting and going back to the woods to the power of Satan (Ether 15:19). And what of the robbers? Were they wiped out? Did they reform? As the nation became more and more involved in a hopeless war, bandits could operate with increasing immunity, their numbers swelled by opportunities and deserters, and as in Asia their depredations would continue unchecked for generations. Nothing is less surprising, then, than to find the direst villain of Nephite history, one whose craft was "to carry on the secret work of murder and of robbery" (Helaman 2:4), whose secret bands lurked in the wilderness and operated as a murderous underground, going under the Jaredite name of Gadianton.

The combing of the land for recruits did not include the entire continent, for it completely overlooked the Nephites, Lamanites, and Mulekites living on it, and who is to say that given *thousands* of years to wander in, plus a great tradition of hunting and nomadism, no Jaredites could have gone to the outermost limits of the continent? Ether is writing the history of one nation only, and Moroni presenting less than one percent of that history (Ether 15:33)—a few renegades are no concern of theirs. Those who drop out of the main picture simply cease to exist for Ether's or any other history. But we would welcome a word from the Book of Mormon that might show us that there actually were such lost and wandering groups on the hemisphere.

As if for the specific purpose of giving us that assurance, a few terse verses in Omni point to the people of Zarahemla, whose history is given so briefly as to be entirely without significance otherwise. Though these people play an important role once they enter the sphere of Nephite history, their whole past is summed up in but three verses (Omni 15-17). That shows us how closely the editors of the Book of Mormon stick to the business at hand, shunning any kind of digression and stubbornly refusing to tell about any people but the announced subjects of their history. The people of Zarahemla are only mentioned because they have to be—since they in time become bona fide Nephites. But the brief and grudging nod to their past is a priceless clue for us. It is a reminder that just because Lehi's people had come from Jerusalem by special direction we are not to conclude that other men cannot have had the same experience. And by the same token the fact that the Jaredites were led to the land of promise at the time of the dispersion gives us no right to conclude that no one else was ever so led, either earlier or later than they. It is nowhere said or implied that even the Jaredites were the first to come here, any more than it is said or implied that they were the first or only people to be led from the tower. Long after the Book of Mormon appeared Joseph Smith quoted with approval from the pulpit reports of certain Toltec legends which would make it appear that those people had come originally from the Near East in the time of Moses;[7] whether such a migration ever took place or not, it is significant that the Prophet was not reluctant to recognize the possibility of other migrations than those mentioned in the Book of Mormon.

The argument of silence bears some weight in considering the possibility of "other sheep." When the Jaredites journey into a land "where there never had man been," our history finds the fact worthy of note, even though the party was only passing through. Now there is a great deal said in the Book of Mormon about the past and future of the promised land, but never is it described as an empty land. The descendants of Lehi were never the only people on the continent, and the Jaredites never claimed to be.

While on the subject, I cannot resist the temptation to quote for you a remarkable passage from Origen's *First Principles,* in which that zealous scholar quotes from Clement, who as you know comes close to being the earliest Christian writer after the Apostles:

> Clement, the disciple of the Apostles, recalls those whom the Greeks designate as *antichthonians* (dwellers on the other side of the earth), and other parts of the earth's sphere (or circuit) which cannot be reached by anyone from our regions, and from which none of the inhabitants dwelling there is able to get to us; he calls these areas "worlds" when he says: "The Ocean is not to be crossed by men, but those worlds which lie on the other side of it are governed by the same ordinances (lit. dispositions) of a guiding and directing God as these."[8]

Here is a clear statement that the *earliest* Christians taught that there were people living on the other side of the world who enjoyed the guidance of God in complete isolation from the rest of the world. The teaching was very soon lost along with other "precious things" and is never approved again after Origen (Augustine definitely opposes it), but it well illustrates how the saints in every age have made due allowance for the dealings of God with all humanity and refused to regard their own limited experience as the only measure of divine providence among men.

In 1898 a farmer grubbing up stumps near the town of Alexandria, Minnesota, turned up a stone slab containing what appeared to be an ancient Runic inscription. Like the Book of Mormon the thing was promptly denounced as a fraud, and the universal consensus of the experts heaped scorn upon the clumsy forgery for forty years. But now it transpires that the Kensington Stone, as it is called, is no fake but very probably the genuine article (so much for the authority of scholarship!). The inscription tells us of bands of Norsemen wandering about in the Middle West at least 130 years before Columbus. Whether true or not, does the Book of Mormon have any objection? Of course not. The Kensington Stone also tells us that these Norsemen suffered a grim and bloody end—quite in keeping, in fact, with the Book of Mormon pattern.[9] We offer this as a test case: for once we have admitted that all pre-Columbian remains do not have to belong to Book of Mormon people, the field is clear to the anthropologist, and the problem of the Book of Mormon archaeologist, when such appears, will be to find in America things that might have some bearing on the Book of Mormon, *not* to prove that anything and everything that turns up is certain evidence for that book. This obvious fact I pointed out in an article in the *Improvement Era* of April, 1947.[10]

There is not a word in the Book of Mormon to prevent the coming to this hemisphere of any number of people from any part of the world at any time, provided only that they come with the direction of the Lord; and even this requirement must not be too strictly interpreted, for the people of Zarahemla "had brought no records with them; and they denied the being of their Creator" (Omni 17), i.e., they were anything but a religious colony. No one would deny that anciently "this land" was kept "from the knowledge of other nations" (2 Nephi 1:8), but that does not mean that it was kept empty of inhabitants, but only that migration was in one direction—from the Old World to the New; for even as Lehi was uttering the words just quoted, the Jaredites were swarming in the east, and the old man refers to others yet to come, "all those who should be led out of other countries by the hand of the Lord." Must we look for all those in the Book of Mormon?

"Men Out of Asia"[11]

Dear Professor F.:

But why all this insistence on the possible survival of a few Jaredite escapees prowling in the woods? Because it would take no great number of such renegades to perpetuate "upon the face of this north country" the ways of the Jaredite nomads and hunters. We have said that when the Asiatics hide in the mountains and the woods their way of life becomes just like that of the Indians. Indeed Professor Grousset can think of no way of life so perfectly like that of the scattered and disorganized tribes of Asia after the destruction of the great nations than that of the North American Indians at the time of their discovery by the whites.[12] And what is more natural than that conditions in the north country, littered with bones and haunted by savage hunters, should present after the passing of the Jaredite nation just the sort of wreckage and savagery that make the Asiatic scene after the passing of empire? In time descendants of Jaredite hunters and robbers would combine with Lamanite riffraff, as their ancestors did with the Mulekites, and the old Jaredite stock would survive, like the Nephite, as a "mixture" only (1 Nephi 13:30). But the ways of the Jaredite hunters, perfectly adapted as they were to conditions of life in this north country, would not only hold their own but remain predominant. This complicates the picture considerably, but for that matter, the anthropologists themselves now begin to detect just such complications in their own picture, as Gladwin has shown us with much spirit and wit.[13]

We need not discuss the well-known affinities between the North Americans and the hunters of Asia—shamans, mounds, peace pipes, scalping, wigwams, and all that. Contacts between the natives on the Asiatic and American shores of the far North Pacific still take place, but that is strictly a local phenomenon.[14] It is the really ancient Asiatic background of the Indians that interests me. In a recent study on the rise of the ancient state in central Asia, I drew evidence equally from the American ethnologists and the Old World sources, and it all fitted neatly into a single picture. But whatever connection there might have been between the Asiatic and the Indians—save for those maddeningly obvious ties with the Near East to which Gladwin draws attention—must have been a very early one indeed, for the Asiatic languages are among the most conservative and widespread on earth, and if the two worlds had been in contact anywhere near as recently as certain authorities believe, the Asiatic nature of the Indian languages should be instantly recognizable. To date no one has been able to recognize those languages as those of the Asiatic steppes.

Now all this is as the book of Ether would have it. That accounts tells us that at the very dawn of history, many thousands of years ago, a party of nomad hunters and stock raisers from west central Asia crossed the water—very probably the North Pacific—to the New World, where they preserved the ways of their ancestors, including certain savage and degenerate practices, and carried on a free and open type of steppe warfare with true Asiatic cruelty and ferocity; it tell us that these people moved about much in the wilderness, for all they built imposing cities, and that they produced a steady trickle of "outcasts" through the centuries. A careful study of the motions of the Jaredites, Mulekites, Nephites, and Lamanites should correct the absurd oversimplification by which the Book of Mormon as a history is always judged. It will show as plain as day that the Book of Mormon itself suggests the Asiatic origin of some elements at least of the Indian race and culture long before the anthropologists got around to it. The scientists *no longer* hold that one migration and one route can explain everything about the Indians. The Book of Mormon *never did* propound a doctrine so naive. Though it comes to us a digest and an abridgment, stripped and streamlined, it is still as intricate and complex a history as you can find; and in its involved and tragic pages nothing is more challenging than the sinister presence of those fierce and bloody-minded "men out of Asia" known in their day as Jaredites.

The Big Picture

The time has come to draw a few conclusions. If you will recall, I set out to prove "that certain strange and unfamiliar things described in Ether could have taken place as described because they actually did take place—characteristically and repeatedly—in those culture areas in which according to the Book of Mormon the Jaredites acquired their culture and civilization." Among such strange and unfamiliar things we mentioned the valley of Nimrod, the confounding of the languages, the great wind, deseret, and the flooded plains of the Old World, while in the New our list includes such items as the great assembly of the nation, the drawing off of followers by bribes, oaths by heaven and earth, secret societies, kings in prison, fine work done in prisons, the dancing princess, strange breeds of animals, plagues of serpents, great national hunts and special hunting preserves, the nation in arms, peculiar strategy and tactics, the formation of armies by forced recruiting, systematic terrorism, the rule of robber bands, wars of extermination regarded as personal duels between rival rulers, with the ritual survival of the king. The list of bull's-eyes is a long one, and if it is not as long as Lehi's, it is because Ether takes fewer shots (1 Nephi, which covers but eight years, can devote much more attention to detail) and at an, if possible, even more difficult target. His percentage of hits is not less staggering.

Individually I find the parallels between the Jaredites and the early Asiatics very impressive, but taken together their value increases as the cube of their number. In the book of Ether they are woven into a perfect organic whole, a consistent picture of a type of society whose very existence has come to be known only in recent years, and which is quite different from that Indian culture into which it later developed. How beautifully integrated this short history is! There is a great calamity, a confusing and confounding of peoples and tongues, a general scattering in many directions from a point somewhere to the north of Mesopotamia.[15] Then a migration into unknown lands covered with swamps and lakes, the dank remnants of the last ice age, and then tremendous winds that overtake the party just as they set sail. Some years after their landing in the New World they hold a general assembly and choose a king; his son in time rebels and inaugurates centuries of bitter warfare, ending eventually in a war of extermination with odd survivors lurking in the woods and deserts. Numbers, distances, and times all fit together perfectly, but the sort of thing that can be most fully checked and is virtually impossible to fake is, as I have often insisted, the *sort* of thing that was done and the *way* it was done. It is the big picture that is really impressive.

But our main purpose in writing these letters, if you will think back to the first one, was to refute the *Einheitstheorie* of a single beginning for the origin of the Indians, since you protested that the Book of Mormon was oversimplifying the story. I think by now it should be apparent that the Book of Mormon account is not as simple as it seems. Ether alone introduces a formidable list of possibilities, few of which have ever been seriously considered. Foremost among these is the probability, amounting almost to certainty, that numerous Jaredites survived in out-of-the-way places of the North to perpetuate a strong Asiatic element in the culture and blood of the American Indian.

To write a history of what could have happened at the very beginning of recorded history would have been as far beyond the scope of any scholar living in 1830 as the construction of an atom bomb would have been. The portrait of the first great states of antiquity is only just taking shape in our own day, and the idea of the original Asiatic nucleus of *all* civilization was undreamed of a few years ago. Our own ideas will have to be revised continually on many points, but the main outlines of the picture are firm and clear—and it is the same picture that meets us in the book of Ether. One of the most surprising discoveries of recent years has been the revelation that wherever the experts search, in Babylon, Thebes, Ras Shamra, Central Asia, or the Far East, they are met at *every period* of history by an almost unbelievable mix-up of physical and linguistic types. And as the biological picture becomes more complex, the cultural one seems to become more simple, the whole civilized world at any moment of its history seeming to share in a general sort of way in a single common world civilization. This is also the picture we get in Ether, where the nations and tribes are already thoroughly "confounded" in Jared's day, while certain institutions and practices are described as being common to "the ancients" as a whole and as flourishing among all nations.

Consistent with this picture is the fact that a number of Jaredite names are also Bible names. You ask in your last letter how that can be if the Jaredite language was the lost Adamic tongue? In the first place let us make it clear that the language of Jared was not the Adamic language at all: Jared asked that his language be not confounded, so that his people might continue to understand each other, not because it was a unique or perfect language or the sacred language of Adam, a thing which would certainly have been mentioned if it were so. Indeed after the Jaredites had made their getaway and their language was safe, the Lord told the brother of Jared: "the language which ye shall write I have confounded" (Ether 3:24). When Moroni tells of the remarkable power of the writings of the brother of Jared, he attributes the mighty words not to the genius of the language but to a special gift from God to the writer (Ether 12:24). As to the antiquity of writing, incidentally, we have not discussed the matter because it is still, so to speak, completely up in the air. At Uruk, where "the parent forms" of writing appear, they do not do so by any gradual process of evolution, but "suddenly and without warning there appear fifteen hundred signs and pictographs scratched on clay. They seem to have been written and used without any signs of hesitancy,"[16] showing that writing was already well-established *somewhere* in the world, and that somewhere would seem to be in the region to the north of Mesopotamia.[17]

As to Jaredite names in the Bible, the general confusion of tongues would not only allow it but also require it; for remember that the vast majority of people who spoke the Jaredite language originally were confounded and their language contaminated, so that while the words remained their meanings did not (Ether 1:34). We would expect, then, to find Jaredite words scattered about all over the Old World. The only way we can trace such words, of course, is in proper names. Few people in our society know what their names mean (though both family names and given names almost all once had meanings), because our names are almost without exception survivals from long-dead languages, having very involved and picturesque histories. Such has always been the case with proper names. It is not surprising that three of the oldest cities in the world, one of them traditionally described as the first city in the world after the flood, all bear the good Jaredite name of Kish, though these cities are widely separated. It is not surprising that the father of the first king of Israel should also be named Kish. It is not surprising that a city rivaling Kish in age and importance in Mesopotamia should be named Lagash, while one of the oldest cities in Palestine was Lakish, both recalling the Jaredite Riplakish, which could mean in Babylonian "Lord of Lakish." A more remarkable coincidence is that the Jaredite king Ahah was the son of Seth (Ether 1:10; 11:10), since Menes, the fabled founder of the First Egyptian Dynasty, bore the name of Aha (meaning warrior), and was supposed to have succeeded Seth as the ruler of the land.[18] A good idea of how mixed up things are may be gained from considering the name of Corihor. We noted above that the name of the high priest who in 1085 B.C. usurped the throne of Thebes (incidentally, the oldest city in Egypt and the oldest city in Europe *both* bear the name of Thebes—how come?) seemed to be identical with that of the Nephite upstart Korihor. But we have seen that Korihor is just as obviously identical with the Jaredite Corihor. What is the tie-up? Not in Egypt, surprisingly enough, for Hur-hor, Heriher, or whatever it was, does not seem to have been an Egyptian name at all, though found in Egypt, but is possibly a late adoption from the Hurrian, through Canaanite; that is, it comes from the original stamping-grounds of the Jaredites![19] The Nephites could thus have gotten it *either* from the Jaredites through Mulek or have imported it directly from their corner of the Egyptian Empire, where its Egyptian form was illustrious among the followers of Ammon.

There is not a name or an event in Jaredite history that does not call for long and serious study. They merit such study because they are names and events of authentic *type*. As with the Lehi story, if this is fiction, it is fiction by one thoroughly familiar with a field of history that nobody in the world knew anything about in 1830. No one is going to produce a skillful forgery of Roman history, for example, unless he actually knows a good deal of genuine Roman history. So if Ether is a forgery, where did its author get the solid knowledge necessary to do a job that could stand up to five minutes of investigation? I have merely skimmed the surface in these hasty letters, but if my skates are clumsy, the ice is never thin. Every page is loaded with matter for serious discussion—discussion that would fizzle out promptly in the face of any palpable absurdity.

But nothing could be more unfair than to treat the book of Ether simply as a history. After our long preoccupation with the sordid and secular side of Jaredite history it is high time to remind ourselves that this text, from which we have been arbitrarily selecting for comment only those verses which might have been found in any ancient chronicle, is one of the greatest treasures that ever came to a generation of men. The sad story of the Jaredites is but a framework for the inspired commentary of Moroni, a mighty tract for our times but more than that for the times ahead.

My dear F.:[20]

Moroni assures us that it is the Lord who is running things, and that men miss the whole point and meaning of their life by failing to recognize the fact: "the winds have gone forth out of my mouth, and also the rains" (Ether 2:24), he tells the brother of Jared—but to men it does not seem that way, for the Lord is constantly showing forth "great power, which *looks small* to the understanding of men" (Ether 3:5, emphasis added). Men simply do not have faith and so deny themselves the blessings and the power that might be theirs—boundless "knowledge, of all things" that is "hid up because of unbelief" (Ether 4:13). Given faith, God will not withhold from us a knowledge of all things. And ironically enough men know that they *should* have faith even apart from the thought of any reward, "for it persuadeth [men] to do good" (2 Nephi 33:4). You begin with hoping—"man must hope, or he cannot receive an inheritance" (Ether 12:32), for "faith is things which are hoped for and not seen; wherefore, dispute not because ye see not, for ye receive no witness until after the trial of your faith" (Ether 12:6). "If there be no faith among the children of men, God can do no miracles among them" (Ether 12:12), for he "worketh unto the children of men according to their faith" (Ether 12:29).

Nothing is harder than to convince a man of a thing he has not experienced: "Ether did prophesy great and marvelous things unto the people, which they did not believe, because they saw them not" (Ether 12:5). Those without faith live in a world of their own which to them seems logical and final; they take the very *un*scientific stand that beyond the realm of their own very limited experience nothing whatever exists! God's works to them look small, and they will never be cured of their myopia until they are willing to face facts and pass a test that only the honest in heart can consider without a chill of aversion. The test is this: "If men will come unto me I will show unto them their weakness. I give unto men weakness that they may be humble; . . . then will I make weak things become strong to them" (Ether 12:27). What man of the world or posturing Ph.D. is ever going to *ask* for weakness? The men of the world seek for the things of the world, the realities they know—and the greatest of these are "power and gain." Through the ages, the book of Ether assures us, men have sought these things as their highest goal and have invariably made the tragic discovery that the key to control over one's fellow men, i.e., to power and gain, lies in three things: secrecy, organization, and freedom from moral scruples, especially from squeamishness in the matter of shedding blood. Of these three things Moroni says: "The Lord worketh not in secret combinations, neither doth He will that men should shed blood, but in all things hath forbidden it, from the beginning of man" (Ether 8:19). These things, the prophet explains, have destroyed one civilization after another, and shall continue to destroy "whatever nation shall uphold such secret combinations" (Ether 8:22).

We seem to be reading Thucydides, who comments on Greek history just as Moroni does on Jaredite: Men who live for this world only invariably become dangerous paranoiacs who destroy themselves and all connected with them. But the Greeks never showed us the other side of the picture. It is here that the book of Ether far surpasses all other commentaries on human history. The greatest of Greeks taught us, wrote Goethe, that "life on this earth is a hell." Farther than that they could not go. But the book of Ether teaches us that life *on this earth* can be heaven, that there actually have been *many* "before Christ came, who could not be kept from within the veil, but truly saw *with their eyes* the things which they had beheld with an eye of faith, and they were glad" (Ether 12:19, emphasis added). Here we are not dealing with the usual platitudes and truisms to the effect that if men would only behave themselves and help each other, they would have no troubles—men have always known that, only too well.

Ether shows us human society divided into two groups, not the good and the bad as such, but those who have faith and those who do not. They live in totally different worlds, the one group in a real heaven, the other in a real hell. In no uncertain terms we are shown just what kind of world the faithless make for themselves to live in. This is Moroni's tract for our times. A generation ago the doings of the grim and bloody maniacs of the Asiatic steppes were as far removed from the thought and experience of western man as the other side of the moon. Today the eery nightmare has become our own history, and we are met in the news with photographs of American commanders striking the appalling attitudes and sporting the huge ear-flaps and quilted jackets of ancient khans of the steppes. Who would have dreamed of such a thing?

On the other side of the picture we have the Lord himself speaking "in all humility" (what a commentary on humility!) to *any* man who is ready to receive him. The Jaredites were not Israelites or even the seed of Abraham: they were simply human beings, apparently a nondescript body of no particular racial affinity. Time and place cease to exist in this story, for many men of whom we have no record spoke face to face with the Lord long before he came to fulfil his earthly mission. This remarkable indifference to any quality but faith is carried in Ether even into the next world, where we learn that the Lord has prepared "among the mansions of [his] Father" *a* house for man (Ether 12:32), where the faithful of this earth shall be at home among the faithful of other worlds. Thus the bonds of time and place are completely dissolved in Moroni's theology, and the same promises and warnings that hung over the world of the Jaredites are handed on to our own world.

In closing let me point out that it is in the Book of Mormon, specifically in Ether, that we read about things beyond the veil, of other worlds than this—many mansions, among which the faithful of this world inherit but one—and of men who talk with Jesus Christ face to face in visions. All this I find published in 1830, when Joseph Smith was but twenty-four years old, and the Church was not yet organized. Yet some of my intellectual friends are even now knocking themselves out to show that all such ideas were the product of Joseph Smith's later thinking, and that the idea of anything like his first vision was first worked out by a committee in Nauvoo in 1843. There is nothing like the story of the Jaredites to show us that the gospel is as timeless as it is true.

If the historical part of the book of Ether were to be put forth to the world as the translation of some text found, let us say, in the Cave of the Thousand Buddhas, the experts on early Asia might think it a work of fiction but would find nothing cultural in it, barring the strange proper names, to make them doubt that it reflected a genuine ancient culture. If you want to be very cautious, you might say there is very *little* in it that would annoy the expert. But bearing in mind that Asiatic studies are still in embryo, and considering the condition under which this work was published, and the fabulously remote probability of the writer's getting anything right at all, I think no further credentials are necessary to establish the authenticity of the book, which repeatedly claims to be reporting the ways of very early Asiatics. The book of Ether, like First Nephi, rings the bell much too often to represent the marksmanship of a man shooting at random in the dark.

Notes

Chapter 1: A Twilight World

1. Part 1 of "The World of the Jaredites," *IE* 54 (September 1951): 628-30, 673-75, began at this point.

2. Richard Andree, *Die Flutsagen* (Braunschweig: Bieweg, 1891); Franz von Schwarz, *Sintfluth und Völkerwanderungen* (Stuttgart: Enke, 1894), 358 & passim.

3. Emil G. Kraeling, "The Earliest Hebrew Flood Story," *JBL* 66 (1947): 290, 280-85.

4. Ibid., 285.

5. Albrecht Götze, *Hethiter, Churriter und Assyreer* (Oslo: Aschehoug, 1936), 11.

6. Bruno Meissner, *Babylonien und Assyrien*, 2 vols. (Heidelberg: Winter, 1926), illustrating the permanent dependence of all later Babylonian civilization on the culture of the early settlers of the valley; e.g., in literature, 2:154-55; cf. Alexandre Moret, *Histoire de l'Orient*, 2 vols. (Paris: Presses Universitaires, 1929-36), 1:130.

7. I. A. Richards, quoted by A. C. Bouquet, *Comparative Religion*, 6th ed. (Baltimore: Penguin, 1962), 24.

8. Siegfried Schott, *Mythe und Mythenbildung im alten Ägypten* (Leipzig: Hinrich, 1945; reprinted Hildesheim: Olm, 1964), 10-11.

9. "La finesse des fils est telle qu'avec nos machines les plus récentes, nous ne l'avons gèure dépassée." Lacasine, quoted by Moret, *Histoire de l'Orient* 1:66. The earliest known cloth shows a high degree of perfection, F.-M. Bergounioux and André Glory, *Les Premiers Hommes* (Paris: Didier, 1952), 388-90.

10. The superiority of the stone-headed arrow has been fully demonstrated by Saxton Pope, *Hunting with the Bow and Arrow* (New York: Putnam, 1947).

11. Wilhelm Schmidt, "The Injury Done to the Study of Primitive Man by Evolutionary Preconceptions," in Edward Eyre, ed., *European Civilization*, 7 vols. (Oxford: Oxford University Press, 1934-38), 1:36-51. "The paleolithic artists," says Moret, *Histoire de l'Orient* 1:23, "must have lived in a time when they could work with continuity, security, and permanence." We might envy them!

12. P. van der Meer, *The Ancient Chronology of Western Asia and Egypt* (Leiden: Brill, 1947), 13.

13. Part 2 of "The World of the Jaredites," *IE* 54 (October 1951): 704-6, 752-55, began at this point.

14. Alfred Jeremias, *Handbuch der altorientalischen Geisteskultur* (Leipzig: Hinrich, 1913), 33-34, 48, 51, 55-57, 92, 128.

15. Hugh W. Nibley, "The Hierocentric State," *WPQ* 4 (1951): 226-53.

16. For the classic treatments of the tower, see Jeremias, *Handbuch der altorientalischen Geisteskultur,* 44-47, 85-86, 149-50, 230, 236, 275, 286-89, 319, citing many authorities; Alfred Jeremias, *Das Alte Testament im Lichte des Alten Orients,* 3rd ed. (Leipzig: Hinrich, 1916), 168-80; Theodor Dombart, *Der Sakralturm* (Munich: Beck 1920); Dombart, "Der Babylonische Turm," *Das Alte Orient* 29 (1930), Heft 2; Eric Burrows, "Some Cosmological Patterns in Babylonian Religion," in Samuel H. Hooke, ed., *The Labyrinth* (London: Society for Promoting Christian Knowledge, 1935), 45-70, and below, n. 19.

17. 1 Enoch 6:2-8; The Book of Jasher 9:20-39; E. A. Wallis Budge, *The Chronography of Bar Hebraeus,* 2 vols. (Oxford: Oxford University Press, 1932), 1:3-4.

18. Hugh W. Nibley, "The Arrow, the Hunter, and the State," *WPQ* 2 (1949): 339-40.

19. Ibid., 339-43; cf. Wilhelm Nestle, "Legenden vom Tod der Gottesverächter," *ARW* 33 (1936): 246-69.

20. The vague "before the Lord" of the Kings James version (Genesis 10:9) conceals the true meaning, rendered "against the Lord" by the Rabbinical and early Christian writers; on this subject see Karl Preisendanz, "Nimrod," in *RE* 17:624. On the crimes of Nimrod, see Nibley, "The Arrow, the Hunter, and the State," 339-41.

21. Under the direction of Nimrod men said, "We will ascend to heaven and smite him (God) with bows and spears; and God knew all their works, . . . and he saw the city and the tower which they were building," Jasher 9:20; cf. G. Sale, *The Koran* (Philadelphia: Lippincott, 1870), 269. The same custom and the same arrogance is reported of the ancient Thracians, Herodotus, *Histories* IV, 94.

22. See the article "Nimrod," *JE* 9:309-11; cf. 1 Enoch 10:7-10 on Azazel the mad hunter to whom "is ascribed all sin," who "led the angels in their pursuit of the daughters of men," etc. Preisendanz, "Nimrod," 624.

23. Clement of Rome, *Homilia (Homily)* IX, 3-5, in *PG* 2:241-44.

24. Chronicon Paschale 36, in *PG* 92:145. Koran 16:5, 66; 33:70-72; 40:79 speak of the eating of animals. Cf. Chronicon Anonymi 3, in *PL* 3:680.

25. Mahbub (Agapius) of Menbij, Alexandre Vasiliev, ed., *Kitab al-Unwan,* in *PO* 5:631; Budge, *Chronography of Bar Hebraeus* 1:8; on Nimrod the usurper who "slew his father and took his mother to wife," Charles M. Doughty, *Travels in Arabia Deserta* (New York: Random House, 1937), 2:32, 657.

26. W. St. Chad Boscawen, "The Legend of the Tower of Babel," *TSBA* 5 (1876): 303-12.

27. A. J. Carnoy, *Indian/Iranian Mythology,* vol. 6 of *Mythology of All Races* (Boston: Marshall Jones, 1917), 321.

28. According to the Persian antiquarian Thaᶜlabi, *Kitāb Qisas al-Anbiyya* (Cairo: Muṣṭafa al-Babli al-Ḥalabi wa-Awlāduhu, A. H., 1345), 33.

29. Ad-Diyarbakri, *Tārīkh al-Khamis* (Cairo, A. H., 1283), 1:67; Clément Huart and Louis Delaporte, *L'Iran antique* (Paris: Michel, 1952), 454-55.

30. Preisendanz, "Nimrod," 626. Kraeling, "The Earliest Hebrew Flood Story," 289, n. 28; Eduard Meyer, *Geschichte des Altertums,* 5 vols. (Stuttgart: Cotta, 1925-58), vol. 2, pt. 2, pp. 31-32.

31. O. Emin, *Izsledovania i Statyi* (Moscow, 1896), 301-3.

32. I have treated this subject at some length in my article "The Hierocentric State," *WPQ* 4 (1951): 226-253. For a survey of various such primordial mountains, Theodor H. Gaster, *Thespis* (New York: Schuman, 1950), 184-85, 169-71; H. R. Hall, "Notices of Recent Publications," *JEA* 10 (1924): 185-87.

33. C. J. Gadd, *Ideas of Divine Rule in the Ancient East* (London: Oxford University Press, 1948), 1-3; Dahhad-Jemshid is a typical example of this, Carnoy, *Indian/Iranian Mythology,* 321-22.

34. Jasher 7:39-46.

35. Jeremias, *Das Alte Testament im Lichte des Alten Orients,* 159-60, citing bin Gorion and the Pirke d' R. Eliezar; "Nimrod," *JE* 9:309; Preisendanz, "Nimrod," 627.

36. Quote is from Jasher 7:24-30; others given in "Nimrod," *JE* 9:309-11, cf. Jeremias, *Das Alte Testament im Lichte des Alten Orients,* 159-60.

37. August F. von Gall, *Basileia tou Theou* (Heidelberg: Winter, 1926), 330, citing 2 Enoch 22:8.

38. Robert Eisler, *Iesous Basileus ou Basileusas,* 2 vols. (Heidelberg: Winter , 1929-30), 2:33-38. Eisler, 33, cites the tradition that John the Baptist wore the garment of raw skin (*ᶜor,* Genesis 3:21) in place of the original garment of light (*ᶜor*) worn before the fall; various early cults, forbidding the slaying of animals, changed the skin garment into a hair garment, ibid., 2:16, 34, 118-19, cf. Friedrich Dieterici, ed., *Thier und Mensch vor dem König der Genien* (Leipzig: Hinrich, 1879; reprinted Hildesheim: Olms, 1969), 22, 97.

39. John Chrysostom, *Commentarius in Sanctum Matthaeum Evangelistam (Commentary on Matthew)* 10, 4, in *PG* 57:188-89; this and the anonymous Life of John the Baptist are both cited in Eisler, *Iesous Basileus* 2:36, n. 6. According to the R. H. Charles, *Book of Jubilees* (Jerusalem: Makor, 1972) 3:30-31 (written in the 2nd century B.C., hereafter cited as Jubilees), "to Adam alone did He [God] give to cover his shame. . . . On this account, it is prescribed on the heavenly tablets as touching all those who know

the judgment of the law, that they should cover their shame, and should not uncover themselves as the Gentiles uncover themselves."

40. Eisler, *Iesous Basileus*, 2:78-81; Josephus, *Antiquities*, 3:182-87, cf. Eusebius, *Historia Ecclesiastica (Ecclesiastical History)* I, 6, in *PG* 20:533-36.

41. Eisler, *Iesous Basileus*, 2:35, 78, 109-10; von Gall, *Basileia tou Theou*, 330-32, cit. Greek Baruch Apocalypse (3 Baruch) 4:16; 1 Enoch 62:15; 2 Enoch 22:8; Revelation 3:4-5; 6:11; the Mandaeans believed the garment of John the Baptist would be given to all who were admitted to salvation, Eisler, *Iesous Basileus*, 2:33, cf. Odes of Solomon 25:8; and the 2nd-century Apostolic writing published by Carl Schmidt, *Gespräche Jesu mit seinen Jüngern nach der Auferstehung* (Leipzig: Hinrich, 1919), 72. Related to the baptismi vestamentum of the Early Christians, Tertullian, *De Baptismo (On Baptism)* 13, in *PL* 1:1323 (1215).

42. See above n. 7; cf. Joseph Poplicha, "The Biblical Nimrod and the Kingdom of Eanna," *JAOS* 49 (1929): 304-5.

43. Abraham's refusal to make the exchange was the real reason for his being expelled from Egypt, according to apocryphal writers. Dieterici, *Thier und Mensch*, 112; A. Wünsche, *Salomons Thron und Hippodrom Abbilder des Babylonischen Himmelsbildes, Ex Oriente Lux* 2, 3 (Leipzig: Pfeiffer, 1906), 26. There is a good deal of Egyptian material dealing with this custom of a royal exchange of garments and honors, but there is not time to go into it here—I only want to call attention to the fact that we are actually moving in a world of established patterns and familiar concepts, however weird they may seem to the uninitiated.

44. "Nimrod," *JE* 9:309: "When the animals saw [Nimrod] clad in them, they crouched before him so that he had no difficulty in catching them."

45. Jasher 27:2-13.

46. Above n. 29; Egyptian priests, royalty, and the dead were all clothed in the classic skin garment of the Egyptian priesthood; cf. T. J. C. Baly, "Notes on the Ritual of Opening the Mouth," *JEA* 16 (1930): 173-86. The *kaunakes* of the Sumerians was a heavy skin garment wholly unsuited to the climate of Babylonia and has for that reason been taken as proof that the Sumerians came from the North, Moret, *Histoire de l'Orient* 1:21, n. 81; vs. George A. Barton, "Whence Came the Sumerians?" *JAOS* 49 (1929): 263-64. Montague R. James, *The Apocryphal New Testament* (Oxford: Clarendon, 1924), 414; cf. p. 412, on the garment of the King of Kings. In 1939 an amber statuette was found showing the King of Assyria wearing the insignia of the Jewish High Priest, "A Unique Example of Assyrian Sculpture: A Portrait in Amber," *ILN* (7 January 1939): 25.

47. In later times the Egyptian priest wore "no real leopard-skin but a close-fitting coat of fine linen in the form of a leopard-skin," H. R.

Hall, "The Bronze Statuette of Khonserdaisu in the British Museum," *JEA* 16 (1930): 1, cf. T. J. C. Baly, "Notes on the Ritual of Opening the Mouth," 178. The Syrian Christians said that the garment given to Adam was of cotton, the "skin" of the tree, Eisler, *Iesous Basileus*, 2:34; this doctrine, they say, was known only to Moses, "who called cotton 'skin' because among trees it takes the place of skin"; hence the idea that John the Baptist took his clothes from trees. The Jews retained traces of the older garment in their phylacteries and in the Sisith, the four strings that every Jew once had on the edge of his garment, Ferris J. Stephens, "The Ancient Significance of Sisith," *JBL* 50 (1931): 59-70. Compare the Irham of the Moslems in John L. Burckhardt, *Travels in Arabia*, 2 vols. (London: Colburn & Bently, 1831), 1:104-05; 163-64.

48. Eisler, *Iesous Basileus*, 2:34, n. 11 for references.

Chapter 2: Departure

1. Among traditions of the dispersion, that story is not lacking of the righteous man whose language was not changed. Certain rabbis, says Bar Hebraeus, in E. A. Wallis Budge, *The Chronography of Bar Hebraeus*, 2 vols. (Oxford: Oxford University Press, 1932), 1:8-9, teach that the "Hebrew . . . was preserved with Abher (Eber), for he was a righteous man and did not agree to the building of the tower." This theory is necessary to defend the belief, popular among the Jews, that Hebrew is the language of paradise. The book of Ether is much more realistic.

2. Jubilees 8:8.

3. Part 3 of "The World of the Jaredites," *IE* 54 (November 1951): 786-87, 833-35, began at this point.

4. John de Pian de Carpini opens his account of his travels in Central Asia in the 13th century with a description of these winds, in Manuel Komroff, ed., *Contemporaries of Marco Polo* (New York: Liveright, 1928), 4. Such modern explorers as G. N. Roerich, *Trails to Inmost Asia* (New Haven: Yale University Press, 1931), 49, refer to them repeatedly, e.g., "We were approaching the great desert basin of inner Asia, and each breath of wind brought dust from its vast sandy expanse," 110, 193-95, 404, etc.

5. Good general treatments of the major weather changes in ancient history may be found in C. E. P. Brooks, *Climate Through the Ages* (London: Benn, 1926); A. R. Burn, *Minoans, Philistines, and Greeks* (New York: Knopf, 1930); Christopher Dawson, *The Age of the Gods* (London: Murray, 1928); J. L. Myres, "The Ethnology and Primitive Culture of the Nearer East and the Mediterranean World," in Edward Eyre, ed., *European Civilization*, 7 vols. (Oxford: Oxford University Press, 1934-38), 1:94-95, 103; J. B. S. Haldane, "A Biologist Looks at England," *Harpers* 175 (August

1937): 284, 286; V. Gordon Childe, *New Light on the Most Ancient East* (New York: Praeger, 1953), ch. 2.

6. Aurel Stein, *Serindia,* 5 vols. (Oxford: Clarendon, 1921; reprinted Delhi: Matilal Banarsidass, 1980-83), 1:369-449; Aurel Stein, *Innermost Asia,* 3 vols. (Oxford: Clarendon, 1928), 1:214-16.

7. Henning Haslund, *Men and Gods in Mongolia* (New York: Dutton, 1935), 106-10.

8. Ibid., 176-77.

9. Ibid., 177.

10. Ibid., 106.

11. Eusebius, *Chronicorum* I, 4, in *PG* 19:116.

12. Theophilus of Antioch, *Ad Autolycum* II, 31, in *PG* 6:1101; virtually the same text in the *Sibylline Books* 3:98-107, in R. H. Charles, *Apocrypha and Pseudepigrapha of the Old Testament,* 2 vols. (Oxford: Clarendon, 1912), 2:380-81. The idea that the tower was built expressly to unify the human race which was tending to become dispersed is found in *Sibylline Books* 5:423: "touching the very clouds and seen of all, so that all the faithful and all the righteous may see the glory of the invisible God." Of this idea Emil G. Kraeling, "The Earliest Hebrew Flood Story," *JBL* 66 (1947): 283, says, "Here is indeed a primitive, yet profound philosophy concerning the nature of the Oriental city." Whether Babel was a tower or a city, ibid., 280-83, is a mere quibble, since the two normally go together. In spite of everything, God cursed the project because it was undertaken by men on their own without consulting him: "Woe to thee, Babylon, golden-throned and golden-sandaled, thou who for many a year wast queen, sole sovereign of the world, of old so great and cosmopolitan." *Sibylline Books* 5:434-5.

13. Jubilees 10:26.

14. Thaʿlabi, *Qiṣaṣ al-Anbiyya,* 43.

15. Budge, *Chronography of Bar Hebraeus,* 1:8.

16. For 'Ad and Thamud, R. A. Nicholson, *A Literary History of the Arabs* (Cambridge: Cambridge University Press, 1930), 1-3; Herodotus, *Histories* II, 31-32. The suddenness of the fall of world-ruling Babylon made an ineradicable impression on the minds of men, who have applied the name of that city as a "code-word" to every doomed world-metropolis since then, e.g., Rome, Alexandria.

17. The magazine article at this point reads: "I suppose that one would only have to find the next major catastrophe before 2300 B.C. in order to date the Tower of Babel with some accuracy. Meantime, I must insist again, we are concerned only with the sort of thing that happened. Not only does the Bible not mention the winds, but the Book of Mormon itself does so casually, albeit very specifically, by way of explaining something else. This very casualness is a strong argument for the au-

thenticity of the record. As we said at the beginning, the Book of Ether leads one into the strangest regions. Now we shall demonstrate the surprising fact that even at its oddest, our story never loses touch with historical reality. That is going to take a good deal of time and paper, so let this suffice for the present and expect more." *IE* 54 (1951): 835.

18. "This dome was the symbol ('alam) of Baghdad, and the crown of the country, and the principal achievement of the sons of Abbas." cf. Genesis 11:4. The passage is in E. Harder, *Arabische Chrestomathie* (Heidelberg: Goos, 1911), 166.

19. Part 4 of "The World of the Jaredites," *IE* 54 (December 1951): 862-63, 946-47, began at this point. Originally, this installment began with the following paragraph, the basic content of which appears as the last paragraph of the preceeding section: "So you think my account of the Big Wind is a bit farfetched. I make no claim that the tower was blown over, but only point out that the ancients had a very old, widespread, and persistent tradition that its fall was accompanied by high winds. This I correlate with the description of the winds in the Book of Ether. To show you that such a thing is possible, however, I will give you one historical parallel. Qazwini in his *Cosmography* says that the great dome of Bagdad was a sign and symbol of the power and unity of the land. Scholars have often pointed out that the Tower of Babel served as a like symbol. Qazwini further informs us that this mighty structure was destroyed by a terrible wind—at least he says it fell during a windstorm and leaves us to draw our conclusions."

20. Alexandre Moret, *Histoire de l'Orient,* 2 vols. (Paris: Presses Universitaires, 1929-36), 1:306.

21. See appendix 1.

22. See Charles E. Chapman, *A History of California: The Spanish Period* (New York: Macmillan, 1926), 21-30.

23. The quotation is from Louis Marin, foreword to G. N. Roerich, *Trails to Inmost Asia* (New Haven: Yale University Press, 1931), ix.

24. V. Altman, "Ancient Khorezmian Civilization in the Light of the Latest Archaeological Discoveries (1937-1945)," *JAOS* 67 (1947): 81-85.

25. George Vernadsky, *Ancient Russia* (New Haven: Yale University Press, 1943), 15-16. In the 12th century it was possible to ward off invasion from the great central Asian kingdom of Khwarazm by flooding the country, Karl A. Wittfogel and Fêng Chia-Shêng, "History of Chinese Society Liao," *TAPS* 36 (1946): 647.

26. Raphael Pumpelly, *Explorations in Turkestan,* 2 vols. (Washington: Carnegie Institution, 1908), 2:286; cf. 1:66, 70-75.

Chapter 3: Jared on the Steppes

1. Hugh W. Nibley, "The Hierocentric State," *WPQ* 4 (1951): 245-46.

2. Ammianus Marcellinus, *Rerum Gestarum* XXXI, 2, esp. sections 18-22.

3. See the vivid description in Priscus Rhetor, *De Legationibus Romanorum ad Gentes,* in *PO* 113:7-9. written in 433 A.D.

4. William of Rubruck, ch. 12, in Manuel Komroff, ed., *Contemporaries of Marco Polo* (New York: Liveright, 1928), 76.

5. Raphael Pumpelly, *Explorations in Turkestan,* 2 vols. (Washington: Carnegie Institution, 1908), 2:260.

6. David D. Luckenbill, *Ancient Records of Assyria and Babylonia,* 2 vols. (Chicago: University of Chicago Press, 1926-27), vol. 1.

7. The sense of being lost and on search for a promised land or an ancestral home has always dominated among the nomads of Asia, as is finely illustrated in a recent study of the Kirghiz, Semen I. Lipkin, *Manas Vyelikodushnyi* (Moscow: Sovietski Posaty, 1947).

8. William M. McGovern, *The Early Empires of Central Asia* (Chapel Hill: University of North Carolina Press, 1939), 73-78. Cf. Pumpelly, *Explorations in Turkestan* 1:39, 41, 67-69.

9. Henning Haslund, *Men and Gods in Mongolia* (New York: Dutton, 1935), 264.

10. William of Rubruck, ch. 2, in Komroff, *Contemporaries of Marco Polo,* 59.

11. T. Wright, ed., *The Travels of Marco Polo* (London: Bohn, 1854), 129 (bk. 1, ch. 47).

12. Xenophon, *Cyropaedeia* VI, 1, 52, 29, where he describes huge wood tower-wagons used in war.

13. For sources, Alexandre Moret, *Histoire de l'Orient,* 2 vols. (Paris: Presses Universitaires, 1929-36), 2:584, n. 150.

14. M. A. Czaplicka, *Aboriginal Siberia* (Oxford: Clarendon, 1914), pl. 16.

15. Xenophon, *Cyropaedia* VI, 1, 27, notes that "in ancient times Medes, Syrians, Aramaeans and all the inhabitants of Asia used to make use of those wagons which today survive only among the Cyrenaeans."

16. Gertrud Hermes, *Anthropos* 31 (1925): 365-94, cf. 32 (1926): 105-27. For Tel Agrab chariot, discovered after Hermes' authoritative study appeared, see Henri Frankfort, "Revelations of Early Mesopotamian Culture," *ILN* (6 December 1937): 794-95.

17. McGovern, *The Early Empires of Central Asia,* 47; Bruno Meissner, *Babylonien und Assyrien,* 2 vols. (Heidelberg: Winter, 1926), 1:93.

18. Part 5 of "The World of the Jaredites," *IE* 55 (January 1952): 22-24, begins at this point.

19. See generally Moret, *Histoire de l'Orient,* vol. 1.

20. Ibid., 1:173.

21. Alan H. Gardiner, *Egyptian Grammar* (Oxford: Oxford University

Press, 1950), 73-74. The sedge is the sign of Upper Egypt and the bee is the sign of Lower Egypt. This topic is discussed in great detail in Hugh W. Nibley, *Abraham in Egypt* (Salt Lake City: Deseret, 1981), 225-45.

22. See the speculations of W. Pleyte, "Le Guepe," *ZASA* 4 (1866): 14-15; Kurt H. Sethe, "Über einen vermeintlichen Lautwerth des Zeichens der Biene," *ZASA* 30 (1892): 113-19; Karl Piehl, "La Lecture du Signe (Abeille)," *ZASA* 36 (1898): 85.

23. Sethe, "Über einen vermeintlichen Lautwerth des Zeichens der Biene," 117.

24. Adolf Erman and Hermann Grapow, *Aegyptisches Handwörterbuch* (Berlin: Reuther & Reichard, 1921), 223.

25. Gardiner, *Egyptian Grammar,* 504. The final "t" in deseret is the regular feminine ending, not part of the root, the root being *dsr*. Nevertheless it may not be omitted in designating the bee, the crown, or the land of Lower Egypt, all of which are feminine. The original text at this point said, "The substitution was a natural one, for the bee like the red crown was identical with the majesty of Lower Egypt."

26. Erman and Grapow, *Wörterbuch der aegyptischen Sprache,* 1:435.

27. Theodor H. Gaster, *Thespis* (New York: Schuman, 1950), 364-67. In his notes on the Telepinu Myth, Gaster points to ties that connect the bee rites all over the ancient world. On the bee in Christian ritual, see L. Duchesne, *Origines du culte chretien,* 5th ed. (Paris: Boccard, 1920), 266; for an English translation, see L. Duchesne, *Christian Worship: Its Origin and Evolution* (London: Society for the Promotion of Christian Knowledge, 1910), 253.

28. Moret, *Histoire de l'Orient,* 1:175-180, 189, 207-22, 230-37, especially 257-58.

29. In Egypt "the kings of the North were incarnated in the totem of Bouto: a bee (bit)"; ibid., 1:178.

30. Eduard Meyer, *Geschichte des Altertums,* 2nd ed. (Stuttgart: Cotta, 1928), vol. 2, pt. 1, p. 36.

31. Erman and Grapow, *Wörterbuch der aegyptischen Sprache,* 1:434.

32. Sethe, "Über einen vermeintlichen Lautwerth des Zeichens der Biene," 118; "Als Determinativ steht es aber, was zu beachten ist, stets allen anderen voran."

33. Moret, *Histoire de l'Orient,* 1:12.

34. Henri Frankfort, *Cylinder Seals* (London: Macmillan, 1939), 311.

35. G. N. Roerich, *Trails to Inmost Asia* (New Haven: Yale University Press, 1931), 123.

36. For a general treatment of this theme see Ellsworth Huntington, *Mainsprings of Civilization* (New York: Wiley, 1945), 187-207.

37. C. J. Gadd, *Ideas of Divine Rule in the Ancient East* (London: Oxford University Press, 1948), 1.

38. George Vernadsky, *Ancient Russia* (New Haven: Yale University Press, 1943), 27.

39. McGovern, *The Early Empires of Central Asia,* 116-17, 124.

40. Part 6 of "The World of the Jaredites," *IE* 55 (February 1952): 92-94, 98, 100, 102, 104-05, began at this point. The original magazine article at this point began: "Dear F.: Continuing the theme of my letter: As to the fugitive who gathers forces in the wilderness by 'drawing off' people from his rival, in the first century there was Lu Fang."

41. McGovern, *The Early Empires of Central Asia,* 224-26.

42. C. C. Mierow, *The Gothic History of Jordanes* (Princeton: Princeton University Press, 1915), 101-3; ch. 35.

43. They were Dinzio, ibid., 129-31; ch. 53, and Mundo, ibid., 137-38; ch. 58.

44. B. Ya. Vladimirtsov, *The Life of Chingis-Khan* (New York: Houghton Mifflin, 1930), 3.

45. Fikret Isiltan, *Die Seltschuken-Geschichte des Akserayi, Sammlung Orientalistischer Arbeiten* 12 (Leipzig: Harrassowitz, 1943), 88.

46. The first quotation from E. S. Creasy, *History of the Ottoman Turks,* 2 vols. (London: Bentley, 1854-56), 1:5, the second from Sven Hedin, *The Flight of Big Horse,* trs. F. H. Lyon, (New York: Dutton, 1936), 16. Cf. Mildred Cable, *The Gobi Desert* (New York: Macmillan, 1945), 222-32.

47. F. E. A. Krause, *Cingis Han* (Heidelberg: Winter, 1922), 13. Michael Prawdin, *The Mongol Empire* (London: Allen & Unwin, 1940), 47-49. A description of the technique of "drawing off" another's supporters is in Al-Fakhari's *Al-Adab al-Sultaniah wal-Daula-l-Islamiah* (Cairo), 5.

48. Prawdin, *The Mongol Empire,* 86.

49. Menander Protector, *De Legationibus Romanorum ad Gentes 8,* in *PG* 113:888.

50. According to Odoric of Pordennone, ch. 18, in Komroff, *Contemporaries of Marco Polo,* 249-50 "the ancient law" of the Khans is, "Thou shalt not appear in my presence with an empty hand," the corollary being that "No Mongol, this day, entered the tent of his ruler without being richly rewarded," Prawdin, *The Mongol Empire,* 86. The strictly mercenary nature of the whole business is well described by Peter Patricius in 230 A.D., in *PG* 113:665-68, and Priscus, in 449 A.D., in *PG* 113:748-52. E. A. Wallis Budge, *The Chronography of Bar Hebraeus,* 2 vols. (Oxford: Oxford University Press, 1932), 1:505, tells how when Baidu the Mongol wanted to supplant his brother on the throne of Asia "he made men rich with gifts, and he made men splendid with royal apparel." And so he bound them to him. Innumerable parallels might be cited.

51. Vernadsky, *Ancient Russia,* 80.

52. Fritz Hommel, *Ethnologie und Geographie des alten Orients* (Munich: Beck, 1926), 22-23.

53. I am following the text of René Labat, *Le poème babylonien de la création* (Paris: Maisonneuve, 1935), 98-101.

54. Ibid., 24.

55. *Memoirs of Louis IX, King of France,* in Lord John de Joinville, *Chronicles of the Crusades* (London: Bohn, 1848), 482. The whole history of Jenghiz Khan is a long succession of terrible oaths, the most solemn being taken by a bag full of blood, to follow Krause, *Cingis Han,* 17-18, 23-24, etc. Herodotus, *Histories* IV, 64, describes the blood-drinking oaths of the Scythians two thousand years earlier.

56. Moritz Hoernes, *Natur- und Urgeschichte des Menschen,* 2 vols. (Vienna: Hartleben, 1909), 1:582, discussing conditions in pre-agrarian societies generally.

57. James Darmesteter, *The Zend-Avesta,* 3 vols. (Oxford: Oxford University Press, 1895), 2:135, 140 (Yasts 15:63; 21:82).

58. Hoernes, *Natur- und Urgeschichte des Menschen* 2:418. The reader is reminded that fellowships and secret societies have always been the foundation of Asiatic government and religion, whether shamanistic (e.g., the Bn), lamist or Buddhist, from Peking to Cairo.

59. Clément Huart and Louis Delaporte, *L'Iran antique* (Paris: Michel, 1952), 399.

60. I have a long note on this subject in my article, Hugh W. Nibley, "Sparsiones," *CJ* 40 (1945): 526, n. 70.

Chapter 4: Jaredite Culture: Splendor and Shame

1. Ether 11:9, 18-19, 23; cf. 10:14, 31; 7:7; 8:3-4; 10:15, 30.

2. E. A. Wallis Budge, *The Chronography of Bar Hebraeus,* 2 vols. (Oxford: Oxford University Press, 1932), 1:495, 500.

3. Benjamin of Tudela, Travels, ch. 56, in A. Asher, ed., *The Itinerary of Rabbi Benjamin of Tudela,* 2 vols. (New York: "Hakesheth," n. d.), 1:95 (italics added); cf. ibid., 1:96: following a rebellion "it was decreed, that all the members of the Khalif's family should be chained, in order to prevent their rebellious intentions. Every one of them, however, resides in his palace; . . . They eat and drink and lead a merry life."

4. Michael Prawdin, *The Mongol Empire* (London: Allen & Unwin, 1940), 424.

5. Ibid., 448.

6. Fikret Isiltan, *Die Seltschuken-Geschichte des Akserayi, Sammlung Orientalistischer Arbeiten* 12 (Leipzig: Harrassowitz, 1943), 41-42. For some picturesque dethronements, see Budge, *Chronography of Bar Hebraeus* 1:147, 163, 176, 178.

7. N. Martinovitch, "Another Turkish Iron Cage," *JAOS* 62 (1942): 140, citing a number of instances.

8. Budge, *Chronography of Bar Hebraeus,* 1:471.

9. David D. Luckenbill, *Ancient Records of Assyria and Babylonia,* 2 vols. (Chicago: University of Chicago Press, 1926-27), 2:155.

10. Ibid., 2:314.

11. A. B. Cook, *Zeus,* 3 vols. (Cambridge: Cambridge University Press, 1914-40), and C. J. Gadd, *Ideas of Divine Rule in the Ancient East* (London: Oxford University Press, 1948) treat this subject at length.

12. Luckenbill, *Ancient Records of Assyria and Babylonia,* 1:270-71, 288; 1:182.

13. Ibid., 1:50.

14. William M. McGovern, *The Early Empires of Central Asia* (Chapel Hill: University of North Carolina Press, 1939), 73. Cf. Herodotus, *Histories* IV, 20.

15. Claudian, *Bellum Geticum* 11, 364-68; C. C. Mierow, *The Gothic History of Jordanes* (Princeton: Princeton University Press, 1915), 128-29; ch. 52.

16. Henning Haslund, *Men and Gods in Mongolia* (New York: Dutton, 1935), 4.

17. Marco Polo, *Travels.*

18. B. Ya. Vladimirtsov, *The Life of Chingis-Khan* (New York: Houghton Mifflin, 1930), 147-48; the quote is from 148. The theory is that "the conquered are the property of the conqueror, who is the lawful master of them, of their lands, of their goods, of their wives, and of their children. We have the right to do what we will with our own," E. S. Creasy, *History of the Ottoman Turks,* 2 vols. (London: Bentley, 1854-56), 1:21.

19. Prawdin, *The Mongol Empire,* 131, 142, 175, 476. Luckenbill, *Ancient Records of Assyria and Babylonia,* 1:182.

20. G. N. Roerich, *Trails to Inmost Asia* (New Haven: Yale University Press, 1931), 232.

21. Prawdin, *The Mongol Empire,* 374; Gadd, *Ideas of Divine Rule in the Ancient East,* 6.

22. Prawdin, *The Mongol Empire,* 374.

23. Under the subtitle "Mountain and Palace," in Hugh W. Nibley, "Hierocentric State," *WPQ* 4 (1951): 235-38. No empire was possible without a palace and city as its center; as in Jubilees 4:9; 7:14. In the most ancient times "every king built himself a new residence: upon mounting the throne," says Eduard Meyer, *Geschichte des Altertums,* 2nd ed. (Stuttgart: Cotta, 1909), vol. 1, pt. 2, p. 145, for the custom was "that every king possess his own 'city.' "

24. A. Wünsche, *Salomons Thron und Hippodrom* (*Ex Oriente Lux* 2:3), 9ff, 22-25. Thaʿlabi, *Qiṣaṣ al-Anbiyya,* 11-12.

25. Part 7 of "The World of the Jaredites," *IE* 55 (March 1952): 162-65, 167-68 , began with this sentence.

26. Budge, *Chronography of Bar Hebraeus,* 1:500.

27. Clément Huart and Louis Delaporte, *L'Iran antique* (Paris: Michel, 1952), 367; Adam Mex, *The Renaissance of Islam,* Salahuddin Khuda Bukhsh and D. S. Margoliouth, tr. (London: Luzac, 1937), 19-20. This golden throne was erected on a golden platform, before which stood a silver platform on which his princes sat in gilded chairs; some say the latter were silver thrones.

28. Carpini, ch. 28, in Manuel Komroff, ed., *Contemporaries of Marco Polo* (New York: Liveright, 1928), 45.

29. Eduard Meyer, *Geschichte des Altertums,* 2nd ed. (Stuttgart: Cotta, 1928), vol. 2, pt. 1, p. 235; Hugh W. Nibley, "Hierocentric State," *WPQ* 4 (1951): 240. The sella curulis was a gilt campstool used by the Roman emperor, but its name shows that it was originally mounted on wheels in the Asiatic fashion.

30. At the Pacific Coast meeting in 1940, *ARAHA* (1940): 90.

31. Hugh W. Nibley, "Sparsiones," *CJ* 40 (1945): 541-43.

32. Ibid., for a preliminary treatment.

33. Budge, *Chronography of Bar Hebraeus,* 1:182, "The sister of the Khalifah had a certain scribe, an Egyptian, in Syria, and he sent and complained to her about Abu Tahir [the ruler of Syria]. . . . And because her brother always paid very great attention to her, she went and wept before him. And she received [from him] the command, and she sent [it] and killed Abu Tahir, and his head was carried to Egypt."

34. Quotation is from P. Van der Meer, *The Ancient Chronology of Western Asia and Egypt* (Leiden: Brill, 1947), 13. The quote does not pertain to glass, but is relevant to matters of historical prejudice.

35. Gerald A. Wainwright, "The Coming of Iron," *Antiquity* 10 (1936): 7.

36. Ibid., 7.

37. Ibid., 8-9.

38. Ibid., 7, 23.

39. Ibid., 22.

40. Ibid., 14; emphasis added.

41. Ibid., 18.

42. Friedrich Spiegel, *Ernische Alterthumskunde* (Leipzig, 1873), 2:152. James Darmesteter, *The Zend-Avesta,* 3 vols. (Oxford: Oxford University Press, 1880-87), 1:93.

43. This subject received some notice in Hugh W. Nibley, "Lehi in the Desert," *IE* 53 (1950): 323-25.

44. Sadr al-Din Abi al-Hasan 'Ali b. Nasir b. 'Ali al-Husayni, *Akhbar al-Dawla al-Saljuqiyya* (Lahore: University of the Panjab, 1933), 1. This might be regarded as a mere ornamental epithet were it not that the name *Iron Arrow* is fairly common and actually refers to such a weapon, Semen I. Lipkin, *Manas Vielikodushnyi* (Moscow: Sovietski Posaty, 1947),

24-25. The implications of steel bows are of course very significant for 1 Nephi 16:18.

45. T. Wright, ed., *The Travels of Marco Polo* (London: Bohn, 1854), 53 (bk. 1, ch. 14). Traveling through central Asia in 568 A.D., Menander was met more than once by primitive tribesmen from the mountains who tried to sell him their native ironware; Menander Protector, *De Legationibus Romanorum ad Gentes* 8, in *PG* 113:884.

46. T. J. Meek, "The Challenge of Oriental Studies to American Scholarship," *JAOS* 63 (1943): 92, n. 73, gives the formula for the Ras Shamra steel.

47. Wainwright, "The Coming of Iron," 16.

48. "The art of forging iron must have been kept secret for a long time by the clans of forgers, in order to preserve their privileges." George Vernadsky, *Ancient Russia* (New Haven: Yale University Press, 1943), 43.

49. D. B. Harden, "Ancient Glass," *Antiquity* 7 (1933): 419; Pliny, *Natural History* XXXVI, 191.

50. Harden, "Ancient Glass," 419.

51. P. E. Newberry, "A Glass Chalice of Tuthmosis III," *JEA* 6 (1920): 159.

52. Ibid., 158-59.

53. Harden, "Ancient Glass," 419.

54. Newberry, "A Glass Chalice of Tuthmosis III," 158; Harden, "Ancient Glass," 420, cf. 426.

55. Harden, "Ancient Glass," 419.

56. Wright, *The Travels of Marco Polo,* 179, n. 1 (bk. 2, ch. 6). The existence of such windows has been hotly disputed, for no good reason. An early traveler "mentions that the windows of some yachts or barges had plate glass" in the East, ibid. It is interesting that the only proven use for window-glass was on vessels.

57. Karl A. Wittfogel and Fêng Chia-Shêng, "History of Chinese Society Liao," *TAPS* 36 (1946): 661.

58. "Silk and Sericulture," *Encylopaedia Britannica,* 24 vols. (Chicago: Encyclopaedia Britannica, 1960), 20:661.

59. Joseph P. Free, "Abraham's Camels," *JNES* 3 (1944): 187-93.

60. Fritz Flor, in Harentz, ed., *Germanen und Indo-Germanen* (Heidelberg, 1934), 1:111ff, 122.

61. McGovern, *The Early Empires of Central Asia,* 77, cf. 27; Raphael Pumpelly, *Explorations in Turkestan,* 2 vols. (Washington: Carnegie Institution, 1908), 1:41-43.

62. James H. Breasted, *A History of Egypt* (New York: Scribner, 1909), 304; Wittfogel & Chia-Shng, "History of Chinese Society Liao," 669.

63. The principal authority on this subject is Max Hilzheimer. See

Max Hilzheimer, "Dogs," *Anitquity* 6 (1932): 411-19; and Max Hilzheimer, "Sheep," *Antiquity* 10 (1936): 195-206.

64. See for example Wittfogel & Chia-Shng, "History of Chinese Society Liao," 662, Haslund, *Men and Gods in Mongolia,* 73.

65. Darmesteter, *Zend-Avesta,* 1:5, n. 3.

66. Herodotus, *Histories* I, 140.

67. James A. Montgomery, *Arabia and the Bible* (Philadelphia: University of Pennsylvania Press, 1934), 50.

68. Isiltan, *Die Seltschuken-Geschichte des Akserayi,* 97-98.

69. Odoric ch. 13, and William of Rubruck ch. 7, in Komroff, *Contemporaries of Marco Polo,* 241, 68. On Oppenheimer, see Nibley, "Hierocentric State," 251.

70. Xenophon, *Cyropaedeia* II, 4, 16-26.

71. E. A. Wallis Budge, *The Mummy* (Cambridge: Cambridge University Press, 1925), plate 2, center.

72. Nibley, "Hierocentric State," 238-44; and Hugh W. Nibley, "The Arrow, the Hunter, and the State," *WPQ* 2 (1949): 343-44.

Chapter 5: They Take up the Sword

1. Part 8 of "The World of the Jaredites," *IE* 55 (April 1952): 236-38, 258, 260-65, began at this point.

2. Hugh W. Nibley, "The Hierocentric State," *WPQ* 4 (1951): 238-44.

3. Ibid., 226-30.

4. James Darmesteter, *The Zend Avesta,* 3 vols. (Oxford: Oxford University Press, 1880-87), 2:265 (Din Yast 1:3).

5. Michael Prawdin, *The Mongol Empire* (London: Allen & Unwin, 1940), 162.

6. The earliest kings are always described as perpetually "going the round." Thus Pharaoh in the Pyramid Texts "goes the rounds" of the Two Regions as of the skies, and the Babylonian gods move from shrine to shrine, i.e., from castle to castle, as Apollo, *Iliad* I, 37-42, and Poseidon, e.g., *Odyssey* V, 381, do in the beginning.

7. Anton Jirku, "Aufstieg und Untergang der Hyksos," *JPOS* 12 (1932): 51-61; William F. Albright, "Egypt and the Early History of the Negeb," *JPOS* 4 (1924): 134; Eduard Meyer, *Geschichte des Altertums,* 2nd ed. (Stuttgart: Cotta, 1928), vol. 2, pt. 1, p. 72. For dates see William F. Albright, *The Archaeology of Palestine* (Baltimore: Penguin, 1960), 84-85, 108-9.

8. Moritz Hoernes, *Natur- und Urgeschichte des Menschen,* 2 vols. (Vienna: Hartleben, 1909), 2:396.

9. E. A. Speiser, "On Some Articles of Armor and Their Names,"

JAOS 70 (1950): 47-49; Hurrian words for armor indicate central Asian origins, ibid., 49.

10. See Appendix 2.

11. Karl A. Wittfogel and Fêng Chia-Shêng, "History of Chinese Society Liao," *TAPS* 36 (1946): 663; Henning Haslund, *Men and Gods in Mongolia* (New York: Dutton, 1935), 236-37.

12. Mildred Cable, *The Gobi Desert* (New York: Macmillan, 1945), 264.

13. E. Nelson Fell, *Russian and Nomad* (New York: Duffield, 1916), 9-10.

14. The whole question is treated in my two articles, Hugh W. Nibley, "The Hierocentric State," *WPQ* 4 (1951): 226-53; and "The Arrow, the Hunter, and the State," *WPQ* 2 (1949): 328-44.

15. F. E. A. Krause, *Cingis Han* (Heidelberg: Winter, 1922), 14-27; Prawdin, *The Mongol Empire,* 147-50.

16. Darmesteter, *Zend-Avesta,* 2:148 (Yasts 27:111). A description of the technique of "drawing off" another's supporters is in Al-Fakhri's *Al-Adab al-Sultaniah wal-Dawla-l-Islamiyah* (Cairo), 5.

17. William M. McGovern, *The Early Empires of Central Asia* (Chapel Hill: University of North Carolina Press, 1939), 143; cf. Nibley, "Hierocentric State," 244-47.

18. Xenophon, *Cyropaedeia* IV, 2.

19. Max Pieper, *Die Ägyptische Literatur* (Wildpark-Potsdam: Akademische Verlagsgesellschaft Athenaion, 1927), 74.

20. David D. Luckenbill, *Ancient Records of Assyria and Babylonia,* 2 vols. (Chicago: University of Chicago Press, 1926-27), 1:57, 60, 40; cf. 2:124: "I seized him alive with my (own) hands," etc., speaking of the rival king.

21. Herodotus, *Histories* IV, 11, 126; Jordanes, in C. C. Mierow, *The Gothic History of Jordanes* (Princeton: Princeton University Press, 1915), 93-95; ch. 30; E . S. Creasy, *History of the Ottoman Turks,* 2 vols. (London: Bentley, 1854-56), 1:46.

22. Krause, *Cingis Han,* 26; Haslund, *Men and Gods in Mongolia,* 155.

23. Herodotus, *Histories* I, 214.

24. George Vernadsky, *Ancient Russia* (New Haven: Yale University Press, 1943) , 298-99; G. N. Roerich, *Trails to Inmost Asia* (New Haven: Yale University Press, 1931), 368; C. R. Beazley, *The Dawn of Modern Geography,* 2 vols. (London: Murray, 1901), 2:267.

25. Bruno Meissner, *Babylonien und Asyrien,* 2 vols. (Heidelberg: Winter, 1926), 1:112; Haslund, *Men and Gods in Mongolia,* 155.

26. Carpini, ch. 16, in Manuel Komroff, ed. *Contemporaries of Marco Polo* (New York: Liveright, 1928), 26.

27. Carpini, ch. 6, in ibid., 12.

28. R. Grousset, *L'asie orientale des origines au XVe siècle* (Paris: Presses Universitaires, 1941), 304-5, 307; quote on 305.

29. Luckenbill, *Ancient Records of Assyria and Babylonia,* 2:99.

30. E. A. Wallis Budge, *The Chronography of Bar Hebraeus,* 2 vols. (Oxford: Oxford University Press, 1932), 1:465.

31. Ibid., 1:124.

32. This is well-nigh the leitmotiv of Arabshah's *Life of Timur, Kitāb ʿAjā'ib al-Maqdur* (Cairo, A. H. 1335); princes when defeated regularly become highway robbers according to Chinese annals, Krause, *Cingis Han,* 24. Attila's descendants became leaders of robber bands though heirs to world empire, e.g., Jordanes, in Mierow, *The Gothic History of Jordanes,* 137-38; ch. 58. That this is the primordial state of things appears from Darmesteter, *Zend-Avesta* 2:171.

33. Budge, *Chronography of Bar Hebraeus,* 1:103, 111.

34. Herodotus, *Histories* IV, 64, 66, 70; Pliny, *Natural History* VII, 2, 10; Ammianus Marcellinus, *Rerum Gestarum* XXXI, 2, 14 and 2, 22; Luckenbill, *Ancient Records of Assyria and Babylonia,* 2:396 (No. 1050); Budge, *Chronography of Bar Hebraeus,* 1:465; McGovern, *The Early Empires of Central Asia,* 54.

35. Arabshah, 4-6, lists great world conquerors who propagated the belief that they were devils.

36. M. E. Moghadam, "A Note on the Etymology of the Word Checkmate," *JAOS* 58 (1938): 662; cf. L. Thorndike, "All the World's a Chessboard," *Speculum* 6 (1931): 461-65.

37. Krause, *Cingis Han,* 26; Grousset, *L'asie orientale des origines au XVe siècle,* 291.

38. Luckenbill, *Ancient Records of Assyria and Babylonia* 2:310-11 (No. 811); 152 (No. 340).

39. Prawdin, *The Mongol Empire,* 191-93, 469, 472.

40. Constantine Porphyrogenitus, *De Administrando Imperio* 47, in *PG* 113:365.

41. Jordanes, in Mierow, *The Gothic History of Jordanes,* 131; ch. 53.

42. Eunapius, *De Legationibus Gentium ad Romanos* 6, in *PG* 113:656-57; McGovern, *The Early Empires of Central Asia,* 366.

43. Haslund, *Men and Gods in Mongolia,* 206-7.

44. Prawdin, *The Mongol Empire,* 221, 329.

45. McGovern, *The Early Empires of Central Asia,* 335-36, 189-91.

46. Carpini, chs. 13, 21, in Komroff, *Contemporaries of Marco Polo,* 22, 37.

47. Krause, *Cingis Han,* 17.

48. Lord John of Joinville, *Memoirs of Louis IX. King of France,* in Lord John of Joinville, *Chronicles of the Crusades* (London: Bohn, 1848), 476.

49. Part 9 of "The World of the Jaredites," *IE* 55 (May 1952): 316-18, 340, 342, 344, 346, began at this point.

50. Joseph Fielding Smith, *Teachings of the Prophet Joseph Smith* (Salt Lake City: Deseret, 1938), 320.

51. Quoted in N. B. Lundwall, *Temples of the Most High* (Salt Lake City: Lundwall, 1941), 301, from *Journal of Discourses* 3:367-68.

52. Smith, *Teachings of the Prophet Joseph Smith,* 331.

53. Ibid., 348.

Chapter 6: A Permanent Heritage

1. Examples of mimation may be found in William F. Albright, *The Vocalization of Egyptian Syllabic Orthography* (New Haven: American Oriental Society, 1934), 7-8, 14-15.

2. At this point the magazine text reads: "Noah was a Jaredite king, and another Noah was a Nephite king, but the latter was not a pure-blooded Nephite, for his father Zeniff was the last leader of the Mulekite colony." The latter part of this comment was deleted in the 1952 book edition. Information about Zeniff is very sketchy.

3. Leonard Woolley, *Abraham* (London: Faber & Faber, 1936), 175.

4. "They flee to the mountains" is the Assyrian formula, e.g., David D. Luckenbill, *Ancient Records of Assyria and Babylonia,* 2 vols. (Chicago: University of Chicago Press, 1926-27), 1:79. "Upon leaving Balach," says Marco Polo, in T. Wright, *The Travels of Marco Polo* (London: Bohn, 1954), 79 (bk. 1, ch. 23), "you traverse a country that is destitute of every sign of habitation, the people having all fled to strong places in the mountains, in order to secure themselves against the predatory attack of lawless marauders, by whom these districts are overrun." In the flat regions of the north "everyone tried to escape into the woods," at the approach of the hordes, B. Ya. Vladimirtsov, *The Life of Chingis-Khan* (New York: Houghton Mifflin, 1930), 20.

5. René Grousset, *L'asie orientale des origines au XVe siècle* (Paris: Presses Universitaires, 1941), 305.

6. Mildred Cable, *The Gobi Desert* (New York: Macmillan, 1945), 278.

7. Joseph Fielding Smith, *Teachings of the Prophet Joseph Smith* (Salt Lake City: Deseret, 1938), 267.

8. Origen, *Peri Archon (On First Principles)* II, 3, 6 in *PG* 11:196.

9. For a complete account of the Kensington Stone, see S. M. Hagen, "The Kensington Runic Inscription," *Speculum* 25 (1950): 321-56.

10. Hugh W. Nibley, "The Book of Mormon as a Mirror of the East," *IE* 51 (1947): 202-4, 249-51.

11. Part 10 of "The World of the Jaredites," *IE* 55 (June 1952): 398-99, 462-64 , began at this point.

12. René Grousset, *L'asie orientale des origines au XVe siècle,* 305.

13. Harold S. Gladwin, *Men Out of Asia* (New York: McGraw-Hill, 1947).

14. M. A. Czaplicka, *Aboriginal Siberia* (Oxford: Clarendon, 1914), 69, 79, 114-16, 203-27.

15. If readers will examine the culture map of Asia published in *Life* magazine for 31 December 1951, pages 8-9, they will notice that the editors have placed the "beginning of civilization" in the mountains to the north and east of Mesopotamia, with the main focal point in the great valleys immediately north of the Plain of Sinear. This is in strict accordance with our own conclusions based on the Book of Ether.

16. W. Andrae, "The Story of Uruk," *Antiquity* 10 (1936): 141-42. On the equally sudden emergence of Egyptian writing, Siegfried Schott, *Mythe und Mythenbildung im alten Ägypten* (Leipzig: Hinrich, 1945; reprinted Hildesheim: Olm, 1964), 3.

17. I have treated this theme in "The Arrow, the Huntei, and the State" *WPQ* 2 (1949): 328-44.

18. Philip K. Hitti, *History of Syria* (New York: Macmillan, 1951), 149.

19. Ibid., for the archaic Hur-, Hor- element in Egyptian names, see Schott, *Mythe und Mythenbildung im alten Ägypten,* e.g., p. 5.

20. The Conclusion of "The World of the Jaredites," *IE* 55 (July 1952): 510, 550, began at this point.

Part 3
There Were Jaredites

1

The Heroic Age[1]

"So you really think there were Jaredites," said Professor F. with a slightly skeptical expression and another pull at his blackened briar. He hated smoking but his profession and institution required tweeds and a pipe unequivocally as they prescribed the lounging attitude and intellectual drawl with which he confronted his visitor.

"So you really think there were Jaredites. Well, well, and what makes you think so now? Of course I read all your letters, but you seem to be worked up over something new."

"It is new," said the visitor, "and yet it is very old. It is the *epic milieu* that makes me think there were Jaredites."

"Epic milieu? Epic milieu? What on earth is that?" queried the man of learning. For an answer, Mr. Blank (a good enough name for the other man) went to the large bookcase against the wall. After a minute of exploration in which he refused help from his host, he returned to his chair blowing the dust from an Oxford text of Homer.

"Do you remember any of this," he asked, "or shall I refresh your memory?"

"About what? A mere thousand pages of hexameters?"

"I mean about these people," said Blank, solemnly holding the book (Munro's elegant India paper edition), "their wars and their journeys, their intrigues and quarrels, their food, clothes, diversions—what they chose to do and how they chose to do it."

"Well," said F., scratching his head thoughtfully, "I still have a fair general idea of what the Homeric world was like . . . "

"That is a good expression, *Homeric world.* Homer has given us a whole world from the past, complete with all the trimmings. But now it would appear that that is more than a poet's world of fancy: it is the actual milieu in which epic poetry took its rise."

"You mean there really was such a world as Homer describes?"

"Apparently there was. Your question, incidentally, is basic to the solution of the Homeric question itself."

"Ah, yes," said the professor trying desperately to remember something about it, "the Homeric question."

"There is hardly a branch of literary criticism or historical analysis, including the higher criticism of the Bible," Blank rejoined, "that did not take its rise in the Homeric question."

"Indeed," replied his host.

"The Homeric question itself is simply, How did these poems come to exist?" Blank tapped the volume impressively, "Did a creative genius make them up out of thin air or are the scenes and characters depicted taken from life? What do *you* think? Was there ever an Achaian host? Did it assault a real city of Troy? Did such heroes as Achilles and Hector ever live?"

"I'm sure I don't know," muttered the professor, thoughtfully stroking his chin, "but then there was Schliemann and all that. I dare say there are ways of finding out. By the way, what has this to do with the Jaredites? And you still haven't told me what the epic milieu is."

"Hand me the big Webster, will you? Thanks. Ah, here it is, the full definition (copyright G. & C. Merriam and Co., 1924): milieu: medium, environment. A milieu is an environment, a complete environment taken with all its own roots and origins; and the epic milieu is the real world in which the events described in epic poems are supposed to have taken place: it is that world and not the poet's imagination which furnishes him with his characters and images. Everyone agrees today that the epic milieu described by Homer was a real one."

"And now you can tell me where the Jaredites come into this," said F.

"With pleasure. The Jaredites have a milieu, too. If there is a Homeric world that vanished thousands of years ago, so also there is a Jaredite world. And if the reality of the one can actually be proved over this great gulf of time, why cannot the other?"

"I'll tell you why. Because the archaeological problem is a totally different one. Whereas every student—"

"Excuse me if I interrupt, but the problem is not an archaeological one."

"Oh, come now!"

"I mean it. Students of the classics never ignore physical remains, of course—"

"Are you joking?"

"—but it so happens that the epic milieu has been most successfully investigated from another angle entirely. I see you subscribe to the *AJA [American Journal of Archaeology]*. That is convenient. Where is that big issue that was devoted entirely to Homer? The year 1948 I think it was. Yes, here it is. You should have read this account of Robert Wood. He was quite a big-wig in his day—Under Secretary of State to Lord Granville, in fact. Over a hundred years before Schliemann went to look for Troy, this man with his friends walked all over the terrain where Homer's heroes are supposed to have fought and fled; and then they traced the routes of the heroes homeward bound from Troy.[2] From this he became convinced and was able to convince some others that the stories in Homer had at least a real geographical background."

"And you think you can do that with the Jaredites?" the professor interposed.

"Of course not. No one has ever identified a single Nephite artifact, let alone a Jaredite ruin! But that is not our problem at all, nor was it Wood's solution to the Homeric question. It was only important as a preliminary step, in fact."

"So what did our Mr. Wood do next?"

"Next he went to Syria, and there came upon 'a type of community strangely remote from the world of contemporary scholarship,' but it was a real world, just the same. You know how many travel classics have given substance to the mysterious Bedouin world since Wood's day. Well, Robert Wood's critical eye detected the same 'combination in the Arab traits of savagery and chivalry which also characterizes the heroes of the *Iliad.*' Was that just a coincidence, he asked himself, or could the ways of the modern Arabs be used to check, of all things, the authority of Homer?"

"*Lehi in the Desert* stuff, eh?"

"You might say. Anyway, Wood thought there was a connection and, as the book says, he 'intended to write a detailed work in which similarities of the cultures exhibited in the Old Testament, in Homer, and in the Near East of his own day should be collected, and prove that the "Heroic Age" is a real and recurrent type in human society and that Homer's picture of that of Greece is reliable.' "[3]

"And did our man succeed?"

"Unfortunately he died before he could carry out the project, but he did publish an essay on the nature of epic poetry that made a big impression on the Germans. That was the time, you know, when the German romantics were busy reconstructing the wonderful misty world of woods and crags from which they fondly supposed their own national epic poetry took its rise. In England Bishop Percy was hot on the trail of another epic milieu. Two years before Wood's essay appeared he brought out the first edition of his *Reliques of Ancient English Poetry.*"

"It's right behind you," said the professor, "third shelf from the top."

"Thank you. Note the acknowledgment to 'the late elegant Mr. Shenstone,' who really started the thing. Here in the introductory essay Percy says that the ancient minstrels 'had before them too many recent monuments of the Anglo-Saxon nation, not to know what was conformable to the genius and manners of that people; and therefore we may presume that their relations prove at least the existence of the customs and habits they attribute to our forefathers before the conquest, whatever becomes of the particular incidents and events themselves.'[4] Note how he goes to the heart of the thing: as a historical source for 'particular incidents and events' these old poems may not be worth a bean, but the *sort* of thing they describe, the things that happen recurrently, familiar scenes, and accepted patterns of behavior may be reliably reported and carefully confirmed in their verses. In other words, it is possible to detect in the early English ballads just such a genuine cultural milieu as one discovers in Homer."

"And where does that get us?"

"To our next point, which is that one not only finds genuine epic milieux (how do you pronounce a final 'x' by the way?) looming behind one ancient literature after another, but also when you compare those different milieux they are all the same!"

"Do you mean to tell me that Bishop Percy's English Heroic Age or epic milieu, or whatever you call it, is exactly like Homer's—two thousand years earlier?"

"That is what I am coming to. For a long time the Germans, for example, insisted that they had a very private epic world of their own. But Schneider, the leader in the field, has shown how they gradually came to recognize that the epic world described in their poems was exactly like that depicted in the epics of other nations: so they finally came to the conclusion that epic poetry in general is not the product of a national spirit or a poet's fancy but before everything else of the *Völkerwanderungszeit*—the time of the Great Migrations."[5]

"So the Teutons were like the Greeks. That's not too surprising."

"But it is only the beginning. At the turn of the century Hugo Winckler in that old classic *Die Keilinschriften und das Alte Testament*—I see you have it here—wrote as follows:

> We now know that the tides of people, such as the Germans at the beginning of the "Middle Ages," [these are the "Great Migrations" we just referred to], the Islamic expansion, . . . and the Turkish-Tartar-Mongol movements . . . were not anything extraordinary, and that the history of the ancient world is likewise composed of a continuous chain of such migrations.[6]

"He is pointing out here a fact that is now being appreciated every day, namely, that the great migrations were by no means confined to one period of the world's history, but have been a recurrent event, involving all of Europe and Asia, throughout historic times."

"But if it is these great migrations that produce epics, shouldn't there be a lot more epic poems than there are?"

"A natural, if hasty, conclusion. A more correct deduction would be that epic literature should be much vaster not than it is but than we have hitherto supposed it to be. Actually investigations now going on are showing that for lo, these many years, the scholars have had all sorts of epic material lying around under their noses without knowing what it was."

"Are you serious?"

"Actually it has only been since the 1930's that the real nature and scope of the epic world has begun to be appreciated. It was the studies of H. Munro Chadwick and Milman Parry in our own generation that first showed the real nature of the epic. Back to our *AJA*—here you have it:

> Poetry is heroic only because it is created by a people who are living in a certain way, and so have a certain outlook on life, and our understanding of the heroic will

> come only as we learn what that way of living is and grasp that outlook. We find, for example, that cattle-lifting is a common theme in the ancient European poetries, but it is found there because of no law of poetry, but because these people happen to live in a way which led them to the stealing of cattle on the one hand and to the practice of poetry on the other. The heroic element in early poetry is not a problem of lore, but one of anthropology and history, and the students of heroic poetry have done a very great deal in showing how the social background is mirrored in the poetry.[7]

"No matter when and where it is produced, genuine epic poetry can be only the product of a particular way of life, and that way of life is our epic or heroic milieu—it furnishes the ideas and images reflected in the poems."

"A very majestic concept, this epic background of the oldest literature. But must you find it everywhere?"

"Of course not, but where we do find it, we are beginning to know where we stand."

"And who, pray, are 'we'?"

"You know what I mean. But there are experts in quite a number of fields who are finding the fact of a world-wide heroic age of great service in helping them interpret their materials. In many cases it is, in fact, decisive, and I think it will prove decisive in the case of the Jaredites."

"How about a concrete example?"

"That, of course, is what I wanted you to ask. I love concrete examples. Well, here is Professor Samuel Kramer, writing in this same useful volume of the *AJA*—"

"He's an orientalist, isn't he?"

"Yes, he is our top Sumerian scholar, and in his archaeological capacity he is the director of the University of Pennsylvania Museum. And here he tells us that our epic milieu provides the only possible means yet devised of reconstructing the history of the earliest Sumerians."

"Wait a minute! When you say our epic milieu, do you mean Homer and the Northmen?"

"Exactly. It is the epic literature of those people that enables him to interpret the new Sumerian evidence."

"What is this new evidence?"

"Kramer says it is contained in the fragments of nine epic poems, which indicate 'that early in their history, the Sumerians had passed through a cultural stage now commonly known as a Heroic Age. . . . Once the existence of a Sumerian Heroic Age had been determined, it was possible to adduce its cultural pattern and historical background on analogy with such long-known heroic ages as those of the Greek, Indian, and Teutonic peoples.' He feels that the reality of the epic milieu has actually 'permitted a reinterpretation of the earliest history of Mesopotamia which may prove closer to the truth than those suggested hitherto.' "[8]

"What about his archaeological activities?"

"They are out. 'Fortunately enough [he writes here] this new evidence has nothing to do with the highly ambiguous material remains of prehistoric Mesopotamia; it is of a purely literary and historical character.' "[9]

"Dear me, that is something! And he actually thinks that Greek, Indian, and Teutonic heroic ages can explain doings of the first Sumerians?"

"They go farther than that; he says they furnish the key 'for the early history . . . of the ancient Near East as a whole.' "[10]

"Including the Jaredites, eh? But your book of Ether is no epic poem."

"That remains to be seen—what it was, that is, before Moroni got through with it remains to be seen. But please remember that epic writing does not always take the same form by any means; but it *does* always talk about the same *things*. And those are the very things the book of Ether talks about. In all essentials it is an epic production."

"Which, as you say, remains to be seen," replied the professor.

"Of course it remains to be seen. Three things in particular remain to be seen: (1) Is the epic milieu old enough, and is its reality well enough established and defined to provide a valid test for the book of Ether? (2) Is the epic milieu truly and unmistakably depicted in the book of Ether? (3) Can it be faked? You will realize that much depends on the last question, which we haven't even mentioned until now."

"You insist on talking about *the* epic milieu as if there were only one. Aren't there really as many of them as there are epic literatures?"

"Like gold, it is the same wherever you find it, the same effects always following the same causes. It is true that one can establish actual historical ties between various epic cultures—even between some that appear very far removed from each other. But whatever its cause, it is the fact of uniformity that justifies one in speaking of the epic milieu as a single phenomenon. It is not a case of coincidences between vague and general aspects of various cultures or between quaint and striking bits of such detail as dress and behavior; what we have is an elaborate and thorough-going identity of practices and institutions, always found together in the same imposing complex."

"It would take an awful lot of work to prove that," the professor observed.

"And an awful lot of work has gone into proving it. Chadwick's your man for that."

"How did he do it?"

"He set three corpuses of epic poetry or literature (it wasn't all poetry) side by side. Here, let me show you . . . "

The tireless Blank scouted through the shelves and took down a *Beowulf*, Finnur Jonsson's edition of *Egils Saga*, and an elegantly bound little volume of the *Dun Cow*.

"Very weak in the Celtic department," he commented, nodding at the latter item as he set the three books up on the desk beside the Homer, "but then most people are in this country—a crime and scandal, too, since half the population has Celtic blood. Translation, too—can't really use translations, you know; romantic balderdash for the most part, nineteenth-century romanticism and Victorian preconceptions warp every line; miss all the main points, to say nothing of the fine points. However, this will have to do for now. Behold!"

He pointed to the books standing in a row. "There they stand four of them side by side, four out of a possible hundred, selected at random, mind you, written in different parts of the world, with a full two thousand years between the oldest and youngest of them—and yet they are as alike as peas in a pod!"

"You exaggerate, as usual," was the professor's comment.

"On the contrary, anyone who reads them side by side is quite bowled over by the resemblances, which rarely come to the attention of one who reads them separately and far apart, and—I can guarantee you this—*never* come to the attention of one who never reads them at all! How many people do you suppose ever get around to comparing the originals of even half a dozen epics?"

"You know the answer to that one. Somewhere between one and three maybe?"

"Apparently nobody did until Chadwick came along. Though he compared just three epic literatures, he gave them a good going over—he was a professor of Anglo-Saxon at Oxford, you know—and he was able to show just how detailed and fundamental the resemblances really were. Then he turned to the nonliterary sources in each case—the histories, chronicles, genealogies, physical remains, etc., and easily showed that they described or depicted the same world that the poets told about. Not only did the three epic literatures tell the same story, but also in each case that story was seen to have a background in solid fact."

"Three aren't so many," the professor intoned.

"A great truth! But three points are enough to establish a curve on a graph. That curve represents a law, one might say, and of course the *more* points we can fix the more certain we will be of our curve and of the law it represents. Dozens of other epic points have been determined or identified since Chadwick's original three, and all fall quite close to the original line. Thus when Dr. Kramer found evidence that would put his proto-Sumerians smack on Chadwick's curve, he did not hesitate to project his limited information along the lines of a general law." Mr. Blank fortified the first curve with another chalk line and then read from the book:

" 'Once the existence of a Sumerian Heroic Age had been determined,'—that was the little 'x' we drew on the line—'it was possible to adduce its cultural pattern and historic background on analogy with . . . long known heroic ages,'—they were represented by the first curve.[11] Kramer gives credit to Chadwick for establishing the original curve: 'It is largely to the credit of . . . Chadwick that it is now generally realized that the so-called heroic ages which we come upon from time to time and from place to place in the history of civilization are not mere figments of the literary imagination, but represent very real and very significant social phenomena.' "[12]

"Has anyone else used the curve?" Professor F. asked.

"You may have heard of the very recent decipherment of all but twenty of the eighty-eight mysterious symbols of the so-called Minoan Script B. Some 4000 tablets written in that script now await interpretation, and to date Chadwick's heroic age has been a most useful guide in reconstructing the world those tablets are talking about."

"How does that work?"

"Once the heroic situation is established, the researcher knows what to look for—he is reassured when he is on the track and admonished when things don't ring true.

Professor Nilsson uses Chadwick in the same way, working in this area. Then in quite another cultural area, Cyrus Gordon has recently detected in the heroic age or epic milieu a sure guide to restoring the historical and cultural background of Abraham and his people, whose true nature, he believes, has escaped the scholars. He gives full credit to Chadwick as his guide."

"And now, my dear sir," said the professor, "if this discussion is to continue, as you seem determined it shall, would you be so kind as to tell me how I can recognize your epic milieu when I see it?"

"Always willing to oblige. By a fortunate coincidence I happened to bring Chadwick with me. We can go through it and list some of the stock characteristics of heroic ages on the blackboard." He took a fat book from his briefcase; it was bristling with page markers. "To begin with," he said, picking out the most conspicuously marked passage and reading didactically, " 'The heroic age coincides with the period of upheaval, . . . the period generally known as the age of National Migrations.'[13] That is point one. Kramer here says much the same thing:

> The factors primarily responsible for the more characteristic features of the . . . Heroic Ages are two. In the first place these Heroic Ages coincide with a period of national migrations, a *Völkerwanderungszeit*. Secondly—and this is by far the more significant factor—these peoples . . . had come in contact with a civilized power in the process of disintegration.[14]

"It is too bad that we have no word in our language that remotely resembles the rich and succulent *Völkerwanderungszeit*. Our 'Swarming Time,' 'Migration of peoples,' 'National Migrations' and all that are weak and unsatisfying."

"Yes," F. agreed, "it's a chocolate-coated word all right. Just what does it mean?"

"A *Völkerwanderungszeit* is one of those periods of vast

and compulsory nomadism that from time to time fill the whole world with commotion. A tremendously important historical phenomenon, and of course the most significant of all the hundred-and-one different types and degrees of nomadism. Most nomads aren't good at keeping records, but a good old *Völkerwanderung* is such a titanic event evolving such masses of people that it can't very well keep out of the record: the reports come from both sides—the victims describe in chronicles of woe how the barbarians move in on them, while the invaders glorify the same exploits in epic song. At any rate real epic poetry always describes conditions prevailing in times of world upheaval and mass migration."

"You can chalk that up as one point for Ether," the professor conceded.

"And a rather neat one," Blank replied. "The book gets off to a flying start. But let's leave Ether out of this until we get a clear image of the epic milieu by itself. Then we can make comparisons if we want to."

"Then let's get on to point number two," said Professor F.

"That is point one of what makes a heroic age.[15] Now consider the second characteristic." Blank drew a figure 2 on the board and read from Chadwick: " 'Feeling for nationality,' says our guide, 'is of no account in heroic poetry and saga. Love of home and the duty of defending it are of course recognized. But the interest . . . is always concentrated upon the doings or experiences of individuals.'[16] Kramer describes the situation succinctly:

> Now the most characteristic feature of all four of our Heroic Ages is this: they represent a rather barbarous cultural stage in the life of a people which has come far indeed from the primitive but has not yet attained the maturity and stability of a civilized society. Its dominant element is a rather numerous military class . . . to whom the underlying bulk of the population counts for very

> little. It is these knightly aristocrats who have freed themselves from the tribal obligations and ideas which govern the more primitive peoples. At the same time they have developed no true national organization and are inspired by little if any national feeling; their success and failure depend on the personal prowess of their leaders and kings whom they follow, . . . but from whom they are ready to drift away if these tend to turn too peaceful or become ungenerous in their rewards.[17]

"Looks like a whole list of points for Ether," the professor observed, and Mr. Blank modestly confessed that it was a remarkably good description of the very conditions described in Ether and pointed out by him in a minor tract on the world of the Jaredites. "But isn't it remarkable," he added, "that this complex and peculiar—we might almost say freakish—state of things turns up complete in epic literature wherever we find it?"

"There is one slip though," said the professor, "Kramer says these are people who have 'not yet attained the maturity and stability of a civilized society,' and yet your Jaredites are supposed to have had everything that belongs to a very sophisticated world, including a library."

"Well, what does Kramer or anybody know about any of these people before their migrations started? Only this, that something in every case *forced* them to move; if they come onto the stage rather shabbily equipped, it is not because they began life that way but because something happened that made them pull up stakes in a hurry and clear out with just enough stuff for a forced march. Remember, these people are *not* habitual nomads—they are moving because they have to, and in every case they are looking for lands to settle in. They have been forcibly evicted from their old homes and grazing lands. Now it is granted that these people *wherever they go* find civilization 'in the process of disintegration,' to quote Kramer—it is a time of *world* calamity. What reason have we therefore to doubt that it was the disintegration of their own less stable civilization that forced them to move in the first place? If they move in on a world in collapse, you can be perfectly sure that they left one behind as well—otherwise they would never have migrated."

"Any evidence for that?"

"The epics are full of it. The mere fact that our heroes do not enjoy what they are doing but want to get the business over with and settle down as soon as possible should be indication enough. Most epic poems are in mood little more than a prolonged agony. Remember what Goethe says about the *Iliad?* That it teaches us just one thing: 'that life on this earth is a hell.' But note what Kramer says here: these people have all 'freed themselves from . . . tribal obligations.' That means the breaking up of old orders and the cracking of old molds. These people have seen their traditional social order collapse, and with it all sense of security. The heroic mood is one of sheer desperation, as E. V. Gordon points out. Do you have him? Good: 'A good resistance against overpowering odds was made the characteristic situation of heroic literature. . . . The gods themselves knew that they would in the end be overwhelmed by the evil powers, but they were prepared to resist to the last. Every religious-minded man of the heathen age believed that he existed for the sake of that hopeless cause,' and so on.[18] That is not, I submit, a permanent, stable, or even tolerable state of things. And what about their military organization? Do you remember how things went in the council of the chiefs in Homer?"

"I seem to recall," the professor shut his eyes, "glorious Agamemnon and godlike Achilles going at each other like a couple of alley cats . . . "

"Exactly. And that is typical. You have a loose military hierarchy, a very mixed army thrown together in a forced campaign of survival under chieftains who quarrel ferociously among themselves and are always trying to decide who outranks whom. It is a tense and unpleasant situation from start to finish, with everybody's nerves strained to the breaking point and all the people running around and asking, 'Who's in charge around here?' I ask you, can this chaotic organization in which no one is sure of his place possibly be the result of orderly growth, settled tradition, or careful planning? It is a desperate makeshift that pleases nobody. As Achilles says right at the outset, the whole thing wasn't his idea, and he had left much better things behind. So had the lady Andromache left a happy world behind—in ashes. The Jaredites didn't travel light, but still they never regarded their own civilization as anything but a pale reflection of the original article *they* had to leave behind."

"Let's get on to our third point," said the professor.

"Which is, that epic is concerned not only with individuals but also primarily with individuals who are princes: the cast of characters, we are told, 'consists almost wholly of princes and their military followers.'[19] Among these 'there is usually one character whose adventures form the chief subject of interest.' "[20]

"That, I suppose, is why the whole thing is called heroic—centers around a hero?"

"Yes, in every epic there are heroes and also *the* hero."

"A sort of superman."

"He is always mortal and human, and he always occupies a position of subordination, taking orders from a relatively colorless king or commander. He has almost superhuman, but never supernatural, strength, and yet from time to time he receives supernatural aid. Altogether a strange and impressive figure!"[21]

"You will forgive me," said the professor, "if I suggest that you have been describing the brother of Jared to the life."

"His overwhelming importance is understandable if one considers that during actual migration the complete preponderance of one strong character is a necessity. Have you seen C. S. Coon's new opus? I have it here, by the way. Here at the beginning he gives us an interesting picture of the human race living for at least ninety percent of its lifetime on earth as wandering hunters; I must admit it is strictly in the H. G. Wells tradition, but anyway he imagines that these 'hunters lived in bands of from two to twenty or so families, all usually related to each other. In each band, while families were independent, the leadership was vested in one man in his prime, distinguished for his skill at providing meat, in preventing and settling quarrels, and in conducting foreign affairs.'[22] If there is anything to that, then the organization of the epic migrations was simply a reversion to normal ways of life. Be that as it may, the portrait of the brother of Jared as a great primal hero and migration leader is a very striking one—remember that the book of Ether as it comes to us is supposed to have been composed from traditions and materials handed down for thousands of years."

"In a way," mused the professor, "it is rather remarkable that the only really heroic figures in the Book of Mormon are found in Ether. Lehi, Nephi, King Benjamin, and the others were certainly great men, but after all they were normal human beings in trying situations. With Ether it is different—you get some positively real heroes in the legendary sense—*überlebensgross*, the Germans would say: the outsized images of real people, like statues of heroic size."

"And yet," his friend added, locating another passage in Chadwick, "there is this interesting thing about them. Chadwick notes that even though the most ferocious and even depraved characters occupy the stage of epic, 'there is no character who appears uniformly in an unfavorable light.'[23] You will find that also true of the Jaredite monsters—one can't help feeling a touch of admiration and sympathy even for Shiz and Coriantumr, and the licentious tyrants like Noah and Riplakish are not real patrons of the arts but have also a touch of real magnificence. Chadwick rings the bell here: 'The behavior of the heroes often strikes their reader as childish or brutal.' "[24]

"No comment necessary," said F.

"In their dealings with one another," the other continued, "a 'dignified and fastidious tone . . . prevails,' even between bitter rivals, that is."[25]

"Rules of chivalry and all that."

"Yes, as is well-known, the rules and the cult of chivalry originated with these people. Fighting was strictly according to the book, with formal challenges and exchange of messengers. When one hero submits to another, his followers are spared. Fighting ceases formally at sundown, with no funny stuff during the night . . . "

"Do you seriously think those old boys actually kept the rules? I seem to remember Achilles and Ajax flying off the handle."

"And do you remember how Achilles was slapped down for it by his divine mother? And how when Ajax sobered up he was so humiliated by what he had done that he committed suicide? Of course they break the rules, but the rules are there. 'Yet, strangely enough,' says Chadwick, 'even the greatest heroes sometimes win their most notable triumphs by means which appear to us unfair.' "[26]

"That sounds like a prize understatement."

"Our heroes fight a lot. I think Gordon is right when he says that the idea that they loved fighting is wrong—they fought only when and because they had to."

"Which was most of the time, it would seem."

"Yes, Chadwick writes, Warfare is 'an essential' rather than an accessory of heroic life.[27] And that leads to our next point: that the scene of action in the epics is confined exclusively to the battlefield, the court, the hunt, or some place of adventure—usually a wilderness."[28]

"Aha! You say wilderness to put me in mind of Ether. But I guess it's fair game."

"No, I am thinking of certain key epics in which the wilderness is the normal background. Of course there is Siegfried, vibrating between the woods and the court—I dare say Wagner's heroic world of caves and forests was not all papier-maché. But bring Ether into it if you must; I will make no objection. In fact the next point almost compels you to think of it: 'Fighting is apt to take the form of single combats between the leading heroes.'[29] Offhand I would say that that is certainly the best-known aspect of epic story."

"And quite well known in Joseph Smith's day," the professor commented.

"For which reason," the other countered, "it is all the more necessary to distinguish between mere eyecatching episodes and the complete epic milieu, which was definitely *not* known in the Prophet's day."

"But after all, he could have read Homer or Robin Hood, or something."

"Homer, yes. But Robin Hood isn't epic. You would be surprised how few epic texts had appeared in print. Homer, in fact, was the only real writer available—people thought Dante, and Camoens, and Vergil were epics, of course, but that only shows how little anyone understood what epic was. While I was still in high school scholars firmly believed that epic poetry was 'deep-browed Homer's demesne,' the product of poetic imagination pure and simple whether of a great individual genius or the spontaneous expression of *Volksgeist*. In that belief many naive souls in the past have undertaken to compose genuine epic poems of their own—with alarming results."

"But what was the scientific view?"

"Until recently it was the universal consensus of the experts that epic poetry had its origin in nature myths, and that the heroes were really faded sun-gods. Some diehards still believe it."

"But what about Bishop Percy and other eighteenth-century scholars?"

"In every case they were students of national literatures pure and simple. Even Robert Wood's comparisons were meant to cast light on Homer only—mere footnotes to the text. The world view, which is the very essence of the epic milieu, had to wait until our own day."

"Let's get back on the track. What comes next?"

"That heroic societies are held together entirely by oaths. The oath is the one social tie from top to bottom, and so the whole heroic world is a constant ferment of secret oaths and combinations. The oaths are strictly personal affairs between individuals, and need I say that the violation of an oath was considered the one unforgivable crime?[30] In this rough society 'the cardinal virtues of a hero are courage, loyalty, and generosity.'[31] The courage is strictly physical—bravery in the field; the 'loyalty is purely personal.' Chadwick says, 'It involves the duty of vengeance, as well as protection.' As to generosity, it is always a matter of policy—the generosity of a chief to his followers, a princely bribe, with the admitted intent of buying and binding supporters by gifts."[32]

"Ether all over again," said the professor.

"We were going to keep Ether out of this for the present," his friend replied, "but anyway it is further significant that all this generosity is paid for by systematic plunder and organized raids. Chadwick says:

> Plunder is a necessity for the hero who wishes to maintain an active force of armed followers. . . . Plundering raids appear to be a characteristic feature of the Heroic Age everywhere—indeed, we may say, an essential feature. The booty derived therefrom enabled active and ambitious princes to attract to themselves and to maintain large bodies of followers, without which they were at the mercy of their neighbors.[33]

"If I do say it myself, that reads like an excerpt from *The World of the Jaredites*. Chadwick even mentions that the normal trophies of heroic enterprise 'consist usually of the accoutrements or heads of . . . foes . . . valued as evidence of . . . prowess.'[34] This is not true of heroic ages everywhere, but it holds in a surprising number of cases—especially with the northern Europeans and Asiatics. The most coveted forms of wealth among these people—objects lovingly and lengthily described in almost all epic poems—are weapons, horses, wagons, jewels, woven stuff, and damsels, the latter usually bought with so and so many head of cattle. It is all portable wealth—the stuff normally prized and cultivated by nomads. And, as you recall from the opening lines of *Beowulf*, the epic people are always heaping up and dispensing wealth: the economy of plunder requires a brisk turnover."

"But you said these people are only reluctant and temporary nomads."

"Yes, in every case they dream of settling down as soon as they can. But even after they have grabbed themselves lands and pinned them down with castles and strong places, they continue a semi-nomadic existence—a merry round of feudal wars and 'abominations.' "

"Just what do you mean by that?"

"The period of migrations is followed immediately by what Chadwick calls the saga time. It is a jockeying for power among the great houses. The great house is the center of everything. Who came right after the epic and elegiac poets when you were reading Greek?"

"The tragedies, of course."

"And you will recall that Aristotle says the tragedies deal with the doings of the great houses because they are 'naturally tragic.' They certainly were a mess: sordid struggles for power, maniacal hatreds, bestial murders—and all within the household. 'The history of the family,' writes Chadwick of a typical cycle of horrors, 'is indeed little more than a catalogue of the crimes committed by one member against another.'[35] Everything is on a personal level, and invariably the antagonists are relatives, with women taking a leading part in the dirty work.[36] To make it even more like Ether's world after the migration, abominations abound: Stories of incest and malicious serving up to a guest at a banquet of his own children occur with surprising frequency.[37] This sort of thing leads in turn to plots and alliances that culminate in wars of extermination, in which not only whole houses but also entire nations are wiped out. All that is left behind is the strange and tragic figure of 'the lone survivor.' "[38]

"That's one I never heard of," said Professor F.

"And yet he occurs with surprising frequency in the epic world."

"You can tell me about him later." The professor surveyed his watch. "I suppose we could go on all night getting things out of Mr. Chadwick."

"We could indeed. But before we break it up, let me point out just a few more things. There is the overwhelming predominance of cattle in every heroic picture; there is the prominence of feasting and drinking—and they always eat and drink the same heroic fare: bread, beer, and beef. They feast each other at great exchange banquets, that lead to some famous quarrels.

"Of course, a subject peasant population is always found in the background. And in the center of every epic looms some mighty and fabulous fortified place, a combination castle, fort, and city like Camelot or Troy. In keeping with the chivalrous pattern we find everywhere the overpowering influence of some great lady, to whom all owe ultimate allegiance; indeed as Chadwick notes, an older substratum of matriarchy is often apparent. Some authorities insist today that the concept of romantic marriage is found *only* in the epic milieu—completely out of place in other societies. The epic people habitually live in tents, yet they are always building mighty cities as well as sacking them: that paradox can be easily explained . . . "

"But not now," the professor pleaded hastily.

"Since these people are migrants to begin with," Blank began stuffing things back into his briefcase, "everybody rides on chariots and wagons in the early epics, the heroes on horseback in the later ones. Well, so it goes. We have an unmistakable pattern: I think there is no more chance of confusing the epic milieu with anything else than there is of confusing a Sioux warrior with a European peasant."

"Oh, I begin to see where you are going," the professor conceded, rising, "but it's my opinion that you still have a long way to go."

"I'll admit we have got in deeper than I thought we would. But now that you have led me on so far, don't you think we should see this thing through?"

"Not tonight," said Professor F. with a touch of panic—there was no telling what Blank would do once he got started.

"Certainly not. In fact, with the limited resources we have here we could not go much farther anyway. How about getting together next Tuesday night in Dr. Schwulst's office?"

"Why there?"

"Because I think he can give us some help, aside from having the only Egyptian collection between here and Puffer Lake."

"That stuff is over my head . . . "

"Which is exactly why we are going to surprise Dr. Schwulst next Tuesday. He works late, you know. He'll be delighted—pathetically eager to oblige anyone who's interested."

"You are a menace to society," said Professor F. at the door, "but Tuesday it is. Eight o'clock at 315 Gohira Hall."

2

Egypt Revisited

"I got your note,"[1] said Professor Schwulst as the three settled down in the magnificent litter of the big room under the eaves of Old Gohira, "but you must explain to me more fully just what it is you want to know."

"It was Blank's idea," F. explained. "I think he wants to show me that the earliest Egyptians were just like some friends of his called Jaredites."

"Not at all," his friend interposed hastily. "It is not Jaredites we are looking for tonight. I simply want to show this skeptical fellow, my dear Dr. Schwulst, that the epic milieu is as old as history itself. You know, sir, how the heroic age is being used by a lot of investigators today to help them reconstruct a plausible picture of the world."

Schwulst nodded benevolently. "Well," Blank continued, "we want to know if that goes for Egypt."

"You mean, whether the Egyptians start out, like the Greeks and the Germans, with an heroic age?" Schwulst inquired. It was a matter of debate among students whether his accent was as thick as his glasses; no matter what language he discoursed in—and as an orientalist he had to know many—he always managed to make it sound like his native Esthonian.

"That's it exactly," the other replied. "We have already taken in Chadwick's views, but his evidence is from the Greeks, Teutons, and Celts. What we want to know now is whether the heroic stuff goes for really old civilizations. Kramer thinks Chadwick's picture fits the earliest Sumerians like a glove, but as yet he hasn't gone into any particulars. It leaves us rather up in the air. What about the Egyptians, for example? Is there a genuine epic literature in Egyptian?"

"There are a number of important pieces that have always been called epics," said Schwulst, scratching his head in thought. "There is *Isis and the Name of Re,* for example, or the *Myth of the Sun's Eye,* or the *Revolt against Re,* or the famous story of *Isis and Osiris*—yes, there are epics in Egyptian."

"Where do they come in the literature," F. asked. "That is, at what period were they composed?"

"At every period and at no period," was the enigmatic reply. "They are prehistoric."

"I always thought that if you had a written record you were *ipso facto* in historic times. Isn't 'prehistoric records' a contradiction of terms?"

"Not necessarily. Egyptian literature is like a fruitcake or a stew: The minute you look at it you can see that it is a lot of stuff mixed up together; and if you look carefully, you can pick out many of the ingredients. If, for example, you were to select with great care all the pieces of carrot in a stew, you could with diligence actually reassemble the vegetables in the very shape and form they had before they were cut up. Now from the very first scholars have thought they could recognize certain distinctive elements in Egyptian literature, and as a rule the older the elements, the more easily recognized. If all the ingredients that look alike are taken out and fitted together, they give us some very convincing patterns of prehistoric history and culture. Today the Germans are busy reconstructing dramatic and ritual texts that may be centuries older than the first dynasty of Egypt. For almost a hundred years the epic or heroic element in the Egyptian tradition has been recognized as among the oldest."

"Most gratifying," murmured Blank. "Just how does the story begin?"

"As far back as we can go, Egypt has always been a land not of one but of two essentially conflicting cultures." Dr. Schwulst took from the crowded shelves that lined his office a volume with the familiar black-and-gold binding of Walter Otto's *Handbuch*. "This is Hermann Kees' standard work on the economy of Egypt. He tells here how one always finds in Egypt the herdsmen with their long hair and coarse clothes, living in tents, shunning the social life of the towns, and viewed by the rest of the population with a mixture of contempt and misgiving. Like the professional hunters, Kees says, these herdsmen lived in a world of their own, retaining 'something of the old independence of the nomad.' "[2]

"That sounds as if all Egyptians were once nomads," F. observed.

"Well, you have to migrate to get into Egypt, as Maspero noted long ago. And it is now known that the Egyptians were certainly not indigenous; their earliest civilization seems to have appeared only a very short time before the full glory of the dynasties."

"No evolution at all?" F. was dubious.

"If there were any, it did not take place in Egypt. I was just reading something that T. E. Peet wrote thirty-two years ago: 'One of the most remarkable phenomena of Egypt is the fact that as far as our knowledge goes at present there is a complete break between the palaeolithic and the predynastic, the latter appearing quite suddenly with a ready-made civilization, including possibly the use of copper. Future research may fill this gap, but at present it is a great gulf.'[3] The future research referred to has made the gap wider and deeper than ever. Here is what Siegfried Schott has just written: 'Again and again in the development of ancient Egyptian culture the monuments of a new epoch present something entirely unprecedented all of a sudden in a state of complete perfection of form.' He cites as examples the *Pyramid Texts*—a complete and magnificent collection of texts appearing out of nowhere; the sudden emergence of a complete temple architecture, the reliefs that appear on walls with their artistic canons thoroughly conventionalized; the great pyramid complex of Sakkareh, the great pyramids themselves, the underground chambers of Zoser, the wonderful mural decorations. All this stuff appears without any groping, experimentation, or changes of style.[4] If these things were ever evolved, nobody knows where. Certainly not in Egypt."

"How does Egypt start out, then?"

"Some think the oldest settlements were those of the Tasians, described as 'nothing more than a hunting camp or temporary encampment.' Yet those people were certainly farmers, and what is more, they made wonderful pottery—and pottery making is a sedentary art.[5] The same combination of nomadism and farming characterizes the Badarian, the first real civilization of Egypt. Ms. Baumgartel says here: 'We cannot even say whether the Badarians were already sedentary in the Nile valley, or whether they were still nomads . . . cultivating their little patch of grain in one place one season and in another the next.'[6] The trouble is that migrating people can be very highly civilized and yet carry relatively little of the furniture of civilization with them—take the Pilgrim Fathers, for example, or some of your western pioneers. Wave after wave of humanity enters Egypt as nomads and ends up as farmers, but the nomads are always there. Kees writes, for example: 'The half-savage farmer of the marshes was classed by the Egyptians with the skinny herdsman of the nomadizing tribes.'[7] Well, which was he, farmer or nomad? It is like that all over the Near East."

Professor Schwulst began a violent rummaging among the papers and journals stacked on the big table and presently emerged with a document. "Here in this new survey on the beginning of history Waechter tells us that with the drying up of the Near East, people were forced to give up nomadic life; 'the period of wandering was over,' he says, with the founding of the first agricultural towns—Jarmo, Jericho, Hassuna, and the rest—'since the hunting and food gathering economy was becoming inadequate.' "[8]

"Meaning that nobody ever wandered any more?" F. queried.

"No. It simply means that the time when *everybody* wandered was over. Lots of hunters and nomads survived, as they do to this day. And so, at Hassuna for example, you get hunting, grazing, and farming, side by side."[9]

"Rather versatile people for primitives, weren't they?" F. remarked.

"Not necessarily. One of the things that has been discovered of recent years is the high degree of specialization in human society as far back as the record goes.[10] To this day varied and conflicting economies meet and mingle in the Near East, and now as always such contacts almost invariably mean trouble."

"But the great conflict is between nomads and farmers?" Blank asked.

"It certainly is in Egypt," Schwulst replied. "Some very interesting light has been thrown on the subject by recent studies of Egyptian architecture. Ricke writes that 'The architecture of historic Egypt arose from the meeting of an Upper-Egyptian architecture of nomadic origin with a Lower-Egyptian architecture of agrarian origin.' He finds that the graves of the prehistoric chiefs or kings at Abydos in Upper-Egypt are simply the typical mound burials of nomad kings, and that the national shrine of Egypt in dynastic times was actually nothing but the elaboration of a royal tent, while the rush-matted palaces of the Pharaohs were but the reproduction 'on a monstrous scale of the tent of a nomad chief.' So Ricke's conclusion is that like the Egyptian people, the Egyptian architecture is not of a single origin; it is the polarization of nomadism and agrarianism.[11] The famous Egyptologist Eberhard Otto has recently written about this polarization; he says it is apparent in the very first civilization, that of Nakada I, where one finds a settled farming population with matriarchal traditions living side by side with later-comers whose culture was nomadic and patriarchal."[12]

"That certainly sets the stage for a heroic age," Professor Blank noted with satisfaction.

"Otto goes so far as to suggest that the well-known struggle between the kingdoms of the north and south in Egypt, the red and the white, was not fought along geographical lines primarily but was actually a conflict of cultures, with the nomads victorious, 'forcing the farmers to adopt their stricter political order.' "[13]

"Most gratifying," Blank observed. "Those are the very words I used in an article five years ago.[14] But granted the stage is set for an heroic age, does the show go on?"

"Oh, most decidedly," Dr. Schwulst replied. "As V. Gordon Childe writes in his latest book, the story of the Pharaohs begins with 'definite hints in the archaeological record of warfare for the acquisition of cattle, booty, or land.'[15] Isn't that your heroic tradition? There is never any doubt as to the role that Pharaoh plays. As Kees notes here, though Egypt was a land of farmers, the ruling class always kept themselves markedly aloof from the interests of agriculture and from the agrarian point of view.[16] Except on brief ritual occasions, the kings fancy themselves only as warriors, hunters, and cattle-raiders. In the early days Egypt presented what Kees calls 'an astonishing contrast' to the intensely cultivated land of later times, being really a vast cattle range, with only scattered cultivation.[17] 'The raising of cattle, especially of beef, was the backbone of the economy,' and the greatest event in the land, from which all other events were dated, was the census of the cattle.[18] Of course fields must be tilled and due attention paid to the old rites of the soil, yet they are hardly mentioned in the Pyramid Texts, where the cattle and the wild-bull parade before us on every page."

"What are the *Pyramid Texts?*" F. queried, "Are they epics?"

"The *Pyramid Texts*," said Professor Schwulst, slapping the two big volumes of Sethe on the table, "were found carved on the walls of the pyramid tombs of the kings of the fifth and sixth dynasties. That means that the texts themselves—here are some photographs of them—that is, these actual writings, must be older than 2175 B.C. at the latest. But many if not all of them must have been very ancient when they were copied out by the royal stonecutters—even if they are not as old as our editor here thinks they are. Here, you might find this helpful; it is almost a literal translation of Sethe's translation." He handed the first volume of Professor Mercer's new work to Dr. F., who read aloud from the first page: " '. . . the oldest large body of written material in the world.' This is what we want. Does this tell about our hero-kings?"[19]

"It certainly does," Schwulst replied, pointing out passages in Sethe (which we designate, as Mercer does, by Sethe's numbers). "Here, for example, the king boasts of his vast herds of cattle and the way he increases them by wide and venturesome raids.[20] At the same time he is no less proud of his prowess as a huntsman. The most significant monuments of predynastic Egypt are the remarkable hunting palettes that show us what the royal hunt was like—a huge affair with great enclosures or parks into which the wild animals were driven. The oldest monument of Egyptian writing, the famous palette of Narmer, depicts such an enclosure.[21] The special hunting and grazing country was the Delta: 'During the Old Kingdom the Delta was still a place to which noblemen went for big game hunting, and whither they sent their herds of large cattle for pasture.'[22] It seems to have been reserved for the purpose."

("A Jaredite custom, by the way," Blank reminded his friend in an undertone.)

"Even in the thoroughly sedentary predynastic civilization hunting was still one of the main resources, as is clear from the surviving pictures and implements. The royal weapon was the bow, in which the king was instructed by the gods Horus and Seth, the traditional first kings of Egypt, in person, and it was firmly believed that no one but the Pharaoh was mighty enough to draw the royal bow—a clear indication of the original qualifications for kingship and the type of culture the kings represented.[23] That is a familiar motif in heroic literature, by the way.[24] The earliest of all Egyptian gods, male and female, were hunters, and their emblems were arrows. The Egyptians always designated other nations by the types of bow they used, and their conventional description of the human race is 'the Nine Bows.' "

"But a heroic age requires not merely hunters but invaders. Do you have them?"

"Most of all," said the Professor, "A classic text for that would be the so-called 'Cannibal Hymn.' Faulkner has made a special study of it so we can follow him, if I can find him. . . . A king of the fifth dynasty, Unis or Wenis by name, here describes himself storming heaven in the role of the great invader. The imagery he uses is obviously not invented. 'We here see him,' says Faulkner, 'as a mighty hunter, slaying and devouring the gods as food,'[25] the whole thing is transferred to heaven but follows a very convincing earthly pattern. As the scene opens, we find ourselves in a time of great natural upheavals and world-wide social disorders—"

"A *Völkerwanderungszeit!*" cried F.

"It looks like it. Listen to the opening lines: 'The sky pours water, the stars are darkened, the Bows (the inhabitants of the earth) rush about, the bones of the Earth-gods tremble. . . .' Man and nature in confusion; the Egyptians often refer to their god Re coming into Egypt with blasts of the north wind. At such a time this primordial king, 'the bull of heaven,' comes on the scene; and he too seems to have been driven by necessity, for he is described as one 'who suffered want and decided to live on the being of every god.'[26] Having perforce taken things in his own hands, this terrible invader is 'the Grasper of the top-knot,' who slaughters and beheads all other lords, who lassoes his opponents, who exterminates all who oppose him.[27] His messengers go before him in all directions, demanding instant submission, ordering all to serve him 'who has made himself mighty in his place: N. (the king) layeth hold on command, eternity is brought to him and knowledge is placed at his feet. Shout for joy to N.: he that won the horizon.'[28] 'The lion-helmet of N. is on his head, his terror on both sides of him, his magic preceding him![29] The Marshes of Reeds, the Horite regions, the regions of Set—all belongs to N.'[30] There is a great deal more to this effect in the texts."

"Then the authority of Pharaoh really rested on violence?"

"In practice it did, but in theory the Pharaohs are constantly protesting their legitimacy, their divine calling, their lawful descent, and so forth. They protest so much, in fact, that anyone would guess that something is wrong. All these elaborate and conflicting legends and legal and doctrinal fictions are aimed at clearing Pharaoh's claim to rule. The famous justification of Osiris goes back to the founder of the line whose claim to the kingdom must be ritually examined, and is never satisfactorily cleared up. Anthes has recently published a study of the formula *maᶜḫrw*, which means that a king's right to rule has been formally cleared with the prehistoric court of Heliopolis.[31] It is obvious that Pharaoh worried a great deal about his divine authority."

" '. . . blessed with the blessings of the earth, and with the blessings of wisdom, but cursed as pertaining to the Priesthood' " (Abraham 1:26), Blank quoted, to the puzzlement of his friends.

"But if the first Pharaoh comes as an invader," said F., "who are the people he moves in on?"

"Obviously the remnants or descendants of earlier invaders. You will remember that Otto said the patriarchal nomads subdued matriarchal farmers. However that may be, the earliest invasion seems to have been led by a woman, who found the land empty and under water when she got there."

"The annual flood, eh?" F. suggested.

"That is doubtful. Most investigators today think the land was under water the year round when the earliest settlers got there. The first villages are all well up on the banks in what is now desert, not down in the valley itself. Here, for example, is a text in which the first king is described as 'inundating the land after it had come out of the ocean; it is N. who pulled up the papyrus; it is N. who reconciled the two lands; . . . it is N. with whom his mother, the great wild cow, will be united.'[32] This dependence on his mother of the first king, who here clears out the papyrus thickets and makes the land arable, is a very conspicuous feature of the texts."

"The cow-lady was Hathor, wasn't she?"

"The lady has a way of changing names. In the *Book of the Dead*, which is the best commentary on the *Pyramid Texts*, she comes 'cutting off the heads of the heads of the rebels in her name of Tep.ahet,' but she settles down in the name of Hathor lady of red water, and is perfumed in the name of Neith.[33] For all her names, the lady who settled Egypt is to this day a mysterious figure."[34]

"What makes you say *she* settled Egypt?" Blank asked with interest.

"She is the star of the first Egyptian epic ever identified. That is the story of the *Destruction of Mankind* or the *Revolt against Re*—it goes by various names. It was found many years ago inscribed on the walls of the tomb of Sethi I, and a few years later in the tomb of Ramses III."

"They were rather famous kings, weren't they?" Blank asked. "The story must have had considerable prestige."

"Yes, it appears to have been a very ancient tradition, among the high arcana reserved for royal tombs. This is the sort of thing that was kept from profane eyes: the inside story, so to speak, of the settling of Egypt." Professor Schwulst unfolded a large lithographic reproduction of the texts and began to explain them.

"The story begins with the great god, 'the god who exists by himself,' summoning to his presence those he calls 'the fathers and mothers who existed with me when I was still in Nun,' that is, the timeless pre-existence. They all come and prostrate themselves and ask why they have been summoned. Naville, who discovered the text, rightly observes that the scene is drawn from real life, a glimpse of a pre-dynastic court-scene: 'Re,' he writes here, 'is no more the world-creating divinity with the ram's head sitting on his ship; he is a king, a Jupiter, who has long been ruling over men and gods and who gives orders to his father and his relatives,'[35]—typically feudal, and, if you will, heroic. That is seen in Re's response: he says the human race has revolted against him, and he wants their advice as to what should be done with them. After due discussion it is decided that rebel humanity should be wiped out."

"So far straight epic milieu," commented F.

"The one appointed to do the task takes the name of Hathor, Lady of Heaven. She carries out her mission of destruction, returns, and reports to Re, who congratulates her. There is a vivid description of the human race perishing in a mixture of blood and water, which reminds one of Hathor's title of Lady of the Red Water. Next, however, Re sends for his messengers in great haste and commands the bringing of a great propitiatory offering to a universal assembly at Heliopolis. There are offerings of fruits and more blood and water, and Re, pleased with the offering, raises his hand and swears that he will never destroy humanity again; at the same time he orders all the land to be flooded with water. . . ."

"That looks like a contamination of motives," Blank observed, "—the flood story backwards."

"Egyptian texts are full of contamination, confusion, and paradox from the very first. Notice this text here: everywhere you see the formula *ky j.t* written in red ink; that means that another version or explanation of a passage is being given. As the Greek writers often observed, the Egyptian priests themselves disagreed about every point of their tradition. So don't think for a moment that this is the old authentic version of what the Egyptians believed about it. The old stuff is imbedded in the text all right but you have to dig it out: remember what we said about the stew or the fruitcake."

"But what happens after the flood?" Blank asked.

"It was then that the lady went to settle the land."

" 'In the morning,' the Egyptian[36] text reads, 'the goddess arrived and found all the land under water; her countenance was joyous; she drank deeply and was satiated. But she perceived no human beings.' Plainly this is the situation that the first immigrants would have found. Only Re greeted her to the new land, saying 'Come in peace, gracious Lady.' Then he established the New Year's rite of the priestesses of Amon-Ra, which all the people celebrated, but especially the women, every year forever after to commemorate the event. From other sources we know that the lady's son was Horus, the first Pharaoh."

"Are there any other indications that the royal line began with a woman?" asked Blank, greatly interested.

"Sethe, here in his *Urgeschichte*, has treated the subject at length. According to him the key to the whole matter is the bee and the red *Dsrt*-crown: the bee, he believes, is the sign of the Lady Neith—whom we have seen identified with Hathor—called 'the Ruling Lady of the Universe'; he says that this figure must go back to a 'prehistoric rule of women in Egypt.'[37] Now the discovery thirty-five years ago of a perfect representation of the bee-crown on a prehistoric jar from Nakada was taken as an indication that the great shrine of Koptos, right across the river from Nakada, which is only a cemetery, may have been the original capital of the lady. That was the shrine of Min, the oldest god of Egypt, who later became Ammon, and whose symbol was an arrow, as was Neith's. Wainwright has shown that Neith was the prehistoric lady of Koptos."[38]

"And where does the bee come in?" F. asked perplexed.

"The kings of Egypt actually bore the title of 'the bee,' but only, according to Sethe, after they had usurped the authority of the Lady Neith. He suggests that the lady's name is actually the title N.t given to the prehistoric red crown, though it is usually called the *Dsrt*-crown."[39]

"Is it specifically the possession of the *Dsrt*-crown that makes the king eligible to call himself 'the Bee'?" Blank asked with great emphasis.

"That is what Sethe maintains," the Orientalist answered, "He finds it 'tempting' as he says, to attribute the formal title of Queen-bees to the ladies who first ruled Egypt.[40] But more recently others have given a different explanation. They say it was the invading heroes who brought the bee symbol with them, uniting it with the red crown and other props of the Lady of Koptos when they found her ruling the country on arrival."[41]

"I would prefer that interpretation," said Blank, to Professor Schwulst's surprise, "since I have already surmised that the bee belonged to the migrants."

Professor Schwulst, who knew nothing about the Jaredites and their honeybee, called *Deseret*, continued his discourse: "Sethe further points out that 'bee' in Egyptian, being a feminine noun, cannot suit with a king as its original possessor, and that the sedge-and-bee title of the Pha-

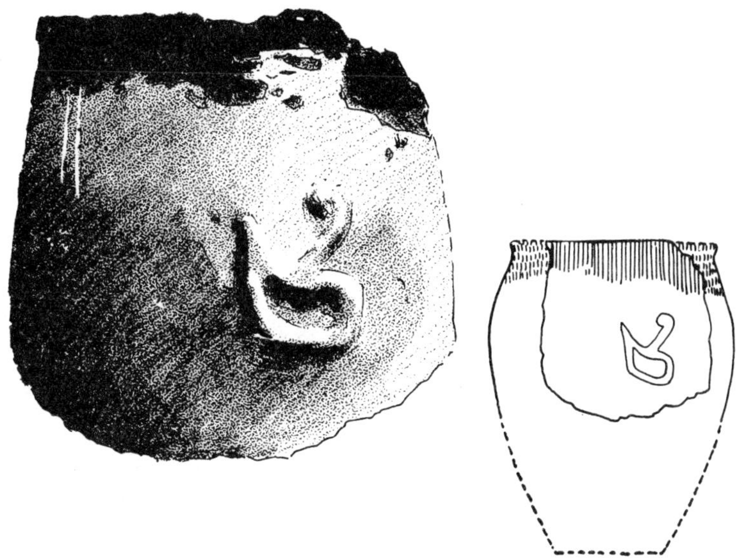

The Red Crown (Dsrt Crown) is clearly depicted on a prehistoric potsherd from Nakada, thus placing it among the oldest known symbols of royalty. It is the crown of the Lady Neith and is often substituted for the sign of the bee. *Journal of Egyptian Archaeology* 9, Plate XX (after Wainwright).

raohs does not designate them as actually being bees but rather as 'belonging to the Bee,' or 'descended from the Bee.' He gives evidence, moreover, that both Geb, the father of the gods, and Osiris were guilty of usurping the bee-crown of the Lady, as they usurped her throne. He finds it significant that the title *h.b.t* 'belonging to the bee' and the *Dsrt*-crown always go together 'as symbols of rule,' being associated as such in prehistoric times, when the royal shrine was both 'the House of the Bee' and 'the House of the *Dsrt*-crown.' It was, he says, specifically in his capacity of 'he who belongs to the bee' that the ruler of the proto-kingdom of Buto wore the *'Dsrt*-crown.' "[42]

"Whatever is behind this," Blank interposed with an air of suppressed excitement, "four things definitely go together at the beginning of Egypt's history: the Bee; the *Dsrt*-crown; the derivation of Pharaoh's authority from a woman; and the identification of that woman with the lady of Koptos, from which or whom Egypt may have got its name."

"Eh?" said Schwulst, somewhat surprised by the fervor as well as the novelty of the last remark.

"If you will excuse me, I have done a little research of my own on the subject. Phythian-Adams has argued, as you may know, that Egypt gets its name not from *Kmt*, 'the black' as is traditionally maintained, but from Koptos, which, as you have suggested, is the oldest shrine and capital of Egypt.[43] Isn't it quite common in ancient times for countries to take the same names as their capitals—Rome, Babylon, Misr itself, to say nothing of Mexico?"

"It is common enough," the Professor observed, "but what are you getting at?"

"One more question: cannot that name also be the name of a person?"

"Many ancient cities are named after persons—hundreds of them, in fact—but only when that person is the founder of the city."

"Exactly. It is agreed today that the great invasions of Egypt in prehistoric times came by way of the Wadi Hammamat. And what is the first place one would settle down on reaching the valley? It is the plain at Koptos, the very place where the Wadi Hammamat opens on the Nile valley. Many scholars have noted this fact. (Blank ruffled a sheaf of notes.) Koptos is not only traditionally but also logically the oldest settlement in Egypt; and just as it could have given its name to the whole land, it could have got that name from the person who led the enterprise."

"It could have, indeed," said Schwulst, with a shrug of impatience, "but no one knows where the name *Koptos* came from. Why does it concern you so much?"

"Because of a text that this discussion brings to my mind. Allow me to read it.

> The land of Egypt being first discovered by a woman,

> who was the daughter of Ham, and the daughter of Egyptus, which in the Chaldean signifies Egypt, which signifies that which is forbidden. When this woman discovered the land it was under water, who afterward settled her sons in it. Now the first government of Egypt was established by Pharaoh, the eldest son of Egyptus the daughter of Ham, and it was after the manner of the government of Ham, which was patriarchal (Abraham 1:23-25).

"What have the Chaldeans got to do with it, I would like to know?" F. asked with a depreciating snort.

It was Schwulst who answered: "A few years ago the Chaldeans would have discredited the whole passage, but not today. There are very reputable Egyptologists who believe that in the beginning Egypt and Mesopotamia were parts of one empire and ruled by one man. The ties between Egypt and Babylonia are better substantiated every day, as in this recent article of Ms. Kantor's.[44] Quite recently Vycichl has argued on linguistic grounds that the Hamites entered Egypt from the East when Egypt was already peopled by a numerous and dense population of the white race who spoke a Semitic language.[45] Even the students of prehistory now hold that all the prehistoric cultures of Egypt represent successive waves of people speaking dialects of the same Semitic language.[46] And now we are being told that the language of the ancient Libyans, which everyone has always believed to represent a prehistoric native African or Berber element in Egyptian, is practically identical with Akkadian, of all things."[47]

"Isn't Akkadian the Semitic language of Mesopotamia?" F. inquired.

"Yes," was the reply. "A few years ago it was called Chaldean. So everywhere we turn the racial and linguistic ties between the Egyptians and the 'Chaldeans' are being tightened.[48] The cattle and the grains of the earliest Egyptians are now believed definitely to have originated in western Asia, and the earliest coronation ceremony that meets us in Egypt is found likewise in Mesopotamia, though neither version is derived from the other."[49]

"Where do they come from then?"

"No one knows. Here is a scholar who tells us that the original home of the Nakada people (your Egyptian predynastics) 'was not far from that of the Sumerians of Mesopotamia,' but where that may have been still remains to be discovered.[50] Here is an indication of how things were stirring in the early days of Egypt: Before the First Dynasty Asiatic visitors came to Egypt. At the founding of the dynasty, however, they came in numbers, bringing a high civilization; they were relatives of the people who spread to Cyprus and the Aegean. After that, according to this authority, 'a new, and highly competent people, came to Egypt. These folk were quickly followed by yet another band of people who imposed their . . . civilization on Egypt [in] the Fourth Dynasty,' only to be followed by several other groups in 'a great and long-drawn-out infiltration.'[51] And the same waves that bring these people into Egypt, moving outward in a circle like ripples in a pond from some mysterious center of disturbance in the north, were at the same time bringing ever new invaders into Mesopotamia. The graves in the so-called Royal Cemetery of Ur of the Chaldees show remarkable resemblance to the first-dynasty graves of Egypt—those 'nomad mounds' that Ricke talks about. And the prehistoric cult of Heliopolis shows many signs of Asiatic, specifically Semitic, origin."[52]

"My head is swimming," said F. "Let's get back to Pharaoh and the epic milieu."

"The Pharaoh of the Pyramid Texts is always on the move: 'O Way of Horus, prepare thy tent for the king'[53]—that is typical; Pharaoh spends his days on the road and his nights in tents.[54] When like the sun he has completed his day's journey, 'the Great Ones in the north side of heaven lay for him the fire,' and they 'cook for him a meal in his evening cooking-pots.'[55] There is a cry of 'come and get it,' so to speak: 'his chef prepares a meal for him; the king runs, his herdsmen run.' "[56]

"Sounds like old times on the range," F. commented.

"You are not so far wrong at that," the Professor replied. "These people are driving cattle, with Pharaoh himself usually described as 'the great wild bull.' Take this for example: 'Greetings to thee, ox of the oxen, when thou makest the ascension . . . [the whole thing is here transferred to the king at his funeral]. O ye milk cows, ye nurse cows there, go around him.'[57] He is 'adorned with the horns of Re, his apron on him is like Hathor.'[58] One thinks of the famous Apis bulls, and indeed, in Pyramid Text 286e, the king catches the sacred Apis with a lasso. Of course in his travels Pharaoh is most often compared with the sun, like whom he moves over all the earth, inspecting his domains in a course which is one eternal round: 'Behold, thou art great and round like the "Great Round"; behold, thou art bent around, and art round like the "Circle which encircles the *nb.wt* [the universe]; behold thou art round and great like the "Great Circle which sets.' "[59]

"Wasn't that circle, which was both the sun and the course of the sun called by the Egyptians *shenen?*" Blank asked.

"Indeed it was," the Professor answered. "In the earliest times it was represented by a circle which later became the cartouche, which is drawn around the name of every Pharaoh. This is what Gardiner says about it: 'The Egyptians called the cartouche *shnw* from a verb-stem *shni* "encircle," and it seems not unlikely that the idea was to represent the king as ruler of all "that which is encircled by the sun," a frequently expressed notion.'[60] The *shni* root is no doubt the same as the universal Semitic root for 'year.' At any rate, the Pharaoh goes about exploring the world, and every beautiful place where the sun goes, he finds the king already there before him.[61] In the evening a tent is prepared for him when he stops to spend the night in his favorite places.[62] He sets boundaries to the nations; he approaches the sea; he advances from one nome to the next and makes sure that all roads are secure for him to travel. He even makes expeditions across the water: 'when he traverses the foaming sea, destroying the walls of Shu.'[63] 'Thou will not be resisted at any place where thou goest; thy foot will not be hindered at any place thou desirest to be.'[64] The worst thing that can happen to a great chieftain is not to be able to travel. Thus when Re overcomes a rival, he says to him: 'Retreat into thy place, thy roads be impeded, thy paths stopped up, be confined in thy place of yesterday!' And thus pronounces the curse on him: 'His blows are decreed; he may not make his courses on this earth according to his will.'[65] *His* touring is at an end, but Pharaoh's world inspection never ceases: 'He comes again; he goes, he comes with Re. His houses are visited by him. The king seizes Kas [spirits or people]; he frees Kas; he covers up evil; he abolishes evil; he spends the day; he spends the night,' and then he is on his way again: 'Nothing opposes his foot; nothing restrains his heart.'[66] This last is not only a good description of a royal progress but also explains the purpose of such, which is to correct ill doing and put the realm in order, redressing injuries, and punishing upstarts. Here also we see the great antiquity of the religious institution of the *Parousia* of 'Coming of the Lord,' who lets his countenance shine first on one community and then on another. Deissmann saw that source of the Christian Parousia doctrine in Hellenistic Egypt, but here we see that it is far older than that.[67] When the king or the great lord visited a district, everybody enjoyed a holiday; all were on their good behavior and received gifts and donatives from the lord. You can readily see how the figure lent itself to the expression of Jewish and Christian religious ideas."

"It is 'heroic' also," Blank volunteered. "Who is the

great arch-type of all your wandering heroes and benefactors of the human race? It is Hercules with his twelve labors—and surely I don't have to remind you of his identification with the sun passing through the twelve houses of the zodiac. It is a very ancient idea; you will find it at home among the Persians, Babylonians, Chinese, or Teutons. Read Bernhard Schweitzer's book on the subject."

"Now that you mention that, there are some interesting descriptions of the royal and solar progress in the *Book of the Dead* here; for example, when Re visits each of the twelve shrines of the gods, their doors fly open, and he brings them joy, 'and when he has passed the doors close again, and the gods inside lament and bewail his departure.'[68] That certainly sounds like an authentic *Parousia;* and so does this old hymn: 'When thou travellest, thou are acclaimed by us; life springs up to us out of thy nothingness. . . . Proclaimed mightily art thou in thy circuit.' "[69]

"Do you really think Pharaoh spent most of his time traveling?"

"It would seem that way. You may recall the magnificent bedroom set of Queen Hetep-Heres, the mother of the king who built the great pyramid: It is all camp furniture—everything light, portable, and hooked together. It is the same with other royal furniture, like that of King Tutankhamen. Many Egyptian kings are definitely known to have been Asiatic invaders, and some scholars suspect that many a 'native' king had very little Egyptian blood indeed: by their portraits, their names, their behavior, the arms and customs, their friends and alliances, the bitter opposition to them of the nationalist party led by the priests, by their ideas of empire and their taste in dress and weapons, these Pharaohs betray an Asiatic and a heroic tradition right down to the last dynasties.[70] From the story of Sinuhe, written about 2000 B.C., we can see how easily the people of the desert and the steppe could overrun Egypt the minute a government lost its grip. One doesn't have to imagine that—there is a whole corpus of Egyptian literature that tells about it—the so-called Lamentation literature."

"So we never lack the stuff of heroic literature?"

"Never. All this touring and inspecting was not a royal pleasure trip: It is the familiar system of keeping control over conquered lands."

"Do you mean that Pharaoh's subjects didn't like him?"

"At first he had to be tough. He kept runners, messengers, and spies at work night and day reporting to him any signs of disaffection.[71] He was the super administrator: 'his abomination is to sleep; he hates to be tired.' He visited his palaces with a whip in his hand and a sceptre on his arm, and all fell on their faces in submission. The war was over and now came the occupation: 'The messengers of the blue-eyed Horus go; his runners hasten to tell him who is lifting up his arm in the East.'[72] Any sign of disaffection is immediately reported. 'Pay attention to Geb,' says this interesting text. 'If thou payest not attention to him, his branding-iron which is over thy head will pay attention to thee!'[73] That is certainly grim enough, and there are many like it: Anyone who earns his frown of disapproval will be instantly put to death, 'his head will not be attached.' "[74]

"But you cannot found a permanent order on violence," F. protested, "and the Egyptian society was the most stable in history."

"Once he has won the day, Pharaoh settles down to govern—exactly as many a usurping king did in historic times. 'The agitations cease after they have seen N. dawning,' the "Cannibal Hymn" says.[75] Now he becomes the civilizing subordinate of his divine father, whose authority and approval he claims for all he does; he is 'the goer and the comer who reports his activities to his father; he desires to be justified in what he has done. . . . He puts an end to battle; he punishes revolt. He goes forth as the protector of truth.'[76] By this beneficent activity he wins the natives over: 'Those who were furious [now] busy themselves for him.[77] . . . O gods of the South, North, West, and East, respect N., fear him, . . . you who might have come to N. as an adversary, come to him now as a friend; . . .[78] he will bring truth with him.'[79] Our Pharaoh, you see, is a shrewd politician. He claims to be the son of Geb, the old native god of the Egyptians, and to be acting under his express orders. He now 'judges as a god after he has listened as a prince.'[80] Instead of pre-empting authority, he 'summons the gods for the four regions to be brought to him, so that they may take the report of him to Re and speak favorable word about him to Horus who inhabits the horizon.'[81] He calls great local assemblies and takes a general census of the population.[82] He makes himself accessible to all, declaring that it would be as bad to deny 'the coming of men to the king, the son of god,' as it would be to bar his own access to the assembly of the gods.[83] He is pleased when men come to him of their own accord: 'to thee come the wise and the understanding,'and they freely invite him to visit them in turn: 'Thou art invited to the southern *'Irt.t* palace; to thee come [those of] the full northern *'irt.t* palace with a salutation.' The world now gladly recognizes his authority: 'Thousands serve him; hundreds make offering to him. A certificate as of a mighty great one is given to him by Sah, father of the gods.' "

"This business[84] of running from castle to castle for week-end visits is certainly in the heroic tradition," Blank observed.

"That was recognized long ago," said Schwulst; "the first Egyptologist called the system feudal. Even in its details it seems to come right out of Homer.[85] There is the same tremendous feasting on bread, beer, and quivering chines of beef: 'Arise, O N., be seated before a thousand loaves, a thousand mugs of beer; the roast . . . from the slaughtering-bench, the *rth*-bread from the broad hall; . . . Thou art come . . . among spirits mighty in his domains, protected by the Ennead in the house of the great prince.' "[86]

"Positively Germanic," Professor F. murmured, "even including the holy Nine."

"And notice that the menu is identical with that found according to Chadwick in all his epic societies," Blank added, "regardless of differences of climate and geography."

"Here is another," said Schwulst. " 'Great lord of food in Heliopolis, mayest thou give bread to N., beer to N.; . . . refresh the slaughtering-bench of N.'[87] And this: 'O *Wr-ka-f*, cup-bearer of Horus, chief of the dining-pavilion [or tent] of Re, chef [or cook] to Ptah, give generously to N.; N. eats as much as thou givest, a generous portion of his meat!'[88] Even so would a Medieval baron instruct his seneschal to regale a noble guest! Hospitality is the first law of any heroic society. What could be more Homeric, for example, than the greeting of the noble traveler at the palace porch by a princess of the house, who sees to it that the proper jars of bath water are provided for the weary guest? Or the way in which that guest, after being bathed and perfumed, is clothed in a fine garment and seated in a place of honor?[89] Or the way he is formally received in the great hall: the big double doors swing open to the honored visitor and all the household—especially the young ladies, who seem, as in Homer, to be a traditional greeting committee—utter formal but cheery greetings of 'Come in peace,' while the lady of the house comes forward smiling and takes both his hands or leads him on her arm into the room,[90] or else the great lord himself 'takes hold of thine arm, after Seker, chief of the *Pdw-sh*, has purified thee, and conducts thee to thy throne.'[91] As the formal act of acceptance into the family, the guest is 'raised up' and told to sit and eat."[92]

"Right out of the seventh book of the *Odyssey!*" cried F. with delight.

"And the sixth of the *Iliad,*" Blank appended. "Do you remember where Glaucus and Diomede tell how their ancestors used to visit each other's castles, and recall the story of Bellerophon's romantic wanderings? Do we have anything in Egypt like the system of feudal alliances described in the Bellerophon story, Professor Schwulst?"

"Indeed we do," the other replied. "The whole society is a system of such alliances between great houses—personal and family ties. A network of busy messengers carrying invitations, letters of recommendation, complaints, and felicitations, keeps the great houses in constant touch with each other. All important people are bound by ties of blood and spend a good deal of time paying formal visits to one another's palaces. In this aristocratic circle one must be accepted; one cannot force or bribe one's way into a great house: 'Disown not N., O god; for thou knowest him and he knows thee. . . . N. is not come of himself. It is a messenger who has come to him [with an invitation]; . . . the palace of the great cannot ward him off. . . . Behold, therefore, N. has attained the heights of heaven.'[93] Here the social pattern is transferred to heavenly realms, but everywhere the earthly counterpart shows through.[94] 'The messengers of thy father are come for thee; . . . go thy course, purify thyself . . . that thou mayest be at the side of the god; that thou mayest leave thy house to thy son.'[95] To be accepted is to be a full-fledged member of the household: 'Horus has grown fond of thee; he cannot part from thee; . . . thou hast united thyself with those of his body [i.e., the family], they have loved thee. . . . Geb has noted thy character; he has put thee in thy place. Geb has brought to thee thy two sisters, to thy side. . . . Horus has caused the gods to unite with thee, to fraternize with thee in thy name of 'He of the two *snw-t*-palaces.'[96] To be identified with this or that palace is to be a made man, for you have the whole house to back you against your enemies;[97] if you can call yourself 'one of the royal castle,' you can count on 'the children of Horus' to fight your battles.[98] The head of the house orders his people to respect whom he respects: 'Children of Horus, put yourselves under this Osiris N., let there be none among you who shall withdraw. Carry him.' "[99]

"That 'withdrawing' business interests me," said Blank, thinking of many passages in Ether. "Is there evidence that people withdrew their support from a lord and went over to another?"

"Lots of it. Like all feudal societies, this one was chronically unstable; great houses bid competitively for followers and beg their people to stay with them.[100] There is constant mention of broken allegiances and bloody feuding. Take this warning, for example: 'Any god who puts out his arm (menacingly) . . . when N. calls to thee on behalf of his person, . . . he shall have no bread; he shall have no cake among his brothers, the gods; he shall send no message; . . . the double doors . . . shall not be opened for him.'[101] Note the feeling of tension and jealousy."

"A strange penalty," F. commented.

"It withholds the things that every gentleman desires: cake, shade, baths, a leg of meat, and to have the earth hoed for him."[102]

"*Just* like Homer's Phaeacians!" Blank laughed. "The model citizens of the heroic age! They never farmed, either."

"There is farming going on all around, as in the heroic world everywhere, but important people take no part in it. The gentleman is depicted in his tomb as inspecting the activities of his field workers, but he never touches a tool.[103] On the other hand, he proudly takes the lead in the hunt and the roundup. A noble wants a good word spoken to the king on his behalf 'to cause food to grow for his dining-pavilion on earth'—it is done for him, not by him. The king himself, on his endless progress, deigns to notice the harvest in passing, but he keeps moving: 'The earth has been hoed for thee, the *wdn.t*-offering has been made for thee; as thou goest on thy way whereon the gods go, turn thou and see this offering.' "[104]

"So the Egyptian lords behave as normal heroes."

"In every particular. The single combat figures conspicuously and, exactly as in other heroic societies, follows strict rules of chivalry. Every great chief must be ready at all times to defend his rank and his honor: 'He accepts ["takes on"] his opponent and stands up, the great chief in his great kingdom,' to defend his claim to dominion;[105] the challenger boasts of his superior skill in accepted epic style: 'He came against thee; he said he would kill thee. He has not killed thee; it is thou who wilt kill him. Thou holdest thine own against him, as the surviving bull of the wild bulls.'[106] In the correct epic tradition, when one hero is bested by another, his followers give up the fight: 'His followers have noticed thee how thy strength is greater than his so that they dare not resist thee.'[107] Actually the classic prototype of all heroic combats is Egyptian: the fight between the brothers Set and Osiris (or Horus in some versions) for the possession of the kingdom. Since liegeman and lord were bound by solemn oaths of mutual support, one combat leads to another: 'I have killed for thee him who killed thee as a wild bull,' boasts one hero, avenging his lord as Horus did his father Osiris.[108] 'Thoth has seized thine enemy for thee; so that he is beheaded with his followers; there is not one whom he has spared.'[109] You can see how these oaths and alliances lead to wars of extermination: 'Horus has caused Thoth to bring thine enemy to thee; he has placed thee upon his back, so that he dare not resist thee. Sit down on him, . . . for thou art mightier than he; do evil to him.'[110] It is not a pretty picture, but it is a convincing one."

"And a very Jareditish one," said Blank, "but didn't king-worship put Pharaoh above the storm, so to speak?"

"Far from it! From the earliest times the king had to share his power with others, both because they wanted it and because he needed their help in the administration of far-flung domains. Recently Professor Helck has called attention in the very earliest monument of Egyptian writing, the famous palette of Narmer, to a figure wearing among other things a garment of skins, the unmistakable badge, according to Helck, of royal priesthood and authority; since this person is not the king, it is argued, he is one to whom royal authority has been delegated. In the beginning, Dr. Helck says, 'Only the King may give orders, by virtue of his power to rule all things as the highest *Weltgott*,' that is, he alone holds all priesthood and kingship. Therefore, anyone to whom his power was loaned enjoyed unique authority, 'mightier than other princes,' and all through the old kingdom the great lords strove to acquire that power for themselves."[111]

"How could they get it?" Blank asked.

"Through a peculiar ordinance which is the subject of Helck's remarkable study, called '*Rp^{c}t* on the Throne of Geb.' "

"The study or the ordinance?"

"Both. Geb 'represents the primal ancestor from whom the King receives his testament,' and from whom all authority is ultimately derived, while '*Rp^{c}t* designates the son of the King who receives his father's testament as successor to his throne and who seizes the rule.' In prehistoric tradition Horus is the *Rp^{c}t* of Osiris, and in the earliest times of all Geb himself was the *Rp^{c}t* of Atum.[112] But this was not originally a father-to-son relationship, but rather an ordinance of adoption. Helck believes the title *Rp^{c}t* was at first the 'designation of the substitute king in the Sed-festival,' and from that at a later time 'was derived, apparently at the beginning of the third dynasty, the idea of the King's son as *Rp^{c}t*, who in particular assignments could give royal commands as the King's substitute *(Stellver-treter)*.' "[113]

"And where does the throne come in?"

"It is apparently by the act of sitting on the king's throne that one becomes a *Rpᶜt*. According to a well-known formula, Osiris sets every man on the throne of his father exactly as his father Re set him on his paternal throne in the beginning.[114] Whoever sat on the throne of Geb became thereby the heir, representative, and embodiment of 'the fathers' or 'the ancestors.'[115] The man who sits on the throne is identical with his predecessor and his successor—not symbolically but actually."[116]

"Then really there is no succession at all," said F., puzzled.

"This business of identity is hard for us to understand, but it was basic with the Egyptians. In the *Book of the Dead* the deceased who has his resurrection assured becomes thereby not merely *like* Osiris, he *is* Osiris. In the case of *Rpᶜt* on the throne, for example, that person 'cannot possibly be portrayed,' according to Helck, because the only person who can possibly sit on the throne is the king himself, therefore 'in his place the King himself must be depicted, who of course mounts the throne as his own successor.'[117] So really you were not far wrong when you said there was no succession at all in our sense of the word: the *Rpᶜt* is the king's self: anybody else would be a usurper. There is one thing that bothers Helck a good deal, and that is that the *Rpᶜt* authority seems to come strictly through the *female* line. He finds it hard to believe that Pharaoh should always have had his authority through women, and yet there is no evidence that it was otherwise."[118]

"Wasn't it the title of *nebty*, 'The Two Ladies,' that gave the king his authority after all?" asked Blank.

"Yes, that was his indispensable title to rule. According to Gardiner that title 'displays the king as identified in his own person with the two principal goddesses of the period immediately preceding Dyn. I.'[119] Though the *Rpᶜt* was a man, the office itself was the 'Ibis-power' which belongs strictly to women."[120]

"I find this most significant," said Mr. Blank. "How would you represent Pharaoh allowing someone else to sit on his throne and enjoy his authority after the manner of Geb?"

"One might answer that from a number of coronation scenes. Bonnet's article on Egyptian coronations says that the king is depicted 'sometimes standing, sometimes sitting on the throne, sometimes kneeling before it.'[121] Lepsius has a beautiful reproduction of the newly crowned Pharaoh seated on a throne immediately below that of Atum and identical with it.[122] In many ways the artists have succeeded in conveying with clarity and majesty the idea of the identity of the king on his throne with the god on his. 'Thou doest what Osiris does,' says a Pyramid text, 'for thou art he who is on his throne.' "[123]

"Here is a picture," said Blank, producing with considerable nervousness a battered Pearl of Great Price opened to Facsimile No. 3 in the book of Abraham, "which some claim to represent a man who is not Pharaoh—that makes him a *Rpᶜt*, I suppose—sitting on the royal throne 'by politeness of the king,' and bearing the emblems of royal authority. Pharaoh and his son, the rightful *Rpᶜt*, are standing by and instructing one of their princely subjects to show obeisance to the man on the throne."

Schwulst took the picture and looked at it hard. "He is wearing the Atef crown," he said, "the oldest and holiest of Pharaoh's many crowns.[124] The two big feathers on it are emblems of spirit and truth, the symbols of Shu, the oldest and most 'spiritual' of the gods, and of Maat, who is truth itself.[125] The Heqat sceptre he is holding is indeed 'the scepter of justice and judgment,' that Osiris must always hold when he sits in judgment. The throne itself is strictly in order, and so is the lotus flower before the throne, signifying, as it often does, that this takes place in Egypt.[126] Is this a recent explanation?"

"It is a century and a quarter old," said Blank.

Facsimile No. 3 from the Book of Abraham as it appeared in the original publication of this series in the *Improvement Era*.

"It *is* rather quaint," Professor F. commented. "Any fool can see, for example, that the figures called Pharaoh and his son are women."

"Yes," Mr. Blank countered, "a myopic moron could see that, and that is why it is so remarkable. It is plainly intentional: when a Pharaoh dressed like a woman and had himself depicted as one 'he by his woman's body honored his god, the mother who had brought forth all the universe.'[127] A Roman emperor adopting Egyptian customs had himself represented as the mother-goddess, 'a combination that strikes the modern mind [including your own] as ridiculous, but that is not so alien from ancient sentiment or unfamiliar in the speculation of the mystics and gnostics,' the latter of Egyptian origin, you need hardly be reminded.[128] The confusing of the sexes in royal ceremonies is a highly characteristic Egyptian usage. Bear in mind now that in their capacity as rightful heirs to the throne, Pharaoh and his son were *completely identified* with the 'Two Ladies,' who are never absent from a coronation scene, no matter who else is missing. What was the expression Professor Schwulst just quoted from Gardiner? The king was 'identified in his own person' with the 'two ladies.' Here you have it very plainly."

"But isn't this simply the well-known Egyptian judgment scene?" F. protested, "the one found so often in funeral texts?"

"If you want to call a 'typical' scene one *from* which the most essential elements have been removed and *to* which conspicuous but totally unfamiliar figures have been added, you might have a case," Blank countered.

"But you can find these figures in any collection of Egyptian drawings—all of them—"

"That is the key to the whole business, I believe. What we have here are conventional figures in an unconventional order. They were obviously drawn by an Egyptian; even the bad engraving cannot conceal the authentic and inimitable Egyptian style; but it was an Egyptian laboring to tell an unfamiliar story using the conventional figures that he had been trained to draw. I can best illustrate my thesis by another picture from the same book." He turned to Facsimile No. 1. "What do you see here?"

"Obviously an embalmer at work," said F. jauntily. But Professor Schwulst shook his head.

"There is something wrong here. As has often been observed, the canons or rules of Egyptian drawing are extremely strict and formal.[129] They specialized in funeral pictures in which there was a proper way to depict every little thing; but this is a highly unconventional scene, though I must admit with Mr. Blank that it was surely drawn by an Egyptian. I am trying to figure out what is wrong."

Blank tried to be helpful: "You will agree that the only

Facsimile No. 1 from the Book of Abraham as it appeared in the original publication of this series in the *Improvement Era*.

way an Egyptian artist could draw was by setting down stock figures he had learned by heart. Now suppose someone asked such an artist to draw a completely original scene. What would he do? He would simply arrange the familiar figures of his repertoire in a new and unusual composition, and that is exactly what we have here. Turn this picture on its side, and Dr. Schwulst will immediately recognize what the man on the couch is doing."

"He is praying," the other answered without hesitation. "He is in the proper and conventional attitude of adoration—right foot thrust forward and hands raised before the face—that is the correct depicting of supplication, no doubt about it."

"So the artist was instructed to draw a man praying, and he did it in the proper way. But he was also told to represent the same man bound on an altar. The victim couldn't be bound if the artist was going to show him supplicating, but he could put him on his back. So here you have the strange incongruity of a man assuming the attitude of prayer in a supine position. 'I lifted up my voice,' it says (Abraham 1:15), '. . . and the angel of his presence stood by me, and immediately unloosed my bands.' If an Egyptian artist was told to represent an angel, what would he do, Professor Schwulst?"

"He would draw a bird. The Egyptians always represent spirits that go and come as birds, even when they are thought of as having human form. The reason for that is obvious: birds are the only visible creatures that can leave the surface of the earth. But more specifically, there is a whole cycle of Egyptian legends dealing with the messenger bird of Ammon, who is the hawk; sometimes it is Ammon in person who goes forth from the shrine, but then he too (who is never otherwise represented in any but human form) takes the shape of a hawk. In the tales it is often hard to tell whether the messenger or angel is a bird or in human form. But certainly no Egyptian artist would or could represent a divine messenger as anything but a bird—preferably a hawk."[130]

"Being asked to show a priest about to offer human sacrifice," Blank continued, "the artist draws a figure like an embalmer with a knife, but he is careful to show by his garb and attitude that he is *not* an embalmer."

"We could go on like this all night," said F., growing uneasy. "How about getting back to the subject? This *Rp*ᶜ*t* rite that the Professor has been telling us about opened the way to the throne to ambitious princes and thereby made much trouble for Pharaoh, wasn't that the theme?"

"Right," said Professor Schwulst. "Pharaoh could never afford to be too trusting, as Amenemhet I once told his son. Already in the Pyramid texts the king puts on a terrific show: 'Introduce N. with trembling; adore N. who has honored you all, even as he commands the human race also to do.'[131] 'He will take his seat on the great throne which the gods made; . . . the gods of the horizon will come to him on their faces, and the imperishable stars bowing down.'[132] (Remember that Joseph to whom the stars bowed down was also an Egyptian ruler!) The throne itself is a thing of wonder, made all of copper or of iron."[133]

"Sounds like the court of the Great Khan," Blank volunteered.

"If you think so listen to this: 'Open the double doors, that thou mayest stand at their head; . . . they enter, they are smitten with fear; they depart, they lift up their heads. . . . Thy brother stands beside thee, thy relatives stand beside thee.'[134] Isn't that right out of Ibn Baṭuṭa? And when the king raises his hand, they must all stand up, 'and if N. lowers his hand towards them, they sit down,' and when he calls for a thousand they hasten to prostrate themselves before him.[135] 'He sits upon that firm throne, whose knobs are lions, whose feet are the hoofs of the great wild bull. . . . "A prince of all princes this is," they say of him; and they appoint N. among the gods.'[136] There is a great deal more in the same vein, and though the imagery may be adapted to a funerary context, it is plainly drawn from observations of real court life."

"In other words, a real and tangible 'epic milieu' behind the imagery?"

"Yes, such court scenes abound in the epics. They are not only real but also typically heroic."

"Would you say that the conflict between men and serpents so often mentioned in the Egyptian texts goes back to real events," Blank asked suddenly, "or is it symbolic?"

"No need to be symbolic about it," Schwulst replied, opening an Egyptian handbook to the part on snakes and reading from it: 'For the protection of human life, the Egyptians had to wage a constant war on snakes and scorpions.'[137] But what is your idea on the subject? You have brought some notes which you want to put into the record. Let's have them."

"Well," said Blank with suppressed enthusiasm, "I have long suspected that there was a great plague of serpents in the days of the first Pharaohs, and the circumstances described in the Egyptian records are so very much like those reported in Ether that I am going to ask you to listen to the two descriptions and judge for yourselves. Here are the pertinent passages from the Mormon record. Early in their history, after only half a dozen or so kings had reigned over them there came a time of

> great dearth upon the land, and the inhabitants began to be destroyed exceedingly fast, because of the dearth, for there was no rain upon the face of the earth.
>
> And there came forth poisonous serpents also upon the face of the land, and did poison many people. And it came to pass that their flocks began to flee before the poisonous serpents, towards the land southward, . . . [and] there were many of them which did perish by the way; nevertheless, there were some which fled into the land southward (Ether 9:30-32).

"Do you get the picture? A great drought, a southward movement of cattle to better pastures, people and cattle both plagued by serpents! Some of the cattle get through to the 'land southward,' apparently a region where tropical rains could be relied on, but a great distance away, since most of them never made it. It was the 'dearth,' incidentally, that destroyed the people, not the serpents. The animals were looking for grass, of course, and the people followed them: 'the people did follow the course of the beasts, and did devour the carcasses of them which fell by the way, until they had devoured them all' (Ether 9:34). After that, it says, the serpents 'pursued them no more,' but they did present a definite barrier to the southern migration of the people, who were able to return to something like a normal economy when it finally rained, 'and there began to be fruit in the north countries, and in all the countries round about' (Ether 9:35). Still it was not until over two hundred years later that 'the poisonous serpents were destroyed' and the people could go into the land southward. That means, of course, that this was no local or temporary condition. It was more than a few miles of snake-infested desert that kept a whole nation out of the lush south country for two centuries and more. In its years of isolation the land southward had become a paradise for game, and it had always been favorite grazing land for the herds (Ether 10:19). We are told that in the days of King Lib, 'who became a great hunter,' 'the poisonous serpents were destroyed,' and the south country was opened up—but not to settlement: 'they did preserve the land southward for a wilderness, to get game. And the whole face of the land northward was covered with inhabitants' (Ether 10:21). Moreover 'they built a great city by the narrow neck of land, by the place where the sea divides the land' (Ether 10:20)—divides it into north and south, that is, for there were no cities in the southland proper. All this activity seems to have been part of a great period of expansion and settlement in the days of Lib."

"Now[138] let me take you to Egypt, and first of all recall what has already been said tonight, that from the earliest times the Delta country was preserved both for grazing and 'for a wilderness to get game,' with Pharaoh himself as the Mighty Hunter.[139] After rain had fallen on the land and the serpents had 'become cowardly,' the great Menes, the first in the line of historical Pharaohs, 'built a great city by the narrow neck of land'—only in this case it was the narrow valley passage right at the base of the Delta, at the spot which at that time 'divided the land' between the Land Northward and the Land Southward. Before the city could be built, it was necessary to drain vast tracts of land to the north, which were still uninhabitable marshes.[140] The city itself was known as 'The Balance of the Lands,' and the 'City of the White Wall' because it controlled all passage between the two lands and barred or permitted access from the one to the other.[141] The founder of another great dynasty at a later date built just such an establishment at the other end of Egypt, calling it 'The Gate of the North,' since it blocked off the southern empire. The classical distinction between the Land Northward and the Land Southward, which first meets us with great persistence in the Book of Mormon, was more than a geographical convenience for the Egyptians: it was a ritual dichotomy in which the Two Lands theme, the red and the white, was carried out with great thoroughness at all times. Eberhard Otto has recently written on the subject.[142] The philologian Joseph Karst has argued that the Egyptian word for the Land Northward, which everyone knows is *Mekhi*, is the same as Mexico, which has the same meaning.[143] Of course we don't have to go along with speculation like that, but I do maintain that some aspects of Egyptian life and history demonstrate that just such things as described in Ether *could* have been on the earth."

"Meaning such things as plagues of serpents?" Professor F. asked. "You just now said something about Egyptian serpents 'becoming cowardly.' What is the story?"

"That is what I was getting to. If Menes is the first historical king, the first legendary king and the leader of the great migration into Egypt was certainly Horus. He was always remembered, among his other exploits, for having overcome the serpents. 'Horus was an ox-herd when he trod on.' Here the old fragment breaks off, but hundreds of representations of Horus treading on serpents and crocodiles enable us to complete it. It ends as a typical charm against serpents: 'O let the beast, O desert, glide away.'[144] Remembering from Ether how 'their flocks began to flee before the poisonous serpents,' it is significant, I think, that Horus fights the serpents as an ox-herd; here is a passage recalling the struggle: 'The bull is fallen because of the *sdh*-serpent; the *sdh*-serpent is fallen because of the bull. Fall, glide away.'[145] Those last words mark it as another charm against snakes; though the Egyptians used many ingenious devices to exterminate snakes, the commonest protection against them was the incantation or charm, of which innumerable examples have been found; they often refer to the war of Horus on the serpents.[146] In the *Pyramid Texts* it is the flame-serpent who withholds bread—drought, heat, famine, and serpents go together, as in Ether's account. 'Be thou watered, O desert, water not sand. Say: The serpent which came forth from the earth is fallen; the flame which came forth from Nun is fallen. Fall; glide away.'[147] That charm seeks to banish drought and snakes in a single operation, as does this: 'O Sesha-w, rain, that the serpent may become cowardly.'[148] The most potent medicine against serpents is the image of Horus treading on snakes and crocodiles, holding snakes in one hand and a lion and a scorpion in the other—always by their tails, for he is not their patron but their enemy."

"But doesn't the water-loving crocodile come in for as much punishment as the flame-serpent?" F. asked.

"That, I believe, is a clear indication that there was a regular campaign against serpents because there certainly had to be against the crocodiles. In places where they swarm, they are to this day a menace to settlers. The *Book of the Dead* describes the crocodile god as 'ravening, dangerous, dwelling in the place of terror, to whom bowings and prostrations are made in Letopolis,' those being originally acts of appeasement rather than worship.[149] Here is a vivid little episode from an old epic wherein a goddess says, 'I advance alone, I go around among the bushes. A very great crocodile is after thy son.'[150] That was no mere symbolism. When Cleomenes was sent by Alexander to be the first governor of Egypt, his servant was eaten by a crocodile, and the priests had to pay a terrific fine.[151] The snakes, crocodiles, lions, and scorpions that Horus overpowers are all the dangerous creatures that prowl in the bush and along the clearings. Here is a typical charm: 'Repulsed is thy crocodile. . . . Thy soul is cut in pieces, thy vertebrae are severed. . . . The Horus children are for smashing thee—destroyed art thou at their season. Back, back, Thou Retreat, . . . Horus makes thy crocodile to go back. . . . The children of Horus give [put] their spears into thee.' "[152]

"That plainly says that the reptiles were destroyed by the Horus children 'at their season.' " Schwulst observed. "I think you are right—there seems to have been a definite large-scale operation. It reminds me now of a snake episode in the story of the lady and the settlement of Egypt—the one I told you about earlier. Here it is: Re charges Geb to go down in haste and take charge of the serpents on the earth who fear and obey him, 'and then you will go to the place of my father Nun,' he instructs him, 'and say to him: Watch carefully the reptiles of the land and the water. . . .' Then follows a charm against snakes."[153]

"There must have been quite a to-do," said Mr. Blank. "One text describes the king and the serpent as biting each other while 'the centipede was smitten by the householder, and the householder was smitten by the centipede.'[154] And this looks like a fight to the finish: 'Who is it who will remain?' Says the text, describing a fight between the king's champion and the serpent, 'It is the King who will remain!' "[155]

"And who, pray, is the king's champion?" F. inquired.

"In this case it is a lynx who springs on the neck of the serpent when he raises it to strike and gives him a bad mauling. The early classical writers report that the Egyptian priests attributed the singular holiness of the cat, the hawk, and the ibis, to the fact that they are the natural enemies of snakes and the allies of the children of Horus in overcoming them.[156] And speaking of snakes who hedge up the way, there are many accounts of how Alexander almost failed to reach the Oasis of Ammon because of the serpents that hindered passage across the desert.[157] In the *Book of the Dead,* the road between this world and the next is supposed to be blocked by serpents which the soul can only pass with special guidance and protection. In one place three serpents hedge up the way of Re himself, whereupon the local gods, who are the equivalent of the local inhabitants, join him in a campaign of extermination in which they smash the heads of the snakes and pronounce charms over them, so that Afu-Re can finally get by."[158]

"Here we have some lively descriptions of community snake hunts, with special attention to the setting of fires in the brush and marsh—which points to a very early date: 'The eye of Horus . . . devours thee, the mighty fire leads it on, the eye of Re prevails over thee, the flame devours thee. . . . Back with you! You are cut to bits, your life is scorched, your name is buried, . . . get back! Go away! You are cut to pieces, . . . you are ground up, . . . Apepi. . . . The fire eats thee; it cuts thy soul,' and so forth.[159] Apepi, or Apopi, was the great snake who kept Horus and Re from occupying the Delta: He is always represented as a huge serpent. One of the best-known of all Egyptian classics is the overthrow of Apopi: there is talk of torches, of hacking and mangling, smashing of backbones, and the rest—'they burn thee upon thy folds, . . . the flame eats into thee. . . . Set puts his spear on thy head.'[160] 'Their flame of fire comes forth against thee; fall back, retreat from the flames of fire coming forth from their mouths! O falling one, wriggler, retreating enemy of Ra, thou art fallen at this moment. . . . Carried off are thy remains; thou art beat up, cut up, slaughtered, thy crocodile is destroyed, . . . thou art pierced, overthrown, thou mayest never again come forth from thy hole forever and ever.' "[161]

"It seems clear that fire is being definitely used as a weapon on a large scale to make the land habitable. The mention of torches proves that, and then all the clubbing and beating and sanitary disposal of remains—really quite convincing." This from Professor Schwulst.

"And there is no shortage of material on the subject. Listen to this: 'Thou art fettered and beaten by tough beaters. . . . Thy crocodile is turned back. . . . Great fire comes forth against thee; its flame is deadly to thy soul, the words of power to thy body, thy spirit. The mistress of fire prevails over thee, hooks flame into thy soul; it makes an end of thee.'[162] And this: '. . . . fire therefore is upon all thy ways. Pechit does evil to thee, she flames, the great fire, lady of slaughter, mistress of the spark, she removes thy flesh, she injures thy soul; the flame burns thee up.'[163] And this: 'Fire comes forth roasting you, frizzling it frizzles you. . . . It bites you in the name of Set. Retreat! Go back ye Sebau!' "[164]

"Enough!" cried F., throwing up his hands. "We get the idea. . . ."

"But the ironical thing is that after all that fuss, it was the coming of the rain with the north wind that put down the serpents—'made them cowardly' as the saying went. 'The breezes of the North winds blow, and at the voice of the thunder-cloud roaring,' the serpents pass away to the east.[165] So the serpents were destroyed, and the land was settled, and the king forever after wore the Uraeus serpent on his brow, to strike deadly terror into his enemies: 'The heat of the flaming breath of his Uraeus serpent is like that of the *Rnn-wt-t* serpent on his forehead. N. has put fear in their heart making massacre among them.'[166] Note the combination of heat, drought, serpents, and massacre. The Uraeus serpent was a life-sized and frighteningly realistic reproduction of the most poisonous serpent known, all ready to strike—it was supposed to paralyze the beholder with fear. The *Pyramid Texts* tell us that its purpose was not only to terrify human enemies, but especially to outface and outfight real serpents—it is the insignia of the first Pharaoh in his capacity of destroyer of the serpents."[167]

"Well, well," said F., rising and stretching, "I guess we do have an epic world or something very much like it, in earliest Egypt."

"Even in the agrarian state of the old kingdom," Dr. Schwulst added, "all the elements are there. Of course we are still far from knowing just what things were like—it is so easy to reconstruct vivid and convincing pictures in the imagination, eking them out with archaeological bits here and there, only to find some day that we have been hopelessly wrong on all the main points. The whole idea of a nomadic or 'epic' element in Egyptian culture is a new one, though it is getting more attention all the time."

"Wouldn't you agree," Blank asked, "that no one, one hundred and twenty years ago, thought it would be like this?"

"No one dreamed of such a thing fifty years ago," was the reply.

"But where has this got us?" Professor F. asked as he put on his coat.

"Just one important step along the way," said Blank, "and the next step should take us to Mesopotamia."

"I thought we had already agreed," said his friend, "the Babylonian origins were Heroic."

"But we haven't said why yet," Schwulst reminded him, "and it would be a shame to overlook all that beautiful Sumerian epic poetry. There's much more of it, you know, than you'll ever find in Egypt. How about a week from Friday?"

3

The Babylonian Background

Two weeks later[1] the three friends met again in Dr. Schwulst's office. No orientalist worthy of the name confines his studies to one culture, and Schwulst was as good at Babylonian as he was at Egyptian. Grateful for a captive audience, he had prepared for the event by piling the texts of a dozen Mesopotamian epics on his table. And now working rapidly through the pile from top to bottom, he virtually monopolized the rest of the evening. The reader must always bear in mind that what we have here is merely academic chit-chat, a setting forth of issues and areas of investigation without any attempt to exhaust anything.

"It has been maintained," Professor Schwulst began in his best lecture manner, "that Babylonia is actually the home of all epic literature, and that 'the true forerunners of the *Iliad* and the *Divinia Commedia* were not Genesis and Exodus but the legends of Etana and Gilgamesh.'[2] Epic stuff is always breaking out in Babylonian texts, even in the ritual literature. The great New Year's hymn called the *Enuma Elish,* for example, is 'a mixture of heroic epic and dogmatic poetry.'[3] So in order not to be here all night, let us just look at the purest and oldest epics.

"Here, gentlemen, is the epic poem of *Enmerkar and the Lord of Aratta*. In it, the first of these two great lords sends a message to the other demanding his homage, only to receive the haughty answer that the Lord Enmerkar is not the vassal of the Lord of Aratta. A showdown follows, and Enmerkar is beaten, but the victor allows him to continue to remain in power in Uruk as his liegeman. But later

Enmerkar refuses tribute to his new lord because Aratta's overlord, one Ensukhkeshdanna, has spoken disrespectfully of a certain great lady to whom Enmerkar has always owed fealty.[4] Do you follow?"

"No," said F.

"It doesn't make much difference," the professor laughed, "because there are conflicting interpretations of the story. I merely give this to you to show you that we begin with the complicated system of feudal alliances which is characteristic of heroic ages everywhere. Aratta's lord is described as sitting grandly enthroned and unassailably secure in his splendid mountain castle; and 'the Lady of heroes' sits in an exalted castle that shines like the sun.[5] Aratta declares that he is 'the properly appointed and sole Ruler of the Steppes, there is none like him!' and he sends out great mule trains moving to flute music and bearing rich gifts 'as a bait' to increase his power by buying support. A messenger comes to him from another great lord to beg humbly for the privilege of buying building materials from him, for his mountains produce timber, stone, and metals; the messenger comes before the great lord with fear and trembling. This is the lord of Aratta's message to the lord of Uruk (often called the oldest city in the world): 'Say to Uruk's king, he must submit to me, he must pay me feudal dues and services, . . . then he may continue to live in his Ishtar temple while I live in mine.' Note that both these men are vassals of the great lady. If Enmerkar submits, he will be allowed 'to shine as Lord of the City, as Prince of the City, as Lord of the Storm, as Prince in the Storm, as the Lord who rages, as the Prince who rages.' "[6]

"Those are certainly not the epithets of peaceful peasant magistrates," Blank observed.

"Not at all," said Schwulst, "and all this is thoroughly typical. Enmerkar thus challenges his rival: 'Since you do not respect my lady, I will destroy your house.' As in all heroic ages, the center of everything is the great house; and these great houses are proud and touchy about their honor and constantly trying to overreach each other. Moreover, they are all related by ties of blood and bound by terrible oaths to each other. In this case when the lord of Aratta is beaten in turn, his subjects promptly and loyally submit to the victor, whom they hail as having proved his superiority by winning 'the jewel of heaven,' that is, the preference of the Lady Ishtar over his rival."

"How medieval it all sounds," mused F.—"the castles, the challenges, the faithful messengers, the vassals, and oaths, the cult of the lady. . . ."

"With echoes of the *Pyramid Texts*," Blank added.

"Even more like the *Pyramid Texts* is the constant Sumerian harping on the nature of gods, heroes, and kings as invaders and cattle raiders. The king is 'the exalted bull, glorious is thy name to the ends of heaven . . . twin brother of the lord of the divine ox of heaven and earth, . . . Father Iskur, lord that ridest the storm, thy name is to the ends of heaven, . . . thy name covereth the land.' "[7]

"Right out of the cannibal hymn!" Blank cried, and the Professor continued:

" '. . . the exalted hersdman, I am the holy cow [confusing genders in the best Egyptian fashion] and the woman who beareth issue.'[8] The king is 'the righteous herdsman,' but no gentle shepherd; he claims to rule the world by force and demands submission of his inhabitants; he sends his arrow-messengers out to exercise vigilance and control, and he himself moves about from place to place with his warlike host: 'Let thy good Utukku proceed me on my way, let thy good Lmassu travel along with me as I travel.'[9] On the famous stele of the vultures, Ningirsu is hailed as 'Lord of the crown of abundance, beast of prey from the steppes!'[10] Reference to the sun and his course and to the horizons, 'the ends of heaven' are common:

'From the rising sun to the setting sun [I] have subdued them unto him, at that time from the lower sea; . . . unto the upper sea his way he made straight for him. From the rising sun to the setting sun Enlil a rival caused him not to have.'[11] Without the name of Enlil as a clue, who would not guess that we were reading from the *Pyramid Texts?* Well, there are volumes of this stuff. But it is more than literary invention. Here, for example, a Sumerian king says that Enlil, king of the lands, has given him a mission, which is to take vengeance on the Guti, who have 'carried off the sovranty of Sumer to the mountains.'[12] Incidentally, if you are interested in the genealogy of the epic milieu, there have been first-rate scholars who have insisted on identifying these Guti with our own Gothic ancestors![13] At any rate, the Guti King Tirigan had in the best heroic manner sent a formal challenge to the chiefs and boasted that no man could stand up to him; he was beaten, however, and fled to one of his castles where, in the best saga manner, he was betrayed and captured."

"How old is all this heroic and feudal stuff?" F. inquired.

"It goes back to the beginning and earlier," was the reply. "It is particularly in the archaic texts that everyone is bound to everyone else by oaths and family ties and given careful heraldic rating in the aristocratic hierarchy. Here, for example, in what Deimel calls 'the oldest known royal inscription,' the king is described as receiving his office from Enlil the king of the lands, who makes him king of Uruk, king of the land, priest of Anu, prophet of Nisaba, son of Ukush (the Patesi of Gish-khu and prophet of Nisba), *approved* by Anu king of the lands, great-patesi of Enlil, endowed with understanding by Enki, *whose name is mentioned* by Babbar, prime minister of En-zu, *shakkanakku* (vassal) of Babbar, *agent* of Innina, *child* of Nisaba, *nourished with holy milk* by Nin-har-sag, . . . *foster-child* of Nin-a-bu-kha-du, the lady of Uruk, etc. etc.[14] Family ties, personal qualification, formal recognition—it is all very elaborate and exacting. Here in another archaic text Gimil-Sin, in his capacity of priest of Anu whom Enlil has chosen as the beloved of his heart, makes a dedication to Shara, lord of heaven (that is also Anu's title) who is the beloved of Ninni.[15] Or again, 'Dungi, the mighty man of Ur' . . . serves his lord Ningirsu, who in turn is 'the mighty warrior of Enlil.' In this hierarchy of allegiance you will always find the heroic combination of personal loyalty and warlike valor. As in Egypt, the favored one is accepted into the noble house, given all the due marks of recognitions, and provided with an adequate income."

"High life in high places all over again," F. observed. "What about the feasts?"

"The *Epic of Nergal and Erishkegal* will tell you all about them," said the professor, opening the appropriate text. "The story opens as the gods meet for one of their usual high feasts; they send a messenger to Lady Erishkegal, a strong-minded damsel who from her grim castle rules the largest but most distant domains of all the family. Since she never leaves her castle to visit the other gods, the messenger is instructed to invite her to send one of her own people to fetch a portion for her from the festive board. Well, when the lady's runner duly arrived and entered the banquet hall to get the promised portion, the merry gods made him the butt of their joking. When she heard of this disrespect shown her emissary, the great lady flew into a passion and demanded the life of the individual who had dared treat her messenger so lightly: it was an insult to a grand dame, and it was not to be borne. The injured messenger was asked to identify the culprit, but again the gods treated the whole matter as a huge joke and got him hopelessly confused. That was the last straw: Lady Erishkegal denied henceforward all access to the water of life that flowed only in her underworld palace, and she built mighty walls around it to see that none of the gods got through to it. This meant death for all, and it was urgent for some hero to deliver the race of gods from their predicament. That hero was the youthful Nergal, son of Ea, the chief of the gods. With a band of fourteen trusted retainers he entered the castle by a ruse, surprised the lady, and threatened to cut off her head, whereupon she offered him her hand in marriage and 'kingship over the wide Netherworld,' along with the Tablets of Wisdom by which he could rule over the universe."[16]

"Shades of a dozen fairy-tales!" cried F. "I thought all that stuff was strictly European—King Arthur, and all that."

"It is," said Blank, "and it is classic, too, because it is right out of the epic milieu: the feasting and rollicking heroes having fun at their elder sister's expense, the constant sending of messengers back and forth with invitations, challenges, and complaints, the visiting of each other's castles, the offended fairy who spoils the party, or if you will, the sinister lady in her dark castle, the young romantic hero with his adventurous band who makes his point with the fatal lady exactly as Odysseus does with Circe. This is certainly no peasant culture, but the ways of great lords and ladies."

Dr. Schwulst took another text from the pile before him. "The *Epic of Irra*," he said, "is more of the same. Like the *Pyramid Texts*, it tells of the invasion and pacification of the land, and it is very old. But the most remarkable thing about it is the fact that it seems to have been composed and sung by a minstrel who went from castle to castle exactly like the minstrels of the middle ages! It divides society into 'gods, kings, warriors, bards, and scholars,' with never a mention of the poor peasant:

> May the [god] who honors this song accumulate riches in his storehouse. . . . May the king who makes my name [the poet's] famous rule [as far as] the [four] rims [of the earth]. May the warrior [or noble-*rubu*] who

> recites . . . the praise of my valor find no match in battle. The bard who sings it shall not die in a *shiptu*, may his words be pleasing to kings and nobles.

"Could you ask for a more 'heroic' statement of values than that?"[17]

"What is a *shiptu?*" Blank asked.

"When there was treason or rebellion against a great lord, instead of punishing individuals, the rulers would take revenge on whole communities; such mass punishment was called a *shiptu*. It reflects a rather desperate state of things."

"No love lost between the princes and their subjects, eh?"

"Rebellion, underground opposition, and savage reprisals are the order of the day. Here is a king who says that his god 'pays no heed to the afflictions of the common people.' And when one great lord curses another he says: 'May the people of his city, having risen in rebellion, strike him down in the midst of his city.'[18] The lords have their 'watchers' busy everywhere.[19] Here is an epic poem which furnishes a good commentary on the way things were run. It is called the *Epic of Ninib*, and according to its editor 'must have been composed soon after the *subjugation* of, and victory over, all those mountains which yielded the several stones here mentioned.'[20] The high lord sits down to call the roll of his followers and reward them for their services by giving them lands and domains. 'Dolerite!' he cries, calling up one—and that reminds one of the 'mentioning of the name' the 'calling forth' and the honoring in high places that we read of in so many Sumerian and Egyptian texts—Dolerite, of course, is a stone, but as the editor observes, 'actions and deeds like these are not those of stones but of living persons.' The chief speaks warmly in Dolerite's praise: 'thou who in my battles forever hast been a hero, . . . who during rebellions hast proclaimed "the lord, he alone a hero is! . . . I, the lord, [thee] the arm of my heroship greatly will I adorn." ' He calls him his right-hand man who has remained true when others rebelled, and adorns him with rich presents.[21] Rough, feudal times indeed; the king is called 'The royal lord, the fearfulness of whose storm is awe-inspiring.' To another supporter he says: 'Eliel stone! wise one, of the mountain, the overpowerer, my awe inspiring fear, with it thou shalt be clothed . . . in the conflict of weapons, warrior, thou who killest, gloriously thou shalt be adorned . . . the people shall gladly look upon thee and greatly reverence thee.'[22] This epic gives us also the point of view of the underdog: 'When ravaging enemies as if with darkness the land with destruction had filled, . . . when the pick and shovel they had made us to carry, when but taxes they had made to be our reward [wages].'[23] Further comment on the social order is unnecessary."

"So Babylonian civilization was not the normal outgrowth of a primitive hoe-culture?" F. asked.

"The common description of Mesopotamia as a river valley is liable to give rise to images of its inhabitants as a race of villagers and truck gardeners. Somebody raised the vegetables, to be sure, but it was not the people who counted. A rereading of Hugo Winckler's classic essay on the essentially nomadic nature of Babylonian civilization at all times should correct such notions, as Kramer's work is doing at present. Recently Delaporte has described the population of the valley as sedentary inhabitants of the towns and nomads encamped along the fringe of the desert.[24] But as in Egypt there was a constant going and coming between the two. After all, from the beginning the important people of Sumer belonged to two classes, the military and the merchants—the priests were merely secretaries of a campaigning and acquisitive priest-king who kept the home office and watched over things generally. Now what Winckler pointed out and others have now confirmed is that a prehistoric net of merchant communications of vast extent actually involved the whole ancient world in a sort of chronic nomadism. The goods were not passed from hand to hand, farm to farm, village to village, as was once thought, but from the remotest times were actually carried immense distances by caravan and ship for specific purposes of trade. 'It is a fundamental error,' Winckler writes, 'to think of the non-sedentary tribes of the ancient East as unaffected by the civilized point of view and way of life. . . . We must abandon entirely, for example, the concept that the Arabs live and lived in a world of their own. . . . The Bedouins still move among ancient cities that preserve to this day the plan and skyline of Babylonian towns—showing how completely at home they were in the Babylonian world.' On the other hand, he reminds us, it is equally false to imagine the ancient city dwellers as stay-at-homes.[25] The ancient Babylonians always pictured their gods as engaged in two main activities, 1) tending cattle, and 2) riding about in wagons.[26] Recently Oppenhiem has pointed to 'the existence of migrant scholars in Mesopotamia' in the earliest times, and many have noted that at all times Asia has been overrun with pilgrims, scholars, missionaries—that is, religious as well as commercial and military travelers, who fondly believe that they are imitating the wandering ways of the gods in the beginning as they move from shrine to shrine."[27]

"Like the wandering Gilgamesh?" Blank asked.

"Thank you for getting us back to the subject so tactfully. The *Gilgamesh Epic* as you know is the greatest Babylonian epic, but it is full of ritual and not so conspicuously 'heroic' as many others. Still, Gilgamesh is undeniably identical with the prototype of all knight-errants and migrating heroes following the course of the sun—Schweitzer, Farnell, Cook, and others have shown that he is our own Herakles."

"I mention this epic with a purpose," said Blank. "Everybody knows how in his wandering the hero Gilgamesh visited Ut-Napishtim, the Babylonian Noah, who told him the story of the flood."

"The *original* story of the flood, by the way," F. commented with devastating emphasis. But Professor Schwulst shook his head.

"For forty years," he said, "scholars were convinced that the Babylonian flood story found by Layard in the library of Assurbanipal at Nineveh was just what you say—the original version of the Genesis flood story. But they were very wrong. Many of the texts found in that seventh-century library contained statements to the effect that they were merely copies of much older originals reposing in a far older temple library at Nippur. When the University of Pennsylvania finally got around to digging at Nippur, they immediately discovered a version of the flood story some fifteen hundred years older than the Assurbanipal text, and this Nippur version 'differs fundamentally from the two Nineveh versions, and agrees most remarkably with the biblical story in very essential details both as to contents and language.'[28] For a generation the educated had proclaimed in loud and strident voices that the Nineveh finds had debunked the flood story once for all, but when the later discoveries debunked them in turn, everyone was expected to preserve a polite silence. I cannot blame you for leaping to conclusions, my friend, since all the experts did the same."[29]

In the next issue Professor Blank places side by side two descriptions of a remarkable type of boat; the one from the book of Ether, the other from Professor Hilprecht's study of the "ark" as depicted in three versions of the Babylonian flood story to which the author adds a fourth text (No. xvi in Gadd's *Reader*).

"With your permission[30] I would like to place side by side before you two descriptions of a remarkable type of boat; the one is from the book of Ether, the other from Professor Hilprecht's study of the 'ark' as depicted in three versions of the Babylonian flood story, to which we add a fourth text (No. xvi in Gadd's *Reader*). First let me present a list of some dozen peculiar features of a Jaredite ship in the words and roughly in the order in which they are given in the second and sixth chapters of Ether:

"First, they were built 'after the manner of barges which ye have hitherto built' (Ether 2:16). That is, except in some particulars these boats were not a new design but followed an established and familiar pattern—there really were such boats.

"Second, they were built 'according to the instructions of the Lord' (Ether 2:16).

"Third, '. . . they were exceedingly tight, even that they would hold water like unto a dish; and the bottom thereof was tight like unto a dish; and the sides thereof were tight like unto a dish' (Ether 2:17).

"Fourth, '. . . and the ends thereof were peaked' (Ether 2:17).

"Fifth, '. . . and the top thereof was tight like unto a dish' (Ether 2:17).

"Sixth, '. . . and the length thereof was the length of a tree' (Ether 2:17), 'And they were small, and they were light upon the water, even like unto the lightness of a fowl upon the water' (Ether 2:16). It is quite plain from this emphasis that the usual type of vessel in those days was some sort of raft, designed simply to float, not to keep out water.

"Seventh, '. . . and the door thereof, when it was shut, was tight like unto a dish' (Ether 2:17).

"Eighth, 'And the Lord said . . . thou shalt make a hole in the top, and also in the bottom; and when thou shalt suffer for air thou shalt unstop the hole and receive air. And if . . . the water come in . . . ye shall stop the hole, that ye may not perish in the flood' (Ether 2:20).

"Ninth, '. . . ye shall be as a whale in the midst of the sea; for the mountain waves shall dash upon you' (Ether 2:24).

"Tenth, '. . . the Lord caused stones to shine in the

> darkness, to give light unto men, women, and children, that they might not cross the great waters in the darkness' (Ether 6:3).
>
> "Eleventh, '. . . their flocks and herds, and whatsoever beast or animal or fowl that they should carry with them . . . got aboard of their vessels or barges' (Ether 6:4).
>
> "Twelfth, '. . . the Lord caused that there should be a furious wind' (Ether 6:5). '. . . they were tossed upon the waves of the sea before the wind' (Ether 6:5). 'The wind did never cease to blow . . . and thus they were driven before the wind' (Ether 6:8).
>
> "Thirteenth, '. . . they were many times buried in the depths of the sea' (6:6). 'When they were buried in the deep there was no water that could hurt them, their vessels being tight like unto a dish, and also they were *tight like unto the ark of Noah'* (Ether 6:7). 'And no monster of the sea could break them, neither whale that could mar them' (Ether 6:10).

"Now with all this in mind, let us go through our thirteen points again, in the same order, but this time with reference to the Babylonian descriptions of the *magur* boat that Ut-Napishtim built to survive the flood. Throughout we shall confine ourselves to quoting Hilprecht verbatim, lest we be suspected of stretching a point here and there. Each feature in the following list corresponds to something designated by the same number in the Ether list.

> "One, 'This class of boats [we are quoting Hilprecht], according to the Nippur version [the oldest, ca. 2100 B.C.], [were] in use before the Deluge.' In historic times the archaic craft was preserved only in ritual, the gods 'in their boats . . . visiting each other in their temples during certain festivals, . . . the Babylonian canals, serving as means of communication for the *magur* boats of the gods between their various temples at certain festival days. . . . Billerbeck and Delitzsch show that a certain class of boats really had such a shape.'
>
> "Two, 'In all three versions of the Deluge Story

Utnapishtim receives special instructions concerning the construction of the roof or deck of the boat.' The manner in which he received the revelation is interesting: the will of father Anu, the Lord of Heaven, was transmitted to the hero through a screen or partition made of matting, a *kikkisu,* such as was ritually used in temples. In the Sumerian version given by Gadd the command is: 'By the wall at my side stand. . . . By the wall a word will I speak to thee. . . . My pure one, my wise one, by our hand a deluge [shall be caused],' etc.

"Three, there was 'of course a solid part, strong enough to carry a heavy freight and to resist the force of the waves and the storm.'

"Four, 'Jensen explains MA-TU as a "deluge boat," . . . adding, that when seen from the side it probably resembled the crescent moon. . . . Moreover, the representations of the sea-going vessels of the Tyrians and the Sidonians . . . show that a certain class of boats really had such a shape.'

"Five, '. . . the principal distinguishing feature of a *magur* boat (was) . . . the roof or deck of the boat. . . . We notice that in the Biblical as in the Babylonian version great stress is laid on the preparation of a proper "roof" or "cover," . . . "Cover it with strong deck," (Nippur Version, line 9). "With a deck as strong as the earth" or "let its deck be strong like the vault of heaven above" '(Second Nineveh Version, lines 2-3).

"Six, the lines containing 'a brief statement concerning the measures of the ark' have been effaced in the Nippur version. The First Nineveh text says simply: 'Its measures be in proportion, its width and length shall correspond.' Since only one ark was built, as against eight Jaredite vessels, one would hardly expect the dimensions to be the same.

"Seven, 'Furthermore in the First Nineveh Version the boat . . . has a door to be shut during the storm flood.' The various names for the boat 'designate "a boat which can be closed by a door," *i.e.*, practically a "houseboat," expressed in the Hebrew story by an Egyptian loanword, *Tevah*, "ark" originally meaning "box, chest, coffin," an essential part of which is its "cover" or "lid." '

"Eight, '. . .the boat has . . . a door to be shut during the storm flood and at least one "air-hole" or "window" (*nappashu*, line 136).'

"Nine, 'The vessel built by Ut-napishtim being such a "house boat" or *magur*, this word could subsequently also be rendered ideographically by MA-TU, a "deluge boat." . . . A *magur boat*, then is a "house boat" in which gods, men and beasts can live comfortably, fully protected against the waves washing overboard, the driving rain from above and against the inclemencies of wind and weather.'

"Ten, '. . . Sin's *magur* boat is called "A bright house" *(esh azag)*, in which at times he dwells, as other Babylonian gods . . . do in their boats, when visiting each other in their temples. . . . The Moon god himself is represented as "sailing in a bright *magur* boat through the midst of heaven." '

"Eleven, in a *magur* boat 'men *and* beasts live comfortably. . . .' Nineveh 2: Ut-napishtim is to take 'domestic animals of the field, with wild beasts of the field, as many as eat grass.' Hermann has recently observed that we are to think of the earliest ships as transports for cattle. The Nippur version mentions 'the beasts of the field, the birds of heaven.'

"Twelve, 'The Storm-winds with exceeding terror, all of them together raced along the deluge, the mighty tempest (?), raged with them . . . and the mighty ship over the great waters the storm-wind had tossed . . .' Thus the Sumerian version. 'Jensen explains MA-TU as a "deluge boat," seeing in it "a boat driven by the wind," "a sailing vessel." . . . But a *magur* boat was written ideographically MA-TU, literally "a deluge boat," not because it was a sailing boat driven by the wind or rather the hurricane *(abubu, shubtu)*, but because it possessed certain qualities which rendered its use especially effective during the deluge, when its exclusive purpose was to carry the remains of life and to protect men and beasts

> against the waters from below and the pouring rains from above.' Though driven by the storm it had 'nothing in common with a boat in full sail, (and) nowhere . . . is a sail mentioned, nor would it have been of much use in such a hurricane as described. . . . Besides, we observe that the pictures of the Tyrian boats referred to have no sails.' A *magur* boat was driven by the wind, but not with sails.
>
> "Thirteen. 'It shall be a house-boat carrying what is saved of life,' says the Nippur version, its purpose being to preserve life and offer full protection 'against the waves washing overboard.' "[31]

"Nothing is more remarkable in my opinion," said Blank, "than the specific statement of Ether that the submarine nature of his ships made them 'like unto the ark of Noah,' since that aspect of the ark has never been rightly understood."

"That is quite right," Dr. Schwulst volunteered. "Ancient, medieval, and modern Bible illustrators have made it perfectly clear that they have not the remotest idea what the real ark was like. The window and the door are the only peculiarities mentioned in the brief three verses in Genesis (6:14-16). Old pictures depict the ark either as nothing but a big box or chest or as a regular boat: attempts to combine the two forms lead to comical combinations that show plainly enough how inadequate information has been on the subject. I think it is remarkable that the word for *window* in the Babylonian texts, *nappashu,* means literally *breather* or *ventilator*. This is also the interpretation in Ether, whereas the window in the ark is called a *tsohar* in Genesis, that is a *shiner* or *illuminator*."

"Which do you think is the older version?" F. asked, "the air hole or the skylight?"

"That would be hard to say," was the reply, "since both are found in the Babylonian texts. As a matter of fact, the rabbis could never agree as to just what the *tsohar* was."

"What did they say it was?"

"Some said it was a window, but others maintained it was some kind of luminous object by which Noah could tell night from day."[32]

"Why would he need a gadget to tell night from day?" Blank asked with interest.

"Because according to some, the ark was completely covered like a tightly shut box, and according to others, it was under the water a good deal of the time."

"Hold on!" said F. with a laugh. "Aren't we getting mixed up with Mr. Jared's ships?"

"And why not?" Blank replied. "Ether himself says the two types of ship followed the same model."

"As a matter of fact," said Professor Schwulst half to himself, "there may be something to that. Now that I think of it, that luminous object in the ark was supposed to have been some sort of shining stone."

"So that's the source of your Jaredite story!" F. cried with satisfaction.

"Not at all," the Professor rejoined. "The Ether version I believe is a much fuller one than that of the rabbinical tradition and contains some very archaic and significant material that is not found in the other. It has been many years ago, but I am almost sure I once saw some important studies on the shining stones."

"I wish you could remember where it was," said Blank. "I long ago gave up hope of finding a parallel to the story anywhere, nor have I ever found anyone either here or abroad who could give me the slightest help on it. This episode in the book of Ether has caused so much sarcastic comment that I have been determined to get to the bottom of it. I must admit it does seem a bit fantastic."

"In the study of ancient things," the Professor intoned with uplifted finger, "it is just the fantastic and incongruous which opens the door to discovery—never forget that. In scholarship as in science, every paradox and anomaly is really a broad hint that new knowledge is awaiting us if we will only go after it. Now as to these shining stones, I seem to remember some rather ambitious comparative studies on the subject, inspired by the Sumerian epic material—the Gilgamesh story, that was it!"

"Do you mean that the shining stone episode is found in the Gilgamesh epic?" Blank asked with surprise.

"No, no! At least not directly. I distinctly remember that there were Greek, Sanskrit, and Syrian versions of the story as well as Babylonian." Dr. Schwulst frowned in consternation, not a little annoyed that his vaunted memory should have betrayed him if only for a moment. Then turning with a gesture of impatience to his friend: "If you gentlemen will give me just a few hours, I am sure I can run this thing down."

"Oh, don't bother," F. said, but it was the wrong thing to say.

"What do you mean, 'Don't bother!' A thing like this is not to be lightly brushed aside. The story of stones that shine is too strange and rare a thing to let go unexamined. What are we doing here if we are not curious about such things—helping lazy young people to get bread-and-butter degrees maybe? So now I am going to bother myself about this little matter, and if you men care to come back tomorrow perhaps I will have some information for you."

Twenty-four hours later[33] the orientalist received his two friends with beaming benevolence and a table piled with old texts and a number of bound periodicals.

"Well, sirs," he began as they sat down around the table, "I have something for you! Not much, of course—that would take some time—but enough. Let us begin by considering the Jewish sources that worried us yesterday, going from the latest to the earliest. The Midrash Rabbah tells us that the various conflicting opinions of the rabbis as to the true nature of the *tsohar*, the light in the ark, simply demonstrates the fact that none of them knew what it was.[34] Rabbi Akiba ben Kahmana, for example, says it means a skylight, while R. Levi says it was a precious stone. R. Phineas, quoted by R. Levi, explains that 'during the whole twelve months that Noah was in the Ark he did not require the light of the sun by day or the light of the moon by night, but he had a polished gem which he hung up: when it was dim he knew that it was day, and when it shone he knew it was night.'[35] To illustrate this odd arrangement, Rabbi Huna tells a story: 'Once we were taking refuge from [Roman] troops in the caves of Tiberias. We had lamps with us: when they were dim we knew that it was day, and when they shone brightly we knew that it was night.'[36] The reference to hiding from the Romans shows that this tradition is at least two thousand years old. But all such stories seem to go back to a single source, a brief notice in the Jerushalmi or Palestinian Talmud, which reports that Noah was able to distinguish day from night by certain precious stones he possessed, which became dim by day and shone forth by night."[37]

"Is it not quite conceivable," F. interposed, "that anyone might embroider these accounts into the Jaredite story?"

"There is no limit to the embroidery that can be put on a tale, I suppose, but it so happens that the peculiar elaboration of the story in Ether follows other and much fuller and older versions—far older, in fact, than anything in the Talmud. And none of those versions was known when I was a boy. That is what makes me wonder. What is more, it seems to me quite unthinkable that anyone writing the Book of Mormon at that time either exploited the Jewish sources or knew about them."

"Why unthinkable?" F. asked.

"Well, first with regard to using the material, you can be sure that anyone who had access to this old Jewish stuff, whether at first or second hand, had a gold mine of useful information at his disposal. Yet he never makes use of any of it with the exception of this one little note. Along with that, the chances of anyone coming across this item seem infinitely remote when one considers where it is found, namely, in the Palestinian Talmud."

"What is so inaccessible about the Palestinian Talmud?"

"Everything. One might have been reading sometime in the Babylonian Talmud, but in the Jerusalem Talmud? Never!—only eminent rabbis ever read or cite it.[38] Do you see these four modest volumes? They represent all the printed editions of the Palestine Talmud that have ever appeared! Two of them came out after 1860, and could not have been used by the author of Ether; the other two are the Bomberg edition of 1523 and 1524 which as you see contains no commentary, and the Cracow edition of 1609, with a very short commentary on the margin."

"How about translations?" Blank inquired.

"Even worse. In 1781 a small section was translated into German—it was not the section in which our story occurs, by the way—and there was nothing after that until the German translation of 1880. Schwab's French translation done between 1871 and 1890 is the best known; Schwab also undertook an English version in 1886 but only completed the beginning of it. But no translation was available in any modern language in 1830, and who could read the original?[39] Who can read it today? It is in the difficult West Aramaic dialect—not the East Aramaic of the Babylonian Talmud, which is close to modern Hebrew—and so many of the words are technical that nobody knows what they mean anyway.[40] It is much smaller and is considered much duller than the Babylonian Talmud—and who reads that? Right now Professor Zeitlin is loudly proclaiming that the host of scholars at work on the Dead Sea Scrolls are one and all unqualified to read medieval Hebrew—which means that he is about the only man in America who can! The scholars and ministers who studied Hebrew in America in the 1830s knew rabbinical Hebrew no better than they do today; their whole interest was in the Old Testament, and if any of them ever looked into the Talmud, you can be sure it was not the Jerushalmi. Then too we must not overlook the fact that the Jewish accounts do *not* say that Noah used the gems for illumination, but only to distinguish day from night."

"That seems like a strange quibble," said F.

"Yet all the sources insist on it. They never come out and say that Noah used the stones for lamps, but only that he used them to tell day from night. That no doubt seems strange to you, but it happened to be a subject of considerable concern and discussion among the ancient doctors, both Jewish and Moslem. They had a good deal to say about distinguishing when it was day and when night by such ingenious methods as hanging up a black and a white thread side by side or by distinguishing certain forms or objects of certain size and certain shape. You see in their way of thinking it is extremely important for ritual reasons to know when it is night and when it is day. There was a whole branch of divine science devoted to the subject, and this naturally was the aspect of the shining stones that would interest any *rabbi*—not the problem of illumination. I can assure you that only a rabbi would ever have read this passage in America a hundred years ago. Apart from all this, it is quite plain to me that the account in Ether was not taken from the Jewish sources. As I said, it is much nearer to a far more ancient source of recent discovery; for example, your book of Ether says that the brother of Jared made transparent stones by 'moltening' them out of rock—the word is perfectly good English, by the way, though archaic. Where do you think he got the idea?"

"I have read the book to oblige Blank here," said F. "As I recall, the Lord is supposed to have told him what to do."

"Nothing of the sort!" cried Blank. "In building his ships there were three problems which the brother of Jared recognized as insoluble by conventional means, namely the problem of navigation under condition of perpetual storm with overcast skies, the problem of ventilation, and the problem of lighting (Ether 2:19). As to the last of these, the Lord told him that the usual methods of lighting by windows and fire would not do—the wording of Ether 2:23 makes it quite clear that those *were* the ordinary methods used. But instead of solving the Jaredites' problem for them by giving them a light on the spot or telling them how to make one, the Lord put the brother of Jared entirely on his own by retorting to his question, 'Lord, wilt thou suffer that we shall cross this great water in darkness?' with another question: 'What will *ye* that I should do that ye may have light in your vessels?' " (Ether 2:22, 25).

"And being thus thrown back on his own resources, what would the great man do?" Schwulst asked with a smile. "He would do what he had done before—follow the example of Noah. So he proceeded to cast some clear transparent stones in the hope that they might be made to shine in the dark."

"Did Noah do *that?*" F. asked with astonishment.

"That is the part I am now coming to, if you will have a little patience. First of all, then, the brother of Jared made some transparent stones by 'moltening' them out of rock, a process requiring a very high temperature indeed. Now the oldest writings of India, reporting her oldest traditions, have a good deal to say about a particular stone that shines in the dark;[41] such a stone, we are told, can be produced only by subjecting a stone or the heart of a person who died of poison to terrific heat—it must in fact be kept in an exceedingly hot fire for no less than nine years! This would turn it to a perfectly clear, transparent crystal, we are told, and this crystal 'would illuminate even the deepest darkness and sometimes shine as brightly as the sun.'[42] Meyer and Printz have traced this strange belief from India to China and the West, where it is mentioned by some of the most celebrated scholars of the Middle Ages. It was even believed in Europe that the Holy Grail was such a jewel and of such fiery power that the phoenix-bird cremated itself in its heat and was thus reborn, for among other things the stone had the power of regeneration."[43]

"And what," said F., "has that to do with the shining stones of the ark?"

"A great deal, if you will follow me. The stone was known to the Greeks and hence to the Middle Ages as the *Pyrophilos* or 'Friend of Fire,' and is most fully described in the Indian sources which say it was a perfectly transparent crystal and also went by the name of 'Moonfriend' and *Jalak-anta* or 'that which causes the waters to part.' For among all its marvelous properties, such as protecting its bearer from poisons, lightning, fire, and enemies, its most particular power and virtue was that it enabled its possessor to pass unharmed through the depths of the waters."[44]

"Dear me!" Blank interrupted. "That is surely something of a coincidence: a transparent stone formed with fierce heat that shines in the dark and guides and preserves its owner beneath the waves! Where do you think the Indians got all that?"

"That has been the subject of considerable search," Schwulst replied, "and it is quite clear that the tradition did not originate in India, though it may have been brought there at a very early time by an offshoot of the same Indo-European people to whom the story has been traced far to the north. But it has been so traced only by following a trail that led to the earliest Babylonian accounts of guess what—the deluge! Later writers quote a letter from the philosopher Aesculapius to the Emperor Augustus, in which he describes the Pyrophilos as the heart of a poisoned man turned into stone by nine years in the furnace; he also says that Alexander the Great possessed such a stone, which he carried in his belt, but that once while he was bathing he laid the belt aside, and a serpent stole the stone and vomited it into the Euphrates.[45] Aristotle tells the same story three hundred years earlier, and other Greek writers know of it many years before Alexander was born.[46] In these older versions the stone is interchangeable with the plant of life—it was a life-giving stone, as the case of the phoenix shows—or the 'medicine of immortality.'[47] In this form the story is identical with the prehistoric Sumerian tale of Gilgamesh and the plant of life, as many scholars were prompt to recognize as soon as the latter was published towards the end of the nineteenth century. Printz points out that this relationship illustrates both 'the immense span of time' over which traditions can survive and the degree to which they can become distorted in the process of transmission and still preserve clearly recognizable traits.[48] This story, in fact, seems to go back to that pre-Sumerian epic milieu that Kramer talks about. In the oldest Babylonian version only one person can tell the hero how and where to get the plant of life, and that person is Ut-napishtim, the Babylonian Noah. He it was who had possessed the plant of life which from the earliest times seems to be confused with a shining stone."[49]

"Where do we find the stone?"

"In the west—in Syria. There we find a most interesting series of ritual texts which for fulness and detail are hardly to be matched anywhere. The actual documents cover a full two thousand years, and the things they deal with are far older, as a little comparative study will show. Through all that period they tell essentially the same story, the now well-known 'Year-Drama' in which the death and resurrection of the hero, his victory over the powers of the underworld, and his marriage with the Mother Goddess are the principal episodes. The hero himself goes by many names, but the ones that concern us here are Attis and Humbaba, whom Stocks has shown to be one and the same person.[50] Everyone knows about Attis who is identical with the Syrian Adonis who is identical in turn with the Egyptian Osiris, but as the pre-Sumerian Humbaba he is less familiar."

"A strange-sounding name," F. commented.

"It is a Hurrian name, like Noah," Schwulst replied. "That illustrates my remark that everything points to a mysterious people of the north. That opens up the way to a lot of investigation and speculation, but now let us consider the Syrian hero. The most celebrated shrine in the East in classical times was the cult center of this hero and his wife the Syrian goddess at Aphek. Lucian visited the shrine which he describes as the greatest cult center in the world. The principal legend of the place and that invoked most often to explain rites and customs observed there was the story of Deucalion and the flood, which Lucian recounts in detail, showing it to be quite close to the biblical account.[51] The vast throngs of pilgrims that came to Aphek from all parts of the world were shown the hole down which the waters of the flood were said to have retreated and told how Deucalion erected at that spot the first temple and the first building to be constructed after the deluge.[52] The most remarkable object in the temple was, according to Lucian, 'a stone which is called *lychnis*, and the name is very appropriate; for by night it gives off a good deal of light, which illuminates the whole shrine just like a lamp, though by day the glow is weak. It looks exactly as if it were burning.' This stone shone forth from the crown of an image of the lady in her capacity of moon-goddess.[53] Nothing could be more natural than to associate with the moon a stone that shines by night and is dim by day. You will recall that the principal designation of the shining crystal in the Indian descriptions is 'Moonfriend.' "

"We may also recall," Blank commented, "that the *magur-boat* of the Sumerian Noah was compared with the moon, not only because it was crescent-shaped and wandered through space for twelve months, but especially because it was illuminated by a miraculous light."

"Then couldn't the whole story of a miraculously illuminated ark have come down from an original moon-cult?" F. demanded.

"A boat may remind anyone of the moon after it is built," Blank replied, "but the moon cannot have supplied the model for any workable boat. The moon is always there for all to see, but one can only compare it with a boat after one has seen not only the moon but boats as well. You can see from that that our whole story must start with a boat. You know as well as I do that the oldest temples in the world contain beautiful and accurate boat-models and sometimes full-sized boats. Whatever the symbolism may be, they are always real boats or scale models of such. Today the experts are playing around a good deal with the idea that these boats refer to some great primal migration, for which the ark of Noah is the archtype. Granted the boat theme, the ancients were free to add any ritual or mythological frills that caught their fancy, the most obvious being the moon motif which every poet discovers independently. But the whole thing began with a real boat, not with the 'nature myths' that were once so popular with scholars but have now been so completely discredited."

"On that point," said Professor Schwulst, "we must insist that the Babylonian coloring of this and many other tales of great antiquity does not imply for a moment that the story itself has a Babylonian *origin*. Take the Greek stories of Deucalion's flood, for example: They go back to prehistoric times and to sources far older than any Bible manuscripts we possess. Yet no one ever suggests that the deluge story originated with the Greeks. Why not? Simply because the Greek versions of the story have been known all along and did not need to be dug up by archaeologists. If they had first been discovered in the nineteenth century, you can be sure they would have been instantly hailed as debunking the Bible! But let us return to our Syrian stone.

"Jirku has pointed out that the moon cult of Syria goes

back to prehistoric times, so that what Lucian is describing is of great age—albeit overlaid, as such old traditions always are, by all sorts of mythologized and rationalized explanations.[54] Macrobius, for example, says the image of the Lady was crowned with an arrangement designed to represent a sunburst of rays 'which symbolize the way in which Mother Earth is made to bring forth life by the fructifying rays sent from above.' In his day the stone was not working, apparently, but the crown on the image was designed to look as if it emitted a life-giving light.[55] Carl Clemen believes that the report that one of the jewels that adorned the image of the Goddess actually shone in the dark is 'naturally an impossibility.' "[56]

"Do you think there actually could have been such stones?" F. asked.

"I think you will find in Athanasius Kirchner that the ancients were familiar with the properties of such fluorescent stones as barite, which will shine for some time in the dark after exposure to the sunlight or after being placed near a fire. The question would require some looking into, but it is notable that all sources describe the shining stones only as *part-time* illuminators: they seem to fade out completely during the day. But after all what we are dealing with here is not scientific or historic fact, but literary and legendary coincidence, which can be just as instructive in its way. Here, for example, Stocks points out that the image of the ark at the great Syrian shrine was represented by an altar with a burning fire on it which seemed to be floating on a lake so that the devout could only gain access to it by swimming."[57]

"A sort of baptism, eh?" said F. with a laugh.

"It is not so fantastic, at that," Schwulst replied. "Remember, we have in things like this a great wealth and intermingling of typology—one thing is the type of another. In the earliest times the shining stone was confused with the plant of life, as we have seen; and we have just noted that Macrobius describes the light of the lady's crown as life-giving."

"I remember," said Blank, "that in the Book of Mormon Lehi had something like the equivalent of Jared's shining stone, and that was the Liahona. And we are told very plainly that there was 'a type in this thing' (Alma 37:39-46).

"That is thoroughly characteristic of oriental thinking," Dr. Schwulst observed. "In a recent study on the Urim and Thummim, Schoneveld has emphasized the idea the Urim does get its name from the root *Or-*, which means light and does imply that it was some sort of shining stone; it was the chief jewel of the twelve gems on the ephod of the high priest, which were nothing less than 'the symbol of God's presence.' According to Schoneveld, these stones were not introduced by Moses, 'but were already known in the times before the institution of the high priest's ritual clothing.'[58] It has also recently been shown that the peculiar endings of the names *Urim* and *Thummim* are not Hebrew plurals at all, but much older endings."[59]

"Strange how everything points to another people," Blank observed.

"Yes, Lucian already gives us a hint when he says that the Deucalion or Noah revered at the Syrian shrine was not a Greek or Oriental but a Scythian—an Indo-European from the north."[60]

"Where did the Sumerians come from," asked F., "if they brought their culture and legends with them into Mesopotamia?"

"No question has been more debated than that one," was the reply, "but as of today we can do no better than to follow Speiser, who has sought the original home of the Sumerians long and diligently, and now concludes (where is that note?): 'The Sumerians arrived at the head of the Persian Gulf . . . from the east, probably by sea, although their original home . . . has to be sought beyond the

Iranian province,' that is, away off in the middle of Asia somewhere—Speiser offers three suggestions: 'Transcaucasia, Transcaspia, or somewhere in Farther Asia.' "[61]

"Then who knows what may lie behind all this?" cried the perplexed F.

"One thing is certain: it is a world we dream not of. If the story of Jared's boats is not a true one, it is certainly a supremely clever tale, incredibly ingenious to have come from anyone in 1830."

"Let us sum up this business of the shining stones as it stands," Blank suggested.

"A good idea," replied the Orientalist, "especially since I have led you on such a tortuous way. Well then, first we found, tucked away in the corner of an old, obscure, and completely neglected Jewish writing, a very brief passage that suggested, along with alternatives, that Noah had shining jewels or stones in the ark, which he used for telling night from day rather than as illumination. That is all the Jews tell us, so far as I can find out, and it is not much. Next we found some traditions about the forming of shining stones by a heat process, and noted that the worldwide dispersion of those traditions indicated their great antiquity. We found then that the shining stone thus produced everywhere went by the same name and was thought to possess the same marvelous properties and powers, the most remarkable of which was its power to enable its owner to pass through the depths of the water. Next it was easy to identify this stone with the very stone that Alexander the Great lost in the Euphrates in an episode which many scholars were quick to identify with a central occurrence in the Gilgamesh epic: the loss of the plant of Life which had once belonged to Ut-napishtim, the Babylonian Noah, who alone could tell the hero Gilgamesh where and how to obtain it. Then we turned to the most renowned survival of a cult of Noah in the ancient world and found that the most remarkable cult object at that shrine was a wonderful stone that shone in the dark—Lucian actually claims to have seen it in operation."

"A monument to human gullibility," F. interposed.

"You miss the point entirely," Blank countered. "This stuff does not rely on its historical accuracy for its significance."

"What would you say was significant about it, then?"

"For one thing it illustrates beautifully a thing we are now pointing out with increasing insistence, namely, that the wild, exotic, unbridled oriental imagination we hear so much about simply does not exist. Where, for example, could you find a more complete and total *lack* of creative imagination? The same old motifs occur over and over again for thousands of years, the only changes being the accretions of equally unoriginal local stuff and the inevitable inaccuracies of transmission. Of originality not a spark! Always the same thing over and over again."

"In other words, the wild excesses of the original fancy are themselves largely an invention of the wild excesses of western fancy!" Schwulst laughed.

"I think that is extremely important, for it shows that when we get a theme like the shining stones, we can be sure that it is not the product of some imaginative village story-teller but began either as a real event or by some unique and forgotten act of general literary creation."

"As a matter of fact," Schwulst commented, "it has been shown time and again that your village story-teller is one of the most reliable depositors of archaic lore, which he preserves intact through the centuries: No one could be less guilty of imagining things!"

"But what if the Ether story is only literary creation?" asked F.

"That makes no difference to its value as evidence. For the question is not, 'How did the author of that book know about those *events?*' but simply 'How could he possibly have known anything about those *stories?*' Remember, the key to the whole thing was the Gilgamesh epic which was not discovered until long after many editions of the Book of Mormon had appeared; without that source all the other materials from East and West remain quite meaningless. But as soon as students had access to that work they began pointing out borrowings and connections on every side, all pointing to a common origin. Knowing nothing, though, about the book of Ether, the scholars have obligingly demonstrated, among other things, that the wonderful Pyrophilus which has *all* the properties of Jared's stones is to be found ultimately in the possession of Noah. Of those same stones the Talmud preserves a dim but unmistakable memory, a mere hint from which the details in Ether could never have been reconstructed, but nonethe-less a witness which puts a final stamp of authenticity on the old story. More than that I cannot tell you now."

4

Epic Milieu in the Old Testament

Having considered Egypt[1] and Mesopotamia, the friends moved by inexorable degrees into the epic worlds of Ugarit and the Hurrians, the Hittites, the Phoenicians, the Greeks, the Persians, the Romans, the Celts, the Germans and Scandinavians, the Slavs, and the heroic cultures of the late Middle Ages, which take their cue from the Arabs and Persians, from whom also come the heroic traditions of modern nations. In some of these areas Professor F. and his friend Blank had the advantage of Schwulst himself, and insisted on prolonging the discussions to such lengths that it is impossible to follow them here. Although we must pass by many heroic epics and ages for want of space to do them justice, some of the newer finds are so significant for the study of the book of Ether that we must give them at least a passing glance on our way back to the Jaredites.

First of all, there is a surprising new development involving the patriarchs of the Old Testament. Recent studies on Abraham have emphasized that great patriarch's dual role as a chief of wandering nomads on the one hand and a highly educated representative of the great and sophisticated civilizations of Babylonia and Egypt on the other. The discovery that Abraham lived in a house as well as a tent came as a great surprise in the 1930s: "We had been accustomed to think of Abraham as a simple dweller in tents," writes Sir Leonard Woolley, "and find him a possible occupant of a sophisticated brick house in a city."[2] This is a reminder that the tent life and city life, far from being mutually exclusive, normally go together in heroic ages. And to follow Cyrus Gordon, Abraham's age was certainly a heroic one.

"Abraham was of Mesopotamian origin," writes Gordon, "and his son and grandson married girls from their kin in Mitanni. At the same time, Egyptian blood was in the Patriarchal household. . . . The Patriarchal Hebrews enjoyed the ideal spot and the ideal time to fall heir to the rich and varied heritage of the entire ancient Near East, when Egypt and Babylon were nearly spent. . . . The pastoral and seminomadic purity of Patriarchal life saved the Hebrews from the decadence of that cosmopolitan age."[3] The age in question, according to Gordon, was the Amarna period, "the pivotal era of the ancient Near East. In it were blended the civilizations of Mesopotamia, Anatolia, Canaan, Caphtor and Egypt."[4] He thus places Abraham a full six hundred years later than conventional scholarship dates him. But the earlier period, *circa* 2000 B.C., was also a typical heroic age like the Amarna period, a time when the whole ancient world was overrun by great mixed hordes under the leadership of chieftains who drove horse-drawn chariots, had formidable new weapons, and bore Aryan, that is Indo-European, names. Both ages were typical migration times, times of world upheaval and collapse of great civilizations. A scholar who places Abraham in the earlier period tells us that his father Terah belonged to "a motley and mobile population," moving among the cities of Mesopotamia, and asserts that "it would not be surprising" to discover at Mari (a city in northern Mesopotamia) a record of "Terah's request of Zimrilim for permission to pass through his territories!"[5]

"Motley" societies, we should note, are not the product of long evolution or stable conditions. Such are only the result of the throwing together of enforced migrants in a time of crisis. The hosts that conquered and occupied both Egypt and Mesopotamia in the early second millennium, and the People of the Sea and their relatives who struck again in the fourteenth century B.C., were such mixed hordes. Abraham has close family ties with the great contemporary "heroic" civilization of the Hurrians, but what puts the genuine heroic stamp on his doings, according to Gordon, is first of all the authentic saga character of the patriarchal biblical narrative. Certain things in those narratives, such as romantic marriage and contests between brothers, are found only in heroic literature and heroic ages. "Just as the social institutions of the Narratives are paralleled in Nuzu, the literary motifs of the Narratives are paralleled often and plainly enough in the legends . . . of Ugarit."[6] Now the Nuzu texts referred to have a Hurrian background, while the Ugaritic texts, though ritual and liturgical in nature, are full of genuine epic material.

Thus in the Ugaritic story of Baal we find that hero passionately declaring: "Whether king or commoner be *invested* with sovereignty *over* the land, *respects* I shall not send to the god Mot, nor *greetings* to Il's beloved, the hero!"[7] This is the old story of the great lord who refuses to pay respects to another great lord lest it look like submission. Meanwhile the position of his bitter rival Mot is clear. He "meditates in his inwards: 'I alone am he who will rule over the gods, yea, command gods and men, even domin[ate] the multitudes of the earth.' "[8] This statement followed a vain attempt to seize Baal's throne of dominion on the cedar mountain. In threatening terms the world is told to submit to Mot: "At the feet of Mot bow and fall. Prostrate yourselves and honor him!" He has a magnificent golden throne made for him and a golden bowl, objects which from their description are like those which have been unearthed at Tepe Gawra, according to our editor, and go back to the middle of the fourth millennium B.C., which may be almost in Jaredite times.[9] Next there is a penalty mentioned against the hero who smote "Lotan, the writhing serpent, didst destroy the crooked serpent, the *accursed one* of seven heads."[10] Again this puts us in mind of the many archaic Mesopotamian seals depicting the hero fighting with a flaming serpent. What is the origin of the Hydra, the seven-headed serpent, whose heads only multiply as fast as they are cut off? The only thing to suggest it in actual experience is the attempt to cut down pestiferous creatures that have one hopelessly outnumbered. It seemed to the pioneers that every cricket killed only made way for seven more. Whenever one looks in the early epics there is the same clear and vivid memory of a great plague of serpents, of which the book of Ether gives us the fullest and best description.

Next our Baal epic reports a great assembly of the gods on *Hmry*, which Gordon identifies with Mt. Hermon.[11] This assembly is often mentioned in the Jewish apocryphal writings as the assembly of the Fallen Ones that took place on Mt. Hermon after the flood. There we are told they founded a world-order which was in imitation and opposition to God's order, but which succeeded in oppressing the human race by its false authority.[12] These apocryphal writings have always been thought to be mere fantasies, the medieval inventions of overwrought oriental imaginations, but the Ras Shamra fragments now vindicate their antiquity. In the end, according to the latter, all the gods finally go and submit to Mot who is the Devil, in the city of Mt. Hermon (*Hmry*), while Aliyan Baal also submits to the haughty and glorious Mot.[13] This submission is by messenger, as in the other heroic tales we have considered.

In the light of these newly found epic texts, our whole idea of Hebrew beginnings must be changed. "The magnificent structure of Old Testament higher criticisms is not to be brushed aside," writes Gordon, "but its individual results can no longer be accepted unless they square with the Hebrew text as we can now understand it in the light of parallel literatures from the pagan forerunners and contemporaries of the Hebrews, in Bible lands."[14] If men have missed the point of Ether entirely, so have they missed the point of the patriarchal narratives of the Bible. Both sources now take us back to the same heroic world.

Of particular interest to students of the Jaredites and the epic milieu is the very recently discovered Phoenician inscription of Karatepe, dated variously between 800 and 725 B.C. The inscription was ordered by King Azitawaddu, who behaves "after the manner of the Assyrians," though his people are the Dananians. "I restored the Dananians," he boasts. "I extended the land of the Plain of Adana from the rising of the sun unto its setting. . . . I established peace with every King. . . . And I built fortresses in all the remotest borders, in the places in which there were lawless fellows, chiefs of robber bands, none of whom had been submissive to the house of Mupshu." It is the old familiar story, including the classification of all who refuse submission to Shiz or Coriantumr as outlaws:

> I, Azitawaddu, placed them beneath my feet [i.e., the robber bands], and I built fortresses in those places so that the Dananians might inhabit them. . . . And I humbled mighty lands in the west. . . . I brought them down; I settled them at my extreme borders in the east.

He sets up a center of control for all his conquests and gives it his own name: "I built this city and I determined [its] name Azitawaddiya, because Ba'al and Rephesh of the he-goats sent me to build . . . that it might be a bulwark for the Plain of Adana and for the House of Mupshu. . . . So I have built this city and I have determined [its] name Azitawaddiya. I enthroned the son of Ba'al . . . and instituted sacrifice."[15] Note that the city does not grow up gradually, but is founded by the great chief, as Jaredite cities were, and given his name. "And this city shall possess grain and wine, and this people, whose children shall dwell [here], shall possess cattle and sheep and grain and wine . . . and they shall be exceedingly mighty, and they shall serve *exceedingly well* unto Azitawaddu and to the House of Mupshu for the sake of Ba'al and the gods."[16]

A clearer exposition of the system and purpose of city founding as we explained it in *The World of the Jaredites* could not be asked.[17] But what rings the heroic note in our inscription is the magic name of "the House of Mopshu." For this Mopshu is none other than the Mopsus who figures so largely in the Greek heroic legends that "scientific" scholarship has always believed to be nature myths.

"In our text," writes the editor, "we thus have a tangible approach to this hero of Greek saga, who, born of Manto, the daughter of Teiresias, came to Cilicia a year before the fall of Troy."[18] In southeast Asia Minor the legendary Mopsus built three famous cities, and here in a tangible inscription we find a descendant of his building and dedicating another city, and a very real one. The German critical method long since decided that the idea of heroes building cities (a very conspicuous theme in the book of Ether) was purely mythological fancy, since cities, like everything else, were required by the prevailing scientific theory to be the product of a slow and gradual evolution.[19]

But to return to our Ugaritic texts of five hundred years earlier. In them "the currents of the Semitic and Indo-European worlds crossed. The Semitic cultural elements . . . included a strong admixture from Mesopotamia. The Indo-European elements embraced the Hittite and especially the Minoan."[20] Since those words were written, we have learned that the Minoans were our cousins the Greeks. All the great races and cultures of antiquity seem here to be mixed up together in an heroic "swarming-time." And the figures of the Old Testament are in it with the rest:

> The importance of the epic tradition underlying prose biblical history down to David's reign, though long surmised, is first beginning to take concrete shape.

> . . . We are now able to see that an *epic* approach (if not an acutal epic stage) underlying our prose accounts has affected the *content* of pre-Solomonic Hebrew history.

In the composition of this history Gordon finds "a distinctive epic attitude," which gives priority in the histories to those things which would "be included in the epic repertoire," events of epic allure which enjoy a conspicuous place in the pre-Solomonic histories.[21]

Until the 1920's all that was known about the Hittites was that Abraham had dealings with them. Now we know them as the oldest representatives of our Indo-European languages and customs and a people quite as ancient as the Egyptians or Babylonians. Their society was remarkably heroic. The king lived in a state of constant migration, in the summer going forth on his sacred mission of conquering and subduing the world, in the winter moving from city to city in a sacred progress which was regarded as a single protracted festival called the *nuntariiashhash.*[22] The king was the ruler of the world, the ever-victorious conqueror who moved forward in the thunder,[23] yet his office was elective as "among the Anglo-Saxons and other Germanic peoples."[24] As a result, Hittite history begins with the grim rivalry between two kings who have been nominated by competing groups of great lords, and the subsequent history of the kingdom is fraught with revolts and rebellions on the part of the king's kinsmen.[25] It is the old Jaredite story all over again!

The Hittite kings, like the Jaredites, exchanged messengers and letters with rivals whom they challenged to personal combat and whose followers they tried to "draw off." Thus the greatest Hittite ruler writes to his equally great Hurrian rival: "The people of Kizzuwatna are Hittite cattle and have chosen their stable, they have deserted the Hurrian and gone over to My Majesty."[26] Among the Hittites "the king's kinsmen, called the 'Great Family,' enjoyed special privileges, which they constantly abused."[27]

The usual things happened: when a Hittite king was actually taking Babylon about 1600 B.C., his son the crown prince was leading a conspiracy of princes against him at home; the unfilial son was banished but his youthful successor was murdered upon returning home from a campaign by *his* brother-in-law. This set off "a sorry period of palace murders and intrigues . . . which lasted for several generations and reduced the kingdom to a condition little short of anarchy."[28] In one letter we read of a noble who came as a fugitive to the Hittite king from the oppression of the great lord Attarissiyas (identified by Forrer with the Greek hero Atreus). The Hittite king bestowed a dukedom on his noble suppliant and saved him when the Lord Attarissiyas tracked him down and attacked him in his mountain domain. And what did our noble do to show his gratitude? He joined forces with the terrible Attarissiyas and raided the lands of his Hittite benefactor![29]

What could ever bind such men to allegiance? Ties of marriage (all the great Hittite houses were intermarried), and especially oaths! The oath is almost an obsession with the Hittites. Every vassal swore to be eternally faithful to his lord and to support him against all his enemies, and every year the eternal oath of fealty was renewed (just to play safe) along with a formal payment of tribute. Anyone who failed in his oath and tribute was brought to the palace and kept in dignified imprisonment there, for in theory no noble could be put to death, being himself a free agent.[30] Nobody else in the state was free, all others existing simply to serve and support the nobles. Workers were bound to the land and could not marry outside the estate on which they lived.[31] "The Hittite state was the creation of an exclusive caste superimposed on the indigenous population of the country."[32] We read of a king who punished a perjurer by taking his sword from his side and making him a farmer.[33] With intriguing princes all about, revolution was always just around the corner, and the king was actually the leader of an army of occupation. We are told that the first Hittite king, after subduing the whole land, sent his sons "each to every part of the land . . . and governed the land, and the great cities of the land were assigned to them."[34] The empire was a mesh of fortified cities, these cities actually being but permanent fortified camps to which the king would summon all his vassals to take the oath to him before setting out on the spring campaign.[35] Each city controlled the very active business and commercial life of the empire (for the Hittites were great businessmen) through its "city messengers," and special commissioners. The more important centers had in each a prince and a palace, the palace being both temple, fortress, and "a transmission and control center for the passage of wares."[36] So let us not imagine that there was anything "primitive" about the civilization of the Hittites: it was rich, sophisticated, mobile, restless, brutal, acquisitive, energetic, and military, in all of which the reader will scarcely need to be reminded of the Jaredites.

From various letters of the Hittites we learn that their great houses had extensive political, economic, and family ties with the lords of the Ahhiyawa to the west. It is pretty certain by now that these were none other than Homer's Achaeans. And so we are back to Chadwick: Since Homer furnishes the yardstick by which other heroic ages are measured, there is not much point in demonstrating that Homer's world is heroic. Yet since we are dealing with the beginning of things, it is not amiss to point out that in those passages of Homer which are admittedly most archaic we have to do with a world identical with the epic milieu of the earliest Egyptians and Sumerians. The Apollo of the opening scenes of the *Iliad* is not the shining youth of the classical tradition but a grim war lord of the steppes, who comes from the far northeast, the land of the Hyperboreans, sweeping like a storm wind across the plain in a shower of arrows—"and his coming was like the coming of night!" "Hear me, Silver-bow," cries his priest in supplication, "thou who travelest the rounds to Chryses [one of his many castles or shrines], and who rulest mightily in Killa and Tenedos, O Sminteus [another title]: if ever I drove peace offerings to thy shrine or burned fat roasts of mutton and beef at thy feasts, grant me now what I ask: make those Danaeans pay for my tears with your arrows!" For all the world this is the typical appeal of the Hittite or Hurrian vassal to his lord. And when Apollo responds, he crouches at a distance from the Greek camp like an Indian fighter and from his invisible position pours poisoned arrows into the camp, apparently from nowhere: he is a typical scourge of the plains. And so is father Zeus, *Nephelēgeritēs*, "the god of the *cumulo-nimbus*," who always moves with the thunder. The thunder is the sound of his chariot, and "all the higher divinities of the Greeks have a chariot and pair ascribed to them."[37] He comes as a conqueror and settles down as a tyrant: "You rule now," Prometheus reminds him through his haughty messenger, "and as new conquerors think to live at ease in your new castle. But have I not seen two such tyrants fall already? You can take it from me that number three who lords it now is not only the worst of the lot, but his rule is going to be the shortest."[38]

Aristotle says the tragic poets concentrated on the doings of a few great houses from the heroic age because their affairs were naturally tragic, were real history, handed down by tradition, no matter how freely the poets may have dealt with details.[39] The plays of Aeschylus show us the sordid and murderous clash of wills and ambitions in the great princely families after the conquest. The dreadful things that go on in the castle on the hill have always held excitement for the rest of us—they are the great stuff of literature. History is no less the child of the heroic age, and the writing of it down to our own times has been in the strictly heroic tradition, with "princes to act, and monarchs to behold the swelling scene!"

Next the friends spent an evening with Professor Sindh and heard about the prehistoric society of those Indo-Iranian invaders who followed their cousins into central Asia and spread abroad with great rapidity about 2000 B.C. The Yashts are the ancient books which describe their way of life as it was in the beginning: "The Yashts are saturated with the spirit of chivalry"; in them "we find ourselves in the Epic Age of the ancient Iranians."[40] There is the king at the head of his victorious migrating host, slaying the great snake and finding water. His royal successor is the "perfect Chief: whose face looks over all the seven Karshvares of the earth; who is swift amongst the swift, liberal amongst the liberal, strong amongst the strong, a chief of assembly amongst the chiefs of assemblies; increase-giving, fatness-giving, cattle-giving, sovranty-giving."[41] Like Mithra, he is "the King, Ruler, and Chief-inspector of the entire world."[42] He is "he of the ten thousand spies, the powerful, all-knowing, undeceivable god" who drives along in his high-wheeled chariot.[43] He was the chief herdsman and the chief hunter of the realm, and all who would not fight him must submit to him.[44] Yet his relatives, the great nobles, were always plotting to get the throne from him, even as Cyrus drew off the retainers of King Cyaxares who cried: "You are now great and glorious, thanks to my retainers! I would rather go down under the earth than be seen weak. . . . But you are on top now, and my own followers are in a position to control me."[45] Even so Mazda, the divine hero, "took from the Daevas both riches and welfare, both fatness and flocks, both weal and glory. Then Mithra seized that Glory . . . the second time when the Glory departed from Yim. . . . Then . . . Threatona seized that Glory . . . who killed the snake Srvara."[46] "From whom shall I take away, without his thinking of it, the awful sovereignty," cries Mithra, " . . . who fells down heads . . . who orders chastisement . . . and his order is done at once."[47] He is "the lord of the wide pastures . . . strong, sleepless, and ever awake; To whom the chiefs of the nations offer up sacrifices, as they go to the field, against the havocking host . . . with the fiend-smiting wind."[48] All his liege men are bound to him by awful oaths, and whoever breaks his oath loses his eyes and ears, and "Mithra sends the heads rolling of those who break fealty to him, and destroys their houses."[49] The Jaredite oath of fealty, it will be recalled, was by one's head. Yet if a king overlooked a threat to his honor or challenge to his power, such defaulting would be interpreted as a confession of weakness and would absolve his followers from their oaths to him while binding them to his adversary.[50] Therefore the king's business was to wage single combat with his enemies. But before attacking any enemy the king would send him a formal message inviting him to submit to Mazda and become his subject.[51] The Persian court, with the great throne in its center, was skilfully stage-managed and furnished the model of European courts and cathedrals.[52]

According to the Iranians, the very first man was also the first king, the killer of serpents, followed immediately by eight rulers bearing the title of *kavi*, and these, says Christensen, "were purely human figures whose deeds . . . have absolutely no mythical character."[53] "Those men . . . are kings of kingdoms," says the Yasht, "that are rich in horses, with large tributes, with snorting horses, sounding chariots, flashing swords, rich in aliments and in stores of food; . . . [they] have houses that stand well laid up, rich in cattle, . . . [they] have their ladies that . . . [wait] for them, . . . [they] have daughters, . . . thin in the waist, beautiful is their body, long are their fingers, . . . [and] hoards of silver and gold brought together from distant regions; and garments of splendid make."[54] In the castle "where whole herds of cattle and hosts of men are at home, there is high feasting and stout portions for everyone."[55] This chivalrous stock, the cultural and spiritual ancestors of the knighthood of Europe, went the usual way of "despotism tempered by dethronement and assassination."[56] These are just a few high points of the earliest Indo-European civilization, but they are enough to indicate that we have here no exception to the general rule of a genuine epic background.

It has recently been claimed that the very first waves of migrants into Egypt spoke Semitic languages, which have been spoken there without interruption to the present day.[57] The Ammorites, Canaanites, Phoenicians, Hebrews, Babylonians, and Assyrians were all Semitic speaking, and this has been taken to indicate a common homeland for all of them in the "Arab cradle." Scholars have long held the opinion that there are two main sources and centers of migration in the Old World, two areas from which, from time to time, waves of invaders move out in all directions to inundate the peripheral areas and revitalize the ancient sedentary civilizations of those areas with fresh blood. The two centers are Central Asia and the Arabian Desert. Significantly enough, Hrozny finds the key to the earliest of all world migrations to be the good Jaredite word *Kish*, whose distribution indicates to this great philologian the spreading of all civilization at one time from a single center, perhaps in west-central Asia, north or east of the Caspian, or what we have always called "Jaredite country."[58] Both regions are potential dust bowls supporting large seminomadic populations of herdsmen, hunters, and farmers. It does not take a violent cataclysm of nature to send these people forth in all directions in a desperate search for grass: Just a few abnormally dry years and the dispersion is on, snowballing as it goes and overrunning the richer and safer civilizations of the periphery. Abraham went to Egypt because he had to: "There was corn in Egypt," and the marginal subsistence for his flocks and herds had been wiped out.

Let us remember that Robert Wood first became aware

of the genuine heroic milieu behind the writings of Homer when he visited the Bedouins of the desert, who reminded him also of the patriarchs of Israel. Here we are in the cradle and source of heroic culture; this is the permanent epic milieu; these people are always on the march and always fighting; they are full-time heroes, experts and specialists in conquest, as their phenomenal record of victory shows.[59] It would be hard to say whether the Central Asiatics or the Arabs are best at the game; for our purpose the most interesting thing is that they represent the most essential element in the culture of the Jaredites and the Nephites, respectively.

The story of Rome begins, according to Livy, with the entrance on the scene of a band of migrants, led by the hero Aeneas, "looking for a place to settle down." At his first stop he expelled the natives and built a city, named after his wife. His grandsons Romulus and Remus lived by hunting, robbing, and cattle-raiding, and their suckling by a wolf was the result of their having been hidden in the woods to escape the plans of a great lord and relative who was determined to keep the rule in his branch of the family. They gathered about them a robber band, not a community of pious farmers, and after killing his brother, Romulus founded a city named after himself to become a shrine and center of dominion. All this, says Livy, was simply following the custom of other great cattle-driving heroes and rustlers—all of them bad men and adventurers.[60] Ancus Martius, the third king of Rome, captured the city of the Latins and transplanted "the entire Roman multitude to it," in the best Asiatic manner, turning their old lands back to grazing and agriculture. Exactly in the middle of his new city overlooking the forum, he built a grim castle, "a dungeon to discourage any rising insolence."[61] Forever after, Rome remains a world of jails, and the history of the kings is typically heroic and utterly full of abominations. Fighting was formally and chivalrously conducted, the winners driving off the cattle of the losers. Sometimes a great lord, accompanied by a huge army of retainers, would go over from one camp to another and be received with recognition of rank and a suitable grant of land.[62] When a people went back on their oath to Rome, their princes were beheaded, their walls torn down, and their fields sold.[63] The kings would distribute all the loot among their followers as a reward for their allegiance.[64] From the time of Sulla, according to Sallust, the great houses "all took to plundering each other, betrayals, coveting each other's houses and lands. . . . It is all a story of parricides, sacrilege, and what not"[65] as when, for example, a great lord could make his retainers drink blood in swearing to him awful oaths to participate in his crimes.[66] Coming down to the time of the empire we read how the emperor "shall hurl his spear beyond the stars, and his course shall lie beyond that of the rounds of the sun. . . . He shall impose peaceful ways, spare those who submit and make war on those who remain proud—that is the man!"[67] It might be the first pharaoh speaking!

5

Our Own People

Of all the epic cultures[1] the three friends considered in their long book-filled discussions, the most involved and interesting were those having to do with our own ancestors. True, their records do not go back to the third and fourth millennia B.C.; yet they are closely related in race and language to people whose records do go back that far; for example, the Hittites and Hurrians seem to be most closely related to the Celts, whose truly epic civilization and heroic literature Chadwick has examined at length.

That scholar, however, is interested in giving us only the evidence found in the Celtic writings; a thousand years earlier classical writers describe the same Celtic heroic culture in far more clear and objective terms. One needs only recall the once familiar pictures from Caesar's *Gallic Wars*: Here we find great nations on the move, princely messengers of great houses constantly coming and going with propositions and challenges; betrayals, plots, coalitions, and conjurations are the order of the day; vast masses of humanity with all their furniture and arms piled on lumbering wagons pour through the passes of the mountains and inundate the plains.

For the classical writers the Celts are the people who are constantly moving about in their painted wagons. In prehistoric times the Latin language borrowed from the Celts a vocabulary "drawn chiefly from the following semantic categories: *riding, driving,* . . . warfare, . . . clothing, . . ."and social hierarchy: common Roman words for serf, and our own word ambassador (German *Amt*: official office) are taken from the Celts.[2] It was strictly a heroic vocabulary. The greatest of all Celtic heroes, King Arthur, built up his body of knightly followers by gifts and grants, and "was so prodigal of his bounties . . . [that] he began to run short of things to distribute among the huge multitude of knights that came to him."[3]

At least a century before Arthur, a classical writer recounts an ancient tale of how one hero rode among all the tribes of Gaul scattering gifts with such lavish hand that people followed his wagon everywhere and elected him king of all the tribes.[4] Since generosity had to unite with prowess in war and noble blood to make kings, it is not surprising that the Celtic mythological cycles are full of horrible deeds of bloodshed and intrigues among the great houses. The most interesting thing about these cycles is the way each great house or nation is completely exterminated—with the exception of one survivor—by the next great house or nation, and so on. One of these lone survivors wandered through the world for fifty years, living on memories, as in a fever dream.[5] These wars of extermination were carried out with ritual formality.

Thus when the Tuatha De Danaan refused to halve all Ireland with the Fir Bolg, their hero formally challenged the strongest of the Fir Bolg to meet him in single combat, while the two armies met at Mag Tured and agreed to spend one hundred days preparing for battle. For the battle "it was agreed . . . that there should be no general engagement, but that an equal number of warriors should go out and fight every day!"[6] Among all the Celts we meet the story of the two brothers who fight a duel in which the winner becomes sole ruler of the land. The king-hero of the Celts is a curious mixture of cruelty and paternity.[7]

A good king would "do what the men of Byrgwin held best, . . . giving of food and drink to everyone who came," while a bad king "makes a progress 'round Ireland, demanding the wives and treasures of his hosts," who are honor bound to receive him since, like Arthur's knights, they have all taken mighty oaths to the king.[8] We have the picture from Joinville of St. Louis as king, going about from place to place in royal progress and sitting under the oak, at which time anyone could approach him as he righted wrongs and chastened the wicked.[9] As in other heroic societies, the queen was independent and had her own palace, which exactly paralleled the king's in all its appointments and arrangements.[10]

In numerous legends that tell how successive waves of invaders come to the islands, the invaders are always described as coming from the Great Plain to the East, the Land of the Living, and laying oppressive tribute on the inhabitants of the lands—the descendants of earlier invaders, demanding a tribute of everything including children, to be paid on the night of Samhain feast: two-thirds of all their produce had to be carried yearly to Mag Cetne, the great shrine at the exact center of the earth.[11] The king gave privilege of refuge (i.e., sanctuary) to the roads . . . leading to the cities and temples, and especially to the royal person, as in Persia.[12] In legend the royal establishment is described as a great and fabulous tower that has contact with the other world.[13] The great Merlin describes the taking over of the land in terms that might have been taken right out of the Pyramid Texts, when he tells how under "the favor of the Thunderer . . . the seats of the blessed shall . . . be renewed throughout the lands, . . . [and] shepherds shall be set in places befitting."[14]

It all seems to be right out of the Egyptian or Babylonian epics, and indeed scholars have long since and often pointed out the extremely close resemblances between the Celtic epic literature, especially the Grail saga, and the Babylonian and Egyptian legends and rituals.[15]

Who as a child has not stood between two mirrors and seen his image repeated with perfect accuracy but diminishing brightness into green and mysterious depths where "nothing is but what is not"? The eerie and disturbing quality of such an experience is the nearest thing to what one feels in reading the Germanic epics and the Norse sagas. Most sagas of the North must be interpreted on a number of different time levels at once. The minstrels of what the Germans call the "High" Middle Ages, themselves living in the completely heroic world of courts and camps, sang the deeds of Richard and Taillefer in romantic times gone by. But Taillefer had led the charge at Hastings as he "with a loud voice animated his countrymen with songs in praise of Charlemagne and Roland."[16] Charlemagne and Roland in turn, like the heroes of the saga time that followed them, had listened to the hero tales not of their own age but of a totally different age of migration 500 years earlier.

But the Germanic heroic tradition does not even begin with Attila and Ermanrich, for there is evidence of a still older Frankish heroic tradition, and a Gothic one before that, while the oldest of the Scandinavian sagas emphatically refers everything back to Troy![17] Every time our northern ancestors have found themselves living under heroic conditions of migration and world upheaval, they have revived an authentic heroic literature, but always they have taken as their subject not the deeds of their own age but some preceding migration-time. But the heroic songs of those earlier times went back to still other migrations, and so on. Hence the bedizening impression of duplication and repetition and the sense of being lost in a maze of time or a hall of mirrors.

Let us go back to the earliest of the old Norse texts, the prose Edda, and take a look at Othinn, the great prototype of the first kings.[18] He comes with the storm, especially in a terrible wind, and whatever his spear or rod is pointed at is instantly dedicated to destruction; he is the arch-*Einherja*—the great destroyer; he is the *Sig-fadhir,* ever-victorious, who having subdued the land builds his castle, Sigtun, the victory fort, where he can sit in a high tower on his high seat, the *Hlithskialf*, and through a special window survey all that goes on in the earth. At the slightest sign of disaffection his arrows dart forth to overcome the most distant opposition in an instant. His rule was won by force and is maintained by force, as Loki once reminded the gods when in their cups at a great feast he challenged the lot as usurpers and invaders.[19]

Othinn is in legend the Wild Huntsman, who leads the terrible host through the sky. The peasantry dread him as a warrior and a wanderer in the earth;[20] sometimes he comes traveling in disguise to spy out the land, coming in a great raincoat and floppy hat with a staff and a patch over his eye—for he has literally given his right eye for knowledge and power. As the god of runes he brings writing with him, and magic, and hidden knowledge, and autocratic rule.

"There is something eery and treacherous" about him, we are told, that suggests "the autocratic daring adventurer." The people do not love him: he is their father and their ruler, but just the same they dread him—"they are afraid of his intellectual superiority and aristocratic daring." No popular oath or prayer of the many that have survived is ever dedicated to him: The common people dread and avoid him.[21]

When Othinn enters the land as an invader, he finds Thor, Frey, and Njord already in occupation: They invaded earlier, and have now settled down to become homebodies and popular gods. But a closer examination has shown that originally they too all did exactly as Othinn is doing. Tyr, for example, goes back to an Indo-European expansion time at least a thousand years before Othinn's day. As Zio he is identical with Zeus as director of wars. His sign, like Othinn's, was the spear, and if Getic, Scythian and Gothic traditions meet anywhere, it is in the worship of his spear, which led the prehistoric migrants as the staff of Moses once led Israel.[22]

The fascinating and frightening figure of Othinn, that reminds us so strongly of the prehistoric kings of Egypt and Babylonia of whom we have said so much, is no invention of scaldic fancy, however. There actually were such men, and one of them was Attila the Hun, the hero of half the Germanic epics and the villain of the other half. For the Franks, Attila is the treacherous tyrant, "pure 'Asiatic,' " while "for the Bavarians and . . . Ostrogoths . . . he is the model of the benevolent protector."[23]

The earliest German epics go back to a time when Attila "collected the children of princes from the lands of all the lords and kept them as hostages at his court, from which they were always trying to escape."[24] This romantic theme was more than poets' fancy: the Roman ambassador Priscus who visited the court of Attila had a good deal to say about these hostages.

As to the sordid and bloody affairs between the princely houses, Schneider says, "There is nothing fictitious about this wickedness; it makes the thoroughly convincing impression of having been actually experienced. . . . The Asiatic tyranny is real." And another authority writes: "We believe that the actual experiences of the Heroic Age often enough found expression in the tragic view of life *(Weltbild)*. Much noble blood was shed, brave nations vanished without a trace after performing mighty deeds, the foundations of great empires collapsed, the noble had to perish and the base to triumph."

Even the fabulous story of Siegfried and Brunhilda, we are told, "could come right out of a typical Merovingian chronicle, in which the deadly hatreds among the royal ladies, the slaying of each other's vassals, treacherous ambushes on the hunts, and so forth, are so richly attested." It is not history, indeed, but it is "a snapshot of the real contemporary world of the Franks."[25] And way back in

Tacitus we still find it: the inherited feuds between the great houses, the riotous banquets, the fighting, gambling, and bloody vows.

Since the writer has read sagas at least once a week for thirty years, he is sorely tempted to exploit the vastness of this neglected field. But since with the progress of education the comic book has superseded all other books, we must be content to present the epic world of but one representative saga. It is the *Thithriks-saga af Bern,* a truly gigantic piece and "a great storehouse of Germanic legend, told in a new style imitated from French romance, but recording old tradition."[26] The great hero of this saga is not Theodoric the Goth, as we might expect, but Attila. And it is the real historical Attila. In the Thithriks-saga, Europe is described as an appendage of Asia—and that is exactly how Jordanes, a Goth who witnessed the events of the time, described it.[27]

Attila sets up his *stath,* or administration center, in Susam (Soest) and there receives a constant stream of embassies from the whole earth, while he sends his messengers abroad to proclaim and execute his will.[28] Priscus, who actually visited the court of Attila on the Steppes, describes it as a wood-and-tent city, dominated by the huge palisade and buildings of the central palace—all of wood.[29] Likewise our saga[30] tells us that the great castles of the time were all of wood. In the royal economy the amount of stuff that changes hands in the form of gifts is enormous: it is acquired on great raids—primarily cattle raids.[31] Attila is the soul of generosity, but he has his motives: "To win a man over to him he would give him clothing, weapons, and a horse."[32] "He took cattle and wealth away from his enemies and gave it to his friends"[33] is a formula that might have been taken right out of the Avesta.

In return his friends were bound to him by terrible oaths.[34] Before a knight could "ride," that is, go forth alone on an adventure, he had to receive royal permission after first explaining exactly where he was going and what he was going to do; and on return his first duty was to go immediately to the royal castle and report.[35] Gifts were proportionate to the value of services rendered, and could even include the classic bestowal of the hand of the king's daughter with half the kingdom as dowry.[36]

In the Thithriks-saga,[37] Attila's admirers admit quite frankly that it was his intention to conquer the world[38]; he cultivated the myth that no one could resist him,[39] and to paralyze all opposition practised a policy of deliberate *Schrecklichkeit*, as did his rivals.[40] When he decided on an expedition, he would summon all his followers and address them from a wooden tower, exactly as the Roman emperors and the Hittite kings used to do. The Book of Mormon students will think instantly of certain Jaredite and Nephite parallels.

The conquest was not fitful but planned and systematic, closely following the procedure attributed to Othinn in the prose Edda: in every newly occupied land a *stath* or administration center was set up, a castle built, and a trusted relative of the king, usually a son, left in charge. The saga makes it very clear that these heroes made no distinction at all between hunting and warfare; and when they were not doing the one or the other, they could be found refreshing themselves at their endless *veitzla*, the reciprocal banquets they would give for each other in their castles.[41] All the nobles of Europe and Asia were invited to Ermanrich's great *veitzla*, where he gave out gilt and purple robes, gold, rings, and treasures, exactly as an eyewitness tells us the Emperor Justinian did when he entertained the Hunnish chiefs while striving his best to adopt their customs.[42]

Of kings in general the saga tells us that they must be rich in cattle, good riders, and generous givers of wealth.[43] For this last a king must needs be acquisitive and shrewd *(afli oc hug)*.[44] The great chiefs themselves were skillful traders and businessmen—to that gift in no small degree they owed their power. The *torg* or market was under their special protection,[45] the horse fair being especially important;[46] and in the saga we see the caravans of merchants moving between Europe and Asia exactly as they had done in the earliest heroic ages.[47] The proper business of a king is to raid other kings' lands, take as many *borgir* (castles, strong places) as possible,[48] and return with lots and lots of cattle.[49] Brides were bought with cattle, as in Homer, and to refuse an offer of marrige was a fatal insult: "If you do not give Attila your daughter to wife," says his messenger to a great king, "he will do damage to your domains."[50]

When Osantrix became convinced that Attila was out to conquer the world, "he gathered together against him all the people of his realm, and no people could stand against them to whatsoever land they came."[51] As the two kings squared off for a war of extermination in the best Jaredite fashion, their affairs were regulated with great formality: the proper challenging letters were duly exchanged and the summoning of the two armies was carried out with ritual decorum.[52] When such armies met, each king would set up his *landtiold* or royal pavilion opposite the other and challenge his rival to a duel.[53]

These single combats between kings were common, and formal rules of chivalry were observed, such as "no striking under the shield." The heroes would fight all day long until evening, then retire to their tents for the night, and renew the contest next morning.[54] On one occasion the kings were so worked up that they went on fighting even after dark, and kept it up until both fainted from loss of blood.[55] The defeated king in such a combat was either beheaded by the victor or fell on his face before him, swearing awful oaths of submission.[56] A regular tribute of cattle was demanded by the victor.[57]

As in other heroic cultures, it is very important for a

noble "that all men may hear his name."[58] It must be spoken of in the great houses and be known at all the places where he stopped for the night, receiving hospitality from his own class, family, and order, with a proper formal exchange of credentials and identification.[59] The knight traveled with his coat of arms and badge of nobility on full display, so that it might be recognized by friend and foe at a distance.[60]

They wore Asiatic dress, the trousers and armor invented by the riders of the steppes.[61] The castles in the saga are most interesting: they are great wooden structures[62] used primarily as *gisting* places—overnight stations and military strong points.[63] The castle was a necessity in a world of robber bands, individual outlaws, and adventurers[64]; yet they as much as anything were responsible for the existence of such classes of people, for their primary purpose was to serve as headquarters for the exploitation of both farmers and merchants.[65]

In the Thithriks-saga the great houses, like the kings themselves, are always attempting to draw off each other's supporters.[66] The burning of each other's castles, as in Froissart, amounts almost to a formality.[67] To put a rival out of the running and yet spare his life by the expedient of mutilation was common,[68] as was the custom of rival lords keeping each other "in strong irons"[69] after having obtained control of the rival's person by some such neat device as a breach of hospitality.[70]

Occasionally some adventurer, having been dispossessed or too poor to own a castle,would seek out some wild region, some forest tract, where he would gather his followers for a series of raids to build up his power.[71] In battle and when gathering or rallying his forces the chief himself would carry his banner.[72] Every retainer swore not to return from the battle until the king did: The king must be by the rules of the game the last to die.[73] And by the same rules his proper opponent had to be a rival king whom, as we have seen, he would challenge to single combat.

The Thithriks-saga was first published in 1853. No English translation has appeared, and so far as we know, it has never been translated into any other language.

The Book of Ether as an Epic

"So now we come back to the Jaredites!" cried Blank one evening a year after the three friends had begun their discussions.

"It has been a most interesting trip," F. conceded, "but I wonder if it was really necessary to go so far. Twenty-two epics is quite a workout."

"I think it was necessary," Professor Schwulst said thoughtfully. "When we are dealing with nonmathematical subjects, it is hard to know at what point we can say a thing has been proved. The only way we can be sure is by *overproving* it."

"And there is more to it than that," Blank added. "Who, for example, authorized Chadwick or anyone else to decide just what things are to be taken as the true hallmarks of epic poetry? How do we know that his list is anything but his own idea? Only by reading the epics ourselves. Each one is an organic whole, and not to be broken down arbitrarily into *Leitmotivs*. Far more important than any statistical checking of recurrent themes is the impression each epic makes as a whole. And that impression can only be learned if you read each masterpiece from beginning to end."

"So it looks as if your most powerful tool for proving the book of Ether is one that nobody can use!" F. observed with a smile.

"Well almost nobody," Blank conceded. "But since we three have gone so far, may I suggest as our last undertaking that we read the book of Ether once more—not as an epic, for it has been divested of its epic form, but as a rich depository of epic materials?"

"What do you mean," said F., " 'divested of its epic form'?"

"Our editor, Moroni, admits the damage," Blank replied. "He says that the men of his day were conspicuously lacking in the peculiar literary gifts of those who wrote the original book of Ether: 'Behold, thou hast not made us mighty in writing like unto the brother of Jared,' he says, 'for thou madest him that the things which he wrote were mighty even as thou art, unto the overpowering of man to read them' (Ether 12:24). This applies not only to the case of two men, however, but also to the gifts of the two civilizations as a whole: 'Lord thou hast made us mighty in word by faith, but thou hast not made us mighty in writing; for thou hast made *all this people* that they could speak much; . . . and thou hast made us that we could write but little; . . . wherefore, when we write we behold our weakness, and stumble because of the placing of our words' " (Ether 12:23-25).

As Matthew Arnold has shown in his wonderful essay on the translation of Homer (the greatest work of literary criticism in the English language, according to Housman), the most remarkable thing about a true epic is the way in which it surpasses all other literature in power and directness, a peculiar force and impact that renders a real epic impossible to imitate or translate. Only a real epic milieu can produce it. All other writing is pale, devious, laborious, and ineffective by comparison. Moroni in editing Ether is keenly aware of his inability to do justice to the writing before him. It just can't be done, he says, and he is right. He plainly tells us that the original Ether is a type of composition unfamiliar to the Nephites, "who like ourselves obviously had no true epic literature."

"Why do you say 'true' epic?" F. asked.

"Because there have been so many false ones," Schwulst volunteered. "Let us remember that clever writers in every age have tried their best to produce epic poetry.

Since everybody always thought such poetry was simply the product of literary genius, no one could see any good reason why a literary genius of sufficient determination could not produce an epic. So Virgil, Dante, Camoens, Longfellow, Apollonius Rhodius, Tegner, Tennyson, and Milton, to name only a few, burned barrels of midnight oil in the production of what they fondly thought was true epic poetry. And you know the answer: No matter how great the poet or how noble his verse, the artificiality of his work is instantly apparent. There is something completely lacking in every case, but until our own generation nobody knew what it was. It is simply that real epics tell the truth. We can thank Milman Parry for showing us that 'a genuine epic can only be the product of a genuine epic milieu.' "

"In other words," Blank concluded, "epic literature cannot be faked."

"Perhaps with what is known today about the epic milieu a better job might be done. It shouldn't be too hard now, for the great 'literary' epics are not merely off the track in their epic details and off-pitch in the epic idiom; they are, every one of them, incredibly misinformed, crude, and clumsy—childishly so. They are often great poetry, but as faithful pictures of the worlds they mean to depict they are commonly misinformed. The best scholar of the would-be epic writers was Sir Walter Scott; yet who does not know today that his works are monuments of inaccuracy? The reason for this fatal defect in all their works is that none of these great men was aware of the fundamental difference between a real epic and every other type of writing. A real epic describes a real world, while they insisted on describing imaginary ones."

"Yet," said F., "the author of the Book of Mormon seems to have been aware of that difference—he must have been, to make Moroni say the things he did."

"And since Moroni has taken the liberty to change the

language and form of the Jaredite record," Schwulst added, "I am afraid our source can no longer be read as an epic."

"It must have been tremendous," said Blank with a sigh, " 'unto the overpowering of man' to read it. And all we have now is Moroni's brief summary, made from a translation and interlarded with his own notes and comments. That means that all that is left to us is the gist of the epic material."

"Still that should be enough for a thorough testing," said Professor Schwulst. "There are forty pages of it, and some of them are amazingly compact. So let us now go back again to Chadwick's list, and this time see how it fits the book of Ether."

"An excellent idea,"[74] said Blank, taking his briefcase as he had done on the night of his first meeting with F. "Let us begin at the beginning."

"Ether starts out on the keynote of all epics, the two factors which according to Kramer are 'primarily responsible for the more characteristic features of the . . . Heroic Ages,' namely, the scattering and wandering of the peoples and the disintegration of world civilization.[75] And here we have it: 'Jared came forth with his brother . . . at the time the Lord . . . swore in his wrath that they should be scattered upon all the face of the earth; and . . . the people were scattered' (Ether 1:33). They went forth with their flocks and herds, friends, and families (Ether 1:41), all alike torn up by the roots and driven out of the land (Ether 1:38), but still hoping, like every heroic people, to become 'a great nation' and equal or surpass all others" (Ether 1:43).

"Philip de Comines gives us an interesting commentary on that last point," F. interrupted, "when he tells us that by the laws of chivalry it is the solemn duty of every nation and monarch to become greater than all others—a rule which makes war the natural state of things. A state of chronic warfare was thus the heritage of the Middle Ages from the times of migration."[76]

"Strictly in keeping with the epic tradition," Blank continued, "the history of the Jaredites is presented in the form of a royal genealogy; the book of Ether is in fact simply a running commentary on a genealogy, with Moroni doing most of the commenting. The story opens with a long list of royal names, and all that follows is a continuation and expansion of that list. In dealing with its heroes, many of whom are 'oversized' figures either for good or for evil in the best heroic manner, the book of Ether scrupulously observes the rule that in the true epic 'there is no character who appears uniformly in an unfavorable light.' Who was the worst of the Jaredites—Akish? Riplakish? Coriantumr? Shiz? No matter which one you pick you will find yourself as much inclined to pity as to hate him; nor can you deny a grudging admiration for the ferocious and abandoned heroism of these terrible warriors who, though they know they are doomed, continue, like Milton's Lucifer, to shout defiance and pursue one another with fierce and unrelenting energy to the end."

The behavior of the heroes in the epics is "often childish and brutal," as we have seen, and even the noblest of them is not beneath gaining an advantage by some underhanded trick. The career of Akish in the eighth to tenth chapters of Ether is a perfect illustration of this, although others are just as bad. On the other hand, in true epic "a dignified and fastidious tone" prevails in the dealings of these men with each other, and strict rules of chivalry are observed, especially in war and duels. So we are told in Ether how Shiz and Coriantumr pitch formal camps and "invite" each other's armies forth to combat by regulated trumpet blasts (Ether 14:28), exchange letters in an attempt to avoid needless bloodshed (Ether 15:4-5, 18), and rest at night without attempting to attack each other, fighting only at the proper and agreed times (Ether 15:8, 21-26). As in all epics, including Ether, "the waging of war is not incidental but essential to the heroic way of life." A great chief gains "power over all the land" only after he has "gained power over many cities," and "burned many cities," (Ether 14:17) in the best Homeric fashion.

Again, as in all true epics, every scene in the book of Ether takes place either on the battlefield (as in chapters 13 to 15), in the court (as in the tales of intrigue in chapters 7 to 12), or in the wilderness, where hunting and hiding play almost as conspicuous a part as fighting (Ether 2:6-7; 3:3; 14:4, 7; 10:21). Fighting takes the proper heroic form of the single combat between heroes, with the personal feud as its motive, the contest being conducted by the established rules of chivalry. This is well illustrated in the career of Coriantumr, who was wounded in a single combat with his rival Shared, whom he dispatched (Ether 13:27-31); then he fought hand to hand with Gilead (Ether 14:3-8), and next with Lib (Ether 14:12-16). Finally he met his bitterest rival, Shiz, in a number of face-to-face combats (Ether 14:30; 15:30). Since in heroic ages one becomes a leader by proving his prowess in open competition, personal rivalry and ambition are the ordinary and accepted motives for war and need no excuse. Throughout our Jaredite history the perennial source of strife and bloodshed is the purely personal rivalry between great leaders, and so it is in all epic literature.

Jaredite society, like every other heroic society, is a feudal organization bound together by an elaborate system of oaths. This is indispensable to the survival of the society in which the followers of a chief are a free ranging, mounted nobility, always on the loose and free to serve anyone they choose. The oath is the only possible control over such men. We are clearly told in the book of Ether that the terrible oaths and conjurations behind every ambitious project for power and gain were imported directly from the Old World (Ether 8:9, 15-18, 22-26; 9:5, 26-27; 10:33; 11:7, 15, 22; 14:8). At the same time, loyalty must be bought with a price. To attract and hold followers every great lord must be generous with his gifts and promises. In Ether loyalty is bought by "cunning words" (Ether 8:2) and by gifts (Ether 9:10-11; 10:10). By such means in heroic societies great chiefs attempt to "draw off" each other's supporters. This is a commonplace in the book of Ether (Ether 7:14, 15; 9:11; 10:32). Gangs were quickly formed and dissolved, and each regarded itself as an independent society whose own aggrandizement was the only law, "every man with his band fighting for that which he desired." (Ether 13:25). Even an unpopular prophet could seek and find personal safety under the protection of a great chief (Ether 11:2), and an unpopular leader could be liquidated by an uprising, no matter what his claim to the throne, "and his descendants . . . driven out of the land" (Ether 10:8).

To defray the expense of lavish and necessary gift-giving, the lords of all heroic ages engage in a systematic and perfectly honorable business of plunder and exaction. It is their prerogative to try to grab whatever does not belong to them already, and that includes the seizure and holding of one another's persons for ransom. The Jaredite brothers, Shez and Riplakish, show us this free competitive economy in action: Shez was well on the way to taking the kingdom away from his father, thanks to his "exceeding riches," when those same riches got him killed by a robber (Ether 10:2-3). Riplakish paid for his royal magnificence by oppressive taxation and extortion, which resulted in getting him, too, assassinated (Ether 10:5-8). Everyone grabbed what he could, and nothing was safe (Ether 14:1), with every strong man leading his own gang to plunder. (Ether 13:25-26.) As to the retaining of each other's persons in honorable captivity, nothing is more characteristic of heroic ages or more familiar to the readers of Ether (Ether 7:7; 8:3-4; 10:4, 15, 30-31; 11:9, 18-19, 23).

The feudal contract on which every heroic society is based is before all else a mutual obligation of fief and overlord to avenge wrongs done to the other. The book of Ether is full of this. The sons of Omer, for example, "were exceedingly angry" against Jared for stealing their father's throne, and "did raise an army" and forced him to give it back again (Ether 8:2-6). In the same way "the sons of Coriantumr . . . did beat Shared, and did obtain the kingdom again unto their father" (Ether 13:24), in whose interest they "fought much and bled much" (Ether 13:19). But this same Coriantumr had to reckon with equal devotion when it was directed against himself at a time when the brother of Lib "had sworn to avenge himself . . . of the blood of his brother" (Ether 14:24), whom Coriantumr had killed in single combat during a battle (Ether 14:16). Blood vengeance is obviously the rule in this as in other heroic societies, where it touches off those long tragic feuds that make up so much of the epic literature, especially of the "saga period." The fights in Ether are nearly all family feuds, sordid quarrels between warring kings, ambitious sons, and avenging brothers (Ether 8:2-6, 9-12; 7:4, 13-16; 12; 10:3-4; 11:4), though typically Asiatic complications must have been introduced by polygamy, an institution reported quite casually by Ether (Ether 14:2) and thoroughly typical of the early heroic periods. The worst plot of all in Ether is engineered by a woman, who employs as her "do-it-yourself" guide to the art of murder certain books of the ancients brought over from the Old World (Ether 8:9-10). As we have seen, nothing is more typical of the post-heroic saga times of settling down after the migrations than these terrible women and their criminal ambitions—the Greek tragedies like the Norse sagas are full of them, and they are not lacking in any heroic literature.[77] When Chadwick describes a typical epic cycle as "little more than a catalogue of the crimes committed by one member [of the ruling family] against another," and further describes those crimes as particularly horrible in nature, we need not apologize for the book of Ether, either for neglecting or overdoing that sort of thing.

Relatively early in Jaredite history a war of extermination took place, leaving only thirty survivors "and they who fled with the house of Omer" (Ether 9:12). A general war of all against all in the Asiatic manner nearly wiped out the race again "in the days of Shiblom" (Ether 11:7), and "utter destruction" was promised by the prophets unless the people changed their ways (Ether 11:20). Finally, in the last great war, the destruction was systematic and thorough, the people laboring under what the Greeks called the spell of Ate, as if they were determined, no matter what happened, to accomplish their own annihilation (Ether 14:19-25). The whole population was cut down to fifty-nine souls (Ether 15:25), and these slew each other in the best heroic fashion, leaving the two kings as the last survivors. This is not a fantastic coincidence at all. We have seen that the common and established rule of heroic warfare *demanded* that the king be the last survivor in any conflict. Since the entire host had taken a solemn oath to die in defense of his person, in theory the king had to be the last to go, and in practice he sometimes actually was. The only way to get around that sometimes inconvenient rule was by another rule which dissolved the nation automatically on the death of the king, as if all had been destroyed with him. In such cases all the former subjects of a king would automatically become the subjects of his conqueror.[78]

"But there is one thing that puzzles me," said F. when the friends were together for the last time. "Where is the archaeological record for all this?"

"I am glad you asked that," Blank replied. "People are prone to expect any civilization described in the records as great and mighty to leave behind majestic ruins. The mighty piles of Egypt and Babylon have fooled us into thinking that the greatness or even the existence of a civilization is to be judged by its physical remains. Nothing could be further from the truth. The greatness of a civilization consists in its institutions, and as Professor Coon has recently observed, 'institutions leave no easily detected archaeological remains.'[79] This has led even the experts to overlook the importance and sometimes the existence of heroic or epic worlds."

"Or rather," Professor Schwulst amended, "it led them for many years to assume that there was no alternative in early history between complete savagery or sedentary life in farms and cities. Actually the ancients were committed to neither type of life. But because farmers and city-dwellers leave remains behind them while the nomads do not, they have always received the credit for coming first. As Professor Childe observes here: 'The nature of the archaeological record is liable to favor [this] view unduly; herdsmen living in tents and using bone tools and leather vessels' leave few remains behind them, and so wherever the remains of the first civilization turn up it is a hundred-to-one chance that they will have been left by townspeople or cultivators, who thus get all the credit for founding civilization.'[80] Actually a little reflection will show that they cannot have come first, and today scholars are agreed in describing the first civilizations in heroic terms rather than agricultural ones. Nilsson warns his fellow archaeologists that they are wasting their time looking for remains from the genuinely heroic—that is, the migration time, of the Greeks: 'No archaeological record is preserved,' he says. '. . . Some archaeologists have tried to find the ceramics of the invading Greeks. I greatly fear that even this hope is liable to be disappointed, for migrating and nomadic tribes do not use vessels of a material which is likely to be broken, as will be proved by a survey of the vessels used by modern nomadic tribes.' This was a period of great importance and activity, and of a really high civilization, yet it has left us no remains at all."

"Isn't that rather unusual?" F. asked.

"On the contrary," Schwulst replied, "it is the rule

when we are dealing with heroic ages and peoples. Like the early farmers, such people, even though their culture and their practices may be very ancient, 'rarely remaining long enough at one site to produce a mound.' "[81]

"Perhaps the greatest[82] and certainly one of the longest of all heroic cultures was that of the East Iranians," F. continued, "yet, though those people 'had already learned to dwell in fixed habitations' (the Avesta has a great deal to say about their magnificent castles), archaeology has not yet brought to light a single edifice built at this early period.[83] One might list a hundred great and mighty nations of old, the reality of whose existence and whose deeds there cannot be the slightest doubt, since literary and historical evidence for them is abundant, yet of whose deeds and buildings not the slightest physical trace remains.

"Of course heroic peoples built much, as all their records tell us they did, but the trouble is that none of the stuff can be identified. The situation is thus stated by Chadwick: 'Archaeological evidence is abundant, though not as a rule entirely satisfactory. Great numbers of raths or earthen fortresses, usually more or less circular, still exist, and very many of them are mentioned in the stories of the heroic age.'[84] The problem is to identify them. Nowhere have these mounds and barrows been more exhaustively studied through the years than in England; yet the diggers still cannot agree on whether a given mound is Celtic, Roman, Norman, Stone-Age, Saxon, Danish, or even late Middle Ages. They have been guessing for hundreds of years, and the game still goes on."[85]

"May I be allowed to point out," Blank interposed, "that 'earthen fortresses, more or less circular' are exactly what used to be found in great abundance all over the eastern United States; and there again it is the same story: a given mound might be almost anything, and every possible age and date has been attributed to some of them, from pre-human to Spanish. It may well be that Jaredite remains still exist: the problem is, as with all heroic remains, to identify them."

"That is what Chadwick says here," Schwulst volunteered, " 'Archaeological evidence can demonstrate the existence of the conditions required by a heroic story at a given place and time, though it can supply no names, unless writing is found,'[86] – and unless, we might add, that writing can be read. Without that, all we can hope for is a general indication of the type of thing indicated – nothing specific. The classic illustration of that is, of course, Schliemann's discovery of Troy. Today every schoolboy knows that the city which Schliemann identified as Homer's Troy was not Homer's Troy; what is not often realized is that *no* city in the mound of Hissarlik has been identified as Troy, and that to this day the ruins of Hissarlik are still properly referred to by archaeologists as 'the presumed site of Troy.'[87] Yet Homer has described the city of Troy at far greater length and in far more detail than the Book of Mormon describes *any* city. In view of that, can we hope for any better luck in America?

"The main trouble seems to be that these people did not build of stone. In all the epics we have mentioned, the great castles are specifically or indirectly shown to have been built of wood. Even the few stone edifices which have survived, such as the first royal tombs of Egypt, display, as Ricke notes, the nomadic nature of their builders, every detail of their construction being in careful imitation of the wooden beams and boards and the matting walls and hangings of the original models. This is equally true of the palaces, as well as the tombs of heroic royalty, whether in Egypt, Persia, or Babylon: they are all faithful reproductions of wood and cloth originals.[88] Again, the few surviving temples of Greece are naturally of stone, yet they still preserve in marble all the meticulous details of the boards, logs, pegs, and joinings of the normal Greek temple, which was of wood.[89] But for a few monumental exceptions, the ancients (save in the Near East) seem almost never to have built of stone; but since those exceptions were the only buildings to survive, they have given the world the impression that the ancients never built of anything *but* stone! Pliny, like St. Jerome, even claims that it is immoral to build of stone, and certainly before his day there was very little stone building in Rome.[90]

"Of course, where there is no wood, that is another problem. In the Near East we know from many sources that the timber shortage was acute in early times: there they had to build of stone.[91] But consider Europe in contrast. Scandinavian bogs have brought forth an abundance of articles in metal, leather, wool, and wood that show the presence of a high, even brilliant, civilization, while the records tell of most wonderful cities and castles, such as the fabulous Jomsborg; yet no traces of those castles and cities have been found save earthen mounds and embankments. The Welsh tales are full of mighty castles, yet long and careful search failed to reveal a single stone ruin older than the time of the invader Edward I, who brought the fashion of stone castles to Britain from the Near East, where he had been crusading.

"An official account of Roman castles from the time of Justinian enumerates five hundred imperial strongholds, and yet, while the stone temples and amphitheatres built at the same time and the same places still survive, not a scrap of one of those castles has ever been found.[92] The explanation is obvious: until the end of the Middle Ages, stone building was almost entirely unknown in Europe. An ambassador of that same Justinian to the court of Attila describes the great imperial city and huge castle of that mighty conqueror as being all of wood."[93]

"But surely there were some great heroic structures of stone!" cried F. "Think of Troy and Mycenae!"

"The mighty Cyclopean works of the Mycenaean and Hittite fortress-palace complexes are the exception that proves the rule," Schwulst replied, "for Cyclopaean masonry is decidedly not a style of construction employed by people long accustomed to working in stone. It is a skillful shift, an intelligent step in the adoption of a new medium, or else, as has recently been suggested, a deliberate attempt to build in the 'megalithic' style, keeping the stones deliberately irregular. But this style is exceedingly laborious, awkward, and expensive, and is never long continued. It never becomes a style."[94]

"Isn't it rather strange that wandering nomads should build cities at all?" F. asked.

"Not if they are engaged in the kind of nomadism we have been describing in these discussions. Actually the strange thing is that the building of cities should never have been attributed to farmers, who neither need nor like them, as the case of many a peasant civilization will show. Cities are primarily administrative and commercial centers, bases of operation for wide-ranging rulers, soldiers, and merchants, rather than market places for truck gardeners. There is a general and growing awareness among students today that ancient cities did not evolve from farming villages as was once thought to be the invariable rule. The names of ancient cities are in themselves evidence enough of their founding by great individuals: They are almost always the names of persons—human or divine.[95]

"From prehistoric Egypt and Mesopotamia to the remotest regions of the North and the farthest stretches of Asia it is the same story: The great conquerors are the great city-builders, and the cities last no longer than their empires. Indeed there is a great deal of evidence for the custom of requiring each king to inaugurate his reign with the building of a *new* capital—a system which adds greatly to the complexity of early Egyptian history.

"There are a few perennial centers, such as Babylon, Thebes, and Rome, but where are the others? In the center of every great epic cycle there looms one great supercenter, with its fabulous castle and its many-gated city—Camelot, Tara, Susat, Troy, Sigtun, Heliopolis, Liere, Assur, etc.; yet after generations of searching, none of these mighty centers has ever been located with certainty. We have already mentioned Troy, but no less persistent has been the search for On or Heliopolis in Egypt. The earliest written records constantly refer to Heliopolis as the religious and political center of everything through long centuries; yet generations of the most exhaustive searching failed so completely to turn up so much as a single button or bead to show where Heliopolis had stood that until the very recent discovery of a predynastic cemetery on the spot, some of the foremost investigators, such as Miss Baumgartel, insisted with fervor and conviction that there *never had been* such a place, though the written documents are full of it! I could give you scores of other examples just like that."[96]

"Wouldn't you say," asked Blank, "that the most significant thing about the Jaredite cities is not that they were great, many, or mighty, but that they were built up all at once, instead of gradually evolving? Here, for example, we read that Coriantumr 'did build many mighty cities,' (Ether 9:23) and later Shez 'did build up many cities upon the face of the land' as the people moved out and 'began again to spread over all the face of the land' (Ether 10:4). Morianton, a descendant of Shez, not only gained power over many cities (Ether 10:9), but he also 'built up many cities' (Ether 10:12) in restoring land after a total collapse and revival; just so, after a great slump and revival, the people under King Lib 'built a great city by the narrow neck of land' (Ether 10:20), just as we have seen that the first Pharaoh did upon establishing a new order in Egypt. Also we find that cities could vanish as quickly as they arose, as when Shiz 'did overthrow many cities . . . and he did burn the cities' (Ether 14:17). Now granted that there may be cities on the earth which have grown up on the evolutionary pattern of hut-to-hamlet-to-village-to-town, and so forth, it must be admitted that our book of Ether cities were not of that kind. They are definitely of the 'heroic' variety, which are now known to have arisen and perished all over the ancient world, but which leave only a very drab and undramatic type of ruins if they leave any at all."

"Professor Nilsson has given us a good description of the type of thing that went on," Dr. Schwulst observed as he sought out a passage:

> For the great expeditions through which the Greeks founded colonies far away and went so far eastwards cannot have been disconnected raids of small roving bands but must needs have been backed by some power, even if it was a loose feudal organization. The seat of this power was Mycenae, at least in the beginning of the Late Mycenaen age, when a great building activity set in and a large palace, the great ring wall with the Lion Gate, the Grave Circle, and the stateliest of the tholos tombs were erected.[97]

"There you have it: the invaders spread into new lands and take them over, but they do it systematically, their movements being controlled and directed from a main center, where a magnificent complex of headquarters buildings, so to speak, is erected. This is what we have found everywhere in our discussions."

"But is it safe to generalize about the ancient world as a whole?" F. asked somewhat dubiously.

"It is the thing that all the leading men are doing today," Schwulst retorted, "and they seem to know what they are about. The best over-all picture to date is that which is at present being presented by Claude Schaeffer, the eminent excavator of Ras Shamra-Ugarit, that ancient center at which all the cultural and ethnic lines of the ancient East came together. Schaeffer carefully compared and correlated the archaeological findings at all the main centers of ancient civilization, from Asia Minor to the heart of Asia (as far as available materials would allow), and came up with most significant and consistent pictures. Six times between 2400 and 1200 B.C., he discovers, all the principal centers of the ancient world were destroyed, and each time they all went up in flames and down in earthquake ruins *together*! Earthquake, famine, plague, and weather were to blame for this series of world-wide catastrophes, according to Schaeffer, who puts most of the blame on earthquakes. After each of these major world-collapses, we find a sharp diminution in population, while people everywhere revert to a nomadic way of life and great invading hordes of mixed racial and linguistic stocks sweep down from the more sorely afflicted areas to the more fortunate ones—the terror they bring with them being actually less than that which they are leaving behind. Of the first of these calamity-driven waves of humanity Schaeffer writes: 'Perhaps the vast movement of peoples which accompanied it was led by a warlike element which, thanks to the superiority of its arms and its physical vigor, was able in spite of numerical inferiority to extend its conquests over vast areas of Western Asia.' "[98]

"In other words," said Blank, "Schaeffer, using purely *non*literary evidence, begins his history with a typical heroic migration, exactly as Kramer does using 'purely literary evidence' while deliberately avoiding the archaeological remains."

"—and exactly as Hrozny does using neither archaeological nor literary evidence, but purely linguistic indications!" F. added.

"It is remarkable how all the types of evidence are beginning to fuse into a single image of the past," Dr. Schwulst observed, "and such a different image from what it used to be! Instead of a long and gradual upward evolution we find repeated regressions as well as advances, and there is no guarantee at all that the regressions even in the aggregate are less considerable than the advances! Those setbacks, as Schaeffer is at great pains to point out, are the result of forces totally beyond human control. 'Compared with the scope of these general crises, . . .' he says, 'the exploits of the conqueror and the combinations of leaders of states appear quite unimportant. The philosophy of history where it concerns the Ancient East seems to us to have been singularly distorted by the too convenient adoption of dynastic patterns, however convenient they may be for chronological classification.'[99] In other words, it is not man who makes ancient history; yet even in strictly human affairs there now appear to be curious ups and downs, with regression quite as normal a part of the picture as progression. Take the case of iron, for instance. Here Schaeffer writes:

> A most curious and intriguing phenomenon would seem to be the disappearance of this metal after its first utilization at the end of the Old Bronze period, and its apparently total eclipse during the entire Middle Bronze. It seems to have been rediscovered anew in the course of the Late Bronze period and, to judge by all the evidence, in the very same region—in Asia Minor.[100]

Here we have an important step in human history that has to happen all over again!"

"And when you have that," said F., "how do you know that it has not happened and unhappened already dozens of times before?"

"You don't," answered Schwulst. "You must not suppose, for example, that the first of Schaeffer's great world calamities with its accompanying heroic migrations was the first occurrence of such an event. Long ago the philologists were able to trace with certainty migrations of people for which there is not the slightest archaeological evidence,[101] and these carry the pattern back and back to the earliest migration of all when, according to the dean of all living philologians, the forefathers of all the languages and cultures of the world scattered in all directions from a single point searching desperately after grass for their cattle."

"We can sum it all up, then," said Blank, "with the safe and conservative observation, that whatever the particulars may be, it is certain that we now have a totally new setting in which to study the book of Ether, a background of whose existence nobody thirty years ago would have dreamed; and the history of the Jaredites fits into that background as if it were made for it. Who can claim that this is merely a happy accident? Consider the new materials, the scope, and detail of the epic sources, now being read with a new understanding and a new sense of reality; place them beside the compact and powerful history of Ether, presenting all the salient features of heroic times of migration and the ages of feuding that follow, omitting nothing vital and including nothing conflicting or trivial—you will at once recognize that there is small room here for luck or chance. Men once denied categorically that Atreus or Arthur or Mopsus or even Moses ever lived, but now we know they were wrong: there was an Achaean host just as surely as there was a Hebrew host of the Exodus,[102] and the very tests that prove it to be so can now be applied fully and rigorously to show that there were Jaredites."

Notes

Chapter 1: The Heroic Age

1. Part 1 of "There Were Jaredites," *IE* 59 (January 1956): 30-32, 58-61, began at this point.

2. H. L. Lorimer, "Homer and the Art of Writing: A Sketch of Opinion between 1713 and 1939," *AJA* 52 (1948): 12-13.

3. Ibid., 14-15.

4. Thomas Percy, *Reliques of Ancient English Poetry*, 3 vols., ed. Henry Wheatley (London: Allen & Unwin, 1885), 1:350.

5. Hermann Schneider, *Germanische Heldensage*, 2 vols. (Berlin: De Gruyter, 19 28-33), 1:14, 3-4.

6. H. Winckler, in Eberhard Schrader, *Die Keilinschriften und das Alte Testament*, 3rd ed. (Berlin: Reuther & Reichard, 1903), 4.

7. A. B. Lord, "Homer, Parry, and Huso," *AJA* 52 (1948): 39.

8. Samuel N. Kramer, "New Light on the Early History of the Ancient Near East, " *AJA* 52 (1948): 157.

9. Ibid.

10. Ibid., 159.

11. Ibid., 157.

12. Ibid., 158.

13. See H. Munro Chadwick, *The Growth of Literature*, 3 vols. (Cambridge: Cambridge University Press, 1932-40), vol. 1 for an extensive discussion of the Heroic Age.

14. Kramer, "New Light on the Early History of the Ancient Near East," 159.

15. Part 2 of "There Were Jaredites," *IE* 59 (February 1956): 88-89, 106, 108, began at this point.

16. Chadwick, *Growth of Literature*, 1:94.

17. Kramer, "New Light on the Early History of the Ancient Near East," 158-59.

18. E. V. Gordon, *An Introduction to Old Norse* (Oxford: Clarendon, 1927), xxx i.

19. Chadwick, *Growth of Literature*, 1:64.

20. Ibid., 1:82.

21. Ibid., 1:80-95; ch. 5.

22. Carleton S. Coon, *The Story of Man* (New York: Knopf, 1954), 6.

23. Chadwick, *Growth of Literature*, 1:82.

24. Ibid., 1:77.

25. Ibid., 1:78.

26. Ibid., 1:87.
27. Ibid., 1:95.
28. Ibid., 1:79.
29. Ibid., 1:95.
30. Ibid., 1:77, 88.
31. Ibid., 1:74.
32. Ibid.
33. Ibid., 1:95, 92.
34. Ibid., 1:95, 92-94.
35. Ibid., 1:184.
36. Ibid., 1:90-91.
37. Ibid., 1:185.
38. Ibid., 1:106.

Chapter 2: Egypt Revisited

1. "II Egypt Revisited," *IE* 59 (March 1956): 150-52, 185-87, began at this point.

2. Hermann Kees, *Aegypten* (Munich: Beck, 1933), 18-19.

3. T. Eric Peet, "Notices of Recent Publications," *JEA* 10 (1924): 67.

4. Siegfried Schott, *Mythe und Mythenbildung im alten Ägypten* (Leipzig: Hinrich, 1945; reprinted Hildesheim: Olm, 1964), 10-11.

5. V. Gordon Childe, *New Light on the Most Ancient East* (New York: Praeger, 1953), 42-43: "Pottery vessels . . . exhibit a perfection of technique never excelled in the Nile valley."

6. Elise J. Baumgartel, *The Cultures of Prehistoric Egypt,* 2 vols. (London: Oxford University Press, 1947, 1960), 1:23.

7. Kees, *Aegypten,* 19.

8. John Waechter, "The Beginning of Civilization in the Middle East," *PEFQ* 85 (1953): 129, 131.

9. Prof. Schwulst is recalling a good general survey of the whole picture given by Stuart Piggott, *Prehistoric India* (London: Cassell, 1962).

10. For the latest treatment of primitive specialization, see the first five chapters of Carleton S. Coon, *The Story of Man* (New York: Knopf, 1954).

11. Herbert Ricke, "Bermerkungen zur ägyptischen Baukunst des alten Reichs I," Heft 4 of *Beiträge zur ägyptischen Bauforschung und Altertumskunde* (Zürich: Borchardt Institute für Ägyptische Bauforschung und Altertumskunde in Kairo, 1944) , 25-27, 36-38, 109-10.

12. Eberhard Otto, "Ein Beitrag zur Deutung der ägyptischen Vor- und Frühgeschichte," *Die Welt des Orients* 1 (1952): 431-53.

13. Ibid., 452.

14. What Blank (Nibley) had written was that the "widely-ranging tribes of the steppes . . . coerce the unwillg tillers of the soil to cooperate

in bringing forth the great state." Hugh W. Nibley, "The Arrow, the Hunter, and the State," *WPQ* 2 (1949): 328.

15. Childe, *New Light on the Most Ancient East,* 78.

16. Kees, *Aegypten,* 18.

17. Ibid., 18-19, 8-9, 31, 34, 43.

18. Ibid., 22, and Alan H. Gardiner, *Egyptian Grammar* (Oxford: Oxford University Press, 1950), 204: "An event which occurred biennially was the census of the cattle, and this became the standard event by which the years were dated."

19. Samuel A. B. Mercer, *The Pyramid Texts in Translation and Commentary,* 4 vols. (New York: Longmans, Green, 1952), 1:vii. Kurt H. Sethe, *Die Altaegyptischen Pyramidentexte,* 4 vols. (Leipzig: Hinrich, 1908-22); and Kurt H. Sethe, *Übersetzung und Kommentar zu den altägyptischen Pyramidentexten,* 4 vols. (Glueckstadt: Augustin, 1935-39).

20. Thus King Merekere speaks of the Asiatics: "I carried captive their inhabitants, I plundered their cattle," Alan H. Gardiner, "New Literary Works from Ancient Egypt," *JEA* 1 (1914): 31.

21. See the discussion by Alexandre Moret, *Histoire de l'Orient,* 2 vols. (Paris: Presses Universitaires, 1929-36), 1:95-96.

22. Baumgartel, *Cultures of Prehistoric Egypt* 1:3-18; quote from 3.

23. A. Wiedemann, *Das alte Ägypten* (Heidelberg: Winter, 1920), 235.

24. Carl Fries, *Studien zur Odyssee I. Das Zagmukfest auf Scheria* (Leipzig: Hinrich, 1910).

25. Raymond O. Faulkner, "The 'Cannibal Hymn' from the Pyramid Texts," *JEA* 10 (1924): 102. Sethe's number is Pyr. 393a-414c.

26. Faulkner is in doubt about the passage, which Mercer renders: "N. is the bull of heaven, who (once) suffered want and decided (lit. gave his heart) to live on the being of every god," Mercer, *The Pyramid Texts in Translation and Commentary,* 1:93 (Pyr. 397a).

27. Ibid., Pyr. 401a, 402a.

28. Ibid., Pyr. 306c-307c.

29. Ibid., Pyr. 940b-c.

30. Ibid., Pyr. 943a-c.

31. Rudolf Anthes, "The Original Meaning of Ma^{c} Hrw," *JNES* 13 (1954): 21-51.

32. Mercer, *The Pyramid Texts in Translation and Commentary,* Pyr. 388a-c.

33. E. A. Wallis Budge, *The Book of the Dead: The Papyrus of Ani,* 2 vols. (New York: Putnam, 1913), 1:185-87; 2:495-97.

34. Ibid., 1:185-86: "A great number of goddesses of the same name were developed from her, and these were identified with Isis, Neith,

Iusaset, and many other goddesses whose attributes they absorbed. A group of seven Hathors is also mentioned."

35. Edouard Naville, "La destruction des hommes par les dieux," *TSBA* 4 (1875): 1-19; quotes from 4-5, 16; the later text is in Edouard Naville, "L'Incription de la destruction des hommes dans le tombeau de Ramses III," *TSBA* 8 (1884): 412-20.

36. "III Egypt Revisited," *IE* 59 (April 1956): 244-45, 252-54, 256, 258, 260, began with this sentence.

37. Kurt H. Sethe, *Urgeschichte und älteste Religion der Ägypter,* in vol. 18, pt. 4 of *Abhandlungen für die Kunde des Morgenlandes* (Leipzig: Deutsche Morgenländische Gesellschaft, 1930), 68.

38. Gerald A. Wainwright, "The Red Crown in Early Prehistoric Times," *JEA* 9 (1923): 26-33.

39. Sethe, *Urgeschichte und älteste Religion der Ägypter,* 68-70.

40. Ibid., 69.

41. Baumgartel, *Cultures of Prehistoric Egypt,* 1:44-47.

42. Sethe, *Urgeschichte und älteste Religion der Ägypter,* 64, 68-70.

43. William J. Phythian-Adams, "Aiguptos: A Derivation and Some Suggestions," *JPOS* 2 (1922): 94-100.

44. Helene J. Kantor, "Further Evidence for Early Mesopotamian Relations with Egypt," *JNES* 11 (1952): 239-50.

45. Werner Vycichl, "Notes sur la préhistoire de la langue égyptienne," *Orientalia* 23 (1954): 222.

46. Thus Zyhlarz, cited by Baumgartel, *Cultures of Prehistoric Egypt,* 1:48-49.

47. O. Rössler, "Akkadisches und libysches Verbum. I," *Orientalia* 20 (1951): 101-7.

48. On "the common ancestry of the Semites, Hamites, and Indo-Europeans," J. J. Gelb, "A Contribution to the Proto-Indo-European Question," *Jahrbuch für kleinasiatische Forschung* 2 (1951): 23-36; on "the prehistoric parent language, which may be called Hamito-Semitic," Cyrus H. Gordon, *Ugaritic Handbook* (Rome: Pontifical Biblical Institute, 1947), 25; cf. Henri Frankfort, *The Birth of Civilization in the Near East* (Bloomington: Indiana University Press, 1951), 109.

49. Baumgartel, *Cultures of Prehistoric Egypt,* 1:49-51; Moret, *Histoire de l'Orient* 1:186.

50. Baumgartel, *Cultures of Prehistoric Egypt,* 1:49.

51. T. Burton-Brown, *Studies in Third Millennium History* (London: Luzac, 1946), 93.

52. Moret, *Histoire de l'Orient,* 1:12, 200-201.

53. Mercer, *The Pyramid Texts in Translation and Commentary,* Pyr. 607a-b.

54. Thus ibid., Pyr. 2100a-c: "O. N., Horus has woven his tent over

thy head; Set has stretched out thy canopy; be enclosed, O father, by the divine tent; thou art brought there in thy beloved places."

55. Ibid., Pyr. 405a-b, 403b.

56. Ibid., Pyr. 1113a-b.

57. Ibid., Pyr. 547a, 550a-b.

58. Ibid., Pyr. 546a-b.

59. Ibid., Pyr. 629a-c.

60. Gardiner, *Egyptian Grammar,* 74.

61. Mercer, *The Pyramid Texts in Translation and Commentary,* Pyr. 919c.

62. Ibid., Pyr. 2100a-c.

63. Ibid., Pyr. 1121b.

64. Ibid., Pyr. 625c-d.

65. E. A. Wallis Budge, "On the Hieratic Papyrus of Nesi-Amsu, a scribe in the Temple of Amen-Ra at Thebes, about B.C. 305," *Archaeologia* 52 (1890): 535-63.

66. Mercer, *The Pyramid Texts in Translation and Commentary,* Pyr. 310c-311d.

67. Adolf Deissmann, *Light from the Ancient East* (New York: Doran, 1927), 368-73.

68. Budge, *The Book of the Dead: Papyrus of Ani,* 1:152.

69. Budge, "On the Hieratic Papyrus of Nesi-Amsu," 461-64.

70. The theme is developed by Moret, *Histoire de l'Orient,* 2:502-6.

71. Mercer, *The Pyramid Texts in Translation and Commentary,* Pyr. 400b-402c.

72. Ibid., Pyr. 253a-d, 260b.

73. Ibid., Pyr. 675a-b.

74. Ibid., Pyr. 682d-e.

75. Ibid., Pyr. 393c-394a.

76. Ibid., Pyr. 316a-d, 319a-b.

77. Ibid., Pyr. 319c.

78. Ibid., Pyr. 321a-322a.

79. Ibid., Pyr. 323c.

80. Ibid., Pyr. 347b.

81. Ibid., Pyr. 348a-c.

82. Ibid., Pyr. 615c.

83. Ibid., Pyr. 1438b-c.

84. "IV Egypt Revisited," *IE* 59 (May 1956): 308-10, 334, 336, 338-40, began at this point.

85. The late Egyptian story of Petubastis, called "The Fight for the Rights of Ammon," reads so much like a typical Indo-European epic that Pieper was frankly suspicious twenty-five years ago, though no evidence has been found to prove that it was not of native Egyptian

origin; see Max Pieper, *Die Ägyptische Literatur* (Wildpark-Potsdam: Akademische Verlagsgesellschaft Athenaion, 1927), 90-92.

86. Mercer, *The Pyramid Texts in Translation and Commentary,* Pyr. 214b-215c.

87. Ibid., Pyr. 695b-696b.

88. Ibid., Pyr. 560a-c; 566a-c.

89. Ibid., Pyr. 1180b-1182d.

90. Ibid., Pyr. 1343c-1345b.

91. Ibid., Pyr. 1472a-1477d; 654a-657e; 1291a-1293a.

92. Ibid., Pyr. 1356a-1357b.

93. Ibid., Pyr. 327a-335a.

94. Re appears from the beginning "in his high castle with a court whose splendor reflects the glory of the courts of earthly kings, and transplants to heaven the life of a king of the Old Kingdom, with its archives, messengers, ceremonies, and the rest," thus Schott, *Mythe und Mythenbildung im alten Ägypten,* 17-18.

95. Mercer, *The Pyramid Texts in Translation and Commentary,* Pyr. 136b-137c.

96. Ibid., Pyr. 609b-610b, 576c-577d.

97. Ibid., Pyr. 648d-650a.

98. Ibid., Pyr. 640b; 643b-c; 651b-653d.

99. Ibid., Pyr. 1338b-c.

100. Ibid., Pyr. 645c-647d.

101. Ibid., Pyr. 484a-485c.

102. Ibid., Pyr. 1322-1323.

103. Egyptian population is described by classical writers as composed of three classes only: priests, warriors, and artisans; thus Plato, *Timaeus* III, 22A; Diodorus, *Bibliotheke* I, 74. The peasants are tied to the soil and belong to whoever owns it; cf. James H. Breasted, *Ancient Records of Egypt,* 5 vols. (Chicago: University of Chicago Press, 1906), 1:285 (No. 630). In a few Pyramid Texts (Utterance 422, line 761), Pharaoh tills the ground ritually, but these pieces stand out sharply from the rest in style and content.

104. Mercer, *The Pyramid Texts in Translation and Commentary,* Pyr. 817a-818a.

105. Ibid., Pyr. 202a-203b.

106. Ibid., Pyr. 944a-c.

107. Ibid., Pyr. 588b-c.

108. Ibid., Pyr. 1544b-1550b.

109. Ibid., Pyr. 635c-d.

110. Ibid., Pyr. 651b-652b.

111. W. Helck, "*Rpˁt* auf dem Thron des *Gb*," *Orientalia* 19 (1950): 417-18.

112. Ibid., 430-31. It should be noted that some Egyptologists, notably Moret, have identified Atum with Adam.

113. Ibid., 418-19, 432-33.

114. Gardiner, *Egyptian Grammar,* 169.

115. Helck, "*Rpꜥt* auf dem Thron des *Gb,*" 433, 430.

116. Mercer, *The Pyramid Texts in Translation and Commentary,* Pyr. 757-764.

117. Helck, "*Rpꜥt* auf dem Thron des *Gb,*" 430-32.

118. Ibid., 422-25, 433.

119. Gardiner, *Egyptian Grammar,* 73; cf. Moret, *Histoire de l'Orient,* 1:185.

120. Helck, "*Rpꜥt* auf dem Thron des *Gb,*" 424-25.

121. Hans Bonnet, *Reallexikon der aegyptischen Religionsgeschichte* (Berlin: De Gruyter, 1952), 397.

122. R. Lepsius, *Denkmäler aus Ägypten und Äthiopien,* 17 vols. (Berlin & Leipzig, 1849-59, 1897-1913), 3:169; reprinted in Bonnet, *Reallexikon der aegyptischen Religionsgeschichte,* 399, fig. 102.

123. Mercer, *The Pyramid Texts in Translation and Commentary,* Pyr. Text, 625a; cf. 622a-625d.

124. Bonnet, *Reallexikon der aegyptischen Religionsgeschichte,* 57-58.

125. Ibid., 685-89, 430-34.

126. As the papyrus symbolizes Lower Egypt and the sedge (*shema*) Upper Egypt, so the lotus represents the whole land, as on a throne-scene in the Papyrus of Hunefer, where a lotus, springing up before the throne, exactly as in Plate 3 of the Book of Abraham, supports the gods of the Four Regions; reproduced in Budge, *The Book of the Dead: Papyrus of Ani,* 1:241, fig. 1.

127. Moret, *Histoire de l'Orient,* 2:528.

128. C. H. V. Sutherland, "The Historical Evidence of Greek and Roman Coins," *Greece and Rome* 9 (1940): 73-74.

129. Interesting commentaries on the rigid canons of ancient art may be found in Kees, *Aegypten,* 265; E. Douglas Van Buren, "Ancient Beliefs and Some Modern Interpretations," *Orientalia* 18 (1949): 498-99.

130. Schwulst is probably thinking of the Necanebos tale and the Pseudo-Callisthenes and some Oriental accounts of the wooing of Olympia, or even of A. B. Cook, *Zeus,* 3 vols. (Cambridge: Cambridge University Press, 1914-40); vol. 2.

131. Mercer, *The Pyramid Texts in Translation and Commentary,* Pyr. 272c-273a.

132. Ibid., Pyr. 1154b-1155c; 1535b-c.

133. Ibid., Pyr. 1992c, 2012a.

134. Ibid., Pyr. 255a-256b.

135. Ibid., Pyr. 1563a-c.

136. Ibid., Pyr. 1124a-1127c.
137. A. Wiedemann, *Das alte Ägypten* (Heidelberg: Winter, 1920), 247.
138. "V Egypt Revisited," *IE* (June 1956): 390-91, 460-61, began at this point.
139. Baumgartel, *Cultures of Prehistoric Egypt,* 1:3.
140. Kees, *Aegypten,* 8.
141. The theme has been treated by Moret, *Histoire de l'Orient,* 1:185-87.
142. Otto, "Ein Beitrag zur Deutung der ägyptischen Vor- und Frühgeschichte."
143. Joseph Karst, *Die vorgeschichtlichen Mittelmeervölker* (Heidelberg: Winter, 1931), 286, who also insists that the Otomic capital of Mamemhi is remarkably similar to the Egyptian name *Memphis*—Momemphis.
144. Mercer, *The Pyramid Texts in Translation and Commentary,* Pyr. 244b, 245b.
145. Ibid., Pyr. 430a-b.
146. Wiedemann, *Das alte Ägypten,* 247-49.
147. Mercer, *The Pyramid Texts in Translation and Commentary,* Pyr. 236a-237b.
148. Ibid., Pyr. 426b-c.
149. Budge, *The Book of the Dead: Papyrus of Ani,* vol. 1, ch. 88, pl. 27. The translation is the author's. This text can also be found, ibid., 2:545-46.
150. Budge, "On the Hieratic Papyrus of Nesi-Amsu," *Archaeologia* 52 (1890): 469.
151. Aristotle, *Oeconomica* 2, 33.
152. Budge, "On the Hieratic Papyrus of Nesi-Amsu," 515-16.
153. Edouard Naville,"La destruction des hommes par les dieux," *TSBA* 8 (1884): 13-14.
154. Mercer, *The Pyramid Texts in Translation and Commentary,* Pyr. 425a-c.
155. Ibid., Pyr. 438c.
156. Cicero, *De Natura Deorum* I, 36, says the Ibis actually ridded Egypt of a pest of serpents; cf. Budge, "On the Hiratic Papyrus of Nesi-Amsu," 578-79. Mr. Blank has many other notes on the subject, which he can't find at the moment: a great deal about cats as snake killers.
157. Thus Nigidius Figulus, cited in Theodorus Hopfner, *Fontes Historiae Religionis Aegyptiaeae* (Bonn: Marx & Weber, 1922), 83-84, see also Plutarch, *Alexander* XXVI, 6.
158. Budge, *The Book of the Dead: Papyrus of Ani,* 1:152; cf. 256.
159. Budge, "On the Hieratic Papyrus of Nesi-Amsu," 519-20.
160. Ibid., 576-78.

161. Ibid., 516-17.

162. Ibid., 518-19.

163. Ibid., 569-79. The quote is from 579.

164. Ibid., 523-27.

165. Ibid., 603-4, 507.

166. Mercer, *The Pyramid Texts in Translation and Commentary,* Pyr. 302a-d.

167. Ibid., Pyr. 238a-b; 244a-b; 442a-c; 443a-c; 444a.

Chapter 3: Babylonian Background

1. "Babylonian Background I," *IE* 59 (July 1956): 509-11, 514, 516, began at this point.

2. T. Eric Peet, *A Comparative Study of the Literatures of Egypt, Palestine, and Mesopotamia* (London: Oxford University Press), 26. Whether Prof. Schwulst was quoting from memory or reading from the text cannot be determined at the present time.

3. Ren Labat, *Le poème babylonien de la création* (Paris: Maisonneuve, 1935), 2.

4. M. Witzel, "Zu den Enmerkar-Dichtungen," *Orientalia* 18 (1949): 273.

5. Ibid., 265, 268; the whole text is translated on 275-80.

6. Ibid., 271-73.

7. C. J. Gadd, *A Sumerian Reading Book* (Oxford: Clarendon, 1924), 145. Rather than loading our notes with references to texts we have never read, we shall lean heavily on Gadd and Deimel for our illustrations.

8. A. Deimel, *Sumerische Grammatik der archaistischen Text* (Rome, 1924), 151. Deimel reproduces all the archaic texts in full.

9. Ibid., 159; cf. Gadd, *A Sumerian Reading Book,* 147: "Let the lightning, thy messenger, go before thee." References to the kings as shepherds and herdsmen are extremely numerous. Cf. Deimel, *Sumerische Grammatik der archaistischen Text,* 243, 246, 243, 144, 151, etc. Gadd, *A Sumerian Reading Book,* 55, 111.

10. Deimel, *Sumerische Grammatik der archaistischen Text,* 143; he is also "the lion of the Desert," ibid., 324.

11. Gadd, *A Sumerian Reading Book,* 105; entirely indistinguishable from the Pyramid Texts is the Sumerian Hymn to the Sun, No. 21, ibid., 148-49; it is the most perfect literary parallel imaginable.

12. Deimel, *Sumerische Grammatik der archaistischen Text,* 278; Gadd, *A Sumerian Reading Book,* 65, 71.

13. H. V. Hilprecht, *The Earliest Version of the Babylonian Deluge Story and the Temple Library of Nippur,* vol. 5, fasc. 1 of *The Babylonian Expedition of the University of Pennsylvania* (Philadelphia: University of Pennsylvania

Press, 1910), 32, n. 4. These Guti had no regular kings but only migratory chieftains; Deimel, *Sumerische Grammatik der archaistischen Text,* 271.

14. Deimel, *Sumerische Grammatik der archaistischen Text,* 133.

15. Ibid., 243-44.

16. A. Leo Oppenheim, "Mesopotamian Mythology III" *Orientalia* 19 (1950): 147-54. The full text in P. Jensen, *Assyrisch-Babylonische Mythen und Epen* (Berlin: Reuther & Reichard, 1900), 74ff.

17. Oppenheim, "Mesopotamian Mythology III," 155-58; quote from 156-57.

18. Deimel, *Sumerische Grammatik der archaistischen Text,* 316.

19. Ibid., 238. Exactly like the conqueror in the Pyramid Texts, the Sumerian lord "lets no sleep come to his eye," ibid., 161; he is "the one with the far-seeing eye," ibid., 162. In the Enuma Elish the four eyes and four ears of Marduk tell him all that goes on in the four directions, Labat, *Le Poème Babylonien de la Création,* 30-31, n. 43.

20. Hugo Radau, *Nin-ib the Determiner of Fates, according to the Great Sumerian Epic Lugal-e Ug Me-Lám-bi Ner-gál from the Temple Library of Nippur* (Philadelphia: University of Pennsylvania, 1910), 28.

21. Ibid., 27, 36-38.

22. Ibid., 42, 44.

23. Ibid., 24, where the king appears as the "Savior" of his people from bondage, ibid., 26.

24. Louis Delaporte, *Le proche-orient asiatique, Les peuples de l'orient mediterranéen* (Paris: Presses Universitaires, 1948), 1:11.

25. Paraphrase of Hugo Winckler, in Eberhard Schrader, *Die Keilinschriften und das Alte Testament,* 3rd ed., (Berlin: Reuther & Reichard, 1903), 169-70, 22-23 . More recently Sir Leonard Woolley has written: "At once there is called up the astonishing picture of antediluvian man engaged in a commerce which sent its caravans across a thousand miles of mountain and desert from the Mesopotamian valley into the heart of India." Leonard Woolley, *Digging up the Past* (Baltimore: Penguin, 1961), 132; cf. A. Leo Oppenheim, "The Seafaring Merchants of Ur," *JAOS* 74 (1954): 6-17; Samuel N. Kramer, "Sumerian Historiography," *IEJ* 3 (1953): 228-32; Andre Parrot, *Mari une ville perdue* (Paris: Je Sers, 1945), 36.

26. See generally, Bruno Meissner, *Die Babylonisch-Assyrische Literatur* (Wildpark-Potsdam: Akademische Verlagsgesellschaft Athenaion, 1927), 34-35.

27. Oppenheim, "Mesopotamian Mythology III," 158.

28. Hilprecht, *The Earliest Version of the Babylonian Deluge Story and the Temple Library of Nippur,* 61.

29. As recently as our own decade the journalist C. W. Ceram could say of the Assurbanipal version of his immensely popular book *Gods, Graves, and Scholars* (New York: Knopf, 1967), 277, that it is "impossible

to question the fact that the primal version of the Biblical legend of the Deluge had been found." Nothing could be further from the truth!

30. "The Babylonian Background II," *IE* 59 (August 1956): 566-67, 602, began at this point.

31. The quotations in the above comparison are all from Hilprecht, *The Earliest Version of the Babylonian Deluge Story and the Temple Library of Nippur,* 52-55.

32. Georges Contenau, *Le Déluge Babylonien* (Paris: Payot, 1952), 84-87.

33. "The Shinging Stones, Cont.," *IE* 59 (September 1956): 630-32, 672-75, began at this point.

34. The rabbis "could not explain [the meaning of Zohar]." H. Freedman & M. Simon, trs., *Midrash Rabbah,* 10 vols. (London: Soncino, 1939), 1:244.

35. Ibid.

36. Ibid.

37. *Talmud Jerushalmi, Pesahim* 1:1, 5:2, cited in E. Mangenot, "Arche de Noé," in F. Vigouroux, *Dictionnaire de la Bible,* 5 vols. (Paris: Letouzey et Ané, 1894), 1:923. Mangenot's own reflection is that "it is ridiculous to say with Rabbi Ahia-ben-Zeira that in the midst of the darkness of the Ark, Noah could distinguish day from night by the aid of pearls and precious stones, whose luster grew pale by day and shone forth by night."

38. Moses Mielziner, *Introduction to the Talmud* (New York: Bloch, 1968), 62.

39. Ibid., 92.

40. The Babylonian Talmud, "so rich in dialectical subtilties, and so full of technicalities and elliptical expressions, offers to the translator almost insurmountable difficulties. . . . It would sometimes require a whole volume of commentary to supplement the translation of a single chapter of the original. . . . This explains why the various attempts at translating the whole of the Babylonian Talmud have, thus far, proven a failure, so that as yet only comparatively few Masechtoth of this Talmud have been translated, and these translations are in many cases not intelligible enough to be fully understood by the reader who is not yet familiar with the original text and with the spirit of the Talmud," ibid., 89-90. Yet this Talmud is far simpler and infinitely better known than the Palestinian Talmud!

41. "The old Indian literature is full of the theme," according to J. J. Meyer, "Das unverbrennbare Herz und der Edelstein Pyrophilus," *ZDMG* 86 (1932): 97. Though many jewels have been suggested as the original shining stone—sapphire, smaragd, etc., the favored candidate

in Indian lore is the ruby, called the sunstone because of its fiery nature. Ibid., 95-97.

42. Regardless of the original substance, it was the hardening and purifying action of fire that achieved the miraculous transformation: it was believed that even hailstones, clear crystalline pellets, could be used to create jewels by fire! Ibid., 95-97. The result was always a clear crystal, ibid., 99.

43. Ibid., 97. About the supernatural powers of such precious stones generally, see Wilhelm Printz, "Gilgamesh und Alexander," *ZDMG* 85 (1931): 196-206.

44. Meyer, "Das unverbrennbare Herz und der Edelstein Pyrophilus," 99; Printz, "Gilgamesh und Alexander," 200.

45. Printz, "Gilgamesh und Alexander," 196-204, quotes relevant passages from Albertus Magnus, Thomas Cantimpratensis, Conrad of Megenberg, Vincent of Beauvais, Volmar, and others, all of whom give slightly varying versions.

46. The Aristotle passage is lost, though it is referred to as a source by later writers and quoted by an unnamed fourteenth century writer in a passage reproduced by Printz, ibid., 197. An earlier version of the Alexander story is given by A. Nauck, *Tagicorum Graecorum Fragmenta,* 2nd ed. (Leipzig, 1889; reprinted Hildesheim: Olms, 1964), 209-10.

47. It is called a *pharmakon agērasias* or "specific against old age" in the fragment cited in the preceding note; see below, n. 49.

48. Printz, "Gilgamesh und Alexander," 198-200.

49. Peter C. A. Jensen, *Assyrisch-babylonische Mythen und Epen,* 11 vols. (Berlin: Reuther & Reichard, 1900), 6:250-53. Lines 282-93, 302-7 from the 9th Tablet of the Gilgamesh Epic will illustrate the remarkable co-mingling of familiar motifs in this very ancient epic:

I will disclose, O Gilgamesh, a hidden thing
    and . . . tell it to you.
That plant is like a thorn in the field.
Its thorn will pierce thy hand like a thorny vine; it will pierce through thy hand.
When thy hands grasp that plant, thou canst return again to thy land.
When Gilgamesh heard this
He opened the. . . .
He tied heavy stones on his feet,
And they dragged him down into the cosmic ocean and he found the plant.
He took the plant and it pierced through his hand.
He cut the heavy stones loose, and . . .
A second one he cast down to his . . .

****

Then Gilgamesh [on the way home] saw a pool of water, which was cold,
He went down into it and washed himself with water.
A serpent smelled the fragrance of the plant,
came up . . . and took the plant away.
Then when he came back he mocked and taunted [Gilgamesh],
Then Gilgamesh sat himself down and wept . . .

Though the stones on the feet are the key to the story, according to Printz, in identifying the plant of life definitely with the shining stone of Pyrophilos, which Alexander lost in the same way, even the casual reader will note in this brief excerpt various striking parallels to the story of man's fall.

50. H. Stock, "Studien zu Lukians 'De Syria Dea,' " *Beyrutus* 4 (1937): 12.

51. Lucian, *De Syria Dea* 12-13. Stock, "Studien zu Lukians 'De Syria Dea'," 7-8, noting that Lucian's flood story is neither Babylonian nor Greek. He maintains, 10, that Lucian rightly refers to Deucalion, the local Noah, as a Scythian. Gilgamesh's friend and double Humbaba is obviously the Kombabus whose legend Lucian here recounts: it is a version of the sacrifice and resurrection motif.

52. Lucian, *De Syria Dea* 13.

53. Ibid., 32.

54. Anton Jirku, "Der Kult des Mondgottes im altor. Palästina-Syrien," *ZDMG* 100 (1951): 202-4, showing that the cult was prominent both at Ras Shamra and Jericho in very ancient times. The prominence of Kombabus alone at the Syrian shrine is enough to guarantee the great age of its rites.

55. Macrobius, cited in Stocks, "Studien zu Lukians 'De Syria Dea,' " 15.

56. Carl Clemen, *Lukians Schrift über die syrische Göttin,* Heft 3-4, *Der Alte Orient,* No. 37 (Leipzig: Hinrich, 1938), 42.

57. Stocks, "Studien zu Lukians 'De Syria Dea'," 6.

58. J. Schoneveld, in *Orientalia Neerlandica,* 222 [further bibliographic information unavailable—ed.].

59. Anton Jirku, "Die Mimation in den nordsemitischen Sprachen und einige Bezeichnungen der altisraelitischen Mantik," *Biblica* 34 (1953): 78-80.

60. See above note 51.

61. E. A Speiser, "The Sumerian Problem Reviewed," *HUCA* 23 (1952): 355.

Chapter 4: Epic Milieu in the Old Testament

1. "Epic Milieu in the Old Testament," *IE* 59 (October 1956): 710-12, 745-51, began at this point.

2. Leonard Woolley, *Digging Up the Past* (Baltimore: Penguin, 1961), 76.

3. Cyrus H. Gordon, "The Patriarchal Narratives," *JNES* 13 (1954): 58-59.

4. Ibid., 59.

5. André Parrot, *Mari une ville perdue* (Paris: Je Sers, 1945), 208-9.

6. Gordon, "Patriarchal Narratives," 56.

7. Baʿal and ʿAnat, Text 51: VII:41-45, in Cyrus H. Gordon, *Ugaritic Literature* (Rome: Pontifical Biblical Institute, 1949), 36.

8. Ibid., 36-37, lines 50-52.

9. Ibid., 37, Text 51:VIII:27-29, 28, n. 2.

10. Ibid., 38; Text 67:I:1-3.

11. Ibid., 39; Text 67:II:10-15.

12. See Hugh W. Nibley, *Lehi in the Desert and the World of the Jaredites* (Salt Lake City: Bookcraft, 1952), 155-60; this volume, above pp. 163-68.

13. Baʿal and ʿAnat, Text 67:2:2-20, in Gordon, *Ugaritic Literature,* 39-40.

14. Ibid., 7.

15. Roger T. O'Callaghan, "The Great Phoenician Portal Inscription from Karatepe," *Orientalia* 18 (1949): 174-83 for the text; quotes are from 175-79.

16. Ibid., 179.

17. Nibley, *Lehi in the Desert,* 205-6; above, pp. 208-9.

18. O'Callaghan, "The Great Phoenician Portal Inscription from Karatepe," 199-200.

19. Guglielmo Ferrero and Corrado Barbagallo have an interesting comment on this in *A Short History of Rome,* 2 vols. (New York: Putnam, 1918), 1:5-6.

20. Cyrus H. Gordon, "Notes of the Legend of Keret," *JNES* 11 (1952): 212.

21. Ibid., 213.

22. O. R. Gurney, *The Hittites* (Baltimore: Pelican, 1952), 65-66; Albrecht Götze, *Kleinasien,* vol. 3, pt. 1, #3c of *Handbuch der Altertumswissenschaft* (Munich: Beck, 1933), 85-86.

23. Götze, *Kleinasien,* 58, 80-89, 124-38.

24. Albrecht Götze, *Hethiter, Churriter und Assyrer* (Oslo: Aschehoug, 1936), 60-63. Quote is from Gurney, *The Hittites,* 63.

25. Götze, *Hethiter, Churriter und Assyrer,* 53-54; Gurney, *The Hittites,* 24.

26. Gurney, *The Hittites,* 78.

27. Ibid., 67.

28. Ibid., 24.

29. Ibid., 47-52.

30. Götze, *Kleinasien,* 91-95.

31. Ibid., 98.

32. Gurney, *The Hittites,* 68.

33. For a discussion of the relationship of the king and vassal, see generally Götze, *Kleinasien,* 89-102.

34. Ibid., 115, 80-81.

35. Ibid., 90-95.

36. Ibid., 110-14.

37. A. B. Cook, *Zeus,* 3 vols. (Cambridge: Cambridge University Press, 1914-40), 1:333-35; 2:830-33.

38. Aeschylus, *Prometheus Bound* 955-59.

39. This is discussed by H. C. Baldry, "Aristotle and the Dramatization of Legend," *CQ* 48 (1954): 151-57.

40. Arthur Christensen, *Die Iranier,* vol. 3, pt. 1, #3c of *Handbuch der Altertumswissenschaft* (Munich: Beck, 1933), 218-19.

41. James Darmesteter, *The Zend-Avesta,* 3 vols. (Oxford: Oxford University Press, 1880-87), 2:295 (Zamyad Yast 7:40); 2:193-94 (Farvardin Yast 14-15).

42. Fr. Spiegel, *Erânische Altertumskunde* (Leipzig, 1873), 2:80.

43. Darmesteter, *Zend-Avesta* 2:131, 135, 140 (Mihir Yast 10:46; 15:63; 21:82).

44. Ibid., 2:148 (Mihir Yast 27:111).

45. Xenophon, *Cyropaedia* V, 5, 8.

46. Darmesteter, *Zend-Avesta* 2:293-94 (Zamyad Yast 7:32-44).

47. Ibid., 2:148 (Mihir Yast 27:111).

48. Ibid., 2:121-22 (Mihir Yast 2:7-9).

49. Christensen, *Die Iranier,* 218.

50. Xenophon, *Anabasis* II, 4, 3-4.

51. See generally Eduard Meyer, *Geschichte des Altertums,* 4th ed. (Stuttgart: Cotta, 1944), vol. 4, pt. 1, pp. 21-22; Darmesteter, *Zend-Avesta* 2:136 (Mihir Yast 16:66; 17:67-68).

52. Hugh W. Nibley, "The Hierocentric State," *WPQ* 4 (1951): 243-44.

53. Christensen, *Die Iranier,* 217.

54. Darmesteter, *Zend-Avesta* 2:272-73 (Ashi Yast 2:7-14).

55. Christensen, *Die Iranier,* 218-19.

56. Clèment Huart and Louis Delaporte, *L'Iran antique* (Paris: Michel, 1952), 399.

57. See Hugh W. Nibley, "There Were Jaredites, Part 3 Egypt Revisited," *IE* 59 (April 1956): 245; above, p. 320.

58. Bedrich Hrozny, *Über die älteste Völkerwanderung und über das problem der Proto-Indischenzivilisation,* in *Monografis Archivu Orientálnìho* 7 (Prague: Orientalisches Institut, 1939), 5-7.

59. A. Müller, *Der Islam im Morgen- und Abendland,* 2nd ser., pt. 4, 2 vols. of *Allgemeine Geschichte in Einzeldarstellungen* (Berlin: Historischer Verlag Baumgärtel, 1885), 1:219-23.

60. Livy, *History of Rome* I, 4-7.

61. Ibid., I, 33.

62. Ibid., II, 16.

63. Ibid., II, 17.

64. Ibid., II, 5; II, 9; II, 43.

65. Sallust, *Bellum Catilinae,* 11, 14.

66. Ibid., 22. "The whole land was filled with robbers." Ibid., 28.

67. Vergil, *Aeneid* VI, 791-92, 852-53.

Chapter 5: Our Own People

1. "Our Own People," *IE* 59 (November 1956): 818-19, 857-58, began at this point.

2. L. R. Palmer, *The Latin Language* (London: Faber & Faber, 1954), 52-53.

3. Geoffrey of Monmouth, *Historia Regum Britanniae* 9, 1; cf. 3, 7.

4. This was Luernius, in Athenaeus, *Deipnosophists* 4, 152.

5. H. D. Jubainville, *The Irish Mythological Cycle and Celtic Mythology* (Dublin: Hodges, Figgis, 1903), 19-21, 71-72, 76-78, 84-94, 146-55; H. Munro Chadwick, *The Growth of Literature,* 3 vols. (Cambridge: Cambridge University Press, 1932), 1:106; Henry Morris, "The Partholon Legend," *JRSAI* 67 (1937): 57-71.

6. Jubainville, *The Irish Mythological Cycle and Celtic Mythology,* 91-92. Geoffrey, *Historia Regum Britanniae* 9, 11.

7. Jubainville, *The Irish Mythological Cycle and Celtic Mythology,* 147.

8. Geoffrey, *Historia Regum Britanniae* 3, 7.

9. Lord John of Joinville, *Memoirs of Louis IX. King of France,* in Lord John of Joinville, *Chronicles of the Crusades* (London: Bohn, 1848), 363-64.

10. Geoffrey, *Historia Regum Britanniae* 9.

11. John Rhys, *Celtic Heathendom* (London: Williams & Norgate, 1898), 608, 584, 412; Jubainville, *The Irish Mythological Cycle and Celtic Mythology,* 15, 57-58, 60-62.

12. Geoffrey, *Historia Regum Britanniae* 3, 5; Rhys, *Celtic Heathendom,* 13.

13. It is also identical with a tumulus and subterranean palace—the

world of the dead to which the ancient Celts were so attached. See Jubainville, *The Irish Mythological Cycle and Celtic Mythology,* 146-55.

14. Geoffrey, *Historia Regum Britanniae* 6, 3-4 for this and a great deal more to the same effect.

15. Rhys, *Celtic Heathendom,* 155-58, 160-75, 562; Mary Williams, "An Early Ritual Poem in Welsh," *Speculum* 13 (1938): 38-51; A. H. Krappe, "Who Was the Green Knight?" *Speculum* 13 (1938): 206-17; Richard Heinzel, "Über die französischen Gralromane," *Denkschriften der Kaiserlichen Akademie der Wissenschaft* 40, pt. 3 (1892), esp. 155-71; and especially Leopold von Schroeder, "Die Wurzeln der Sage vom heiligen Gral," in vol. 166 of *Sitzungsberichte der kaiserliche. Akademie der Wissenschaft in Wien. Philosophisch-Historische Klasse* (Vienna: Hölder, 1910), pt. 1.

16. Thomas Percy, "Essay on the Ancient Minstrels in England," in *Reliques of Ancient English Poetry,* 3 vols. (London: Allen & Unwin, 1885), 1:354.

17. This whole theme is treated at length by Hermann Schneider in two works which clearly illustrate the complete change of thought that has taken place on the subject of the epic milieu between the two dates of publication. They are Hermann Schneider, *Germanische Heldensage,* 2 vols. (Berlin: De Gruyter, 1928-33), 1-42; and *Heldendichtung, Geistlichendichtung, Ritterdichtung,* vol. 1 of Julius Petersen & Hermann Schneider, *Geschichte der deutschen Literatur* (Heidelberg: Winter, 1943), 1-37.

18. The description is from the *Formali,* the original introduction to the Prose Edda.

19. In the *Lokasenna,* the eighth poem of the Poetic Edda.

20. Jacob Grimm, *Teutonic Mythology,* James S. Stallybrass, ed., 4 vols. (London: Bell, 1882-88), 3:918-50.

21. This description of Othinn is from D. Nathan Sönderblom, *Tiele-Söderbloms Kompendium der Religionsgeschichte,* 5th ed. (Berlin-Schöneberg: Theophil Biller, 1920), 486-89, 483.

22. Ibid., 481-86.

23. Schneider, *Heldendichtung, Geistichendichtung, Ritterdichtung,* 12.

24. Ibid., 26-32. Quote from 31-32.

25. Ibid., 30.

26. E. V. Gordon, *Introduction to Old Norse* (Oxford: Clarendon, 1927), liv.

27. Hugh W. Nibley, "The Hierocentric State," *WPQ* 4 (1951): 247-49.

28. C. R. Unger, ed., *Saga Didriks Konungs af Bern* (Christiania: Feilberg & Landmarks, 1853), chs. 47, 48.

29. Priscus Rhetor, *De Legationibus Romanorum ad Gentes,* in *PG* 113:724, 732-33, 737.

30. Unger, *Saga Didriks Konungs af Bern,* ch. 282.

31. Ibid., ch. 51.
32. Ibid., ch. 132.
33. Ibid., ch. 185.
34. Ibid., ch. 268.
35. Ibid., ch. 139.
36. Ibid., ch. 154.
37. "Our Own People," *IE* 59 (December 1956): 906-7, began at this point.
38. Unger, *Saga Didriks Konungs af Bern,* ch. 134.
39. Ibid., ch. 249.
40. Ibid., ch. 45.
41. Ibid., ch. 49.
42. Procopius, *Anecdota* 8, 5.
43. Unger, *Saga Didriks Konungs af Bern,* ch. 39.
44. Ibid., ch. 182.
45. Ibid., chs. 68, 300.
46. Ibid., ch. 83.
47. Ibid., ch. 109.
48. Ibid., ch. 39.
49. Ibid., ch. 3.
50. Ibid., ch. 44.
51. Ibid., ch. 136.
52. Ibid., ch. 322.
53. Ibid., chs. 45, 204.
54. Ibid., chs. 118, 212, 215, 219, 312.
55. Ibid., ch. 214.
56. Ibid., ch. 48.
57. Ibid., ch. 278.
58. Ibid., ch. 122.
59. Ibid., chs. 90, 94.
60. Ibid., chs. 172, 92.
61. Ibid., ch. 81.
62. Ibid., ch. 282.
63. Ibid., chs. 54, 88, 273.
64. Ibid., chs. 88, 102.
65. Ibid., ch. 102.
66. Ibid., chs. 39-40.
67. Ibid., ch. 282.
68. Ibid., ch. 72.
69. Ibid., ch. 144.
70. Ibid., ch. 54.
71. Ibid., ch. 47.
72. Ibid., ch. 308.

73. Ibid., ch. 324.

74. "Our Own People," *IE* 60 (January 1957): 26-27, 41, began at this point.

75. Samuel N. Kramer, "New Light on the Early History of the Ancient Near East," *AJA* 52 (1948): 159.

76. The highest compliment Philippe de Commynes can pay his master, Louis XI of France, is that "as for peace, he could hardly endure the thought of it." Philippe de Commynes, *Memoirs* I, 10.

77. Chadwick, *Growth of Literature,* 1:90-91.

78. Albrecht Götze, *Hethiter, Churriter, und Assyrer* (Oslo: Aschehung, 1936), 128-32. A number of examples of this have been given in the course of these articles.

79. Carleton S. Coon, *The Story of Man* (New York: Knopf, 1954), 103.

80. V. Gordon Childe, *New Light on the Most Ancient East* (New York: Praeger, 1953), 24-25.

81. Coon, *The Story of Man,* 142.

82. "Our Own People," *IE* 60 (February 1957): 94-95, 122-24, began at this point.

83. William M. McGovern, *The Early Empires of Central Asia* (Chapel Hill: University of North Carolina Press, 1939), 78.

84. Chadwick, *The Growth of Literature,* 1:173.

85. Typical are O. G. S. Crawford, "Burrows," *Antiquity* 1 (1927): 413-34, and E. C. Curwen, "Neolithic Camps," *Antiquity* 4 (1930): 22-54.

86. Chadwick, *The Growth of Literature,* 1:134.

87. Winifred Lambe, "The Site of Troy," *Antiquity* 6 (1932): 71-81.

88. Nibley, "Hierocentric State," 238-41.

89. Leonard Whibley, *A Companion to Greek Studies* (Cambridge: Cambridge University Press, 1931), 261.

90. Pliny, *Natural History* XXXVI, 1, 3-XXXVI, 2, 6.

91. Robert J. Braidwood, *The Near East and the Foundations for Civilization, Condon Lectures* (Eugene, Oregon: Oregon State System of Higher Education, 1952), 13.

92. These points are all made by Edward King, "Observations on Antient [sic] Castles," *Archaeologia* 4 (1777): 364-413; Daines Barrington, "Observations on the Welsh Castles," *Archaeologia* 1 (1774): 278-91.

93. Priscus Rhetor, *De Legationibus Romanorum ad Gentes,* in *PG* 113:732-33, 737.

94. For a good description of this type of architecture, see O. R. Gurney, *The Hittites* (Baltimore: Pelican, 1952), 145-50, 210, with interesting illustrations.

95. A perfect example of this is the city building operations of King Azitawaddu as described in the newly discovered Karatepe Inscription:

"And I builded for tresses in all the remotest borders, in the places in which there were lawless fellows, chiefs of robber bands, . . . I Azitawaddu, placed them beneath my feat, and I built fortresses in those places so that the Dananians might inhabit them. . . . And I built this city, and I determined (its) name Azitawaddiya [after himself], . . . that it might be a bulwark for the Plain of Adana and for the House of Mupshu. . . . So I have built this city, named it Azitawaddiya, . . . and instituted sacrifices." Note that the city was founded by the great chief and given his name, as a means of control, a "bulwark," "and this city shall possess grain and wine, and this people whose children shall dwell (here) shall possess cattle and sheep and grain and wine . . . and they shall be exceedingly mightly." Note how exactly this system corresponds to that described in Ether! The inscription was quoted and discussed in Nibley, "There Were Jaredites: Epic Milieu in the Old Testament," *IE* 59 (October 1956): 711-12; above, pp. 384-85. The text with photographs may be found in Roger T. O'Callaghan, "The Great Phoenician Portal Inscription from Karatepe," *Orientalia* 18 (1949): 173-205, plates 22-25.

96. Elise J. Baumgartel, *The Cultures of Prehistoric Egypt,* 2 vols. (London: Oxford University Press, 1947, 1960), 1:3-9. The eminent Lord Raglan has recently maintained that Troy never existed! The Jomsborg is a classic example. "Lyonesse" is another, for which see O. S. G. Crawford, "Lyonesse," *Antiquity* 1 (1927): 5-14.

97. Martin P. Nilsson, *The Minoan-Mycenaean Religion and Its Survival in Greek Religion* (Lund: Gleerup, 1950), 11-17, the quote is from 15.

98. Claude Schaeffer, *Stratigraphie comparée et chronologie de l'asie occidentale* (London: Oxford University Press, 1948), 537.

99. Ibid., 565.

100. Ibid., 546.

101. Werner Vycichl, "Notes sur la préhistoire de la langue égyptienne," *Orientalia* 23 (1954): 218.

102. Cyrus H. Gordon, "Notes of the Legend of Keret," *JNES* 11 (1952): 213: "The Exodus is the epic of the Birth of a Nation, even though most of the text is now in prose form. Fortunately, chapter 15 of Exodus preserves a sizable poetic fragment. . . . The narrative content includes epic episodes."

Appendix 1: East Coast or West Coast?

Whether the Jaredites crossed the Atlantic or the Pacific is not fundamental to the thesis of their Asiatic origin, since in either case their culture was fully developed at the time they left their homeland. President Milton R. Hunter has kindly called the writer's attention to certain statements in the writings of Ixtiloxochitl and Sahagun that seem to cast light on the subject of the Jaredite landing. The pertinent passages as given in Hunter and Ferguson, *Ancient America and the Book of Mormon,*[1] are as follows:

> Sahagun's comment on the remarks of Ixtiloxochitl: "It is the common and general opinion of all the natives of all this Chichimeca land . . . that their ancestors came from *Occidental parts,* and all of them are now called Tultecas, Aculhuas, Mexicanos; and other nations that are in this land say that they are of the lineage of the Chichimecas, and are proud of it; and the reason is, according as it appears in their histories, that the first king they had was called *Chichimecatl,* who was the one who brought them to this New World where they settled, who, as can be inferred, came from the great Tartary, *and they were those of the division of Babylon.* . . . And they say that they traveled for 104 years through different parts of the world until they arrived at *Huehue Tlapallan* their country."[2]

Sahagun further says:

> "Concerning the origin of these peoples, the report

> the old men [of central Mexico—where Sahagun lived many years] give is that they came by sea from the north [i.e., down the Gulf Coast of Mexico]. . . . It is conjectured . . . that they came from seven caves, and that these seven caves are the seven ships or galleys in which the *first* settlers of this land came. . . . The people first came to settle this land from the direction of Florida, and came coasting along the coast disembarking in the port of Panuco which they call *Panuco,* which means 'place where those arrived who crossed the water.' This people came in search of the terrestrial paradise and they had as a family name Tamoanchan, which means 'we are looking for our home.' "[3]

And again: "and this . . . king, as he traveled on with them through the greater part of the world, arrived in this land."[4]

Here *two* distinct phases of the Jaredite migration are indicated. First, there is the original exodus of the ancestors from Occidental parts under their first chief, "Chichimecatl, who was the one who brought them to this New World where they settled who . . . came from great Tartary, and they were those of the division of Babylon." Tartary is defined in the *Oxford Dictionary* as "the region of Central Asia extending eastward from the Caspian Sea,"[5] i.e., the very area to which we have assigned our Jaredite wanderings in the Old World. When Sahagun, writing in Mexico in the sixteenth century, speaks of Occidental parts, he means regions to the West. In those days the word *Occident* was used in its literal sense, and Jesuit missionaries, writing their reports from Mexico in the time of Sahagun, refer to Asia as the Occident, since it was Asia and not Europe that lay to the west of them. The writer was puzzled when, in an early and premature attempt to translate certain Jesuit letters, he first came upon this natural but unfamiliar use of the word *Occident*. Sahagun removes all ambiguity on the subject by specifically mentioning Babylon and great Tartary, neither of which was "Occidental" in the European sense, as being the very "Occidental parts" from which the settlers came.

Then there is a *second* landing, that of the people who reached Huehue Tlapallan after 104 years of wandering. These people, specifically described as the first settlers of *Mexico*, came "by sea from the north," coasting along the Gulf of Mexico "from the direction of Florida." We are not told where they came from nor are we told that they had just crossed the ocean, but we are told that they landed in Mexico over a century after the great migration began, i.e., long after the Jaredites had arrived in the New World. Moreover, a moment's reflection will make it apparent that the landing at Panuco can hardly have been the original Jaredite debarkation. After 344 terrible days at sea the Jaredites, or anyone else, would waste no time in stepping ashore on the first land that offered. Indeed it is clearly implied in Ether 6:12-13 that they did just that, and only later continued their expansion and exploration (Ether 7:4-11). But the Panuco people "came coasting along the coast," sailing, perhaps for many days, in full sight of land. Either they had not been at sea very long or they had already landed somewhere, else in their dire need for fresh meat, fresh water, and fresh fruit, they would have landed immediately instead of "coasting along the coast." Had they sailed into the gulf from the Atlantic, they could hardly have avoided sighting islands and touching at them. There is no mention of any terrible storm that might have kept them from landing, and at any rate, people do not "coast along the coast" in terrible storms. The statements that they "come from the north," and "from the direction of Florida" are strangely localized. If the Panuco people had just crossed the ocean, they certainly would have known it, and it would have been the main part of their legend, but no Atlantic crossing is mentioned.

The landing in Mexico is obviously one of the later developments of the great Jaredite migration, which, as we have often noted, did not come to an end with their landing in the New World but continued in many directions. We know that the Jaredites in their wanderings crossed many bodies of water and so made *many* landings like the one at Panuco, which need not be described in the Book of Mormon.

Furthermore, Sahagun tells us that the original migrants under their first chief had traveled "through the greater part of the world," and that those who landed in Mexico had "traveled for 104 years through different parts of the world." If they had passed from the Near East into the valley northward, across Asia and the Pacific, and then traversed this continent to reach the gulf coast in Florida or at the mouth of the Mississippi, hence following the gulf coast to Mexico, this would certainly be true. On the other hand, a journey westward from Babylon to the Mediterranean and out over the Atlantic does not take one through the greater part of the world and is far harder to visualize than the eastern route.

In the writer's opinion, the most attractive interpretation of the evidence is this: From Babylon at the time of the great dispersion came a group of wanderers under their first king. They wandered "through different parts of the world" (that is important for our Old World background) and then left "great Tartary" (Asia) and crossed "from Occidental parts" to the New World, where they presently continued their exploration (Ether 7) by land and water, one family or tribe of them, the Tamoanchan, coming cautiously down along the coast of the Gulf of Mexico to land, over a hundred years after the departure from the tower, on the east of Mexico. Such a view is by no means the only possible one to be taken from Sahagun's evidence, but it seems to reconcile all the known facts, while the assumption that the original landing was at Panuco overlooks some important things, to wit, (1) that the original settlers came to the New World from the west, not from the east, (2) that they apparently had been in great Tartary, or Asia east of the Caspian, (3) that they had traveled through many lands—through most of the world, in fact, (4) that they were anxious to land, whereas the Panuco people were coasting, (5) that the Mexican party is not said to have crossed the ocean on this occasion—a thing that would certainly have been recorded were it the case—but only to have come "from the direction of Florida" and from the north—which definitely localizes the picture, and above all (6) that the landing at Panuco took place 104 years after the beginning of the great migration, whereas the Jaredites landed well within one generation after leaving the tower.

The problem is a fascinating, but not a vital one. The writer's opinion on the matter, excluded as he is from any deeper knowledge of the subject by an invincible ignorance of any of the native languages of Central America, must continue to be regarded as pure, unalloyed speculation, at best a particle of truth—not an article of faith.

Notes

1. Milton R. Hunter and Thomas S. Ferguson, *Ancient America and the Book of Mormon* (Oakland, Ca: Kolob, 1950).
2. Ibid., 25.
3. Ibid., 30-31.
4. Ibid., 38.
5. *Oxford English Dictionary,* 12 vols. (Oxford: Clarendon, 1953), 11:100; s.v. "Tartar."

Appendix 2: How Far to Cumorah?

To Mr. Eugene L. Roberts and Mrs. Eldon Reed Cluff in their fascinating book *Benjaman Cluff* (Provo, 1947) we are indebted for valuable chapters (7 through 12) on the Brigham Young Academy Expedition to South and Central America. In those pages the reader may find a clear answer to the question: What geographical barriers would definitely bar an army from passing from Central America to the north country? The answer is—*none*.

On April 17, 1900 a troop of twenty-five men with mules and wagons left Provo, Utah, with the purpose of seeking information casting light on the Book of Mormon in lands to the south. Upon reaching the Mexican border the expedition was disbanded (August 12, 1900) by order of the General Authorities—not because it had reached impassable terrain, but because of the expense involved in a large-scale operation. Proceeding into Mexico with a reduced force of nine men and without wagons, the party found far easier and more pleasant going than they had had in Arizona. Oaxaca they describe as a very Eden, a hunter's paradise, through which they were able to make eighteen to twenty miles a day. Even the terribly rugged Sierra Madre Mountains were crossed in three weeks.

Since the object of the expedition was to gather information, it moved very slowly. Each of the nine men was a specialist, and each was allowed to do a thorough job. Thus C. Van Buren made one of the finest collections of South American birds in the world, J. B. Fairbanks "frequently remained at some camp or city to paint" and took long trips to the coast to ship his pictures back home, Cluff and three others made one side-trip of four hundred miles to inspect the ruins of Palenque, and after passing Mexico City the whole party climbed Popocatepetl. It was such activity rather than any terrors of the road that made progress slow. When in Guatemala Professor Wolfe dropped out, it was not because going had become impossible but because he had never liked the idea of marching beyond Nogales and had been persuaded only with great difficulty to accompany the party as far as he did. Nowhere is the jungle described as an impenetrable barrier: There were always trails and ancient roads to follow. Swollen streams seem to have presented the only serious obstacles to travel, yet they were all successfully crossed, and had the party not been unwise enough to attempt Central America during the rainy season, they could have been avoided almost entirely. When Brother Magelby fell sick in Salvador, all but Cluff and Kienke stayed with him. At one time or another every member of the expedition came down with fever—but all survived. Had Brothers Cluff and Kienke been able to afford a ten-man escort (extremely moderate by explorer's standards), they would have made better time on their journey to Panama. As it was, they got through without serious mishap, and what delayed their entry into the city of Panama was not jungle but a revolution, which also obliged them to go part of the way by boat. In Panama City they were joined by other members of the expedition (so far were they from being downhearted), and then some of the men took the mules across the isthmus to Colon in only three days, though they had only "uncertain and indefinite trails" to follow. From Colon the party went to Colombia by boat—solely because of Indian troubles, and not because of geographical obstacles, for the worst of the jungles and streams were already behind them. In Bogota the expedition finally came to an end not because the country had become impassable, but because the Colombian government advised them against proceeding further, since "south of Bogota the Americans would most likely have all their possessions confiscated by revolutionists before they had traveled far and they would almost certainly be killed."

Two aspects of B.Y. Academy Expedition are particularly pertinent to the question of Book of Mormon logistics: the actual travel time of the party and the nature of the obstacles that slowed it down. As to the first, if we subtract time taken off for missionary work, resting on the Sabbath, side-trips and exploration, receiving the endless and exuberant hospitality of Saints and natives along the way (a very demanding and time-consuming obligation), caring for the sick, collecting, preparing and shipping specimens, negotiating for passports, duty-exemptions, guides, etc., we find that the actual time on the road is to be measured rather in weeks than in months. If one chooses to stop off in Elko for three weeks on a trip from Salt Lake to San Francisco, one cannot rightly describe the journey as taking three weeks—and the explorers from Provo deliberately and constantly delayed on the road. Even when actually under way the group made no effort to move quickly—to set a record for speed was the one thing farthest from their thoughts.

Yet even with all these things to slow them to a crawl, the party reached the first "Narrow Neck of Land" on February 16, 1901, less than ten months after leaving Provo. Fully four of these months had been spent in Utah and Arizona, while more than a month more had been wasted in negotiations on the Mexican border. The second "Narrow Neck" was reached April 13, 1901, less than a year from Provo, and the narrowest neck of all was entered but two weeks later—it was a revolution that delayed arrival at Panama City until the fall of the year.

As to the nature of the obstacles, it will be readily seen

that they are not such as any Jaredite or Lamanite army would have to cope with. Official delays, swollen streams, care for the sick, social obligations, ignorance of the country, hostile Indians, revolutions, lack of guides, lost and strayed pack animals, the labor of preparing scientific collections—such hindrances could all be avoided by the means and experience at the disposal of seasoned armies. The B.Y. Academy Expedition occasionally ran across ancient roads some of which they took to be Nephite. Needless to say, such jungle ways would have been in infinitely better repair in the days of old. The marching of armies would in a very short time establish a system of clearly marked and easily traveled strategic roads, and these would improve from year to year after each campaign. Tough native troops, adequately supplied with every means of accomplishing rapid forced marches, could easily pass from the Narrow Neck of Land to the North Country in a matter of *days*. In World War II, the Japanese demonstrated that the "impenetrable jungles" of Malaya, on which British strategy relied very heavily, were simply a myth. As Professor Spears points out in his book *Deserts on the March*, there are no "impenetrable jungles" in nature. According to the famous military maxim of Suvorov, "where a deer can go, a man can go, and where a man can go, an army can go." It has been proved time and again.

Without committing us to any particular Book of Mormon geography, the remarkable journey of the B.Y.A. Expedition, made more than fifty years ago by a very poorly equipped company during the rainy season through territories of hostile Indians and revolutionaries, proves that Jaredite or Lamanite armies could easily have followed the old established patterns of making yearly raids of continental scope.

Scripture References

2 Nephi

Jacob

Omni

Abraham

3 Baruch

1 Enoch

2 Enoch

Jasher

Jubilees

Koran

Sibylline Books

Index